E. M. FORSTER: A HUMAN EXPLORATION

THE GOTHAM LIBRARY
OF THE NEW YORK UNIVERSITY PRESS

The Gotham Library is a series of original works and critical studies, published in paperback primarily for student use. The Gotham hardcover edition is primarily for use by libraries and the general reader. Devoted to significant works and major authors and to literary topics of enduring importance, Gotham Library texts offer the best in literature and criticism.

Comparative and Foreign Language Literature:
Robert J. Clements, Editor
Comparative and English Language Literature:
James W. Tuttleton, Editor

E. M. Forster: a photograph taken in the late 1950s by Edward Leigh of Cambridge

E. M. Forster: A Human Exploration

Centenary Essays

Edited by
G. K. Das and John Beer

New York · New York University Press · 1979

Contents

Preface and Acknowledgments

The present volume has been compiled to commemorate the centenary of E. M. Forster, who was born on 1 January 1879. The original idea for the volume came from the first editor, who also issued the invitations to contributors and has acted as co-ordinator for the contributions from India; the general editing, standardizing of references and so on has largely been carried out by the second editor. We are particularly grateful to Mr Oliver Stallybrass, who made available an advance text of the Abinger *A Passage to India* so that all references could be standardised to what will be the definitive edition of that novel, and tô Miss J. L. Fellows who compiled the index. Acknowledgments are gratefully made to the Trustees of the Forster Estate—the Provost and Scholars of King's College, Cambridge—for permission to quote from unpublished manuscript material (acknowledged at the appropriate places in the text) and to the Provost and Scholars of King's, the Estate of the late Mrs Frieda Lawrence Ravagli and Lawrence Pollinger Ltd for permission to reproduce an extract from *The White Peacock* in Chapter 18, and some brief passages from unpublished letters by D. H. Lawrence in Chapter 23. The Librarians and staff of King's College, Cambridge and the Humanities Research Center of the University of Texas at Austin are particularly thanked for their assistance at various stages.

The editors also wish to express their appreciation to the contributors for their co-operation and enthusiasm in making this tribute a fully international one.

Just before going to press, we heard with deep regret of the death of Oliver Stallybrass. No one has done more for Forster studies in recent years, and he will be greatly missed.

G. K. D.
J. B. B.

Delhi and Cambridge, 1978.

List of Abbreviations

(i) E. M. FORSTER
Where a work by Forster has not, at the time of writing, appeared in the Abinger edition, a date or some other identifier is attached to the abbreviation to assist ready identification of the text being used. In the case of *Maurice*, however, it is assumed that the pagination of the Abinger text, when it comes, will correspond with that of the first edition.

WAFT	*Where Angels Fear to Tread* (1905) Abinger edition, edited by O. Stallybrass, 1975.
LJ (WC)	*The Longest Journey* (1907) World's Classics edition, 1960.
RWV	*A Room with a View* (1908) Abinger edition, 1977.
HE	*Howards End* (1910) Abinger edition, 1973.
AHG (1922)	*Alexandria: A History and a Guide*, Alexandria, 1922.
PP (1923)	*Pharos and Pharillon*, 1923.
PI	*A Passage to India* (1924) Abinger edition, 1978.
AN	*Aspects of the Novel* (1927) Abinger edition, 1974.
GLD	*Goldsworthy Lowes Dickinson* (1934) Abinger edition, 1973.
AH (1936)	*Abinger Harvest*, 1936.
CSS (1947)	*Collected Short Stories*, 1947.
TCD	*Two Cheers for Democracy* (1951) Abinger edition 1972.
HD (1953)	*The Hill of Devi*, 1953.
M	*Maurice*, 1971.
LTC	*The Life to Come and Other Stories*, 1972.
Furbank	P. N. Furbank: *E. M. Forster: A Life* volume I (1879–1914), 1977; volume II (1914–1970), 1978.

(ii) VIRGINIA WOOLF

AWD   Virginia Woolf: *A Writer's Diary*, edited by Leonard Woolf, 1953.

Bell   Quentin Bell: *Virginia Woolf, a biography*, two vols, 1972.

Diary   Virginia Woolf: *Diary*, introduced by Quentin Bell, edited by A. O. Bell, 1977– .

Essays   Virginia Woolf: *Collected Essays*, edited by Leonard Woolf, four vols, 1966–7.

Moments   Virginia Woolf: *Moments of Being*, unpublished autobiographical writings, edited by J. Schulkind, 1976.

Key to references for
A Passage to India

Since a number of editions of *A Passage to India* are in circulation, all page references have been standardized to the Abinger Edition of it, the one most likely to be found in libraries in the future. The page-numbers of each chapter there are listed below; this should enable readers without access to that edition to locate references fairly easily in the versions they are using.

Temple

Notes on the Contributors

Oliver Stallybrass edited *Aspects of E. M. Forster* (1969), and was, at the time of his death, editing the Abinger Edition of E. M. Forster. He was co-editor, with Alan Bullock, of *The Fontana Dictionary of Modern Thought*, and translated many books by Norwegian and Danish authors, notably Knut Hamsun.

Judith Scherer Herz, who formerly taught at Cornell and holds a Ph.D. from the University of Rochester, is Associate Professor of English at Concordia University. She has written articles on Chaucer, Shakespeare, Milton and Marvell, as well as several studies of E. M. Forster.

George H. Thomson is a Professor of English at the University of Ottawa. He is the author of *The Fiction of E. M. Forster* (Detroit Mich., 1967) and the editor of *Albergo Empedocle and Other Writings* (New York, 1971), a gathering of Forster's early uncollected writings.

S. P. Rosenbaum is Professor of English Literature at the University of Toronto. He has edited books and written articles on Henry James, Emily Dickinson, Virginia Woolf, and the Bloomsbury Group, and is currently writing a literary history of Bloomsbury.

R. N. Parkinson, who is Senior Lecturer in English at Exeter University, has also lectured widely in Germany, France and the USA. A critical study of *Edward Gibbon* appeared under the Twayne imprint in 1973; he is currently working on Eliot and Pound and on William Robertson.

Wilfred Stone, who is Professor of English at Stanford University, has taught at Harvard, Minnesota and Vermont, as well as at Stanford's overseas campuses in Britain and Italy. In addition to his writings on prose style and the short story, he is the author of *Religion and Art of William Hale White ('Mark Rutherford')* and *The Cave and the Mountain: A Study of E. M. Forster*, which won the Christian Gauss Prize.

Mohammad Shaheen was formerly a research student at King's College, Cambridge, where he had many opportunities of talking to Forster, and is now Assistant Professor of English at the University of Jordan. In addition to various articles and notes, he has written a book on Meredith which is to be published by Macmillan.

John Drew, who has lived in India and lectured in Canada, is at present a research student at Cambridge, working on India and the English imagination.

J. Birje-Patil, who took his M.A. and Ph.D. at Manchester University, is Professor and Chairman of the Department of English at M.S. University, Baroda. His publications include an essay on *Measure for Measure* in *Shakespeare Studies* (USA), Vol. V, and a book on T. S. Eliot entitled *Beneath the Axle-tree* (New Delhi, 1977).

V. A. Shahane is Professor of English at Osmania University, Hyderabad. He is the author of *E. M. Forster: A Reassessment* (Allahabad, 1962), and *E. M. Forster: A Study in Double Vision* (New Delhi, 1975).

John Colmer was educated at Oxford and has taught at Khartoum, Birmingham and Adelaide, where he is now Professor of English. He has published widely on Coleridge, and is the author of *E. M. Forster: The Personal Voice*, *E. M. Forster: 'A Passage to India'*, and *Coleridge to 'Catch-22': Images of Society*, which contains a discussion of Forster's political ideas.

Benita Parry, who was born in South Africa, was educated there and in England. She is the author of *Delusions and Discoveries: Studies on India in the British Imagination 1880–1930* (1972) and is working on a study of Conrad.

Michael Orange, a graduate of Cambridge, is a lecturer in

English at the University of Newcastle in Australia. He was awarded his Ph.D. at Sydney University for a thesis on *Bleak House* and is preparing a book on Dickens's involvement with the theatre.

P. N. Furbank is Senior Lecturer in Literature at the Open University and author of *Samuel Butler 1835–1902* (1948), *Italo Svevo: The Man and the Writer* (1966), *Reflections on the Word 'Image'* (1970), and *E. M. Forster: a Life* (2 vols., 1977–8).

Evelyne Hanquart graduated from the Sorbonne, where she is at present a Lecturer. As a research student of the University of Cambridge in 1971, she was given the opportunity of reading the newly released Forster Collection at King's. This has been the occasion of a series of articles – published both in England and France – and has provided material for the thesis she is writing on 'E. M. Forster: A Humanist in the Modern City'.

May Buckingham is the widow of Robert Buckingham, whose long relationship with E. M. Forster is described in the second volume of P. N. Furbank's *E. M. Forster: A Life*.

Carl Baron, Fellow and Director of Studies in English at Downing College, Cambridge, was awarded his Ph.D. for a thesis on D. H. Lawrence and has written several articles on twentieth-century literature. He is also a member of the Editorial Board of the Cambridge University Press's forthcoming Complete Critical Edition of the Works of D. H. Lawrence.

Alan Wilde is Professor of English and graduate chairman at Temple University. He is the author of *Christopher Isherwood* and *Art and Order: A Study of E. M. Forster*, as well as various essays on British and American literature, and is currently at work on a book to be called *Depths and Surfaces: Studies in Twentieth-Century Irony*.

G. K. Das is Reader in English at the University of Delhi. He gained his Ph.D. from the University of Cambridge for research work on E. M. Forster, and is the author of *E. M. Forster's India* (1977). He was a Commonwealth Staff Fellow at Queens' College, Cambridge, during 1975–76.

H. K. Trivedi is a Lecturer in English at St. Stephen's College, Delhi. He obtained his Ph.D. from the University of Wales and is currently writing a book on 'Virginia Woolf and the Tradition of the English Novel'.

James McConkey is a Professor of English and American Literature at Cornell University. His books include *The Novels of E. M. Forster*, *Night Stand*, a collection of short stories, and three novels including (forthcoming) *The Tree House Confessions*.

John Beer is Reader in English Literature at Cambridge and Fellow of Peterhouse. In addition to *The Achievement of E. M. Forster* he is the author of *Coleridge the Visionary*, *Blake's Humanism*, *Blake's Visionary Universe*, *Coleridge's Poetic Intelligence* and *Wordsworth and the Human Heart*.

Frederick P. W. McDowell, who is Professor of English at the University of Iowa, is the author of *E. M. Forster* (Twayne English Authors Series, 1969) and *E. M. Forster: An Annotated Bibliography of Secondary Writings on Him* (Northern Illinois University Press, 1977), as well as of various essays, reviews, etc. on him. In addition to books on Ellen Glasgow, Elizabeth Madox Roberts and Caroline Gordon he has published a number of essays on other authors and has done extensive work on Bernard Shaw.

The Piazza della Signoria, Florence, from *The Cave and the Mountain* by Wilfred Stone (Stanford University Press)

1 Introduction: The Elusive Forster

John Beer

When he published the life of his friend Goldsworthy Lowes Dickinson, Forster commented on the difficulty of what he had been trying to do. He had wanted, he said, to render the 'uniqueness' of Dickinson.[1] If that was difficult in Dickinson's case, it is still more so in his own. With Dickinson, we are made to believe, there was a golden thread running through everything he did and thought: he had aligned himself with a particular tradition – that of Plato and the Platonists – and his career was to be understood as a long attempt to remain true to the insight of that tradition through the unpropitious circumstances of his time. Forster had no such single and identifiable allegiance. He was, as he himself confessed, a fragmented being. 'My defence at any Last Judgment', he once wrote, 'would be "I was trying to connect up and use all the fragments I was born with."'[2]

That last comment typifies something important in him, a kind of self-asserted vulnerability, which makes it all too easy to quash him critically, but which may also seem from another point of view to be refracting a gleam of arrogance. It is a trait which shows itself also in his final decision to leave a body of writing, some of which he knew to be below the level of his best, to be published after his death. Where another writer would have feared to compromise his established reputation Forster evidently thought it worth preserving the whole—even if it displayed weaknesses as well as strengths. (No doubt if he had followed his earlier inclination to destroy *Maurice* the legend of a lost masterpiece would soon have grown up about it).

It was equally typical of the man that he should have anticipated the present occasion by writing, in 1927, a piece entitled 'My Own Centenary'.[3] Prompted by the fact that the centenaries of Blake and Beethoven were both being celebrated in that year, he projected an article in *The Times* for the year 2027 which might commemorate the hundredth anniversary of his own death. It contained, among other things, a sermon by the Dean of Dulborough devoted to his memory in which he would be held up as an example to those later times. The irony here was projected around the little that would have changed. Forster's period would be looked back to as a time of corruption, but the Dean's windy oratory would give slender assurance that things had really altered, as he moved inexorably on to his final note of shared self-congratulation: '. . . in commemorating him we can yet again celebrate what is best and most permanent in ourselves.'

The major ironies are typical of Forster; it is when the Dean sets him confidently at the side of Beethoven and Blake that one picks up a hint of something else. For we know that if he could have chosen men with whom to be placed it would have been precisely those. We can put this piece with his discussion of greatness in *Aspects of the Novel* (a discussion which by implication denies that quality to his early novels, but not necessarily to *A Passage to India*),[4x*] or against the complaint that his mother had 'cramped and warped my genius',[5] and divine that the question of his own greatness, or lack of it, was one to which he was not entirely indifferent. 'I am perfectly certain that I am not a great novelist', he told an interviewer on his eightieth birthday;[6] but his works sometimes hint that 'not to be great' might have been a vocation which he felt to be peculiarly in keeping with the conditions of his time.

Sometimes his worldly incapacities extended that vocation to the point of farcical caricature. Convinced by his mother at an early age that he was delicate he protected himself carefully—not realising until well into middle age that he actually had quite a strong constitution.[7] Although he clearly knew a good deal about physical love and its expression it was not until he was thirty and had published several novels that he fully understood how copulation took place—a fact which in so bookish a man must indicate lack of interest rather than lack of opportunity to acquire the necessary information.[8] His attitude to money was especially individual. In his early years he was not well off—even flying so far in the face of conventional behaviour as to tell the Woolfs on one occasion that he could not visit them unless they paid his train fare;[9] yet he also gave large sums to his friends from time to time when he knew them to be in need. In his later years he grew rich almost without noticing it,

* See rubric to Notes (p. 283) for explanation of 'x' notes.

until in 1964 he enraged a Fellow of King's by revealing casually that he had £20,000 lying unused in his current account at the bank. In spite of his spirited self-defence he was evidently jolted by the reaction, for he began giving away large sums of money to his friends immediately afterwards.[10]

Since his death the most striking addition to knowledge about him has been in the form of information about his homosexuality, conveyed both through the publication of *Maurice* and some later short stories, and more directly in Furbank's biography. This large new array of knowledge has, indeed, given a sharp turn to his literary reputation, encouraging commentators to treat much of his fiction as displaced accounts of homosexual relationships. The latter inference seems to be misguided, however. It would be truer to say that Forster was drawn to those aspects of love which were common to all human relationships, heterosexual or homosexual. Knowledge of his private sexual nature helps to explain certain features of his fiction: the occasional preoccupation with physical cruelty, for instance, and the failure to depict a happy marriage in action. When he writes positively about human love on the other hand, his remarks remain valid for all kinds of relationship: his portrayals of women are often strikingly convincing. It is more important to recognize the degree to which Forster's homosexuality gave him an 'outsider's' view of things, making him look at the world from a point of view which did not regard marriage and the procreation of children as central.

From this unusual vantage-point, he became (to use his own description of Cavafy[11]) a man who stood 'at a slight angle to the universe'. ('Nobody', his friends said, 'came at things from queerer angles'[12]). It also made him elusive—a characteristic not only of his personal life but of his presence in the novels. Virginia Woolf, who imaged him as a butterfly, put the matter well, if critically, when she said: 'He is like a light sleeper who is always being woken by something in the room. The poet is twitched away by the satirist; the comedian is tapped on the shoulder by the moralist . . .'[13]

Her comment brings out the difficulty of aligning Forster with any preceding tradition. The Hardy in him, we might say, was twitched away by the Meredith; the Jane Austen tapped on the shoulder by the George Eliot. Yet it is easy to exaggerate his failures of consistency. If one looks generally at his work one can trace four distinct waves of achievement – even if they stretch a little confusingly across different dimensions of his art and life. In the early works his comic gift was at its strongest, and may well come to rank higher as the Edwardian age recedes from living memory. Forster was shrewd enough to have seized upon areas of society where 'Victorianism' was still preserved in a pure form. All over England in his time the spirit of Victorianism was being overtaken by the spirit of a more open liberalism, but it was for the most part a gradual and acceptable process. Forster spotted the places (the pensione in Florence, the Surrey suburb) where the two forces could still clash more purely and directly. The result was some memorable scenes of comedy which also touched the basic concern of the time. At that period an unusually vivid sense of new potentialities was abroad. For a short time, before the First World War swallowed up such hopes, there was a strong belief in the possibilities of human betterment through education and liberalization of attitudes. Forster did not enter the mainstream of this movement (it is represented better in the early career and setting of D. H. Lawrence and his friends); but he caught something of the excitement, which filters into the speech of characters such as the Emersons and the Schlegels.

'The War', Lawrence later wrote, '. . . was the spear through the side of all sorrows and hopes.'[14] Yet even before its outbreak, anyone who looked outside the life of England was bound to see that the true problems of the century would be posed in the international sphere, and that these were already beginning to dwarf questions of manners and morals in any particular society. That disturbing fact, expressing itself mainly as an uneasiness in the early novels, was not faced squarely by Forster until the writing of *A Passage to India*, when he passed beyond the British – or even European – view of things to look dispassionately at the phenomenon of imperialism. While the novel conveys a searching look at the phenomenon of the British in India, however, it is also much more, and for that reason has not become dated with the decline of colonialism. Discussing it in 1960, Forster said that it was absurd to say that he had been writing about 'the incompatibility of East and West': he had been 'really concerned with the difficulty of living in the universe'.[15] And this deeper concern, once perceived, sets the novel back into direct alignment again with the earlier ones, since in them too he was aiming to find grounds of human existence deeper than those suggested by most contemporary societies.

This further concern is explored in many of the contributions to the present volume. The short stories are here dealt with less as comedies of situation than as fictions in which Forster explores the tenability of various 'mythologies'; *The Longest Journey* is examined for its 'philosophical' enactments; *A Passage to India* – which rightly receives the greatest attention – emerges from the combined scrutiny of various contributors as an unusually rich work, yielding a series of themes (language and silence, promise and withdrawal, documentary report and symbolic statement, for instance) which are each handled with equal subtlety.

A Passage to India marks the highwater mark of Forster's achievement, and some of the journalism of the 1920s is disappointing at its side. The interplay of whimsical irony and seriousness is still to be found, but in far less complex form. Only with the passing of time did it become clear that Forster had something further to offer his age, as the rise of totalitarianisms in Europe brought a new kind of challenge. The cultivation of personal relationships, which could sometimes seem to be a form of weakness in the face of large political threats, was then found to nurture, in someone who took it as seriously as he did, a core of individual resistance, coupled with a welcome resilence of critical intelligence.

In the 1930s the movement towards totalitarianism of some kind, whether of the left or of the right, seemed at times irresistible. The very conditions of industrialism, calling as they did for the development of larger and larger units, seemed to demand a matching organization in society at large. The flaws in that reasoning were not properly seen until further experience demonstrated that such monolithic organizations, having at their apex individuals who were as subject to fear and error as any others, would be likely to maintain themselves with an equally total and inhuman violence.

Forster's own upbringing and reflections had preserved him from such contemporary acquiescence in dictatorial organizations. His own experiences as an isolated individual had made him aware of the imbecilities that may be perpetrated in the name of an institution which tries to impose its own structure upon the world at large (' "School", said Herbert Pembroke, " . . . is the world in miniature" '[16]). While many intellectuals felt the need to commit themselves to a particular cause, Forster reserved his position, except to resist all forms of totalitarianism firmly. As a result, he came out of the period with an unusually clear reputation.

If this side of Forster's achievement is not fully brought out in the present collection, it is for a peculiarly appropriate reason. Iain

Wright, of Queens' College, Cambridge, had originally planned to write a piece on Forster's political writings between the wars. As he came to examine the evidence, however, he found that it extended much further than he thought, and that the resulting study soon exceeded the proper confines of a simple article, so that in the end it seemed better that he should write a more extended study for separate publication. When that appears, it will be found to complement the treatment of the period in Furbank's biography valuably by showing in detail how politically alert and independent Forster remained during a period when the situation was changing so rapidly and bewilderingly that it was hard not to be drawn into one of the many movements of the time.

If the collection had been arranged in strictly chronological fashion it would have been natural to conclude it with the pieces which deal with his later years, when he occupied an honoured place in the culture of his time—a fourth phase in which some of his best essays, including those on the nature of artistic experience, were written. To do so, however, would have had a muting effect; the collection concludes therefore with several pieces which grow naturally out of the appraisal inherent in some of the earlier essays of the collection, where the emphasis is not on successive phases of development but on the various strands which went to make up his expressive persona at its best. Such discussions invite one to turn from the previous literary tradition and the cultural conditions of his time to examine certain influences which were closer to him— and notably those of the Cambridge to which he went in 1897.

The virtue of that Cambridge lay not simply in giving him freedom from relatives and schoolmasters; it also offered fulfilment, the fulfilment possible in a place where the reading in which he had long immersed himself was no longer regarded as freakish but as a natural activity. First and foremost among the seminal influences must be counted his tutor, Nathaniel Wedd, who communicated his sympathy with the new radicalism that was coming into fashion, his passion for egalitarianism in society, his irreverence towards authorities of all kinds—and his own great love of Italy. While Forster did not take over his tutor's forthrightness of manner, the associated attitudes touched him deeply, nourishing the scepticism that peers out of all his writings.[17x]

While the irony and scepticism gave him one ready resource for coping with the world, however, they could not in themselves satisfy him completely. For that reason the influence of Goldsworthy

Lowes Dickinson was crucial. We have mentioned already his confessed aim to communicate the 'uniqueness' of Dickinson in his biography; in the end he could encompass what he was trying to say only by using the word 'charm'. 'Charm in most men, and nearly all women, is a decoration . . . Charm in Dickinson was structural. It penetrated and upheld everything he did, it remained into old age, it conferred on him a beauty which cannot be given that rather patronizing label of "spiritual" . . .'[18] Forster finds it hard to think of an alternative word, in spite of that, but he gropes further towards expressing what he means when he writes,

> He was an indescribably rare being, he was rare without being enigmatic, he was rare in the only direction which seems to be infinite: the direction of the Chorus Mysticus. He did not merely increase our experience: he left us more alert for what has not yet been experienced . . .[19]

The quality that Forster is grappling with here is like that which informs Mrs Wilcox in *Howards End*, or Mrs Moore in *A Passage to India*—a unifying vision which so suffuses every part of the sensibility as to offer to those who experience it a momentary guarantee that the values associated with it are permanently valid. In the end Forster was bound to acknowledge that that kind of sensibility, at least in the form in which he knew it in the West, could survive only under certain conditions. Even Dickinson on visiting India had found his own humanism challenged by the weight of meaningless, or even cruel processes in nature;[20] he was also oppressed rather than stimulated by the architecture of the temples. 'I remember,' says Forster, 'how he used to cower away from those huge architectural masses, those pullulating forms, as if a wind blew off them which might wither the soul'.[21] Mrs Moore's breakdown in an Indian cave evidently represents a more radical failure of the same kind.

Yet Forster (who in any case enjoyed himself more in India) did not give up so easily. In his case the 'alertness for what has not yet been experienced' was backed by a subsisting vitality which made its presence felt more strongly as he grew older. It is as if there remained in him something of the raw longing for experience, the ability to remain true to instinctual sources and find in them a ground of truth which is sketched out (however inchoately) in the character of Adela Quested; and, at the other extreme, something of

the musical passion and sense of yearning expectancy which is
rendered masterfully in the character of Godbole. If Fielding and
Aziz could not be friends, then and in India, there was a sense in
which Adela Quested and Godbole *could* meet—if not in life, at least
in the depths of the novelist's own being. The same qualities that
carried him beyond investigation of the defects of reason and
sensibility in his greatest novel gave him the interlocking tastes for
enquiry and music that were characteristic of his old age.

The older Forster is in some ways more difficult to seize than the
younger, however, for by now the cross-strands of his personality
were very complex. Furbank comments that he could be by turns
'gruff and scout-masterly, grave and prophetic and feline and
flickering in a mercurial and "camp" manner'.[22] Even the nature
of his homosexuality is not clear. Although on many occasions he
sought physical gratification, it seems as if he was more often looking
for a reciprocal warmth of affection, coupled perhaps with the
presence of physical beauty in some form. This could sometimes
bring him into states of depression when the looked-for conditions
were absent.[23]

Coupled with this, however, the sustaining intellectual elements
just noticed had their counterpart in a feeling for the forces of
vitality in nature and mankind—as sketched briefly in the palm-
trees that waved farewell to Mrs Moore in his novel.[24] Furbank puts
the matter well when, towards the end of his biography, he remarks
on the impression Forster made on his friends as that of a man with
'a secret':

> It had to do with the fact that, to a rather special degree, he lived
> the imaginative life and, whether in company or in solitude, was
> attending to imaginative impressions. He did this consciously,
> feared to lose the power of doing so, and rebuked himself for
> slackness in it. It was, for him, the rule and aim of his existence
> and was entwined with his sense for what—for want of a better
> word—he called 'life'. He felt as if, on occasion, he could see
> through to 'life': could hear its wing-beat, could grasp it not just
> as a generality but as a palpable presence.[25]

It is this inner existence which underlies Forster's habit of
'standing at a slight angle to the universe'. He might miss, or wilfully
refuse to see, certain obvious facts about marriage and parenthood,
but he had a correspondingly sharp insight into the nature of love

between human beings. He looked also to the inner life for liberation from self, for that artistic anonymity which is true freedom and which he could find best in the music of Beethoven and other romantics.[26] (Although he was not drawn to women he remarked on, as an attractive feature in them, the occasional beauty of their voices in singing. 'The male, even at his best, has a fruity complacency. A woman can forget herself there.'[27]) This side of him might be said to correspond with the best of Adela Quested and the best of Professor Godbole. If in his depressions he sometimes touched on the despair of Mrs Moore, there was also a strong questing element—an element which insisted, like Adela, on dis-covering the 'real India', and which, in spite of the recognition that 'Nothing embraces the whole of India, nothing, nothing,' would not finally relent but rather found an exhilaration in continual exposure to new experiences.

The quest was still, in an important sense, metaphysical; while it could not realize itself in allegiance to a particular religion, it could honour each religion in turn. He could show such sympathy for the Hindu way of life as to encourage a Hindu to hope that Hinduism might be his true religion;[28] yet his early love for Syed Ross Masood and for Mohammed el Adl had given him an equal, or even deeper feeling for Mohammedanism. On his 1945 visit to India his friends several times saw him 'go down on his knees in mosques, like a believer', and on at least one occasion emerge with a radiant face.[29]

Christianity after his early upbringing, had no such emotional attraction, yet some of its teachings went deeper than he himself perhaps realised. Wilfred Stone notes how he would still quote the New Testament on the love of riches; nothing raised the moralizing strain in him more readily than signs of a grasping nature.[30] One Christmas, a few years before his death, he wrote a dispirited letter to *The Guardian* asking, on behalf of those non-Christians who found in Christmas an opportunity for the expression of personal affection and generosity, 'When has the entrance to the Temple been so effectively impeded by the commercial advertisers, the expense-accounters and the syndicalized sellers of doves?'[31] There were some features in Christianity which he could not easily root out of himself, and without them he would have lost some of his essential quality.

One of the elements in Christian tradition which remained with him most firmly was the conception of life as a human pilgrimage—transmuted in his case, however, into a view of life as a human exploration under the aegis of an unknown god.[32x] For this reason it is natural to conclude the present collection with a series of essays which set him in turn against four writers who readily invite comparison on that score: Virginia Woolf, T. S. Eliot, Anton Chekhov and D. H. Lawrence. It is perhaps in the company of these writers (one of whom could think of life in terms of 'building the ship of death', and another of whom wrote 'Old men should be explorers') that the nature of his own enterprise begins to define itself. He touched at times the astringent clericalism of Eliot, the fluid translucency of Virginia Woolf, the sardonic vitalism of Lawrence, but refused to take them to so extreme a form (and was criticized by each writer in turn for failing to do so). And it is in his drawing back from such extreme positions, in art as in politics, that the nature of his own achievement again becomes clearer. There is an implicit assertion that while such aspirations are always honourable, humanity itself cannot be so contained—and may in the end be excluded by them. In that negative affirmation, that process of recognition and withholding, the key to Forster's own consistency is perhaps most readily to be found. By comparison with Dickinson's steady if embattled, lighthouse-like affirmations, his was an illumination that came by way of continuing process. No doubt the unknown god he honoured possessed, in his eyes, a corresponding radiancy and elusiveness.

2 A Quorum of Quotations

Oliver Stallybrass

Invited to contribute to this volume, I asked if I might be unscholarly, even frivolous, and was granted permission. Nothing could be less scholarly than a selection of quotations, and this one has no object but to give pleasure—including for some readers, no doubt, that of making their own far superior selection.

It was this competitive urge, in fact, that got me going: I felt I could do better than *The Oxford Dictionary of Quotations*, whose latest edition has *one* quotation from Forster: the opening sentence of chapter v of *Howards End*, to the effect that 'Beethoven's Fifth Symphony is the most sublime noise that has ever penetrated into the ear of man'. Those are the words quoted—which, since they are preceded in the original by 'It will be generally admitted that', is rather like quoting as the first sentence of *Pride and Prejudice* 'A single man in possession of a good fortune must be in want of a wife'.

What is a quotation? At times I suspect that it is what has got into a dictionary of quotations—or at least into 'Sayings of the Week'. *ODQ*, however, insists that its contents are all 'actual current quotations . . . *familiar* quotations'. Familiar to whom? Why, in the circles I move in—fellow-contributors to this volume and the like— we never stop quoting Forster at each other and anyone else within earshot: I cannot even go out to bat without some wag crying 'Only connect!', followed by gales of laughter that show an easy familiarity with the quotation as well as legitimate doubts whether the injunction will be obeyed.

For me, then, Forster is as full of quotations as an egg is full of meat (which, as all good Shakespeareans know, is very full indeed), and the only problem has been that of selection. In twice reducing (the second time with the help of John Beer) the number of quotations that constitutes a quorum, I have tried to concentrate on those items that depend least upon their context, and to maintain roughly the original balance I struck between Forster's various ooks. Thus *Howards End* was and remains the largest single source – not because it is his greatest work (which in my view it isn't), but because it is the richest in memorable *sententiae*, or in what the *Subject-Index of the London Library* charmingly groups as Maxims, Aphorisms and Apothegms. It would have been nice to include something from each and every book; but there were no serious competitors from the Egyptian volumes or from *Maurice*, while the final round saw the elimination of *The Hill of Devi*, *Marianne Thornton* and the short stories. The Commonplace Book is, as it ought to be, eminently quotable; but since it is being published for the first time only on the same celebratory occasion as the present volume, it hardly qualifies yet as a source of 'actual current quotations'.

Then the pernicious charm of Italy worked on her, and, instead of acquiring information, she began to be happy.

A Room with a View, ch. ii

A call to the blood and to the relaxed will.

RWV, ch. xii

She gave up trying to understand herself, and joined the vast armies of the benighted, who follow neither the heart nor the brain, and march to their destiny by catchwords. . . . The night received her, as it had received Miss Bartlett thirty years before.

RWV, ch. xvii

'Everyone to his taste!' said Harriet, who always delivered a platitude as if it was an epigram.

Where Angels Fear to Tread, ch. i

As Philip once said, she had bolted all the cardinal virtues and couldn't digest them.

WAFT, ch. i

A young man who had the figure of a Greek athlete and the face of an English one. . . . Just where he began to be beautiful the clothes started.

The Longest Journey, ch. iii

Cambridge, according to her custom, welcomed her sons with open drains.

LJ, ch. vi

Rickie suffered from the Primal Curse, which is not—as the Authorized Version suggests—the knowledge of good and evil, but the knowledge of good-and-evil.

LJ, ch. xviii

In Paddington all Cornwall is latent and the remoter west; down the inclines of Liverpool Street lie fenlands and the illimitable Broads; Scotland is through the pylons of Euston; Wessex behind the poised chaos of Waterloo.

Howards End, ch. ii

'I felt for a moment that the whole Wilcox family was a fraud, just a wall of newspapers and motor-cars and golf-clubs, and that if it fell I should find nothing behind it but panic and emptiness.'

HE, ch. iv

'To think that because you and a young man meet for a moment there must be all these telegrams and anger.'

HE, ch. iv

All men are equal—all men, that is to say, who possess umbrellas.

HE, ch. vi

The remark 'England and Germany are bound to fight' renders war a little more likely each time that it is made, and is therefore made the more readily by the gutter press of either nation.

HE, ch. vii

It is private life that holds out the mirror to infinity; personal intercourse, and that alone, that ever hints at a personality beyond our daily vision.

HE, ch. x

With infinite effort we nerve ourselves for a crisis that never comes. The most successful career must show a waste of strength that might have removed mountains, and the most unsuccessful is not that of the man who is taken unprepared, but of him who has prepared and is never taken. On a tragedy of that kind our national morality is duly silent. It assumes that preparation against danger is in itself a good, and that men, like nations, are the better for staggering through life fully armed.

HE, ch. xii

'More and more do I refuse to draw my income and sneer at those who guarantee it.'

HE, ch. xix

Only connect! That was the whole of her sermon. Only connect the prose and the passion, and both will be exalted, and human love will be seen at its highest. Live in fragments no longer. Only connect, and the beast and the monk, robbed of the isolation that is life to either, will die.

HE, ch. xxii

'I don't think I understand people very well. I only know whether I like or dislike them.'
    'Then you are an Oriental.'

A Passage to India, ch. ii

She felt increasingly (vision or nightmare?) that, though people are important, the relations between them are not, and that in particular too much fuss has been made over marriage; centuries of carnal embracement, yet man is no nearer to understanding man.

PI, ch. xiv

The echo began in some indescribable way to undermine her hold on life. Coming at a moment when she chanced to be fatigued, it had managed to murmur: 'Pathos, piety, courage—they exist, but are identical, and so is filth. Everything exists, nothing has value.' If one had spoken vileness in that place, or quoted lofty poetry, the comment would have been the same—'ou-boum'.

PI, ch. xiv

Nothing enrages Anglo-India more than the lantern of reason if it is exhibited for one moment after its extinction is decreed.

PI, ch. xvii

They had started speaking of 'women and children'—that phrase that exempts the male from sanity when it has been repeated a few times.

PI, ch. xx

Ronny's religion was of the sterilized public-school brand, which never goes bad, even in the tropics.

PI, ch. xxviii

Sir Gilbert, though not an enlightened man, held enlightened opinions.

PI, ch. xxix

We may divide characters into flat and round.

Aspects of the Novel, ch. iv

'The king died and then the queen died' is a story. 'The king died, and then the queen died of grief' is a plot.

AN, ch. v

That the public school is not infinite and eternal, that there is something more compelling in life than teamwork and more vital than cricket, that firmness, self-complacency and fatuity do not between them compose the whole armour of man, that lessons may have to do with leisure, and grammar with literature—it is difficult for an inexperienced boy to grasp truths so revolutionary, or to realize that freedom can sometimes be gained by walking out through an open door.

Goldsworthy Lowes Dickinson, ch. vi

Well-developed bodies, fairly developed minds, and undeveloped hearts.

'Notes on the English Character', *Abinger Harvest*

He [the Englishman] must not express great joy or sorrow, or even open his mouth too wide when he talks—his pipe might fall out if he did.

Ibid.

He [Ibsen] reminds us too often of father at the breakfast table after a bad night, sensitive to the defects of society as revealed by a chance glance at the newspaper, and apt to blame all parties for them indiscriminately. Now it is the position of women that upsets father, now the lies people tell, now their inability to lie, now the drains, now the newspaper itself, which he crumples up, but his helpers and servers have to retrieve it, for bad as are all political parties he must really see who got in at Rosmersholm.

'Ibsen the Romantic', AH

It is pleasant to be transferred from an office where one is afraid of a sergeant-major into an office where one can intimidate generals, and perhaps this is why History is so attractive to the more timid amongst us. We can recover self-confidence by snubbing the dead.

'The Consolations of History', AH

I do not believe in Belief.

'What I Believe', *Two Cheers for Democracy*

My motto is: 'Lord, I disbelieve—help thou my unbelief.'

Ibid.

I hate the idea of causes, and if I had to choose between betraying my country and betraying my friend I hope I should have the guts to betray my country.

Ibid.

So two cheers for Democracy: one because it admits variety and two because it permits criticism. Two cheers are quite enough: there is no occasion to give three. Only Love the beloved Republic deserves that.

Ibid.

Ancient Athens made a mess—but the *Antigone* stands up. Renaissance Rome made a mess—but the ceiling of the Sistine got painted. James I made a mess—but there was *Macbeth*. Louis XIV—but there was *Phèdre*. Art for art's sake? I should just think so, and more so than ever at the present time. It is the one orderly product which our muddling race has produced.

'Art for Art's Sake', TCD

3 The Narrator as Hermes: a study of the early short fiction

Judith Scherer Herz

Perhaps we can even identify the god. In a marvellous group in the British Museum he stands beside Alcestis. The S curve of his body accentuated by his slightly raised left foot, he seems, caduceus in hand, to be urging the group forward. Almost contemporary with the Hermes of Praxiteles, he shares the same languid beauty; indeed, he seems even younger. To the left of Alcestis, if, in fact, the draped female figure between the two beautiful boys *is* the wife of Admetus, stands Death, apparently beckoning her forward. His arm, broken at the hand, his head tilted slightly back, he is framed by two full-length wings that are raised only slightly (much less so than the drapery of either Alcestis or Hermes, more a tracery than a relief) from the marble surface of the column base. To the right of Hermes, but badly broken, is another female figure, possibly Persephone. If that identification is correct, she is well located, for the group as it now stands is directly opposite the seated Demeter of Cnidus. The mother, at once dumpy and divine, is alone on her fragmented throne, although the shrine at Cnidus was, we are assured, dedicated to Demeter and Kore, so that originally a standing figure of Persephone was at her side.

In 1903, when Forster visited Cnidus, he took a wry comfort in knowing that while he was wet and muddied where 'the sea ran into the sky', Demeter was 'at that moment, warm and comfortable in that little recess of hers between the Ephesian Room and the Archaic Room, with the electric light fizzling above her, and casting blue shadows over her chin'.[1] He will not, he explains, turn sentimental on the theme of her exile; rather he appropriates her and makes her a living part of his imaginative world: 'Demeter alone among gods has true immortality. The others continue, perchance, their existence, but are forgotten, because the time came when they could not be loved. But to her, all over the world, rise prayers of idolatry from suffering men as well as suffering women,

for she has transcended sex.' He granted her immortality and took
from her the special comfort of her double sexuality. Perhaps he
responded to her Chthonic nature as well, for, especially in her
identification with her daughter Persephone, she is a life/death
figure, like Hermes, 'conductor of souls'.

There is certainly no disputing the goddess, but is the Ephesian
Hermes across the way part of Forster's active repertoire of images?
In a diary entry at about the same time as the 'Cnidus' essay, Forster
speaks of the Greek sculptures in the British Museum, in particular
of 'that wonderful boy with the broken arm – who I suppose is to be
called sugary because he's neo-Attic – [who] stands all the afternoon
warm in thick yellowy sunshine. He simply radiates light: I never
saw anything like it. Right across the Assyrian transept he throbs
like something under the sea. He couldn't have done it in Greece.'[2x]
To be sure, the figure on the drum that fits this description is Death
rather than Hermes, but the two were essentially interchangeable in
Forster's imagination, as indeed they are mythologically. One need
only think of Mann's Tadzio, in gesture very like this 'wonderful
boy'. Moreover, the winged figure of death is iconographically close
to Eros both as he is traditionally referred to and as Forster imagines
him at the moment of his birth in *The Longest Journey*. We have here
a nucleus of important associations for Forster – Hermes, the
beautiful young friend and guide, particularly a guide to the dead,
and young death, also beautiful and ardent ('I have and hope to
keep the power of thinking of death as beautiful.' Diary, 1912),[3]
both merged in Eros as a figure of love *and* death. The chain of
associations here is similar to Mann's in *Death in Venice* and it is
interesting that Mann, whom Kerényi called Dr Hermeticus ('Your
work and your nature represent a revelation of that God'), observed
in a letter to Kerényi thirty years after the story: 'I could not help
being pleased to note that the psychopomp is characterized as
essentially a child divinity. I thought of Tadzio in *Death in
Venice*.'[4]

Indeed Kerényi's analysis of the Hermes figure is particularly
resonant for a reading of Forster's mythic imagination. Kerényi
speaks, for example, of the close relationship between Eros and
Hermes and of 'the eternal relationship of love, thievery and trade.'[5]
He sees the figures of Eros and Aphrodite as essentially one and
emphasises their wingedness and bisexuality. The Hermetic span, in
his analysis, moves 'from the phallic to the psychopompic' and
Hermes is seen, 'like every trickster', as one who 'operates outside

the fixed bounds of custom and law'. He is a 'hoverer-between-worlds who dwells in a world of his own'.[6]

Hermes, in Forster's fiction, is both a figure with a name, and a point of view, a way of seeing and acting. He is one of a trinity of male mythological figures, and by far the most significant. Pan, his son, was for a time more in fashion, but, as Patricia Merivale has shown, he had become rather trivialised by the first decade of the twentieth century.[7] Although Pan was still important for Forster, particularly as a figure of sexual awakening, a rough country boy, urgent and importunate, he was easily sentimentalised, not resonant enough mythologically as was his father. Even in his most important appearance, in 'The Story of a Panic', he belongs to a larger pattern shaped by Hermes.

The third figure in this trinity is also a countryman, the hunter Orion, shining in a cold sky, his frosty glories both a promise and a negation. Orion, 'the central star of whose sword is not a star, but a nebula, the golden seed of worlds to be', is older than either Hermes or Pan. He rises in autumn recalling youth and adventure ('The Point of It'). For Kuno in 'The Machine Stops', Orion provides the pattern of man and that image more than anything else is the source of his desire to reach the surface: 'The last thing that I saw ere the stopper closed after us were certain stars, and I felt that a man of my sort lived in the sky.' Orion provides a recurrent image in Forster's fiction, a promise of freedom, a vision of the enlarged male self, the rough woodsman. Any attempt to chart Forster's myth-making must place him, but it is, none the less, 'the mystifying son of Maia, that enticing divinity who calls forth ever renewed attempts at interpretation',[8] that must claim our attention.

Neither a heavenly presence nor an eruptive natural force, he is Hermes *philanthropotatos*, most friendly of gods to man.[9] For Forster he is an essential component of the double-sexed spirit of fantasy: 'She or he. For fantasy, though often female, sometimes resembles a man, and even functions for Hermes, who used to do the smaller behests of the gods – messenger, machine breaker, and conductor of souls to a not-too-terrible hereafter.'[10] It is this 'lightly built' figure who introduces the stories gathered together in *The Eternal Moment*. Again some years later he leads forth *The Collected Tales*. To him Forster dedicated *Pharos and Pharillon* and he concludes that book as well, presiding over the descent into the asphodel, even though Menelaus, who escaped death on his wife's account, remains with the cotton brokers, as he 'leads forth the pageant with solid tread'.[11]

Forster's association of Hermes and fantasy anticipates Kerényi's much later description of the type of experience symbolised by Hermes. It is that 'which expresses itself not scientifically but mythologically . . . [and] is open to the possibility of suprasensual guide and psychopomp, capable of affording impressions grounded in sense experience, which do not contradict the observations and findings of science, and which yet transcend the scientific view of the world. With Hermes as our guide through life, the world is viewed under a special aspect. This aspect is utterly real and remains within the realm of natural experience.'[12] Hermes belongs neither to the realm of life nor death. His true space – and the one most frequently evoked in Forster's stories – is the space between worlds.

Once we recognise this space as the natural setting for the tales, we still have the tasks of showing how the fantasies evoke this space, how the Hermetic presence operates. This hermeneutics of Hermes requires that we recognise the tales as being strong fictions, by no means juvenilia or whimsical exercises in fashionable turn-of-the-century Hellenism. They are structures in which language and myth cohere and where the reader plays the role of translator and of expositor of the story's argument. Determining the roles of narrator, characters and reader and thereby identifying the presence of the god will thus be the major concern for the remainder of the essay.

Although the narrators are often dull and uncomprehending, the reader is placed in the privileged position of initiate in a solemn mystery as he distinguishes between false story and true. As a result the controlling narrative point of view in many of these tales is distinct from the teller of the tale. It will be useful to give that point of view the name Hermes (indeed in 'The Celestial Omnibus' he even appears under his sign) and watch the forms he takes and the tricks he plays. His repertoire of jokes, for example, allows a Tytler or an Inskip to imagine he is telling a story, whereas, in fact, this putative narrator is totally unaware of the story that is really happening. We are witness to a process of transformation that the teller is ignorant of. The stories that Inskip narrates and Bons experiences (he could have been the narrator except for his nasty fall) never happen. But their pupils, who become in the stories the poetry their teachers imagined themselves to have read and understood, enter the realm of Hermes – death in the world, rebirth in the spirit.

Both 'Other Kingdom' and 'The Story of a Panic' use the obvious device of a stupid, obtuse narrator who is treacherously involved in the story's events, but who is unwittingly instrumental in the triumphant conclusion. Tytler in his temptation of Gennaro precipitates the leap that frees Eustace and returns him to his vision of Pan, experienced both as epiphany and human touch. Gennaro is both god and boy, the human evidence of the rapt vision. He is the true shaper of the tale, although, as mere actor, corruptible and weak. 'I made the new note crackle in my pocket; and he heard it. He stuck his hand out with a jerk; and the unsuspecting Eustace gripped it in his own.' Even from the Tytler perspective (although we are not to imagine that he intends any pathos in his use of 'unsuspecting'), there is an intimation of the larger meaning of the embrace. Gennaro, of course, sees it all the more sharply because of his own complicity: 'He longed for a friend, and found none for fifteen years. Then he found me, and the first night I – I who have been in the woods and understand things too – betray him to you and send him in to die.' Ironically it is through his apparent treachery that he provides Eustace with his only means of escape and interprets that escape rightly as salvation. 'He has understood and he is saved. . . . Now, instead of dying he will live!' Although lower-born than Hermes and younger, Pan, too, is conductor of the dead, and dwells, as is carefully glossed in 'Other Kingdom', 'most places, as name implies'.

Inskip, the perpetrator of such useful pedantry, is, in many ways, a more interesting figure than Tytler and less of a caricature. He is passionless, neutral, totally the embodiment of the practical world that Miss Beaumont absolutely escapes from at the end. It is those two poles, absolutely/practically, that are in many ways the governing polarities of Forster's fiction. The world of fantasy is absolute, reality is 'practically', in the sense both of 'almost' (i.e. tentative, pre-formed, not yet realised) and of 'useful in the ordinary ways of the world'. In the last sentence of 'Other Kingdom' the contrast and the triumphant escape are given visionary authority: 'She has escaped you absolutely for ever and ever, as long as there are branches to shade men from the sun.' Ford, whose private joke was to keep a diary called 'Practically a Book', is the spokesman for the absolute, the witness to a transformation so total that it escapes the world of sexuality altogether. We may imagine Eustace re-enacting eternally the gesture of awakening to his true sexual identity. But Evelyn in her transformation presides over just such a pre-fallen vegetable world that the Marvellian lover might have given to his coy mistress had there been world enough and time.

The narrative tension is thus between pupil and teacher, between Ford and Inskip, and translation, the ostensible activity of the story's opening, functions finally as a metaphor of its achievement. 'Ah, witless fellow! Gods, I say, even gods have dwelt in the woods ere now.' Inskip, the 'demens, the silly ass' tells a story of an odd, impetuous girl, a handsome wedding present, a clever and cynical ward, an indulgent employer; but in the end it is the gods who inhabit the woods whose deed Harcourt owns in perpetuity and it is Ford who sees them and speaks their tongue.

The different narrative strategy of 'The Celestial Omnibus' is the result of a slight shift in emphasis and is more apparent than real. Inskip and Tytler have been absorbed into the story as Mr Bons while the nameless narrator plays out a story before his nose which he cannot, he will not, see or hear.

The Celestial Omnibus is under Hermes' direction, as the sign-post in the dark alley tells us. The company will not 'be responsible for any negligence or stupidity on the part of Passengers, nor for Hailstorms, Lightning, Loss of Tickets, nor for any Act of God'. The signature is the caduceus, the emblem 'For the Direction'.

The story records a double journey, the boy's toward enlightenment and vision, Mr Bons's through darkness into death. The primary action is, of course, a literal version of the journey metaphor, and the two conductors are figures for the narrator himself. At the last, the boy (as nameless as his narrator) is caught up on the shield of Achilles and raised aloft, made to stand upright, while Mr Bons, unheeding of the words of Dante whom he has bound in vellum, sees only London and plummets to his death. It is indeed a conclusion of Dantesque tonality. His punishment is to see and not know how to believe, so atrophied has his library-bound imagination become; his fall and mutilation, emblematic of spiritual death.

In mythic terms, this story is probably the most satisfying, the most completely worked out. The shield of Achilles is the perfect emblem for the boy's exaltation. It is figuratively the entire world, but is bounded, shaped, indeed a shining version of that enclosed space – dell, cave, cabin, womb – that figures in almost every story and novel, and here made to stand for all experience consecrated by the imagination.

The stories move between two worlds. In them Hermes functions as the mythic analogue of the authorial presence, a device that diminishes the necessity for direct intervention, or rather, turns such intervention into a species of masquerade where, in the person of the god, the narrator can manifest truths and reshape reality. The short story, in Forster's hands, becomes genuinely an epiphany. The god himself inhabits there.

But two crucial aspects of the god remain to be examined: his actualisation as the beautiful young boy whom we saw exiled from Ephesus to the British Museum, and his connection for Forster, via his role as psychopomp, with death and memory. In both of these roles he has a ready place in late-nineteenth-century writing. He is Housman's 'merry guide' and related, too, to Pater's Denys L'Auxerrois, although that figure is, perhaps, more Dionysian or Orphic. He leads the *danse macabre* in *Zuleika Dobson*, but for the purposes of this argument, he makes his most interesting appearance in Henry James's 'The Great Good Place', a story with marked affinities with Forster's 'The Point of It'.

There is no establishing with certainty whether Forster read James's later stories shortly after they were published, nor is it necessary to argue any direct connection or influence. Using James as a touchstone should serve primarily to remind us that Forster was working within an acknowledged aesthetic, even as he shaped it to his own special voice. None the less the resemblances between the two stories are certainly striking, both in their tonality and the shape of the action. In both stories the central character recapitulates a lifetime as the other acts as a guide. In both there is a calculated blurring of the boundary between reality and fantasy. An event occurs that is neither wholly within the soul or within the world. Where does George Dane go? Who is the young man who takes over his life, whose voice, whose face merge with the voice and face of the Good Brother of the dream? 'I just dropped my burden and he received it', Dane tells the brother as a total explanation.[13] To be sure, the central experience of 'The Point of It' seems more overtly allegorical, but the vision of a lifetime leading to death and back is vouchsafed to Micky in much the same Hermetic fashion as it is to Dane.

Such a reading of 'The Point of It' is, at first glance, hard to sustain, but an unpublished version presently in The University of Texas Library confirms it in important ways.[14] The story has always troubled its readers, who echo the title with uncertainty, not quite able to complete the sentence. What is it that Micky finally learns? What is his final transformation? However, the story originally ended with four lines that were cancelled before publication:

'Well rowed,' cried Micky to the ferryman. 'Three more and easy.'
The order was obeyed.
'Ship.'
Harold shipped his oars.

These lines, inasmuch as they imply that Harold did not die, remind us that the sunset with which the story closes locates the same moment in time as the story's opening. The friends are now returning at sunset to the shore they set out from earlier in the day, and this realisation transforms the central part of the story, Micky's life and death, from narration to vision.

Described mythologically, the story arrests the flow of time. In a flash all of Micky's life is unfolded before his eyes. Harold, functioning as Hermes, is the stimulus of a vision which allows both for failure and salvation, death and return. Micky sees, simultaneously, the probable course of his life and that action or gesture which could yet transform it. Thus as he is excited by the total commitment to the moment which Harold's rapt straining at the oars signifies, he is able to transcend the mediocrity that will otherwise characterise his life and return in the blazing sunset, having successfully crossed midstream. No time passes at all, or no more than that split second which it takes for the boat, working against the ebb of the tide, to cross the channel. Harold is at the oars. 'The ferryman', these lines call him, but that identification with Charon serves only to emphasise his role as Hermes. There were many precedents for the conflation of the two names, not the least being Housman's epigraph to 'The Merry Guide'. In that subtitle, subsequently cancelled, the phrase 'Hermes guide of souls' appears, but the line from Euripides generally regarded as the source of the quotation refers instead to Charon.[15] That Forster should have merged the two names is no surprise. For whether his name be Hermes or Charon, Harold remains the psychopomp, the spirit of fantasy itself. He is, however, a silent character, whose function as conductor of souls is taken over by the narrator. For it is the narrator who unfolds and interprets the process whereby Micky transforms his life and becomes capable of that absoluteness which is the total antithesis of the Tomlinson life that would otherwise be his. And – this is the point! – this transformation occurs in the realm of fantasy, it does not occur in reality. *No one dies.*

Thus 'The Point of It' contains two stories; one lasts a moment, the other a lifetime. Even without the cancelled ending, one could maintain such a reading. The framing sunset remains. Moreover, Micky enters the visionary realm early in the story when on the second page we see him transform the farmhouse on the shore into 'a star and the boat its attendant satellite'. 'Micky had imagination', Forster tells us. In his eyes 'the tide was the rushing ether stream of the universe, the interstellar surge that beats forever.' It is within this frame that the rest of the story unfolds.

Death is, however, not only the beautiful boy all wings and muscle, but retrospect, memory. Twelve years later, in a letter to John Middleton Murry on the death of Katherine Mansfield, Forster wrote: 'Death interests me for more than one reason. It is largely connected for me with the problem of remembering. Sorrow I find indirectly rather than directly painful; it obscures.'[16] In the story, dying is re-living and the pain of death is particularly the pain of the failure of memory. In another portion of the story that was removed before publication, this is made explicit:

Ah time, is it not enough to snatch the present? need you ruin the past as well? here is your highest crime against man, that man forgets. Even as a [*sic*] write memories are fading, sweet moments are ghostly in the gathering grey, places and friends are passing from my brain as they have long since passed from my eyes; until in the final twilight even this dimness will be a memory, and I shall but remember that once I remembered.

One can more easily guess why Forster cancelled this passage than give reasons for his cancelling of the final lines. The tone is, perhaps, too sententious; the 'I' merges with 'a' in a more than typographical error. The contrast in the story is certainly sharper without it: 'The shades were silent. They could not remember.'

But why did Forster choose to blur the outlines of the finished tale and leave the impression at the end that the channel Micky crosses is the spiritual analogue of the real one, but, for all that, not the same? Perhaps the decision to leave the ending ambiguous had more to do with his own unresolved feelings about death than with purely literary concerns. Certainly, as we learn from Furbank's biography, 1910 to 1911 was a particularly dark time for Forster; in many ways his 1637. And while I make no claims that 'The Point of It' ranks with *Lycidas* as art, the urgent wrestling with death that both story and poem record are comparable. The 'declaration' to Masood which gets him nowhere, the disappointing New Year's Eve that follows, the illness and death of his grandmother, his own illness that might be tubercular (his father had been not quite two years older when he had died), a birthday shadowed with death. Although 'The Point of It' was not published until November 1911, it had been completed by March.[17] Without the final lines it is a darker story, or, at least, the terms of the triumph are less certain, the point of it more in doubt.

Return is, none the less, part of the Hermes myth and Alcestis on the temple drum will shortly retrace her journey, Hermes still her guide. The story, in similar fashion, holds life and death in equal suspension, its driving urgency, the sense that life must be seized, followed even to the gates of death, as if only in that heroic straining can there be salvation. Harold is, thus, a purer Gerald Dawes, seen more sculpturally, without the crankiness he wore in the novel. And Micky seems, especially from the vantage afforded by the manuscript version, more fit than Rickie to grasp the point of it, to know that he has been in the presence of the god and that, henceforth, his life must be changed.

The god leaves his traces throughout Forster's writing in his many disguises, from Puck the phallic trickster in 'The Obelisk' to the angry god in 'The Road from Colonus'. For Forster he seems to be simultaneously a mythic mode, an artifact of unsettling beauty and a psychological reality. As myth, marble and desire, he presides in the tales. He knows more than the mere narrators, although he sometimes speaks with their voices. Mercurial, elusive, he gives the fiction its shape and informs it with his spirit.

Thus the effectiveness of the tales is in large measure due to their mythic coherence. To say that Hermes inhabits there may be fanciful speech but of the sort congenial to Forster's way of imagining. For, finally, Hermes in his triple incarnation – Hermes, Eros, Death – was for Forster, as he was for Whitman, that 'crown and point which all lives have reference to'. Indeed his evocation in the 1876 Preface to *Leaves of Grass* has many echoes for the present occasion:

I still feel to keep *Passage to India* for last words even to this Centennial dithyramb. Not as, in antiquity, at highest festival of Egypt, the noisome skeleton of Death was also sent on exhibition to the revellers, for zest and shadow to the occasion's joy and light – but as the perfect marble statue of the normal Greeks at

Elis, suggesting death in the form of a beautiful and perfect young man, with closed eyes, leaning on an inverted torch – emblem of rest and aspiration after action – of crown and point which all lives and poems should steadily have reference to, namely, the justified and noble termination of our identity, this grade of it, and outlet-preparation to another grade.

4 Where was the Road from Colonus?

George H. Thomson

The main events in E. M. Forster's short story 'The Road from Colonus' take place in a grove of plane trees in Greece. Within the grove is a small inn or khan and near it an exceptionally large hollow tree from whose roots a spring flows. It is here that old Mr Lucas has his vision of renewed youth. It is here that Mrs Forman says she is reminded of the Colonus of Sophocles. It is here then that the road from Colonus begins.[1x]

The place, we are told later, is Plataniste in the Province of Messenia. That an insignificant inn should have an official name is explained by the habits of rural nomenclature. The action takes place around the turn of the century, when it was still not uncommon to name a khan after the village nearest to it, even if the distance was substantial. For instance, Baedeker mentions the Khan of Piri, which was a ferry-ride plus a full hour's journey from the hamlet of the same name. As for the date, Forster visited Greece and wrote the story in 1903. It was published in June 1904. The action takes place on Tuesday, 18 April. If this conjunction of day and date is accurate, the year must be 1899.

Mr Lucas has already been to Athens, Delphi, Thermopylae, and presumably Sparta, though the reference to the River Eurotas is rather general. While at Plataniste where they make their lunch, Ethel says to her father: 'You know we have to get to Olympia to-night.' They are then going on to Patras – one night's delay will cause them to miss the boat there.

So much for the road *from* Colonus. Where is this Plataniste with the hollow tree and running water? The awkward fact is that any point in Messenia must be in excess of 30 miles from Olympia over some of the most rugged terrain in the Peloponnesus. On its easterly border the province juts northward and comes close to Andritsaena.

From there to Olympia – according to Baedeker – was a stiff journey of ten hours at least. From any other part of Messenia, except this northern spur, the journey would take more than a day. In either case it would not be possible for Mr Lucas's party to reach Olympia in an afternoon.

Two explanations of this anomaly are possible. The first, Forster made a mistake: the account of the disaster should not have specified Messenia or Ethel should not have spoken of reaching Olympia so soon. The second, Forster for some reason deliberately fudged the account of the location, thereby making it impossible to identify or rationalise its geographical setting.

We may, by investigating the territory around Olympia, be able to throw some light on these alternatives. Place-names with the root *platanos* or in its early form *platanistos* (plane tree) are not uncommon, because springs and streams with a grove of such trees are rather frequently met with in the Peloponnesus.

I have been able to locate four potential sites for Plataniste, though each has one or more serious drawbacks. Since the investigation of these sites is rather technical, I have placed the account of them in the notes. Here I will summarise only the most obvious results. Platanos near Olympia in the Province of Elis is too close to Olympia, half-an-hour's journey, let us say, to be compatible with the details of the story and particularly with the fact that after lunch, as the travellers wind their way round the mountainside, they are surprised by an unexpected view: 'the place they had left an hour before suddenly reappeared far below them.' The other three locations suffer from precisely the opposite difficulty: they are Platanos near Patras in the Province of Achaia, Platania near the river Neda in the Province of Messenia, and Plataniston, a stream near Megalopolis, in the Province of Arkadia. All have the disadvantage, give or take a few hours, of being a two-days' journey from Olympia.[2x]

Against these facts we may set Forster's statement in the 1946 Introduction to the American edition of *The Collected Tales of E. M. Forster*, published by Knopf in 1947, that in 1903 'the whole of *The Road from Colonus* hung ready for me in a hollow tree near Olympia.' In the 1947 Introduction to the English edition of *Collected Short Stories* Forster revises this to read 'not far from Olympia'. The change suggests that he wanted to express himself precisely and that the shade of meaning implied by 'not far from' came closer to the truth than did 'near'. Since the *genius loci* had inspired Forster directly only three times, as he informs us in the Introduction, we have good reason to trust his memory of these occasions. Not only does the character, Mr Lucas in this case, have a vision, but the author himself received the story through a visionary or ecstatic experience. It is characteristic of ecstatic experience that every detail is exceptionally vivid and memorable. Thus when Forster says, even after more than forty years, that the moment overtook him 'not far from Olympia', we should believe him.

But this information does not take us very far, though it is of considerable biographical interest. It tells us that the actual geographical setting of the author's experience was not that represented in the story, since Mr Lucas and his party are clearly at some remove from Olympia. In other words, Forster took the moment of experience upon which the narrative is based and removed it from the environs of Olympia. He did so, I would speculate, to reinforce the feeling of isolation and apartness characteristic of ecstatic experience. Once he had removed it, there were no limits to its new location other than those imposed by the story itself.

If we suppose Plataniste to have been a real place represented with some degree of accuracy, none of the four locations mentioned above and described further in the notes is very satisfying. Substituting Elis for Messenia only gives us Platanos, too near Olympia to be possible. Of the three more distant sites, the stream Plataniston, lying fairly near to the border of Messenia, may seem the most tempting, but at more than two days from Olympia it represents an error, by Ethel and the author, of a rather improbable magnitude. The truth, as we know, is that whatever the place chosen, some details will not fit. For that reason and in the absence of any positive evidence to support the claim of any one of these sites, I incline to the belief that the geographical location of the scene is imaginary.

Even so, the incongruities persist, for which the following alternative explanations may be offered.

(1) Forster mistakenly believed that Messenia lay further north and that he was devising a setting fulfilling the needs of the story.
(2) Forster knew he was wrong about Messenia but perpetrated the mistake as an amusing little anomaly which only a fit audience of a few would appreciate.
(3) Forster knew he was wrong but deliberately injected con-

tradictory indicators to convey to the sophisticated reader the truth that Plataniste is everywhere and nowhere.

It is not easy to choose between these alternatives. With respect to (1), it may not seem credible that Forster was so ignorant of basic Greek geography. On the other hand, he was subject to gaps in knowledge like everyone else; he liked guidebooks but did not believe in taking them too seriously; and Baedeker's map does not show provincial demarcations consistently or clearly, nor does his text mention them in a more than casual way. With respect to (2) and (3), it may be noted that 'The Road from Colonus' is both a social satire and a spiritual allegory. This ironic contrast is carried to the very end. In the last sentence but one Ethel makes a fatuous remark about Providence, in the last Mr Lucas complains about the drains, a deadly urban parody of the earlier life-giving running water at Plataniste. In light of this double aspect of the story, (2) and (3) might well be compatible.

Between (1) and (2)–(3) I do not know how to choose unless new facts emerge concerning Forster's intention. What is obvious and striking is his desire to distance his 'not far from Olympia' experience, to isolate it by allowing Mr Lucas an hour later one last view of 'the dangerous scene' far below. For the others it has been a wayside stop on the road to Olympia. For Mr Lucas it has been a rite of passage from old age and an 'old self' to renewed youth and significance and the acceptance of death. But he is torn away from this midday turning point of his existence on the other side of which lies salvation. For the modern Oedipus, the road leads *from* Colonus to a life of meaningless dotage . . . Olympia, Patras, London . . .

5 *The Longest Journey*: E. M. Forster's Refutation of Idealism

S. P. Rosenbaum

Too much has been made of the influence of the philosopher G. E. Moore on E. M. Forster, according to Forster's authorised biographer, Mr P. N. Furbank. Forster never read Moore, a cardinal tenet of whose ethics Furbank says was 'that the only things in the world possessing intrinsic value were good states of mind. . . . ' And though he was a member of the Apostles during the period that Moore dominated the Society,

> he was not, however, a Moore-ite. In fact he always believed himself incapable of abstract thought; and so far as the actual discussions were concerned, he usually found them extremely tedious. Indeed he often didn't listen very closely – which helps to explain, what might appear puzzling, how it is that the problem which Ansell and his friends are discussing in that opening scene [of *The Longest Journey*]—about the cow in the field, and whether it is there when no one is looking—seems to belong more to the age of Berkeley than to that of Russell and Moore.[1]

It may be that too much has been made of the influence of Moore's *Principia Ethica* but Furbank's comments on the matter suggest that more needs to be known about Moore and that influence before we can properly evaluate it. It is a mistake, first of all, to say that a cardinal tenet of Moore's ethics was that only good states of mind possess intrinsic value; Moore, Forster, and Bloomsbury all maintained that works of art were of intrinsic value, and to equate them with states of mind is to make that fundamental error in philosophy that Moore attacked in his criticism of Idealism.[2x] Forster has been quoted by several interviewers as saying he never read Moore (he also said he never read Freud or Jung) but what Forster wrote on the subject indicates that he did not need to:

> I did not receive Moore's influence direct – I was not up to that and have never read *Principia Ethica*. It came to me at a remove, through those who knew the Master. The seed fell on fertile, if inferior soil, and I began to think for myself. . . .[3x]

Hugh Meredith and A. R. Ainsworth were the friends who taught him most about Moore, Forster said in an interview,[4x] and Furbank's biography shows how influential Meredith was on Forster. As for Forster's not being a 'Moore-ite', Leonard Woolf, who knew Forster and Moore and the Apostles well, has stated that, ' . . . under the surface all six of us, Desmond, Lytton, Saxon, Morgan, Maynard and I, had been permanently inoculated with Moore and Moorism. . . .'[5]

Finally, the puzzle that Furbank finds in the opening discussion of *The Longest Journey* reveals that Forster knew his Moore better than his biographer believes. The opening discussion about whether the cow is there or not when no one perceives it is a fairly direct allusion to one of the most famous early papers Moore wrote. Entitled 'The Refutation of Idealism', it appeared in *Mind*—the same philosophical journal Ansell's sister waves about, complaining of its criticism of her brother – in October 1903, which was around the time, Furbank shows, that Forster was beginning to formulate his ideas about Cambridge for his novel. The essay came out at the same time as *Principia Ethica*, which makes use of its arguments. In 'The Refutation of Idealism' Moore attempts to refute Berkeley's assertion that *esse* is *percipi*, for this he says is the basic premiss of modern Idealism. It was not Forster, then, who was looking back to the age of Berkeley but Moore and Russell, who found Berkeley's idea being used to support Idealism at the turn of the century in Cambridge. Their refutation of this Idealism is part of the revolution they worked in philosophy, and Forster's novel is an imaginative interpretation and extension of that refutation. Indeed, Bertrand Russell's account of how liberating Moore's refutation was could have come from *The Longest Journey*:

> With a sense of escaping from prison, we allowed ourselves to think that grass is green, that the sun and stars would exist if no

one was aware of them, and also that there is a pluralistic timeless world of Platonic ideas.[6]

Whether or not we classify Forster as a Moore-ite or a Moorist is in itself unimportant, but when overlooking his significance leads to the misunderstanding of one of his novels, it is time to assume that Forster meant what he said when he wrote, in an introduction to the novel more than half a century after it was first published, that Rickie's Cambridge was,

> the Cambridge of G. E. Moore which I knew at the beginning of the century: the fearless uninfluential Cambridge that sought for reality and cared for truth.   (p. xi)[7]

Throughout his career, Forster's general philosophical outlook is derived mainly from Moore's ethics and epistemology, and the clearest illustration of this influence is *The Longest Journey*, where Forster's adaptation of Moore's philosophical Realism can be seen as the organising basis of the novel. In his introduction to the novel Forster mentioned seven distinct ideas that were whirling around him as he wrote and that may well have impaired his sense of direction in the book. The original idea was 'that of a man who discovers that he has an illegitimate brother'; the subsequent ideas that intervened between this inspiration and the finished work are listed as follows by Forster:

> There was the metaphysical idea of Reality ('the cow is there'): there was the ethical idea that reality must be faced (Rickie won't face Stephen); there was the idea, or ideal, of the British Public School; there was the title, exhorting us in the words of Shelley not to love one person only; there was Cambridge, there was Wiltshire.   (pp. ix–x)

Perhaps the simplest way to show how Moore's rejection of Idealism for Realism is changed into something rich and even strange in *The Longest Journey* is to go through, one by one, the ideas that followed the original inspiration. Such a procedure runs the risk of making the novel appear too schematic, but it has the advantage of showing that *The Longest Journey* is a more comprehensively organised novel of ideas than has been recognised.

We need to begin with the initial inspiration, however, for it may well have come to Forster from another of his valued intellectual resources.

A MAN WHO DISCOVERS THAT HE HAS AN ILLEGITIMATE BROTHER

The original inspiration for *The Longest Journey* is that staple of fiction, the birth-mystery, complete with the problems of love and money that express its concern with personal and social identity. The idea could have come to Forster from anywhere, but the most plausible literary source may be the sequel to *Erewhon* that Samuel Butler published in 1901. Critics have commented on the affinities between *The Way of All Flesh* and *The Longest Journey*, and Forster himself has testified how influential *Erewhon* was on him in both its form and ideas.[8] The story of *Erewhon Revisited* is told by a man who wished for a brother and then discovers that he has an unknown half-brother – his father's son, though the illegitimate half-brother's mother is in a situation not unlike Rickie's and Stephen's mother. The unknown brother lives in Erewhon and his occupations are like Stephen's: he is a ranger. In *Erewhon Revisited* the question is whether the illegitimate brother George will accept his father rather than whether brother will accept brother. But the general resemblance of George to Stephen Wonham is interesting. (Forster said he took the name 'Wonham' from a place but there is also a likeness to 'Erewhon'.) Samuel Butler's iconoclasm permanently influenced Forster's thinking, and in *The Longest Journey* this can be seen in the ideas of Rickie, Ansell, Stephen, and Mr Failing.[9x] The high-minded conventions of the Pembrokes and Mrs Failing form one aspect of the idealism that *The Longest Journey* repudiates—for the novel criticises both of the principal meanings of the word 'idealism'. Idealism in the sense of altruism and Idealism as an epistemology are both 'refuted' in Forster's novel.

The meanings of brotherhood in *The Longest Journey* are far more complex than anything suggested by Butler's Erewhon books. They begin with the novel's one-word dedication 'Fratribus' and include everything from friendship and homoerotic love to Mr Failing's notions about the brotherhood of man – and not excluding what it means to have Herbert Pembroke as a brother-in-law. The distinction between friendship and homoerotic love is not easy to make in the novel, as the following passage shows. It begins with Rickie's thoughts about friendship but then merges indistinguishably with Forster's:

He was thinking of the irony of friendship – so strong it is, and so fragile. We fly together, like straws in an eddy, to part in the open stream. Nature has no use for us; she has cut her stuff differently. Dutiful sons, loving husbands, responsible fathers—these are what she wants, and if we are friends it must be in our spare time. Abram and Sarai were sorrowful, yet their seed became as sand of the sea, and distracts the politics of Europe at this moment. But a few verses of poetry is all that survives of David and Jonathan.

'I wish we were labelled,' said Rickie. He wished . . . there was a society, a kind of friendship office, where the marriage of true minds could be registered.　　　　　　　　　　　　　(vii, 74)

The astonishingly contemporary reference to the politics of Europe probably alludes to the rehabilitation of Dreyfus that finally took place in 1906, when Forster was writing his novel. But when the context of the allusion is taken together with the fact that Ansell is Jewish, the reference to male friendship 'passing the love of women' is reinforced.[10x] And Rickie gets his wish. The male he loves best bears the label of half-brother. How symbolic of homoerotic or homosexual love Forster wanted to make this brotherly love is finally unclear in the novel. At times the symbolism seems unmistakable, as with the Oedipal limp that ought to have kept Rickie from trying to procreate.

'Fratribus' is among other things a dedication to The Cambridge Conversazione Society, alias The Apostles, which Forster joined in 1901 and whose members addressed each other as brothers. Forster's brothers recognised the opening of *The Longest Journey* as an Apostolic scene. The very language of The Apostles was inherited from their Victorian Idealist brothers, but by Forster's time the distinctions between the timeless reality of the Society and unreal 'phenomena' apparently existing outside had become ironic. This change brings us to the influence of G. E. Moore.

THE METAPHYSICAL IDEA OF REALITY ('THE COW IS THERE')

The uses of philosophy in *The Longest Journey* are various. Characters are judged by the attitudes they have toward philosophy. Herbert

Pembroke cannot see what it is for; the Elliots can and they offer Rickie's mother 'views', 'emotional standpoints', 'attitudes towards life', which they call philosophy, instead of the facts she hungers for (xxix, 269–70). Ansell's father, on being assured that philosophy lies behind everything because 'it tries to discover what is good and true', knows that it is more important than money or social position and therefore urges his son to take it up seriously (iii, 33). Stephen feels he has to get himself fixed up philosophically before starting life properly and follows the ideas of Robert Ingersoll into atheism and materialism. But the ideas and symbols associated with Rickie and Ansell are the ones that most centrally involve philosophy in the novel, and they are derived from the Cambridge of Moore that Forster belonged to at the turn of the century. The opening philosophical discussion in *The Longest Journey* about the existence of objects, whether or not they have an existence of their own when no one is looking at them, and therefore whether reality is subjective or objective, is about the same general topic as Moore's celebrated refutation of Idealism. Moore's paper is a critique of the argument used by Idealists to maintain that everything is mental because *esse* is *percipi* – to be is to be perceived. He emphasises that he is not denying that reality is spiritual – indeed he hopes it is; what Moore wants to deny is the truth of the Idealists' argument for it. Their argument is false because the ambiguous meanings of the copula contradict each other. That is, Idealists argue that *esse* is identical with *percipi* and at the same time that they are distinct. In Moore's example, if yellow and the perception of yellow were identical, then the statement that yellow was being perceived would mean only that yellow was yellow. Something else is obviously meant, and therefore Moore concludes that we must distinguish between perceiving and what we perceive. The distinction is the basis for Moore's general position of philosophical Realism: he is not an Idealist, because he finds no reason for denying the existence of objects apart from our consciousness of them, and he is not a Materialist, because he finds no reason for denying the existence of our consciousness apart from the objects it is conscious of.

Ansell is, with some inconsistencies, a philosophical Realist in *The Longest Journey*, and Rickie's waverings between Idealism and Realism mark crucial stages in his education. Yet little of Moore's actual argument finds its way into the novel. Ansell's critic is right, in the opening scene, when he says Ansell has not proved the existence of cows by lighting matches and asserting 'The cow is there'. (Ansell's matches are the beginning of the light imagery that is associated throughout the novel with reality, as well as with love.) Moore did not try to prove the existence of external objects; he simply denied that they could be disproved. 'The question requiring to be asked about material things,' he wrote at the end of his paper,

> is thus not: What reason have we for supposing that anything exists *corresponding* to our sensations? but: What reason have we for supposing that material things do *not* exist, since *their* existence has precisely the same evidence as that of our sensations?[11]

Ansell indirectly concerns himself with Moore's question when he denies the reality of Agnes Pembroke, but this takes us away from epistemology to ethics. Moore's 'The Refutation of Idealism' is an essay in epistemology only. In *The Longest Journey* Forster imaginatively converts an epistemological point from the essay into a moral one. To understand this we need to be aware of what the epistemological point was.

Before going on to the next idea Forster listed, which has to do with the ethical implications of philosophical Realism, it is worth emphasising that Moore's Realism lies behind his ethics and can be found in his rejection of Kantianism, in his emphasis on the value of true belief, and elsewhere. (It was his valuing of true belief that resulted—to Clive Bell's despair—in Moore's asserting that it was better to contemplate a natural rather than a painted scene because the natural one was real.) 'The Refutation of Idealism', as its title indicates, is essentially a negative piece of analysis, but implicit in it and in *Principia Ethica* is that seeking for reality and caring for truth that Forster found in the Cambridge of G. E. Moore. Stephen 'must be told such a real thing', Rickie at first insists when he discovers he has a half-brother (xiv, 159), and Moore together with Bloomsbury would have agreed with this stress on the significance of something because of its reality. The epigraph to *Principia Ethica*—Bishop Butler's 'Everything is what it is, and not another thing'—expresses very well Moore's passionate affirmation of the importance of knowing what is real, what is true. It also expresses Forster's idea of Cambridge truth, as his biographer admits.[12]

Finally, it is also worth noting that Moore's Bloomsbury disciples connected his refutation of epistemological Idealism with the general repudiation of Victorian altruism that was taking place in the works of writers like Samuel Butler. Moore's attack on Idealism did not, however, affect his maintaining, along with his friends, that 'The Ideal' as propounded in the last chapter of *Principia Ethica* was 'the rational ultimate end of human action and the sole criterion of social progress. . . .'[13]

THE ETHICAL IDEA THAT REALITY MUST BE FACED (RICKIE WON'T FACE STEPHEN)

One of the two central lessons taught in Forster's *Bildungsroman* has to do with the consequences of not believing in the objective existence of other people and other societies, of nature, and of time. The other lesson is concerned with love, as we shall see, where again Idealism needs refuting. At one time or another in *The Longest Journey* all the important characters, except possibly Stephen Wonham, act like epistemological Idealists in denying the objective existence of people whom, for one reason or another, they do not wish to be aware of. The reasons are metaphysical, moral, psychological, social, or sexual. Rickie's wife, father, aunt, and brother-in-law all practise that class kind of Idealism that recognises the existence of inferiors only when they impinge upon the consciousnesses of their superiors. They are vulgar Idealists, in the sense of Mr Failing's distinction between coarseness and vulgarity—'coarseness, revealing something; vulgarity, concealing something' (xxvi, 241). 'Procul este, profani' (xxvi, 243) is their motto and no-trespassing sign. The effects of their Idealism extend from snubs to gross social injustices.

The arguments of 'The Refutation of Idealism' have little to do with these moral extensions of Moore's criticism; he nowhere suggests that Idealists behave worse than Materialists or Realists. How Forster fashions a moral symbolism from an epistemological dispute appears most clearly in the case of Rickie Elliot. Initially Rickie tries to love everyone, which in its way is a denial of human individuality, as Ansell implies. At times he knows how important it is to face reality, as when he insists that Agnes *mind* the death of Gerald; but after refusing to acknowledge Stephen's identity, Rickie finds the world becoming unreal. His depression is expressed in the little joke 'that the cow was not really there' (xix, 205). Later the partial acceptance of Stephen makes him happy again, he says to his incredulous aunt,

'because, as we used to say at Cambridge, the cow is there. The
world is real again. This is a room, that a window, outside is the
night—'
'Go on.'
He pointed to the floor. 'The day is straight below, shining
through other windows into other rooms.'   (xxxiv, 317–18)[14x]

But Stephen breaks his promise not to get drunk, and Rickie decides
he has only been pretending again that people were real. His end,
which follows immediately afterwards, is ironical: he throws his life
away to save that of a person whose reality he has again just denied.
Mrs Failing, consistent to the end, buries Rickie, pretending that he
had once been alive, and it is part of the novel's pathos that her
pretending is more justified than Rickie's.

One of the reasons why Rickie has so much difficulty with both
the metaphysical and ethical ideas of reality is his imagination. 'The
Refutation of Idealism' sheds little light on the reality of imagined
things. What Moore wrote about the experience of things also
covers the imagination of them:

> From the fact that a thing was real we should be able to infer, by
> the law of contradiction, that it was experienced; since the latter
> would be *part* of what is meant by the former. But, on the other
> hand, from the fact a thing was experienced we should *not* be able
> to infer that it was real; since it would not follow from the fact that
> it had one of the attributes essential to reality, that it *also* had the
> other or others.[15x]

Rickie's difficulty as a person is how to accept the full objective
reality of other people, but his difficulty as a writer is how to make
his imaginative conceptions fully real. Epistemological Idealism has
been attractive to writers since the Romantics, for it offers a reality
to their imagined creations that is comparable to the perceived
realities of the external world. Thus Idealism has a special
attraction for the artist in *The Longest Journey*. As a writer Rickie is
involved in yet another meaning of the word 'idealism'. His creative
imagination tends to produce ideal forms; his stories are about
outmoded idealisations of nature such as Dryads, and they do not
convince, says the editor, because their creator has not gotten inside
life. Forster seems to be suggesting here, perhaps autobiographi-

cally, that the refutation of Idealism has benefits for aesthetics as well as for ethics and metaphysics. Rickie's last and perhaps best story, written after he has left the Idealism of his Sawston marriage, differs from those included in the posthumous *Pan Pipes*; Rickie describes it as being 'about a man and a woman who meet and are happy'. 'Somewhat of a *tour de force*, I conclude,' says Mrs Failing (xxxiv, 317).

It is, of course, not necessary to know anything about Moore's 'The Refutation of Idealism' to see that *The Longest Journey* is a novel about appearance and reality. What an awareness of Moore's philosophy can do for criticism of the novel is to help it avoid misinterpretations. This is best illustrated with the ideas of Stewart Ansell. Throughout the book Ansell's criticisms of Rickie's attempts to cope with reality are essential to Rickie's education. He points out to Rickie how his imaginative, romantic idealising of people prevents him from judging their real worth. But *The Longest Journey* also shows that Ansell's notions of reality need correcting. His distinction between two kinds of phenomena – those such as the cow, and 'those which are the subjective product of a diseased imagination, and which, to our destruction, we invest with the semblance of reality' (i, 19) – have frequently been taken by critics as authorial. The distinction is an answer to Moore's question about the reasons we have for supposing that anything corresponding to our sensations does not exist. Agnes's behaviour and Rickie's idealisation of her give Ansell ethical reasons, in other words, for supposing Agnes exists only when she is perceived by diseased imaginations such as Rickie's. This is not exactly what Moore had in mind. Ansell's fellowship dissertations, the first one of which was 'about things being real' (xv, 167) both fail at Cambridge. The giving of ethical answers to epistemological questions indicates where Ansell might have encountered some difficulties from his teachers, but the reason given is that he has read too much Hegel. Hegel's Idealism, as represented in Cambridge chiefly by J. McT. E. McTaggart, was part of the philosophical tradition that Moore and Russell revolutionised early in the century. (Moore is untypically polemical in his attack on the Hegelian doctrine of organic unities in 'The Refutation of Idealism'.[16x] Ansell's quasi-Idealistic distinction between kinds of phenomena is undercut a little later in *The Longest Journey* when Forster notes that Ansell did not apply it to those for whom *he* had a special affection:

Mr. Ansell, a provincial draper of moderate prosperity, ought by rights to have been classed not with the cow, but with those phenomena that are not really there. But his son, with pardonable illogicality, excepted him. He never suspected that his father might be the subjective product of a diseased imagination. From his earliest years he had taken him for granted, as a most undeniable and lovable fact.   (iii, 32)

The issue here is not Ansell's inconsistency or even the fallacy of giving ethical answers to epistemological questions. *The Longest Journey* does that throughout for its own imaginative and moral purposes, and among the latter is Forster's point that although our love for people may lead to our idealising them, we are not justified in refusing to acknowledge the independent existence of people we do not care for. When we subjectively idealise people and when we deny their objective reality, we endanger our own sense of reality. Honest, intelligent, and moral, Ansell realises this better than almost anyone in the novel, but he too is flawed with Idealism; his perceptions are also altered by love, which partly accounts for his antagonism towards Agnes. We shall find this connection between love and the perception of objective reality again when we come to Forster's use of Shelley.

Ansell's mandalas are also symbols of his incipient Idealism. The first occasion on which he draws one in the novel is just after he has denied Agnes's existence; Rickie asks him if the drawing is real and Ansell replies that only the undrawable, unperceivable middle is. Later in the British Museum Ansell's sense of reality receives a shock when he learns that Rickie, who Ansell fears has become unreal, and that figment of Rickie's imagination, Agnes, are going to have an undoubtedly real baby. Ansell has been drawing a diagram in the margin of his dissertation, while discussing Rickie and explaining to their friend Widdrington that the way to fight Agnes is not with philosophy but with poetry—not, that is, with distinctions about kinds of phenomena, but with what he calls the poetic 'Spirit of Life'. After the news he admits, among the carved Greek gods and goddesses (including the Cnidian Demeter) he dislikes, that there are powers he cannot cope with or yet understand. In the very next chapter Rickie thinks of a mandala as a symbol of continuity, with the new inner circle or square becoming the son he will forget himself in. But the baby turns out to be a daughter maimed with the hereditary defect of the Elliots that should have kept Rickie from having children. Rickie has tried to idealise the future as he idealised the past.

Ansell's sense of reality is finally corrected and completed by Stephen Wonham. Ansell, in one of his Idealistic moods, ignores Stephen when first addressed by him; afterwards he describes their fight as 'a momentary contact with reality' (xxvii, 259). Stephen's view of reality is quite simple:

> He only held the creed of 'here am I and there are you', and therefore class distinctions were trivial things to him, and life no decorous scheme, but a personal combat or a personal truce.
> (xxx, 281)

In its ethical denial of Idealism—the way, that is, it faces the objective reality of other people—Stephen's creed is closer to Forster's than Ansell's or Rickie's. But it too needs to be widened. When Stephen repeats the creed to Rickie and adds from his philosophy of atheistic materialism, 'the rest is cant' (xxxiii, 307), the author disagrees and says that Stephen will come to realise this in time. The epilogue to *The Longest Journey* intimates that Ansell and Stephen are educating each other in the metaphysical and ethical implications of philosophical Realism. The final sentences of 'The Refutation of Idealism' apply to both of them as well as to all the other principal characters of the novel:

> The only *reasonable* alternative to the admission that matter exists *as well as* spirit, is absolute Scepticism—that, as likely as not *nothing* exists at all. All other suppositions—the Agnostic's, that something, at all events, does exist, as much as the Idealist's, that spirit does—are, if we have no reason for believing in matter, as baseless as the grossest superstitions.[17]

THE IDEA, OR IDEAL, OF THE BRITISH PUBLIC SCHOOL

In his introduction to *The Longest Journey* Forster explicitly endorses Ansell's refutation of the Idealism that is manifested in the assumptions of Sawston. Here the epistemological and altruistic meanings of idealism converge. Sawston's ideals are patriotism, athletics, learning, and religion. Herbert Pembroke's promulgating of them to educate rich boys rather than the poor ones that the school was originally to serve is justified by his conviction, which he shares with others of his class and profession, that the school is an unreal miniature copy or anticipation of the great, that is real, world. The boys themselves are not to be taken as fully real human beings; they are to be taught by personal influence rather than the personal intercourse that Rickie prefers to engage in, and among the consequences of these ideals is the cruel treatment of Varden. Ansell denounces to Rickie the idea or ideal of the British public school because it lies about the reality of other worlds, just as Idealists in the novel like Mrs Failing and the Pembrokes lie about the reality of other people:

> 'There is no great world at all, only a little earth . . . full of tiny societies, and Cambridge is one of them. All the societies are narrow, but some are good and some are bad. . . . The good societies say, "I tell you to do this because I am Cambridge." The bad ones say, "I tell you to do that because I am the great world". . . . They lie. And fools like you listen to them, and believe that they are a thing which does not exist and never has existed, and confuse "great," which has no meaning whatever, with "good," which means salvation.'   (vii, 72–3)

Salvation in *The Longest Journey* is a matter of facing reality. 'Will it really profit us so much if we save our souls and lose the whole world?' (xxviii, 264), Forster asks rhetorically in the little essay on spiritual coinage at the end of the Sawston section.[18x] Agnes thinks she and Rickie are saved when Mrs Failing conceals Stephen's identity from everyone except them, though they are really lost. Real salvation occurs when Rickie throws away his life to save Stephen, in whom he says he does not believe. In the final chapter Stephen then demostrates to Pembroke the difference between the natural world and the unreality of public school Idealism—both its ideals and its metaphysics—when, echoing what Ansell has presumably taught him, he seizes Pembroke and forces him to look at nature: '. . . that's the world and there's no miniature world. There's one world, Pembroke, and you can't tidy men out of it' (xxxv, 329).

The plurality of real societies and people is connected in *The Longest Journey* to another idea—one that is as important to the novel as that adapted by Forster from Moore's 'The Refutation of Idealism', and this brings us finally to Shelley.

THE TITLE EXHORTING US IN THE WORDS OF SHELLEY NOT TO
LOVE ONLY ONE PERSON

The passage from Shelley's *Epipsychidion* that gives *The Longest
Journey* its title refers to an Idealism of love that Forster is most
concerned fictively to refute in his novel. Rickie reads the passage
out loud to himself the day after his ride with Stephen, during which
he fell asleep and dreamt of the world dissolving as he and Agnes
rose to the throne of God—and from which he awoke in a valley full
of men. Immediately after reading Shelley's lines (which he used to
think very good but now finds a little inhuman), he is told by Mrs
Failing that Stephen is his half-brother; with Agnes's indispensable
help and Mrs Failing's co-operation, he proceeds to ignore his
brother's identity. Shelley's words, then, are a commentary on
Rickie's relationships with Stephen and with Agnes:

> I never was attached to that great sect
> Whose doctrine is that each one should select
> Out of the world a mistress or a friend,
> And all the rest, though fair and wise, commend
> To cold oblivion,—though it is the code
> Of modern morals, and the beaten road
> Which those poor slaves with weary footsteps tread
> Who travel to their home among the dead
> By the broad highway of the world,—and so
> With one sad friend, perhaps a jealous foe,
> The dreariest and the longest journey go.[19x]

When these lines are read in the context of Moore's 'The Refutation
of Idealism', the central connection in *The Longest Journey* between
reality and love becomes clear. The monogamous ideal of modern
morals results in the practice of an Idealism that denies the
independent human reality of all but the loved or hated one. Like
the cows when not perceived, all but the one are commended to the
cold oblivion of non-existence. Thus the longest journey is a trip into
subjective unreality. After his denial of Stephen and marriage to
Agnes, Rickie becomes attached to the sect, begins the longest
journey, and as a consequence the mists rise and the world begins to
become unreal. He prays to be delivered 'from the shadow of
unreality that had begun to darken the world' (xvi, 177); in the end
even Agnes, 'like the world she had created for him, was unreal'

(xxiii, 218). Moore pointed out in 'The Refutation of Idealism' that if the object of an Idealist's sensation 'really were an inseparable aspect of his experience, each Idealist could never be aware either of himself or of any other real thing'.[20] Moore adds that furthermore the Idealist could not avoid the possibility of solipsism. Shelley's passage describes a solipsism *à deux* which, in *The Longest Journey*, ultimately makes the solipsists themselves unreal. Rickie, after he has begun to accept Stephen, summarises for him this journey into unreality:

> 'Two years ago I behaved badly to you, up at the Rings. No, even a few days before that. We went for a ride, and I thought too much of other matters, and did not try to understand you. Then came the Rings, and in the evening, when you called up to me most kindly, I never answered. But the ride was the beginning. Ever since then I have taken the world at second-hand. I have bothered less and less to look it in the face—until not only you, but every one else has turned unreal. Never Ansell: he kept away, and somehow saved himself. But every one else.'   (xxxi, 292)

Forster's combining of philosophy and poetry into a novel about love and reality is not as paradoxical as it might at first seem. It certainly sounds a little odd to maintain that in *The Longest Journey* Forster is using Moore's analytic refutation of Idealism to support the poetic ideas of an altruistic Platonist. But Moore was attempting to refute modern not Platonic Idealism, and the dualism he assumes can be found in both *Epipsychidion* and *The Longest Journey*. As we have seen, Moore concluded in 'The Refutation of Idealism' that the only reasonable alternative to Idealism or agnosticism was absolute scepticism or a belief in matter and spirit—and Moore was no sceptic. The spiritual love of *Epipsychidion* is described in metaphors of sexual passion. Dualism in Forster's novel is clearly present in his account of Rickie's unhappy fate. Orderly people, Forster writes in the opening of Chapter vii, say love 'can be fallen into by two methods: (1) through the desires, (2) through the imagination' (vii, 70). The English add that the first is the inferior method, and Forster comments that the second breeds a tragedy like Rickie's. The love-tragedy of Rickie Elliot is the result of his inadequacy, symbolised by his limp, in the love of desire, and his inability to avoid the longest journey in spiritual or imaginative love. Shelley describes the loved one who helps him to avoid the longest journey with his other love in *Epipsychidion* as a sister and twin as well as a spouse. In this respect Stephen is more Shelleyan than Rickie; he eventually has a brother to love and, despite his parentage, 'love for one person was never to be the greatest thing he knew' (xxx, 278). He wants to marry, he tells Rickie ('Does it disgust you?', he asks) near the end of the novel because something outside of himself makes him want to. Forster intervenes to comment on the nature of romantic love and qualify the title passage from Shelley a little:

> Romantic love is greater than this. There are men and women— we know it from history—who have been born into the world for each other, and for no one else, who have accomplished the longest journey locked in each other's arms. But romantic love is also the code of modern morals, and, for this reason, popular. Eternal union, eternal ownership—these are tempting baits for the average man. (xxxiii, 312)

Agnes is an average woman, yet she is also the kind of person, we are told, who loved only once. In that love she was more real for Rickie than in any love she bore him; only Stephen invokes it in her again. Rickie is not the average man but his physical and spiritual limitations help him to succumb to the ideal of modern morals until rescued by Ansell and Stephen. But his treatment of Stephen after he accepts his identity shows that he has not yet granted him his full objective reality, that he is still idealising him and preparing for another longest journey.

The Longest Journey, to repeat, connects love and epistemology, Shelley and Moore, by 'refuting' the Idealism of romantic love in which the lovers become oblivious to the reality of other people. The ethical facing of reality that Forster derives from Moore's refutation becomes the basis for true loving in the novel. But the precise nature of that loving remains ambiguous in Forster and perhaps in Shelley and Moore as well. The brotherly loves of Rickie, Ansell, and Stephen are erotically tinged in *The Longest Journey*, as is the Platonic love in *Epipsychidion*. 'The Refutation of Idealism' has nothing to do with love, but the ideal in *Principia Ethica* does. The association of homoerotic and spiritual love in the *Symposium* was not forgotten by those Apostles whose Socrates was Moore.

CAMBRIDGE

The Cambridge section of *The Longest Journey* occupies more than half the novel. Because of the scepticism that has been expressed, it should be emphasised again that Forster described this place as the Cambridge not of Lowes Dickinson or Nathaniel Wedd but of G. E. Moore. It has even been stated that Ansell was modelled on A. R. Ainsworth, Moore's closest friend among the Apostles at the turn of the century and later his brother-in-law, though Hugh Meredith also seems to have been a source for Ansell.[21] Forster describes Ansell in his introduction as 'the undergraduate high-priest of that local shrine' in Cambridge (p. xi). In assessing his role in the novel, it should not be forgotten that he is only an undergraduate, that he has his own problems with reality, and that he fails to become a philosopher at Cambridge. He is nevertheless Forster's spokesman in denouncing the Idealism of the great world and upholding the fearless, uninfluential values of Cambridge in contrast to those of Pembroke at Sawston, whose criterion for worth is ultimately just success.

Cambridge is described as Rickie's 'only true home', (p. xi) yet even there 'he was frightened at reality; he was frightened at the splendours and horrors of the world.' (vi, 68) He tries to love, or at least not hate, as many people as he can, instead of distinguishing between the worth of individuals, as Ansell argues he ought to. When Rickie falls in love with Agnes, Ansell warns him that he has now substituted Agnes for humanity in his quest to hang all the world's beauty on one peg:

'You are not a person who ought to marry at all. You are unfitted in body: that we once discussed. You are also unfitted in soul: you want and you need to like many people, and a man of that sort ought not to marry. "You never were attached to that great sect" who can like one person only, and if you try to enter it you will find destruction.'

(ix, 94)

This is the novel's first allusion to Shelley's lines, and they have been interpreted by Forster's biographer as expressing a central anti-thesis in *The Longest Journey* that is found in a debate among the Cambridge Apostles between a King's and a Trinity College attitude toward other people. Furbank cites an Apostle paper entitled 'King's or Trinity?' that was written in the autumn of 1903

by Forster's fellow Kingsman J. T. Sheppard. Quoting from
Epipsychidion in support of a Christian love of man that was to be
preferred over the Trinity attitude of contempt for stupid men,
Sheppard argued, before referring to Shelley, that Trinity seemed
to believe

> that a certain amount of capacity for liking people is dealt out to a
> man at birth, & that every grain of liking given to one person
> means a grain less for somebody else.[22x]

Sheppard's point is developed later by Forster in his essay 'Notes on
the English Character', where he quotes the lines from Shelley that
begin the stanza following the one quoted in *The Longest Journey*:

> True love in this differs from gold and clay,
> That to divide is not to take away.[23x]

But in the novel the antithesis between Trinity intolerance and
King's tolerance is not borne out in the disagreement between
Ansell and Rickie after Rickie leaves Cambridge. It is Rickie the
Kingsman, after all, not Ansell, who goes the longest journey that
Sheppard warns Trinity about. Rickie's tragedy is not that he
refuses to hate people, as Furbank says, but that they become unreal
for him after he joins the great sect. The lines in which Shelley
restates the consequences of loving just one person apply, in the
novel, again, not to Ansell but to Rickie:

Narrow
The heart that loves, the brain that contemplates,
The life that wears, the spirit that creates
One object, and one form, and builds thereby
A sepulchre for its eternity.   (ll, 169–74)[24x]

WILTSHIRE

The idea of Wiltshire that Forster listed among the sources of
inspiration for *The Longest Journey* includes the refuting of Idealism
through an affirmation of the beautiful objective reality of nature as
well as human beings. The cow is the basic rural female symbol in
the novel for the reality that exists whether we acknowledge it or

not. Throughout the book the reality or unreality of people for
Rickie is tied to the reality or unreality of the natural world. Rickie
begins the longest journey into unreality while riding with Stephen:
as he dreams of ascending to God with Agnes, the lark stops singing,
the earth dissolves—and he awakes in a valley full of men. After his
second, complementary ride with Stephen near the end of the novel,
Rickie believes that

> the earth had confirmed him. He stood behind things at last, and
> knew that conventions are not majestic, and that they will not
> claim us in the end.　　　　　　　　　　　　　　　　(xxxiv, 319)

As Forster originally put it in the manuscript of *The Longest Journey*
'one by one Stephen stripped him of his illusions, until the world was
again real.'[25] The 'things' Rickie stands behind are conventional
ideals of right and wrong; what confirms him are the realities of
people, nature, and love. For a little while before his pathetic lapse,
he is able to refute Mrs Failing's Idealism, which relies on these
conventions and leads her into dishonesty and injustice because, as
Rickie said to her earlier, she has forgotten what people are like. Her
indifference to the existence of other people is reinforced by her
hatred of the ways of the earth.

Wiltshire stands for the ways of the earth in *The Longest Journey*. A
chance encounter with a young shepherd in the Figsbury Rings in
Wiltshire, recorded by Forster in his diary in September 1904, was
trivial in itself, Forster noted in his introduction, but 'it fructified my
meagre conception of the half-brothers, and gave Stephen Wonham, the bastard, his home' (p. x). Furbank has printed some of
Forster's entries concerning this experience, and one of the things
that emerges is that the original shepherd of Forster's inspiration
had a club foot. Forster's imaginative transfer of this defect to Rickie
illustrates the way Forster reworked his material to give it greater
significance—and that material includes not only experiences but
ideas as well. Wiltshire, Cambridge, and Sawston, the names for the
three divisions in the novel, represent for Rickie and his creator
types of existence. They have sometimes been described as a
Hegelian triad, yet the third part is hardly a combination of the first
two. Wiltshire synthesises nothing from Sawston. Stephen and
Ansell are together at the end, educating each other; Ansell is
presumably having his Idealist tendencies corrected further, and
Stephen's handling of Herbert Pembroke shows what he has learnt

from Ansell. But Rickie fails finally to accept the reality of other people and of nature; he breaks Mrs Failing's conventional coffee-cup of experience but he cannot accept in Stephen the beer of life. Stephen had once scoffed at Rickie's Forsterian fable in which the girl who turns into a tree is identified by Agnes as 'getting in touch with Nature'. (xii, 141) *The Longest Journey* is not entirely free of this kind of allegorising. Stephen, the natural son, is in touch with instinct, Ansell with reason, Rickie with imagination. All need one another, but if there is a synthesis at the end of the novel of natural beauty, rational truth, and imaginative art, it is only a partial one.

The assertion of the objective existence of nature is finally also an assertion of the reality of time in *The Longest Journey*. Throughout the novel the natural and temporal symbolism go together. Rickie retells his past to his 'brothers' in the Madingley dell, and then finds out more about it in the Rings where he is literally encircled by the ancient past. (The Rings and dell can also be seen as mandalas whose centres are the past instead of the future.) Rickie's subsequent refusal to face the reality of his past is a refusal as well to face human and natural realities. And Rickie, furthermore, avoids confronting the reality of the future until the child he should never have had dies. One of the means Forster uses to convey the reality of time in his novel is classical symbolism. The Roman road that intersects the railroad represents the past that is violated by the present—a present that is destroying the future when children are killed at the level-crossing. This oversimplified summary shows the preoccupation of *The Longest Journey* with the continuity that is an inseparable aspect of nature. All the major characters have to learn to accept this continuity, to recognise that the past really has existed and that the future really will exist, whatever their abilities to perceive these times. The river symbolism in the novel is one of the ways in which the realities of time and change are associated with nature, and, in the scene where Stephen and Rickie float the burning ball of paper under the bridge, with love.[26x] Some of the river symbolism is rather subtle, as when Ansell leans against the pedestal of the Athenian river god Ilissus after hearing that Agnes is pregnant, or when Forster uses a river metaphor to describe how unlabelled friends 'fly together, like straws in an eddy, to part in the open stream' (vii, 74). When Ansell returns to his dissertation, he walks past part of a temple devoted to the goddess of childbirth and past the famous Cnidian Demeter. His dislike of these sculptures suggests his inadequate response to nature and to art. Forster uses the Demeter effectively in the novel to foreshadow the relationship of Stephen and Rickie. This most beautiful of Greek earth-mothers has a smashed nose, which mars her ideal beauty; Rickie's mother is also flawed. The Demeter's knees are smashed, just as Rickie's legs will be when he rescues Stephen – Stephen the atheistic materialist who nevertheless hangs her picture in his room. Love, again, as well as nature, art, and finally the continuity of all of these are symbolised by the 'stone lady'. The phrase is that of Stephen's daughter who, we are told in the last line of the book, has been named after the mother of Rickie and Stephen.

The realities of the past and the future that are connected by the characters of the novel as they journey by the broad highway of the world or by other paths are essential parts of the refutation of Idealism in *The Longest Journey*. The philosophical background for the novel's emphasis on the reality of time and on the ethical importance of facing this reality is again to be found in Forster's Cambridge. Time was famously denied in Cambridge in the early years of the twentieth century by McTaggart, who was an Apostle as well as a Hegelian, and who dominated the Society until the advent of Moore. McTaggart's argument was first published in *Mind* in 1908, the year after the publication of *The Longest Journey*, but it was well known among his friends and students, including Moore, long before then. (Moore recalled in his autobiography that it was his shocked attempt to deny McTaggart's denial that led to Russell's encouraging Moore to become a philosopher.[27]) The details of McTaggart's abstruse argument are irrelevant to *The Longest Journey* as well as to 'The Refutation of Idealism', except perhaps for the general Idealist assumption about perception that Moore attacked in his essay. It is worth noting, however, that in his original 1904 sketch for the plot of a novel that turned into *The Longest Journey*, Forster's first version of Ansell is described as a 'brainy uncouth undergraduate, soaked with idea of mutability'.[28]

The argument of this essay is that G. E. Moore's 'The Refutation of Idealism' provided E. M. Forster with a philosophical argument about the perception of reality that he used to connect the central concerns of *The Longest Journey*. This use involved converting the refutation of epistemological Idealism into an ethical conclusion about accepting the objective reality of other people, of other loves, of other societies, of nature, and finally of time. From Moore's interest in arguments against the existence of objective reality Forster develops his own novelistic interest in the objective and subjective assumptions that his characters act upon in their lives. In his own fictional terms Forster 'refutes' their idealisms – both epistemological and altruistic – by showing their consequences, especially in love.

It is not necessary to know much about Moore's philosophy to see how Forster is using it. But for a novel in which, as Virginia Woolf said, 'everything is accentuated',[29] it is useful to be clear about the philosophical organisation of the accents, even though this clarity may make the novel appear simpler than it is.

Forster's use of Moore will undoubtedly strike some philosophers and even some critics as hopelessly naïve. *The Longest Journey* will never rank as a great philosophical novel. But it should not be forgotten that Russell's personal reactions to Moore's freeing him from what he felt was the prison of Idealism were not that remote from what Forster is expressing in his novel. Forster may not have understood the philosophical significance of Moore's refutation, but *The Longest Journey* suggests that he recognised a revolution in thought when he saw one—or, since he did not read Moore, when he heard one. Some of the ethical implications of that revolution are crucial to Forster's novel. Understanding them may not necessarily lead to a higher evaluation of the novel as a work of art, though it may. There are many things wrong with *The Longest Journey*: the sudden deaths that his plot needed, the sentimental characterisation of Stephen, the authorial essays and purple patches, the ambivalence about Rickie's inadequacy and priggishness, the uncertain conflict between homoerotic and heterosexual love.[30x] Forster has admitted his painful awareness of some of these difficulties. But there are more things right about the novel than is often recognised. *The Longest Journey* is a far richer, subtler, and finally more serious book than many readers realise. One of the reasons why the novel has been so dispraised appears to be an unawareness of its philosophical basis.

Years after he wrote *The Longest Journey* (but some time before he wrote his introduction), Forster discussed, in a paper for Bloomsbury's Memoir Club, the experience in Wiltshire that was so important a part of the inspiration for the novel. After noting how the inspiring experience may in itself be of no importance, merely a transient part of living that we make glamorous because it is unfamiliar, Forster went on to mention an exception to this:

But now and then, before the experience dies it turns a key and bequeaths us with something which philosophically may be also a glamour but which actually is tough. From this a book may spring. From the book, with the violence and persistency that only art possesses, a stream of emotion may beat back against and into the world.[31]

Furbank quotes this passage at the end of his discussion of the sources for *The Longest Journey* as Forster's summary of the ways books and life affect each other. It is an admirable summary but it needs to be applied equally to ideas as well as to 'life'. Moore's refutation of Idealism also bequeathed *The Longest Journey* something that had a philosophical glamour and toughness about it.

6 The Inheritors; or A Single Ticket for Howards End

R. N. Parkinson

In her hurry of body and agitation of mind, Margaret Schlegel asks for a single ticket to Hilton, the station for Howards End. She has just rushed on to the platform at King's Cross in her eagerness to let Ruth Wilcox know that she wishes to accept the elder lady's invitation to visit the house. This haste is Margaret's acknowledgement that Mrs Wilcox's passion for her house is a real and important fact of their joint experience. After a relatively short acquaintance, they share a similar awareness of what is important: their friendship had really begun with the shared perception (they call it an instinct) that it would not have been helpful for Helen and Paul to meet again. As it happens they are both prevented from catching the train and the single ticket is not used, but this piece of pasteboard has a far greater significance than Margaret recognises at the time, for she is eventually to become both the mistress and the owner of Howards End. In this double sense, she is to be her new friend's successor, for Ruth Wilcox realises, before she dies, that she wishes to leave her house to Margaret, and the bereaved Henry Wilcox will discover that he wishes to marry Margaret. The single ticket, to which Forster draws our attention in passing, is one of many quiet, prophetic, symbolic touches which suggest the power of the house to choose worthy heirs and owners to and for itself. These people alone go to Howards End without needing or wanting the return half of the ticket.

It is apparently by a series of accidents and coincidences that people come to ownership of the house, for there is no direct line of family inheritance. Ruth Howard's grandmother leaves the house to her because Ruth's brother Tom, the obvious heir, is disappointed in love, goes off to the Boer War and is killed. In her turn, Ruth passes over the claims of her husband and children and leaves the house out of her family altogether, to her new friend, Margaret Schlegel. This bequest is written in pencil on a scrap of paper and is not legally binding, so that Ruth's husband Henry becomes the new owner. Without hearing of the bequest, Margaret marries Henry Wilcox and becomes the mistress of Howards End. They plan to live elsewhere but accident determines that it shall be their permanent residence. Henry then bequeaths the house to his second wife, and, since they have no children of their own, they agree to leave it eventually to that curiously collateral descendant, the baby of Helen Schlegel and Leonard Bast. For all the appearance of chance, the line of descent is not accidental. Howards End chooses its owners and it chooses them for their individual qualities. Forster tells us explicitly that to Ruth Wilcox the house 'had been a spirit, for which she sought a spiritual heir'.[1] In tracing the line of heir-ship Forster tells his readers what is most important to him in human life – the awareness of the spiritual element. It is because he so perfectly embodies the idea in the whole structure of the novel that a study of *Howards End* is a peculiarly appropriate centenary tribute.

As late as 1958 Forster confided to his Commonplace Book that he thought *Howards End* his best novel:[2] a year later he was to say 'I think *Howards End* is alright. But I sometimes get a little bored with it';[3] and near the end of his life he noted in his diary that he had been reading both *Howards End* and *A Passage to India* and had found them both very good.[4] It is not surprising that he should have done so, for, if the Indian novel offers to its readers an additional historical interest in the form of a distinctive series of attitudes to the British Empire, *Howards End* offers something of even more permanent interest. Some of the preoccupations of the novel have as strictly contemporary a relevance to the thought of the nineteen-seventies as they had to the advanced thinking of the first decades of the century. A later phrase of Forster's which is often cited from the essay 'What I Believe',[5] the phrase 'Tolerance, good temper and sympathy', has an earlier and variant formulation in *Howards End* (iv, 25). 'Temperance, tolerance and sexual equality' are in-telligible cries to the Schlegel sisters. Their concern with social justice is every bit as 'real' as any of the political concerns of the Indian novel. The relations between the classes, the interrelation-ships between money and culture, and the examination of possible steps towards the achievement of sexual equality, all are taken seriously. An even more important idea, which is voiced frequently by the author in his comments on the destructive pace of change in modern civilisation, is stated clearly by Margaret at the end of the book when she is trying to explain what the house and their life there mean to her:

> 'Because a thing is going strong now, it need not go strong for ever,' she said. 'This craze for motion has only set in during the last hundred years. It may be followed by a civilization that won't be a movement, because it will rest on the earth. All the signs are against it now, but I can't help hoping, and very early in the morning in the garden I feel that our house is the future as well as the past.'   (xliv, 337)

Such ideas speak clearly to a period which not only looks with sympathy upon conservation movements but also questions seriously the whole concept of economic growth and the need for increased productivity, which is typified in the novel by the successful Wilcox rubber business.

The first Mrs Wilcox did not find it easy to express such ideas. She needed a Margaret Schlegel to formulate them for her; but their influence is implicit in her conduct, in her love of Howards End, and in her ability to help others intuitively. Upon occasion Margaret goes as far as to use 'the methods of the harem' (xxvi, 227) in her efforts to help others, but there is a credible and probable progression in the novel towards the implementation of such ideas in the private lives of the characters – a progression which Forster's handling of his characters makes entirely acceptable and apparently natural. This kind of naturalness is, of course, rooted in artifice. Much of the strength of *Howards End* arises from the presence of an almost symmetrical artistic pattern beneath the plot of the story. 'Where, for the complete expression of one's subject, does a particular relation stop?', asks Henry James in his preface to *Roderick Hudson*, as he searches for artistic completeness.[6] Forster's novel seems to offer two kinds of completeness: the completeness of a carefully meditated symbolic pattern and the completeness of a comprehensive picture of human nature; and the two kinds are played against one another much as a poet will play the rhythms of speech against those of metre.

The ways in which such patterning works are suggested by a brief episode at the end of chapter 4 of *Howards End*, where Forster is revealing some of the national influences upon the temperaments of the two sisters. At first sight there is nothing new in this. Forster always loves to use national characteristics as a means of illustrating the emotional deficiencies of the English middle classes. He gives Gino Carella an Italian sincerity of emotional response which drives the intelligent English to recognise their own lack of it; or he shows that the Italian cab driver (Phaethon) has an instinctive appreciation of Lucy Honeychurch's real feelings – feelings which the English girl is afraid to acknowledge even after he has led her to the moment of revelation on a bank of violets. We might expect him to use the Germans of *Howards End* in the same way: there is, however, a significant difference in the fact that the Germans are not simply opposed to the English in order to expose English deficiencies. In the scheme of the novel it is necessary that the Schlegel sisters should be neither *echt Deutsch* nor properly English, but Anglo-German.

Forster underlines this fact with care and good humour. When he describes the upbringing of the little girls he lays proper stress upon both sides of their heritage. The paragraph describing their father opens: 'A word on their origin. They were not "English to the backbone", as their aunt had piously asserted. But, on the other hand, they were not "Germans of the dreadful sort" ' (iv, 26). Here national differences are apparently reduced to the level of a family quarrel which the rational will dismiss as foolish, if entertaining. The description of their father as an idealist, inclined to be dreamy, who had nevertheless 'fought like blazes' when given the opportunity, seems to sustain the tone, but Forster treats him more seriously when 'he abstained from the fruits of victory and naturalized himself in England.' The serious purpose of the paragraph and of the chapter is indicated by the next sentence: 'The more earnest members of his family never forgave him, and knew that his children, though scarcely English of the dreadful sort, would never be German to the backbone.' The syntactical repetition may appear simply to intensify the comedy: we are presented with equal, opposite and ridiculous prejudices whose complacent extravagance is antithetically absurd. The real aim of the antithesis is not, then, to relate the history of the Schlegels and their mildly intellectual father: its aim is the maintenance of a reasonable perspective by means at once serious and comic, affirmative and ironic. It is the maintenance of this double perspective which persuades the reader that the author is reliable and enables him to accept the important statement about Margaret which follows further comedy – 'Her conclusion was, that any human being lies nearer to the unseen than any organization, and from this she never varied' – almost without noticing that he has done so; and to accept an equally important statement about Helen, without suspecting its significance at all – 'the younger was rather apt to entice people, and, in enticing them, to be herself enticed' (iv, 28). Here Forster's apparent tolerance, good temper and sympathy put us off our guard, as they are intended to do, and allow him the sort of almost didactic interference which we might expect from an earlier novelist, but which we do not expect from him. When Forster appears to be at his most light-hearted, he is in fact instructing and informing.

The process which is at work in such a paragraph as the above is at work in the novel as a whole. The construction of *Howards End* uses a similar symmetry to draw the reader's attention to important truths. It appears to simplify in order to show that the simplification is not the whole truth. When we consider carefully the symbolic patterning which underlies the behaviour and relationships of the characters, our appreciation of what the novel is doing is changed and enhanced; and one of the things we learn is that the meaning of the novel is not contained in any one pattern. Yet it is by setting his characters in a context of antithetical patterns that Forster tries to persuade us that the baby has been given its single ticket to *Howards End*. By revealing the interaction of nationalities, of classes and of temperaments he prepares us to accept the baby's inheritance as a re-establishment of the kind of order which Ruth Wilcox had loved and cherished. We know that the house is a spiritual as well as a material inheritance. Possession of it – or, more properly, possession by it – denotes imagination as well as sympathy: the house enshrines the sentiments of the past which help to give meaning to the present. Forster lets us know that the Schlegel sisters are peculiarly susceptible to this sort of spiritual influence: when they realise that they must leave Wickham Place, 'Round every knob and cushion in the house sentiment gathered.' Forster laments their separation from their past, declaring that 'historians of the future will note how the middle classes accreted possessions without taking root in the earth, and may find in this the secret of their imaginative poverty' (xvii, 146). Howards End will offer them a refuge, a home for their furniture and a base from which to re-order their lives. For the Wilcox children, Howards End is simply a piece of property and they are not conscious that they or their mother may have owed anything special to it; it appears to have no associations for them, and none of them wants to live there. It marks a division between the sensitive and the insensitive. It is at the centre of any attempt to represent the dialectical pattern of the novel.

In fact Forster seems to have felt in terms of antitheses. The Schlegels have German and English inheritances: the house has Wilcox and Schlegel heirs; it divides and unites the two families; polarises their differences and joins their complementary qualities. In the surviving first drafts of the novel as in the printed version, Helen's opening letter is a description of the surprisingly unpretentious country home of the wealthy Wilcoxes.[7] It is the house with which we must begin, and here it is helpful to see Forster's antithetical pattern in terms of a diagram: Howards End must run up the centre of our diagram like a tree. At the top of it as presiding genius and most important heir must sit Ruth Howard Wilcox, who is an aristocrat of the emotions because 'she worshipped the past' and, in consequence, had 'the instinctive wisdom the past can alone bestow' (iii, 19). She understands other people's feelings without them telling her anything and she moves through the life of telegrams and anger without being touched by it. She is the unpretentious and instinctive mistress of the life of personal relationships. On either side of her, and of the house, are grouped the two families, the Schlegels and the Wilcoxes, with their various relations and connections.

Here Forster gave himself the opportunity of constructing a symmetrical system of marriage relationships between the two families, but refused to take advantage of it. The Schlegel parents have two daughters and a son: the Wilcox parents two sons and a daughter. If his novel had simply been intent upon balancing the complementary qualities of the characters and of their families, what better structure plan could there have been than to marry Helen off to Paul (the emotional, enticing enthusiasm of Helen being balanced by the practical businessman's fear of emotion in Paul); Margaret to Charles (intelligence to stupidity); and the intellectual Tibby to the golfing Evie? What a tidy pattern it might have made! – and what a facile novel. The speculation reminds us that Forster's novels are more naturalistic than this, for all his love of symbolic touches. The symmetry of *Howards End* is not that of the genealogical table or of the Victorian novelist. His construct must allow for disparities of personality and temperament, of upbringing and education which make up the individual man and produce disquality rather than equality.

Nevertheless, in the presentation of the two families Forster strikes a careful and deliberate balance, for the qualities he admires are not easily acquired or often inherited. In this novel, a character's possession of them is indicated by the nature of his relationship to the house. Much though Forster admires the Schlegels, they are as fully and as freely criticised as the Wilcoxes. Amused and irritated by Wilcox obtuseness though the Schlegels may be, Margaret at least realises how dependent upon the practical qualities of the businessman (with whom we shall only be able to dispense 'in the millennium') is the Schlegel life of cultured leisure; and their life of the mind and of the emotions has as many dangers for the human spirit as the life of commercial calculation and imperial preference. This is immediately apparent if we attempt, in terms of our diagram, to lay out each family on either side of Howards End and to look at the similar composition of each, as well as at the opposed qualities of corresponding individuals on either side.

In this diagram, Helen would lie at the extreme left of the three Schlegel siblings: a girl excited by ideas and imagination; overcome by the beauty of Howards End and over-reacting to it by imagining herself in love with Paul ('animal contact at dusk', perhaps?); ready to espouse the cause of Leonard Bast and to swallow him up, in her enthusiasm for bringing home to the now detested Wilcoxes their social responsibilities; ready to offer herself to Leonard as a kind of consolation prize for all the things that his poverty deprives him of; only too easily dominated by 'that tense, wounding excitement that had made her a terror in their nursery days' (xxvi, 221); using her beauty thoughtlessly to 'entice people and . . . be herself enticed' (iv, 28); indulging the emotions excited by art for the sake of the excitement; and only at the end of the novel seeing and accepting her responsibility for the harm that her unworldly irresponsibility has done, when she can at last 'like Henry because he does worry' (xliv, 334) about practical things. No wonder that Paul is dismayed the morning after his proposal by the power of the forces which he has released into his own life and that he is only too glad to pass out of the Schlegel orbit into the safer and easier task of Empire-building. When he has to return to the family business after Charles's imprisonment, he brings with him all the crude prejudices of the kind of Empire-builder whom Forster detests ('piccaninnies included' (xliv, 339) is what gives him away): clearly Paul is at the extreme right of the Wilcox clan.

At the extreme right of the Schlegels is Tibby, as near to the

Wilcoxes as possible: he has the intellectual equipment upon which to build a little cold culture (indicated by his intellectual appreciation of the Beethoven score); he even has the kind of appreciation of good food which might be a Wilcox quality; and, seeing human beings as types rather than as individuals, he is unable to enter very deeply into the feelings of his fellows – or even of his sisters. He appears to have all the worldliness of the successful scholar whose success is built upon the ignoring of human claims: his is the leisure without sympathy. He lacks warmth, lacks emotion itself, not just the ability to express it. Evie, his counterpart on the Wilcox side, has a similar incapacity for real feeling throughout the novel and remains the 'old girl', the overgrown schoolgirl of her father's affectionate greeting, doing what she can for her personality by taking an interest in tweeds, golf and dog breeding, and marrying for companionship and convenience her sister-in-law's not-so-young uncle. The curious spiritual thinness of the Wilcox children when compared with the Schlegels is particularly evident in her, for she hardly affects the plot at all, unless it be in helping her father to manoeuvre Margaret into a luncheon party at Simpsons. She cannot help either of her brothers as Tibby can and does help his younger sister, and she is certainly unlikely to have Tibby's ability to discover a flaw in his own equipment as the result of a family scene.

In our diagram Margaret and Charles are the leaders of their own generation and structurally each is at the centre of his sibling group. They are also a strongly opposed and contrasting pair. (Charles views the Schlegels as the enemy almost from the first.) And the contrast points to a fact which many critics have had difficulty in recognising – the appropriateness of Margaret's marriage to Henry. Charles, we know, is physically and mentally like his father, but his marriage to Dolly (who 'was a rubbishy little creature and she knew it' (xi, 89–90)), like his conduct of the quarrel with Mrs Munt at the beginning of the novel, shows him to have a severely limited allowance of his father's good qualities. It is something of a surprise to learn that Charles (and the other Wilcox children) had affection and 'had it royally' (xlii, 325): their author tells us this and, on the evidence of Charles's desire to protect his father from predatory Schlegels, we must, I suppose, believe it. Charles's ill-directed and limited business abilities, his failures of relationship with his servants and his well-meaning misjudgements of character and situation need the foil of an understanding and spiritually superior wife to turn him into a proper human being: only a woman as perceptive and as intelligent as Margaret could possibly have supplied the gifts and the tact to complement his defects and, perhaps, to reform his character; and, of course, no such woman should ever have found him attractive; though we may note Lionel Trilling's suggestion that what had attracted Helen to the Wilcoxes originally was sex. Certainly both sisters in their different ways feel the power of the love that is of the body.

If, then, we see Charles as the central Wilcox child in our diagram, it is as a rather strident echo of his father, without any of the qualities which his mother might have transmitted to him. With Margaret it is totally different: although she, too, occupies at first a central position in her own family, she is destined for greater things from the moment that Ruth Wilcox invites her to Howards End. At first her practical (Wilcox?) concern for Ruth Wilcox's health makes her decline the invitation, but she has the sensibility which enables her to realise how important it is to her friend. Initially, she appears to be half-way between the emotional extremes of Helen and the intellectual clarity of Tibby: before she develops into the mistress of Howards End, she is the embodiment of all that is good in the Schlegels, inheriting the common sense which we may justly attribute to her moneyed English mother, as well as the mild intellectual light and the combativeness which she may owe to her German father. We come to see that Margaret's strength does not arise from being half-way between anything: it arises from her own unique individuality (unlike the Wilcox children she *has* individuality). She is what Helen recognises at one of the crises of the novel as 'always Meg' (xxxvii, 296), a person with an inner life which affects the outer, a person with a spiritual identity. This is a Howards End quality which she possesses from the beginning of the novel and it stems from her awareness of 'the unseen'.

Such awareness of spiritual realities is nowhere seen in terms of any kind of religious orthodoxy – like most of the authors of his day, Forster is shy of attributing any of his characters' virtues (or vices) to the presence of any religious influence in their upbringing. What distinguishes Margaret, and distinguishes her even from Helen and Tibby is her ability (in Helen's phrase) to 'keep proportion' (xxiii, 191). She is ultimately successful in her assumption of Ruth Wilcox's place in the novel, not only because she can feel the conflicting claims of businessman and mystic, but also because she knows from experience that 'affection, when reciprocated, gives rights' (xxxvi, 288); and she is able to act upon this knowledge without needing to rationalise it. Although Margaret uses this phrase in speaking to Henry of Helen, she might equally have used it to describe to her sister the quality of her relationship to her husband. The reader knows, if Helen does not, that Margaret penetrated into the depths of her husband's soul and approved of what she found there: her insight could find what was good and worthy in him when Helen could not even imagine the possibility of such worth in a Wilcox. Margaret admires the Wilcox life for the kind of practical virtues it fostered: 'such virtues as neatness, decision and obedience' (xii, 101). The catalogue is bald, but Margaret's comment to Helen after she has formulated this list, is revealing: 'Don't brood too much on the superiority of the unseen to the seen . . . Our business is not to contrast the two, but to reconcile them.'

Margaret's ability to reconcile people and ideas is what makes her Ruth Wilcox's spiritual heir: after her death Margaret moves gradually into the central position which she had occupied. In terms of our diagram, she becomes the Schlegel counterpart of Henry, senior to her brother and sister by experience as well as age: and, after Henry's proposal, she earns her position as the real mistress of the house by her ability to reconcile Henry to Helen and Helen to Henry. She can enable the two people she most loves to appreciate one another. She obtains her single ticket to Howards End from Ruth Wilcox and uses it when she marries Henry. She only earns it subsequently (as Ruth must have foreseen), by settling her extended family down at Howards End and resolving their most serious misunderstandings. She tidies up, as her predecessor had done, the different kinds of muddle resulting from the two contrasting kinds of life: the life of telegrams and anger and the life of passion and intellect.

One only of the Wilcoxes obtains a similar ticket to the house, and that is Henry. Many critics have been so mesmerised by his moral obtuseness that they have failed to recognise either his spiritual acuteness or his charm, and have underrated his common sense and clear-sightedness. To substantiate his spiritual acuteness is easier than might appear. What in Ruth Howard accounted for Henry's love of her? After her death he remembers 'his wife's even goodness during thirty years . . . the unvarying virtue that seemed to him a woman's noblest quality . . . Her tenderness! Her innocence!' (xi, 88). Whatever we may think of the words in which he attempts to describe to himself his love for his wife, we should be able to see that Henry is as well able to recognise and to prize spiritual qualities as is a Schlegel, and to feel instinctively what he can only imperfectly express. As for his charm, this is the word which Margaret uses to describe the qualities in him which attract her (xv, 129), and they include the self-confidence and optimism of youth. It is only in times of sorrow or emotion that his inadequacy pains her. Henry's common sense is normally far more practically sensitive than the blind rationality of Charles. Henry will not let Charles pursue a feud with his chauffeur: he has a rudimentary sense of responsibility which recognises the interdependence of the extended family group even when it applies economic laws to those outside it. He has 'tact, of a sort – the sort that is as useful as the genuine, and saves even more situations at board meetings' (xxvi, 217). Henry is far-seeing in his business and he also foresees some of the consequences of Charles's self-righteous anger: he soon realises that Charles will be sentenced for the death of Leonard. Perhaps more important than all these qualities is the fact that it is Henry who has saved Howards End itself. He has put it to rights and refused to sell it: without seeing its real value, he is aware that it has a value. He has earned his right to live there, and live there he does, to recover from the shocks which his obtuseness in other areas has brought upon him.

So far, Margaret's reconciliations have all been within her own class. She even appears to have very little sympathy with the lower classes, and yet, when she actually meets one of them, her habit of treating all men as individuals helps to turn him into a human being and to explain his role in the story. The sisters' interest in Leonard Bast raises him out of the class which suffers in order to make the money upon which the cultured (and the Philistine) may live, for they ensure that the Basts do in the end inherit the earth. Leonard and Jacky are the representatives of 'life's daily grey'; and yet Leonard has a deep, painful and lasting involvement with the Schlegels, Jacky a temporary, half-forgotten and casual liaison with Henry Wilcox. Jacky's ghastly merriment recalls the miserable fallen women, the Martha Endells and Esther Bartons of the previous century, and in doing so it reminds us that even she has a tenuous connection with the realities which help to give Leonard importance: the fallen women are all originally of country stock. Whatever we may imagine about Jacky, Forster assures us that the ancestors of Leonard were the shepherds and ploughboys whom 'civilization' had sucked into the town (xiv, 113). Moreover,

Leonard's cousins, the countrymen who still remain in the country, 'half clodhopper, half board-school prig . . . can still throw back to a nobler stock and breed yeomen' (xli, 320). Leonard's ancestors are also cousins to the owners of Howards End. Perhaps this is what gives such sincerity to his strivings, such poignancy to his aspirations: he comes ultimately from the same class as Ruth Wilcox and his aspirations to culture are also aspirations to truth and honesty – to greater self-knowledge. As a result of his midnight walk, and of telling the Schlegels about it, he goes further: 'He had hitherto supposed the unknown to be books, literature, clever conversation, culture . . . But in that quick interchange a new light dawned. Was that "something" walking in the dark among the suburban hills?' (xiv, 122). We may believe that he had heard the Forsterian Pan pipes, for, when he is sincere, he has something in common with Henry Wilcox: charm – the charm which is in the end fatal to him. The 'naïve and sweet-tempered boy' who appears occasionally to the Schlegel sisters through layers of affectation and bogus refinement (xiv, 118), has a spirit so attractive that it encourages Helen to seduce him and thereby provide the appropriate father for the baby who inherits the house – the house which had been built, and had for so long been owned, by yeomen. His charm and his honesty earn for him and for his baby a single ticket to Howards End.

During the whole of this discussion a face has been looking on, 'shrewd and humorous . . . capable of scathing wit and also of high but unostentatious nobility' (xxxiii, 269), the face of the Miss Avery who did not marry Tom Howard but has remained as guardian of Howards End and interpreter of its intentions. All her prophecies come true. The first time she sees Margaret Schlegel she takes her for Mrs Wilcox: Margaret becomes Mrs Wilcox. Miss Avery unpacks the Schlegel furniture to make the house into a home, and home to the Schlegels it becomes, against all probability. While Helen and Margaret are debating whether to spend the night there, Miss Avery sends up the milk which provisions them, and they stay. It is even she who has put the sword within Charles's reach and who pronounces over Leonard a kind of tender benediction: 'No one ever told the lad he'll have a child' (xliii, 327). Miss Avery is the last central figure to complete our diagram.

Lesser mortals may have their place as ballast to the two families but the view of the novel we are left with will look something like this:

```
                        Miss Avery
                        Ruth Wilcox
     SCHLEGELS          H                    WILCOXES
                        O
                        W                    Henry
     Margaret           A
                        R                    Charles
                        D
Helen        Tibby      S      Evie          Paul

Frieda Mosebach  Mrs Munt   E   Col. Fussell      Mrs Warrington
Liesecke                    N   Dolly                 Wilcox
                            D   Percy Cahill
                      the baby
        Leonard      THE  BASTS          Jacky
```

The symmetry of the two families, grouped around the house, is the superficial part of Forster's message: Schlegels balancing Wilcoxes, English balancing Germans: the real truth is that only those who are worthy find their way to the house permanently. The real inheritors, and the house itself, grew from the earth, both literally and metaphorically. Others may earn their way in, some unconsciously, like Henry, others with some sense of what they have been admitted to, like Margaret and Helen. The Schlegels earn their way in by the sincerity and the self-knowledge which are required for a genuine inner life: Henry earns his way in by the hard work and vitality which achieve useful practical things in the outer life. Mrs Wilcox alone, of the older generation, was born with the intuitive sensibility which is the rightful heritage of the owners of Howards End. The novel appears to say that she is of yeoman stock and she has the qualities of the gentlewoman: a sensibility to the feelings of others ('the instinctive wisdom the past can alone bestow . . . that wisdom to which we give the clumsy name of aristocracy . . . assuredly she cared about her ancestors and let them help her' (iii, 19)); a sense of responsibility for others which produces practical action (she heard her ancestors say, 'Separate those human beings who will hurt each other most. The rest can wait' (iii, 19) and no Howard ever turned any one away without food (xxxiii, 271)); and a sense of continuity – continuing life and continuing culture – which is rooted deeply in a sense of place ('To be parted from your house, your father's house. . . . It is worse than dying' (x, 81)). Forster uses this idea of rootedness in a typically modern way: he implies that the rootedness – the traditional wisdom – of Ruth Wilcox gives her the security and the intuition which enables her to help and understand others. At the same time he attributes mysterious qualities to Howards End, and to those who understand and interpret it.

In some respects Howards End is Forster's symbol for God and his expression of religious feeling. This should come as no surprise, in spite of Forster's attitudes to organised religion. He has faith – the humanist faith in higher human possibilities – and he needs in this novel a way of expressing it. His friend W. J. H. Sprott remembers Forster as objecting to the idea of any religious commemoration of him after his death. He would not even like a concert in King's College Chapel: 'Oh no, not the *Chapel*, that would smell too much of religion. It would be letting the humanists down,' he is quoted as saying.[8] In repudiating organised religion, Forster perpetuated a common confusion about religion, the confusion which is rectified by citing two of the *OED* definitions: number four, 'A particular system of faith and worship'; and number five, 'Recognition on the part of man of some higher unseen power as having control over his destiny and as being entitled to obedience and worship; the general mental and moral attitude resulting from this belief . . .'. If Forster rejects the particular system of Christianity, he accepts its results. His 'aristocracy of the sensitive, the considerate and the plucky'[9] has classical roots and it also has Christian ones, but he seems to want to go back to an archetype behind both. The house (the home of traditional wisdom), the wych elm (superstition on its way to faith) and the meadow (the beauty, joy and dignity of labour) are his attempt to embody them. He professes to be interested not in the Ideas or the gods but in human witnesses to their reality.

At the end of the novel Forster leaves us to suppose that the baby of the new generation will be the inheritor of all the Howards End qualities (what practising humanism, practising Christianity and practical farming have in common). The baby will become a sturdy farmer by his actions, he will have faith in higher powers, and he will be a gentleman in his considerateness. To Forster the most important thing appears to be that the baby is at once the herald of a new order and a continuation of the old: the order of instinctive wisdom, living on the land and drawing its strength from it. The baby is not half-way between anything. The baby needs no ticket: he is born there. The baby of Helen Schlegel and Leonard Bast is he whose right it is, intuitive inheritor and yeoman inheritor, and it needs the whole novel to persuade us that this must be so.

7 Forster on Profit and Loss

Wilfred Stone

Throughout his life, Forster worried about money. He worried not about how to get it (he was well off) but how to possess it, how to be an honourable *have* in a world of *have-nots*. The morality of money, what the ownership of money does to the character, were issues that haunted him throughout his career; and always ringing in the back of his mind were four passages from *Matthew*: (1) 'For what is a man profited, if he shall gain the whole world, and lose his own soul?' (2) 'If thou wilt be perfect, go and sell that thou hast, and give to the poor.' (3) 'It is easier for a camel to go through the eye of a needle, than for a rich man to enter into the kingdom of God.' (4) 'Render therefore unto Caesar the things which are Caesar's, and unto God the things that are God's.'[1]

The division between earthly and spiritual coin, earthly and spiritual possessions, becomes virtually Forster's basic metaphor— symptomatic of the dualistic bent of his mind and a model (to use a current word) against which he continually tested his conscience. Any reader of Forster is aware of those numberless formulations – the seen *v.* the unseen, the public *v.* the private, the conscious *v.* the unconscious – with which he worked in trying to negotiate the divide between the everyday world and an ideal world of value. 'Only connect' is his prayer (competing always with rival ideals of exclusion), and *Howards End* – the novel where connection was first seriously tried out – is one long experiment in bringing Caesar's coin and God's into some sort of common market. 'Has the soul offspring?', he asks – and the question has to do with whether a piece of earthly real estate can be probated in spiritual terms:

To them Howards End was a house: they could not know that to her it had been a spirit, for which she sought a spiritual heir. And – pushing one step further in these mists – may they not have decided even better than they supposed? Is it credible that the

possessions of the spirit can be bequeathed at all? Has the soul
offspring?   HE xi, 96

Forster acquits the Wilcoxes for their blindness: 'the problem is too
terrific, and they could not even perceive a problem' (xi, 96–7). Yet
we know he does not forgive them in his heart. In working his
'connections', Forster is the inveterate seeker for ideal value, always
tugging the material towards the spiritual and never the other way.
'The inner life had paid' (xxxvii, 296) is the conclusion of the
Schlegel sisters, and the commercial language ('paid') is Forster's
subtle way of yoking the real to the ideal in one sentence. But to see
connection as a victory, a pay-off, rather than as an equal marriage
of inner and outer, is to confess that connection has not worked. For
connection to have a fair trial, body and soul must be equal values in
the scales.

The struggle, however, did not end with this novel, as it did not
start with it. The attempt to make Caesar's coin and God's the same
currency occupies a central passage in *The Longest Journey*. 'The soul
has her own currency', the metaphor begins, and Forster goes on to
consider the value of that coinage when it is stamped with a human
face. It is unreliable, for that human image, however beloved, is also
mortal and imperfect, and 'the soul can . . . have her bank-
ruptcies.' But when stamped with God's image, it is equally
unreliable:

> There is . . . another coinage that bears on it not man's image
> but God's. It is incorruptible, and the soul may trust it safely; it
> will serve her beyond the stars. But it cannot give us friends, or the
> embrace of a lover, or the touch of children, for with our fellow-
> mortals it has no concern. It cannot even give the joys we call
> trivial – fine weather, the pleasures of meat and drink, bathing
> and the hot sand afterwards, running, dreamless sleep. Have we
> learnt the true discipline of a bankruptcy if we turn to such
> coinage as this? Will it really profit us so much if we save our souls
> and lose the whole world?[2x]

The humanist, alive to the pleasures of the senses (and in this
instance to awakening homosexuality) cannot settle for spiritual
coinage alone. Still, that does not solve the problem of how to find
one kind of coinage that will purchase both spiritual and material

goods – nor does it solve the problem (that worried Forster acutely in the 1930s and 1940s) of what to do about people who had no coinage at all, the poor and the exploited.

With the coming of the post-war and depression decades, Forster's concern about money took a strong down-to-earth bent. People were unemployed and going hungry. Social circumstances were calling the Christian bluff: it was no longer enough to talk about selling all one had and giving it to the poor, it was (for a serious moralist like Forster) a decision that had to be realistically faced. Though Forster was no orthodox Christian in an organisational or theological sense, he never ceased being one in an ethical sense; he could laugh at the church and at clergymen (witness Mr Kingcroft, the curate with damp hands in *Where Angels Fear to Tread*) because he saw them, to paraphrase Delmore Schwartz, as the clowns of the spirit's motive, parodists of a Christian morality that, in its non-institutional form, Forster still deeply respected. What influence the modern church retains, Forster said in 1939, 'is due to the money behind it, rather than to its spiritual appeal'[3] and the church's hypocrisy over money was, Forster believed, a main reason for its decadence. In writing of Tolstoy in 1925, he faced the issue of money-corruption directly. Should one, like Tolstoy, attempt to become one with the poor, work and love with them, and thus save one's soul? Forster will not do it:

When the Dean of Durham (officially representing the carpenter Jesus) enjoins poverty upon me, I answer readily enough, 'Yea, Dean, yea,' because I know that when his sermon is over the Dean will go back to an excellent lunch, and leave me free to do the same. It is a put-up job between us, a farce that has gone on century after century, ever since Christianity became respectable. But Tolstoy is not like that. He does not go off to his lunch. He, too, had his insincerities of action, but they were not of the suave organised sort promoted and practised by clergymen. The bulk of him is sincere; he demands a sincere response, and that is why he is so painful to read. He exacts (in my case) a definite refusal. I believe that he is right, that poverty has been caused by wealth, and that it is impossible to help the poor without becoming poor oneself. But I will not do it, I will not part with the whole of my surplus. Will you? If so, discontinue (among other things) your subscription to the *New Leader*. . . . [I]t is better that we should make this reply than remain vague, self-satisfied, and unseeing.[4]

It is a statement George Eliot might have made – the voice of the sincere apostate, the honest doubter – and it spells out in clear terms Forster's self-imposed demand for honesty on this issue. Many economists (though not Maynard Keynes or E. F. Schumacher) and most businessmen would disagree with Forster's statement that poverty has been caused by wealth, but a good case can be made for the argument, even though much depends on how one defines 'wealth'. The issue here, however, is not the validity of the argument but the insight it gives into Forster's set of mind: the issue for him is not primarily one of secular economics but one of Christian – or at least liberal – morality. And so it was that through the thirties Forster worried publicly about his investments. He got rid of some South African mining stock and some shares in Imperial Chemicals, since these companies were in his opinion either sweating labour or contributing to war preparations. But he feels 'hopeless' about investments:

> It seemed impossible for a small private investor like myself to know where his money had actually gone or whether it was doing harm or good. When I ask those who are better informed than myself, they usually laugh at me and tell me not to worry, and I have got to feel that the world of finance is so complicated that—ethically speaking—it doesn't matter what I buy.
>
> In a sense this is true. It is impossible for any one to have clean hands. I will wash my hands in innocency and so will I go to thine altar? Impossible. There's nowhere to wash. We are all messed up together in a civilization which is going badly askew and which may, as the Communists think, be skewing because of the institution of private property. No individual, however humble, can be guiltless. Yet resignation is a mistake, there are degrees of guilt, and now and then I have tried—very incompetently—to overhaul my investments and to direct them into more plausible channels.[5]

Certain critics would doubtless take pleasure in reminding Forster of more 'plausible' – more applaudable – channels than these, and might argue that Forster's sensitivity helped not at all the shareless and the jobless – who could well look on Forster's delicacy with

something like rage. Even the Forster partisan could ask if this were
not a case of the liberal conscience eating its cake and having it, of
making the inner life 'pay' without making any real sacrifice. That
radical argument must be respected but so, I think, must Forster's
conscientious worry be respected – not as a call to action, but as a
call to thought. Forster, like Jean Genet, continually played with
ideas that were 'treason' to the respectable. They are not revolutionary ideas, but in their Horatian way they attack complacency and smugness; and they give flashes of insight into the
moral contradictions of capitalism that can have revolutionary
implications.

Take, for example, his idea that our civilisation may be 'going
badly askew . . . because of the institution of private property'. His
essay 'My Wood' (1926) is a study of this problem in its personal
aspect: 'What is the effect of property upon the character?' And in
asking this question he plumbs, with comic yet devastating effect,
the corruptions that attend the modern (for it is a relatively recent
phenomenon) lust to *own*. In the first place, the ownership of his
wood (the first property he ever owned, purchased with royalties
from *A Passage to India*) made him feel 'heavy' and unable, therefore,
to pass through the eye of the needle:

> Property produces men of weight, and it was a man of weight who
> failed to get into the Kingdom of Heaven. He was not wicked,
> that unfortunate millionaire in the parable, he was only stout; he
> stuck out in front, not to mention behind, and as he wedged
> himself this way and that in the crystalline entrance . . ., he saw
> beneath him a comparatively slim camel passing through the eye
> of a needle and being woven into the robe of God.[6x] . . . Men of
> weight cannot, by definition, move like the lightning from the
> East unto the West, and the ascent of a fourteen-stone bishop into
> a pulpit is thus the exact antithesis of the coming of the Son of
> Man.   AH 23–4

In the second place, his property makes him feel 'it ought to be
larger' – in short, it induces greed for more. In the third place,
'property makes its owner feel that he ought to do something to it',
and here Forster, with a simple directness, goes to the heart of much
that critics like E. F. Schumacher, Barry Commoner, or the Club of
Rome (in *The Limits to Growth*) have explicitly pointed out – the
tragedy of endless expansion and 'improvement':

Creation, property, enjoyment form a sinister trinity in the human mind. Creation and enjoyment are both very good, yet they are often unattainable without a material basis, and at such moments property pushes itself in as a substitute, saying, 'Accept me instead—I'm good enough for all three.' It is not enough. It is, as Shakespeare said of lust, 'The expense of spirit in a waste of shame': it is 'Before, a joy proposed; behind, a dream.' Yet we don't know how to shun it. It is forced on us by our economic system as the alternative to starvation. It is also forced on us by an internal defect in the soul, by the feeling that in property may lie the germs of self-development and of exquisite or heroic deeds. Our life on earth is, and ought to be, material and carnal. But we have not yet learned to manage our materialism and carnality properly; they are still entangled with the desire for ownership, where (in the words of Dante) 'Possession is one with loss.'

AH 25

The management of our materialism and carnality was what Jesus was concerned about when he said, 'If thou wilt be perfect, go and sell that thou hast, and give to the poor.' That advice haunted Forster, as we have seen, and he wrote an early short story, 'The Rock', in an attempt to deal with it. The theme came to him in a moment of inspiration just after he had dropped some of his surplus, but not all, into a collecting box of the Royal Life-boat Institution in Cornwall in 1906. This charitable impulse followed upon the success of two other stories, 'The Story of a Panic' and 'The Road from Colonus', but 'The Rock', as Forster tells us, was a complete flop. 'Not an editor would look at it. My inspiration had been genuine but worthless, like so much inspiration, and I have never sat down on a theme since.'[7] It is not hard to understand why the editors scorned it: though the story is an eloquent confession of how conflicted Forster was over this biblical admonition, the narrative does little to resolve the conflict. It is the story of a man rescued from drowning by some fishermen off the Cornish coast. The question is, how shall he reward them or – to remember the rest of *Matthew 16:26* – 'what shall a man give in exchange for his own soul?' How much is a life *worth*? Though there was an established tariff for rescues, and though he could have dispatched his obligation by the gift of a lifeboat or of almost any sum of money, he could not settle the issue thus simplistically. While most people have their lives as a 'right', this unfortunate's life had been 'saved' – so he had to decide on its worth. (Or so he claimed; this casuistry is one of the defects of the story.) It was not a purely 'practical' question, for, as his spokesman says, 'Every question springs straight out of the infinite, and until you acknowledge that you will never answer it' (LTC 63). After prolonged thought, he discovers the answer: Nothing. 'Such things' were worth 'Nothing; and nothing is my reward to the men who saved me.'[8x]

However metaphysically profound this solution is, the men who saved his life neither understand it nor appreciate it; not only does he pay them nothing but, after selling all his goods and giving the value of them to the poor, he goes down to the village penniless and becomes a charge on their charity. The point is, of course, that there is a spiritual as well as material side to such debts, and that some elect souls can see this and make their payment in this transcendent extra-legal tender. (It is interesting to note that in Forster's stories such elect souls are always upper-class people.) The narrator dissociates himself from this solution, however, and prays to be delivered from such spirituality: 'as long as I have flesh and blood I pray that my grossness preserve me' (LTC 64). The rescued man's 'solution' is, of course, preposterous, but so is Jesus's advice to the rich man – and Forster, however unwilling he was to follow suit in his own life, was continually tempted in his fiction to test these radical solutions.

The body must be honoured as well as the spirit; the flesh must not suffer mortification in the name of any ascetic ideal – Forster is clear on these points. Nevertheless, his use of the word 'grossness' is not merely ironic, but is an indication of how hard it was for him to live with this conviction. Though 'only connect' remained his lifelong ideal, he increasingly realised in his later years that he had been too easy an idealist before the First World War. In that brilliant essay 'The Challenge of Our Time' (1946), he tells how the education he had received in that 'fag-end of Victorian liberalism' had made him, on the subject of money, morally blind: 'In came the nice fat dividends, up rose the lofty thoughts, and we did not realise that all the time we were exploiting the poor of our own country and the backward races abroad, and getting bigger profits from our investments than we should' (TCD 55). Even Margaret Schlegel – bold and brave as she tries to be about money – can be indicted on that charge, for her connections were made via 'lofty thoughts' more than via any painful self-sacrifice. If we are to meet the challenge of our time (this in 1946), we must combine 'the new economy with the old morality':

> The doctrine of *laissez-faire* will not work in the material world. It has led to the black market and the capitalist jungle. We must have planning and ration books and controls, or millions of people will have nowhere to live and nothing to eat. On the other hand, the doctrine of *laissez-faire* is the only one that seems to work in the world of the spirit; if you plan and control men's minds you stunt them, you get the censorship, the secret police, the road to serfdom, the community of slaves. . . .
>
> . . . We want the New Economy with the Old Morality. We want planning for the body and not for the spirit. But the difficulty is this: where does the body stop and the spirit start? In the Middle Ages a hard and fast line was drawn between them, and according to the mediaeval theory of the Holy Roman Empire men rendered their bodies to Caesar and their souls to God. But the theory did not work. The Emperor, who represented Caesar, collided in practice with the Pope, who represented Christ. And we find ourselves in a similar dilemma to-day.   (TCD 55–6)

Still the old dualisms, still the familiar divisions between the material and the spiritual, Caesar's world and God's! In spite of the ideal of connection, the guiding metaphors of Forster's thought are always dual and never unitary. Can Forster have been asking too much in seeking one coinage that would serve in both God's and Caesar's realm? (That hope is clearly implied in the doctrine of 'only connect'.) Perhaps so; as Forster himself said, 'the problem is too terrific.'

Yet terrific as the problem is, I think that Forster could have moved closer to a solution had it not been for one overriding inhibition: the problem of class. To sell all one has and give to the poor is to become poor oneself, to give up class privileges and prerogatives, to forfeit all the comforts of social election. This solution, as we have seen, Forster could not adopt – as who among us, save for an occasional Tolstoy, could? Certainly few readers of Forster have any right to be smug on this issue. But Forster could have gone further than he did. In a 1917 letter to Bertrand Russell from Alexandria where Forster, 'harmless and unharmed', was a non-combatant engaged in Red Cross work, he wrote: 'I love people and want to understand them and help them more than I did, but this is oddly accompanied by a growth of contempt. Be like them? God, no.'[9] When one remembers that the 'people' Forster is discussing are wounded veterans of a war he is escaping through a relatively cushy job, one realises the depth and seriousness of his class prejudices. It is an honest letter, but the fastidiousness that makes him repudiate any likeness to these people is of the same cut as his refusal to give up his 'surplus'. *Mon semblable, mon frère?* If the question relates to the lower classes, Forster's private answer is 'God, no.' Publicly Forster gives two cheers for democracy, privately he may have given even fewer, for his whole scheme of value is fundamentally aristocratic; he wants the doors to his aristocracy to be open to all who qualify, an 'aristocracy of the sensitive, the considerate, and the plucky' – an aristocracy based on character rather than simply on caste. Yet it is an exclusionary notion. And he cares about the caste as well; he will not relinquish the money that, along with other needful values, gives him his standing in it.

In short, spiritual elitism is not finally separable from social elitism with Forster. That disturbing statement in *Howards End*:

> We are not concerned with the very poor. They are unthinkable, and only to be approached by the statistician or the poet. This story deals with gentlefolk, or with those who are obliged to pretend that they are gentlefolk. (vi, 43)

is a measure of the book's failures in connection – for there is no successful joining of either the sexes or the classes: the love celebrated is implicitly homosexual (that of the Schlegel sisters for each other), and the only class connections attempted are between extremes of the middle class, and those are failures. The elect are saved not by connection, but by quarantine. Forster saw the problem, for in *Maurice* he makes the necessity to 'overleap class'(M 207) the condition for Maurice's success in love with Alec Scudder; but psychologically he overleaps it only in fantasy, in that mythy 'greenwood', and even physically there is an enormous distance between Maurice and his lower-class lover. As P. N. Furbank says of Forster: 'He achieved physical sex very late and found it easier with people outside his own social class, and it remained a kind of private magic for him – an almost unobtainable blessing, for which another person was mainly a pretext . . . and by romanticizing them he managed to keep them at a distance.'[10] That 'distance' was, with Forster, a condition of salvation.

These sexual issues may seem remote from the worry over money, but actually they are not. The problem of connecting sexually put Forster's class prejudices to the test just as did the problem of connecting socially, and in all his fiction Forster identifies with the privileged characters – with those connected to money and power. He wants the money and power to be used responsibly and generously; but he also wants to keep his own membership in that club, albeit as a critical member with very modest personal claims. Forster also read in *Matthew* (26:11) that 'ye have the poor always with you', but he faced that unpalatable fact painfully, reluctantly, with profound moral embarrassment. He never overcame the habit of thinking in terms of 'high' and 'low' and – almost in spite of himself – he gave the spirituality and the 'lofty thoughts' solely to the gentlefolk or to those 'obliged to pretend' that they were gentlefolk. And since he could not 'overleap class', he is finally stymied in his attempts to solve the money problem. For unless Caesar's coin is fairly distributed among the people, any attempt to equate it with God's coin is bound to be specious: you cannot bring man and God together if you omit vast numbers of God's children from the experiment.

Perhaps the problem lies in the metaphor itself. Perhaps there is no such thing as 'God's coin' and can never be, perhaps there is only the money of this world and what we do with it. Perhaps the division into matter and spirit, Caesar and God, is itself false – even pernicious. But Forster inherited those Christian dualisms and wrapped some of his deepest thinking around them. Part of our debt to him, as artist and thinker, is his role as an adapter of that Christian inheritance (what he could take from it) to a modern world. As he said, we want the Old Morality, but along with it we want the New Economy – by which he did not mean capitalism. Forster's ideal New Economy would be run by love rather than by competition, and it would require a new coinage, stamped with, to borrow the words of Blake, 'the human form divine'. Just how that minting would be done is one unsolved problem; another, and a far greater, is how the coin would be distributed. Forster gave us no answer to this problem, but he shared his trouble over it with remarkable honesty and sensitivity. Though he was no economist, Forster has probably given us as much help on this 'terrific' issue as we are likely to get.

8 Forster's Alexandria: the Transitional Journey

Mohammad Shaheen

Forster's sojourn in Alexandria was not less needed than his previous visit to India. The mixture of futility and exaltation generated by that earlier journey had subsequently been superseded by feelings of self-disgust and misery. Firstly, the domestic affairs of his female relations became too chaotic for him to deal with without becoming depressed. Secondly, *Maurice*, which Forster had just finished and which he had decided to leave unpublished, did not bring with it satisfaction, or the cure to his troubles which he had anticipated while writing it. Thirdly, there was the general mood of the war, in which he found a parallel to his own affairs.[1]

Late in 1915 Forster arrived in Alexandria as a volunteer in the Red Cross, and, to use his own word, *stuck* in the job for over three years. Modern Alexandria provided little interest for him. On one occasion (1968) Forster said to me that he did not like the place. When he was there and taking a look at the city from the air, the houses of Alexandria 'looked like decayed teeth, . . . all the buildings are quite ugly enough to be pulled up by the roots and flung into the sea.'[2] Despite the fact that he loved its climate and its sea, in which he enjoyed bathing (an activity which he probably regarded as more concerned with the Mediterranean than with Alexandria) he did not find the city attractive.

Forster viewed modern Alexandria, if not modern Egypt as a whole, as being sterile (though this sense of his may have been partly associated with the general sterility of wartime). When he came across vitality springing up from the middle of this sterility, he would immediately try to justify its existence, and would often do so by regarding it as a kind of vitality in exile. For example, Enrico Terni, an Italian composer living in Alexandria, 'is emphatically a musician in Egypt, not an Egyptian musician'. He remarks that

79

Enrico may be talented; yet the environment prevents the growth of his talent.

His discussion of Enrico's milieu directly or indirectly extends his picture of the man's dilemma, therefore:

> It is not a heroic talent [Enrico's], but we do not live on heroic soil, nor, with all respect to the great war, in a heroic age. We are exiled here in Egypt for the purpose of doing various little [jobs] . . . and out of a population of exiled little jobbers it is impossible that a heroic art should be raised.[3]

Forster was also able to see Alexandria, or as he called it, coastal Egypt, in perspective, however:

> But what coastal Egypt can do and what from time to time it has done is to produce eclectic artists, who look for their inspiration to Europe. In the days of the Ptolemies they looked to Sicily and Greece, in the days of St Athanasius to Byzantium, in the 19th century it seemed they would look to France. But there was always this straining of the eyes beyond the sea, always this turning away from Africa, . . . [4]

One might suggest that Forster himself was practising a 'straining of the eyes beyond the sea'. At this time in his career (perhaps more than at any time before) Forster realised the need to turn away from the life of Weybridge, if not from England altogether.

In his discussion of Enrico Terni Forster points out three strata of civilisation in Egypt. The first is the Egypt of the Pharaohs, which he sees as a source of attraction for tourists and popular novelists. Another is 'the Arab Egypt in which we more or less live and less or more have our being – a real civilization this, but static and incomprehensible'. A third is the civilisation of the coastal strip which has proved attractive to the European mind. Forster, who considered himself European, identifies himself with this third stratum.

However, Forster has something in common (though not to an equal degree) with the other two strata – both with the antiquarian, which he had left behind and to which he anticipated no return, and with the 'static and incomprehensible', whose situation resembled his own static and puzzled state of mind, in which creative vitality, he felt at the time, was being stifled by the sterility of circumstances.

To judge from the writing he undertook during the three years of his stay in Egypt Forster's situation may be described in terms of a quest for detachment, and the coastal strip seemed to be the appropriate haven for this purpose. Since Forster was neither enchanted as a tourist nor impressed as a more popular novelist might have been, he was happily able to observe, and, with the comic spirit in which he had already been trained, to capture the gay spirit of Egyptian life.[5x] For example, he tells the reader that 'Sunday music at San Stefano is for the eye', and warns him not to expect to hear the music because of the overwhelming noise. Further on, the humour becomes quite biting: 'A sparrow in a German concert hall betrays no emotion except fear, but the sparrow here lives and loves and nests and fights close above a sixty-man-power orchestra.'[6]

In 'Photographic Egypt' Forster records comic scenes, most of which have been characteristic of Egyptian life up to the present day. He remarks that an authentic picture of Egypt cannot be derived from the exotic pictures of the country. Such practice by the photographer recalls 'the tradition that has produced the grill-room at Shepherd's Hotel and the novels of Robert Hichens'. Forster continues:

> Queen Victoria, had she permitted her imagination to luxuriate, would have conceived the East as thus. To her, as to the photographer, there could have been cushions in front and the Pyramids behind, and maidens going with pitchers to the well in the middle distance, perhaps. It is doubtful whether such an Egypt ever existed.[7]

The typical sights that Forster wishes to record are rather the people walking in the streets carrying chickens, turkeys and ducks; Alexandrian ladies passing by with their high heels and ditch hats; the slow brown streams of *gaffirs* (night-guards) coming out of the station in the evening; *tarbooshes* (fezzes) covered with handkerchieves to prevent them getting wet; or, close to the Pyramids, a charming child who has fallen asleep close to his donkey with his head resting on its snowy shoulder.

More typical scenes of Egyptian life are discussed in 'Diana's Dilemma' where Forster comments on Egyptian films in terms of the idiosyncrasies of the actors as well as those of the audience. Similar scenes occur in 'Cotton from Outside', 'The Den' and in 'The

Solitary Place', which are included in *Pharos and Pharillon*.

Scenes from the history of the coastal strip are exhibited in the same spirit of gaiety, for Forster's observation remains detached. In his essay 'Pharos', on the history of Alexandria, for example, he produces three gay pictures of the races who made their way into the city at one period or another. First, the Jews:

> Deeply as they were devoted to Jehovah, they had ever felt it their duty to leave his city when they could, and as soon as Alexandria began to develop they descended upon her markets with polite cries. They found so much to do that they decided against returning to Jerusalem, and met so many Greeks that they forgot how to speak Hebrew. . . .

Of the Arabs he says:

> Though unable to maintain the lighthouse on earth, the Arabs did much for it in the realms of fancy, increasing its height to seven hundred feet, and endowing it with various magical objects, of which the most remarkable was a glass crab. . . .

The essay concluded with a picture of the British:

> The dominant memory in the chaos is now British, for here are some large holes, made by Admiral Seymour when he bombarded the Fort in 1882 and laid the basis of our intercourse with modern Egypt.[8]

Before Forster came to Alexandria he had written in his diary (August 1914) that only gaiety was bearable, and wondered if he could get work in a hospital.[9] So far, Forster's city happily accommodated those two needs.

'Modern Alexandria is scarcely a city of the soul.' This is how Forster introduces his tribute to Cavafy's poetry.[10] Like Cavafy, Forster made his journey to the past in search of her soul, if not of his own. When Cavafy received from Forster his own copy of *Pharos and Pharillon* Cavafy wrote back (10 July 1923) to express his deep appreciation of the book, referring particularly to his delight at finding 'Pharos' first in the collection, and to the sentence from 'The Return from Siwa' which he actually quotes: ' . . . the Greek spirit still lived. But it lived consciously, not unconsciously in the past.'

Forster himself was conscious of what he was doing when he called Alexandria, in the third section of *A History and a Guide* (which includes 'Neo-Platonism'), 'The Spiritual City'.

But unlike Cavafy, Forster was not able to recapture in poetry the spirit of the city, nor would he have wished to be its historian, a role which, by comparison with that of the novelist, he considered as that of recorder rather than of creator.[11] Had his creative powers not been for the time paralysed, Forster would probably have liked to write a novel about Alexandria (Three novels were to remain unfinished.) A middle course between history and fiction seemed to be the answer.

The result was an unusual sort of history, together with a guide (perhaps less unusual) of the city. Introducing the American edition of the book in 1960 Forster says:

> And visions kept coming as I went about in trams or on foot or bathed in the delicious sea. For instance, I would multiply the height of the Fort of Kait Bey by four and so envisage the Pharos which had once stood on the same site. At the crossing of the two main streets I would erect the tomb of Alexander the Great. I would follow Alexander in imagination to Siwa, the oasis of Jupiter Ammon, where he was saluted as the Son of God. And I would follow the monks too, to the desolate Wady Natrum whence they burst to murder Hypatia.[12]

Forster's account of Alexandria is subjective and bellettristic in tone, in that he draws less on the narrative of the historians than on the imaginative recreation of the past in literature: his Cleopatra owes as much to Shakespeare and Dryden as to more conventional historical sources. The same attitude leads him to append to his section on the modern period Cavafy's poem 'The God Abandons Antony'.

The result is a lack of proportion in the amount of attention given to the various periods, the Hellenistic and Christian periods—i.e. the periods which have most interested European poets and novelists—being emphasised at the expense of other periods. Hence the sketchy nature of his treatment of the Arab period and modern times: they hardly appear in sources of the kind with which Forster felt most at home. Thus he dismisses the nationalist campaign led by Urabi (not Arabi as always – wrongly – in Forster) in a sentence: 'The details – like Arabi's motives – are complicated.'[13]

Forster's passion for Hellenism and his interest in Christian theology may be explained by his earlier training in the Classics, and by the fact that he feels at home with the past. Critics sometimes have related such enthusiasms and interests to his desire to escape the dreary present and substitute for it a harmless past; or they may generalise the issue and explain it in terms of Forster's attempt to connect two different ends.

These explanations have some measure of validity, but they ignore the larger pattern of thinking which guides Forster's approach to Alexandria.

Forster approaches his *Alexandria* with the selective eye of an artist who, though not at the time creative enough to be able to write a novel, was sufficiently alert to review the ideas of fiction. He then goes on to examine certain classical ideas which he may have hoped to demonstrate later through fictional characters of his own.

The idea of deity was one which preoccupied him at this time. The Greek god (or gods) appealed to him most, perhaps on account of the very varied nature of its manifestations. He was further attracted by the question of the distance (close or otherwise) between God and man, and particularly remarked how this issue troubled Alexandrian thinkers:

> It never occurred to these Alexandrian thinkers, as it had to some of their predecessors in ancient Greece, that God might not exist. They assumed that he existed. What troubled them was his relation to the rest of the universe and particularly to Man. Was God close to man? Or was he far away? If close, how could he be infinite and eternal and omnipotent? And if far away, how could he take any interest in man, why indeed should he have troubled to create him? They wanted God to be both far and close.[14x]

In the course of his discussion of Neo-Platonism Forster refers to the problem, as presented by Plotinus in the *Enneads*, as the greatest thing Alexandria ever produced. He tries to simplify Plotinus's three grades of God (which may sound like the Christian Trinity but greatly differ from it) by producing a very brief account of each grade:

> The first and highest grade in it he [Plotinus] calls the One. The One is – Unity, the One. Nothing else can be predicated about it,

not even that it exists; . . . it has no qualities, no creative force, it is good only as the goal of our aspirations. But though it cannot create, it overflows (somewhat like a fountain), and from its overflow or emanation is generated the second grade of the Trinity – the 'Intellectual Principle.' . . . It is the Universal mind that contains – not all things, but all thoughts of things, and by thinking it creates. It thinks of the third grade – the All Soul – which accordingly comes into being. . . . [15]

Forster then gives another summary of Plotinus's conception of the relationship between God and man:

We are all parts of God, even the stones, though we cannot realise it; and man's goal is to become actually, as he is potentially, divine. Therefore rebirth is permitted, in order that we may realise God better in a future existence than we can in this; and therefore the Mystic Vision is permitted, in order that, even in this existence we may have a glimpse of God.[16]

Another idea which engaged Forster's mind was that of good and evil, and their relation to God. He shows that the Neo-Platonic School did not recognise the eternal existence of Evil, despite the fact that it recognised its presence. The School believed that Good and Evil were aspects of God, and that the presence of one simply meant the absence of another.

These two ideas are worked out further in *A Passage to India* and form the core of the novel's metaphysics. They are represented by Professor Godbole, the Indian Brahman.[17x] Godbole surprises the other characters by his attitude towards the nature of the crisis at the Marabar Caves:

'I am informed that an evil action was performed in the Marabar Hills, and that a highly esteemed English lady [Adela] is now seriously ill in consequence. My answer to that is this: that action was performed by Dr Aziz.'

Then, with alternation of silence and emphasis, he goes on to say that the action was performed by the guide, by Aziz, by himself, by his students, by the lady herself:

'When evil occurs, it expresses the whole of the universe. Similarly when good occurs.'[18]

The relationship between man and God again appears in the last part of *A Passage to India*, where Godbole undertakes a celebration of the birth of Krishna. This relationship can be described in terms of God's manifestation in the animate lives, as well as in the inanimate objects of this universe. In his conception of God, Godbole (as well as Forster) is neither committed to a concrete reality of existence nor to an abstract one:

> God is not born yet – that will occur at midnight – but He has also been born centuries ago, nor can He ever be born, because He is the Lord of the Universe, who transcends human processes. He is, was not, is not, was.[19]

The celebration is carried out in a simple manner with Hindus sitting at the sides of the carpet, and God and Godbole standing at opposite ends of the same carpet. Godbole and the audience sing a song with a simple repetitive sound addressed not to God but to a saint. In the course of the ritual Godbole happens to remember Mrs Moore, and a wasp which was blessed by her, and a stone to which it clung – and he loves them all.

The Neo-Platonic God can be seen as close to that of the Hindu in being an all-embracing love which yet remains incomprehensible. Forster speculates that Plotinus had contact with Hindu merchants who came to Alexandria.

After Forster's passage between Alexandria and India there emerges an important development in his fictional technique, largely concerned with point-of-view. I believe that this aspect of Forster's aesthetics is deeply rooted in the thinking about God and the question of good and evil which had exercised him in Alexandria, and which bore fruit later on in *A Passage to India* and *Aspects of the Novel*.

The final vision of reality, as *A Passage to India* may demonstrate, lies with the narrator, who, like God, stands in full control. Incomprehensible in itself, it overflows into the characters and then becomes more comprehensible.

In answer to a question about what happened in the Caves, Forster answered that he did not know. Godbole evokes God by saying 'come' several times. But whether God comes or not is another matter, as he explains to his Christian friends. God is a desire and not a promise, he suggests. In *Alexandria*, Forster indicates the difference between Christianity on the one hand, and the Neo-Platonic and the Hindu by remarking that the Christian promise is that a man shall see God. This is further demonstrated in the character of Mrs Moore, whose vision of Indian reality proves to be more than her Christian belief can accommodate; and her appearance during Godbole's celebration can be justified on the basis of her attempt to free herself from the limitations of the Christian God.

In *Aspects of the Novel* the question of point-of-view receives specific treatment. Forster here suggests that the narrator should be neither too close nor too detached from his characters: 'The novelist who betrays too much interest in his own method can never be more than interesting; he has given up the creation of character and summoned us to help analyse his own mind, and a heavy drop in the emotional thermometer results.'[20] Similarly with the novelist who would be too much the detached historian, merely recording facts. He describes what is called the aesthetic distance as a power of expanding and contracting the vision of reality. He finds this shifting power 'one of the great advantages of the novel-form, and it has a parallel in our perception of life.'[21]

It was within the framework of this belief that Forster was gaining freedom in life and art. From the final compromise of *Howards End* (which D. H. Lawrence blamed him for as 'glorifying those *business* people') Forster was moving to a viewpoint which was seen as *essentially* shifting.

For Forster, Alexandria meant more than a place he disliked – or even the people he said he liked after having expressed that dislike for the place. It gave him a time and a space in the middle of suffocation in which to breathe. He turned to its history without the expectation of being able to connect past and present. The conclusion he draws from the history of Alexandria sounds like the prophetic voice of a narrator:

> Since the bombardment of 1882, the city has known other troubles, but they will not be here described. Nor will any peroration be attempted, for the reason that Alexandria is still alive and alters even while one tries to sum her up.[22]

On one occasion he wrote to Cavafy that Alexandria often turned up in his thought and occasionally in the flesh.[23x] On another he wrote saying that he wished he could have stayed longer in Alexandria as there was so much to say.

Alexandria had become for him the very embodiment of the shifting point of view.

9 A Passage via Alexandria?

John Drew

In *Alexandria: a History and a Guide*, Forster expressly commends the translation by Stephen MacKenna of the *Enneads* of Plotinus, the first volume of which, published in 1917, included a useful note on Terminology and a valuable Conspectus of the Plotinian System composed of important passages from all the *Enneads*.[1] MacKenna's work is particularly important to *Alexandria* since Forster suggests not only that in the Neo-Platonists the later city found her highest expression but that Alexandria produced nothing greater than the *Enneads*. *Alexandria* was published in 1922, just two years before *A Passage to India*, and it may be of interest, therefore, to note how Forster, in contrasting the Neo-Platonic promise that a man shall be God with the Christian one that he shall see God, likens it to the Indian. Forster was aware that the primary impulse left with Plotinus after his training in Alexandria was to travel East to get in touch with Persian and Indian philosophy and points out that, whether or not he met Hindus on the quays of Alexandria, his system can be paralleled in the religious writings of India.[2]

The unresolved question of whether or not Neo-Platonism was ever influenced by Hinduism need not concern us any more than it concerned Forster. A reading of the biography of Apollonius of Tyana, written by Philostratus during the lifetime of Plotinus and held in high esteem by the later Platonists, suggests the question may be irresolvable in that it is impossible to tell whether the book represents a projection on India of the Pythagorean view or an Indian influence on the Pythagoreans.[3x] At the time of Alexander's invasion of India a strong resemblance between Indian philosophy and the tradition associated with the names of Pythagoras and Plato had been indicated by the earliest commentators to shape the Western image of India, Onesicritus and Megasthenes.[4] In recent times J. F. Staal has demonstrated how very close to Neo-Platonism is the Advaita Vedanta of Sankara, traditions which, as he is aware,

point back, respectively, to the Pre-Socratics and to the Upanishads.[5] Another modern academic philosopher, J. N. Findlay,
prefers to think in terms of a common Indo-Pythagorean-Platonic
tradition[6] and, in so doing, echoes a point made long before, in a
literary context, by the Turkish Spy.[7] The imaginative India of Sir
William Jones, more influential on English literature, perhaps,
than any other, is conceived wholly in terms of Pythagoras and
Plato.[8x] Forster, therefore, is far from being eccentric when, in his
biography of Lowes Dickinson, he notes that his subject, who in his
youth had supposed there was much esoteric Buddhism in the
Phaedrus, had been happy in India only when he had attuned the
prevailing Vaishnavism (or devotional worship of Krishna) to his
own Platonism.[9] It may be that this remark is as revealing of Forster
as it is of Dickinson and, bearing in mind also the remarks about
Plotinus in *Alexandria*, a reading of *A Passage to India* in terms of the
Enneads might illuminate the novel and determine what, if any,
dimension beyond Alexandria, India represents.

The character who, in *A Passage to India*, accords most closely with
the Ideal Sage of the *Enneads*, the man for whom happiness consists
not in action but in wisdom,[10] is Professor Godbole. On first meeting
him we learn that for him tranquillity appears to swallow up
everything whereas the rest have no reserve of tranquillity to draw
upon.[11] The word 'tranquil' is precisely the one used in
MacKenna's translation of the *Enneads* to describe the contemplative state the Sage must attain to if he is to be Vision itself.[12]
Furthermore, the whole tendency of the *Enneads* is towards that
abstract thought which, we are told, an encounter with Godbole's
mind will cause an experience akin to,[13] and Godbole also attracts
the sort of instinctive trust which Plotinus makes a prerequisite for
Vision.[14] Even Fielding, exasperated as he is by (what to his rational
perception is) Godbole's obtuseness, none the less wants to have
Godbole's opinion about the moral propriety of his behaviour at the
club.[15]

The occasion for Fielding's exasperation is Godbole's denial of his
competence to decide either whether or not the Marabar expedition
has been a catastrophe or whether Aziz is innocent or guilty. As far
as he is concerned legal evidence determines matters of guilt and
innocence, but society's laws are no more ultimate than the personal
opinion he refuses to give: both are grounded on a faith in individual
perceptions. According to his philosophy, neither good nor evil are
performed in isolation by an individual – they express the whole of

the universe. Both are 'aspects of my Lord. He is present in the one, absent in the other . . . Yet absence implies presence, absence is not non-existence . . .'[16] This Hindu position, as baffling to some of Forster's readers as it is to Fielding, is in fact that of Plotinus:

> From none is that Principle [The Good] absent and yet from all; present, it remains absent save to those fit to receive, disciplined into some accordance, able to touch it closely by their likeness and by that kindred power within themselves through which, remaining as it was when it came to them from the Supreme, they are enabled to see in so far as God may at all be seen.[17]

Godbole's explanation of his philosophy to Fielding also provides a perspective on the song at the tea-party which had proved equally bewildering to the guests there. Again Plotinus is pertinent. Referring to the All, in a central passage on the One Life, he writes: 'Not that it has to come and so be present to you: it is you that have turned from it.'[18] Krishna, Indian image of the All, neglects or refuses to come: it is we who have to go to Krishna or rather, less dualistically, actually take on the form of Sri Krishna and assimilate ourselves to him.

In his summary of the *Enneads* in *Alexandria* Forster makes a distinction between what might be termed the philosophical and mystical sides of Plotinus. He notes that, for the philosopher, the All-Soul comprehends the whole sensible world down to the animals, plants and stones and that the Matter 'that seems so important to us' is really its last and feeblest emanation. These gradations Forster finds 'abstruse' and his attraction is to what he refers to as the 'more emotional side' of the *Enneads*. This is the side which, in treating of the universal urge to return to God (a striving that includes 'even the stones') speaks of the inner withdrawal through which we realise the 'Mystic Vision' of our Identity as God.[19] The vision vouchsafed to Professor Godbole and his fellow Hindus during the festival at Mau, as well as the peculiar, and relatively happy, ending to the Marabar trial, may be read in the light of this more mystical side of Plotinus.

Initially, however, *A Passage to India* appears to fly in the face of the argument which causes the idealist, as philosopher, to sound abstruse: that concerning the non-existence of Matter. Forster prefaced his remarks on Alexandrian thinkers by saying that it never occurred to them that God might not exist.[20] Given his awareness of this, we might expect his novel to pit the possibility of the non-existence of God, or pure Materialism, against the Neo-Platonic (consistent with the Advaita Vedantin) Idealism which asserts that God's absence is indicative of His presence. In fact, even in his exposition of Materialism, Forster is wholly consistent with Plotinus and, what is more remarkable, all the difficulties experienced by Mrs Moore, Adela, Fielding and Aziz can be seen to be a result of their failure to live the life of a Neo-Platonic sage such as is lived by Godbole.

In the opening chapter of the Caves section of his novel, Forster depicts the world before the advent of the gods as a primal ocean, pure matter 'older than all spirit'.[21] But Plotinus, too, conceives of the universe before it was ensouled: 'it was stark body – clay and water – or, rather, the blankness of Matter, the absence of Being, and as an author says, "the execration of the Gods".'[22] If an unopened Marabar cave appears to be the centre of a wholly material universe, it may be remembered that the extreme Idealist position, which denies any reality to the effect, is so perfectly the converse of Materialism, which denies any reality to the cause, that their terminology is identical: the Essential Existence of Plotinus is defined wholly in terms of negatives. Thus Plotinus writes that 'you must turn appearances about or you will be left void of God'.[23] Matter is Essential Evil, Authentic Non-Existence,[24] and it is only when, like an opened Marabar Cave, it is perceived that it pretends to a participation in Being it does not really have: 'Its existence is but a pale reflection, and less complete than that of the things implanted in it.'[25]

According to Plotinus, the whole Kosmos strives towards the Good, even all 'that you may judge inanimate. But there are degrees of participation . . . We have no right to demand equal powers in the unequal: the finger is not to be asked to see; there is the eye for that; a finger has its own business – to be finger and have finger power.'[26] The fists and fingers of the Marabars neither see nor permit sight, very little sunlight penetrates a Marabar cave and, unless a match be lit, it is devoid also of fire,[27] that derivation of sunlight which permits the back wall of Plato's Cave to participate in Reality as a distinct, if faint, image of it.

The sun, like the cave, Forster would appear to cast in a role the very reverse of that which it has in the Platonic theology. As the sun returns to preside over the Hot Season and its sinister events, his 'excess of light' portends power but not beauty. He is not 'the unattainable friend', 'the eternal promise' (of Platonism), 'the never-withdrawn suggestion that haunts our consciousness'. He is merely 'a creature' – i.e. material.[28] Sunrise over the Marabars is consequently uninspiring: 'It was as if virtue had failed in the celestial fount.'[29] But if Adela's sunstroke is to be read as the very converse of Platonic enlightenment it is because she has sought in the sunrise, as in the caves, something of scenic, or material, interest. She and Mrs Moore are looking at the wrong India or, rather, looking at India in the wrong way. Plotinus, consciously using the sun as an image for the Intellectual-Principle, also says that it is difficult to tell, as it is difficult to tell approaching the Marabars, whether or not the sun has risen but that, on that account, it is the more important to wait its rising with tranquillity, confident that the contemplating Intellect, above which it alone can dawn, will be filled with power and take a new beauty to itself.[30] Forster is consistent with Plotinus: the image cannot have the power that is also beautiful except in the contemplative Intellect.

Likewise, the Caves have no evil but what they are permitted to propagate by the hearts and minds of those whose souls are not ready for them. While Mrs Moore's experience of the cave leads her to accord to it an independent and eternal principle – the undying worm[31] – Plotinus draws the opposite conclusion. The moment Matter, itself bodiless and formless, is penetrated by Form, the moment a Marabar Cave is opened up, it begins to image Reality. Since Matter is an absolute lack of all Being its initial imaging will be so faint as to be a mockery:

> Its every utterance, therefore, is a lie . . . it is like a mirror showing things as in itself when they are really elsewhere, filled in appearance but actually empty, containing nothing, pretending everything. Into it and out of it move mimicries of Authentic Existents, images playing upon an image devoid of Form, visible against it by its very formlessness . . . they might be compared to shapes projected so as to make some appearance upon what we can only know as the Void.[32]

The intellectual context of this passage is as evocative of Forster's description of the inside of a Marabar Cave as the passage itself is evoked by Plato's Cave, elsewhere, along with the Cave of Empedocles, cited by Plotinus as an image for this universe (the corporeal ensouled).[33]

Writing of Matter participating in Form, Plotinus says 'The

entrant Idea will enter as an image, the untrue entering the untruth.' This is

> a pseudo-entry into a pseudo-entity – something merely brought near, as faces enter the mirror, there to remain just as long as the people look into it . . . All that impinges upon this Non-Being is flung back as from a repelling substance; we may think of an Echo returned from a repercussive plane surface; it is precisely because of the lack of retention that the phenomenon is supposed to belong to that particular place and even to arise there.[34]

Both here, and shortly after, Plotinus stresses that Matter has no existence: 'though Matter is far-extended – so vastly as to appear co-extensive with all this sense-known Universe – yet if the Heavens and their content came to an end, all magnitude would simultaneously pass from Matter with, beyond a doubt, all its other properties.'[35]

After her experience of the cave Mrs Moore has come to exactly the opposite conclusion: Matter alone has existence and it is from the huge scenic background of the Heavens that all magnitude has passed.[36] Yet she understands that nothing evil (in the Christian sense) had been in the cave.[37] She has experienced the emptiness of the universe, vision presents itself as nightmare and it is she more than Fielding who needed to hear Godbole say that absence implies presence, that absence is not non-existence.[38] In fact she has heard the old Brahmin say as much in his song and in his explanation of it at the end of the tea-party, she has shaken off enough of her limited English Christian background and come close enough to enlightenment to experience its prerequisite converse, disillusionment, and this makes it possible for her ultimately to be 'seen' psychically by Godbole at Mau.[39]

Adela is less well prepared. She had gone into the cave with her mind half on sight-seeing and its boredom and half on marriage,[40] and, as a result of doubts about the propriety of her own marriage, proposed as a result of 'esteem and animal contact at dusk', asks Aziz an unconsciously offensive question about his marital state. Plotinus writes that when the partial or individual soul is set on self 'it produces its lower, an image of itself – a non-Being – and so is wandering, as it were, into the void, stripping itself of its own determined form.'[41] Adela's doubts about her own personal relationships, like Mrs Moore's doubts about the efficacy of

Christian values, are reflected in the cave at their most de-spiritualised extreme.

The peculiar circumstances of Adela's, no less than Mrs Moore's, recovery from this nightmare suggests how closely *A Passage to India* may have followed the antithetical movement Forster saw in the *Enneads*. Plotinus makes clear that the soul can liberate itself from a descent and become illuminated by assimilating itself to the Soul above it. There are two phases of the soul, the lower, tied to sense-impressions, and the higher, free of them:

> When the two souls chime each with each, the two imaging faculties no longer stand apart; the union is dominated by the more powerful of the faculties of the soul, and thus the image perceived is as one; the less powerful is like a shadow attending upon the dominant, like a minor light merging into a greater: when they are in conflict, in discord, the minor is distinctly apart . . .[42]

This explanation would account both for the shadow which bottles Adela up in the cave and for the single vision which comes to her in court following the cessation of the crowd's chant and her insidious echo (the evil double, as that is, of her original harmless sound). At this point, Adela's higher, or Impersonal, soul had been assimilated to the Impersonalism of Mrs Moore above it: her lower, or personal, soul which takes the Cosmic personally is now not dominant but subordinate – and so Aziz does not appear in the cave.

That even Adela can salvage enough from her ghastly Marabar experience to feel indebted to India[43] suggests that the *Enneads* may, however coincidentally, bear on something more than her surname: those who seek the Authentic, we are told, do not necessarily find it: 'it chooses where it will and enters as the participant's power may allow . . . it remains the quested and so in another sense never passes over.'[44x] As the novel moves on from the Hot Season to the Rains and from the Mosque and Caves to the Temple we have increasingly to consider just how totally Forster has come round to accepting Plotinus even at his most abstruse: 'without evil the All would be incomplete. For most or even all forms of evil serve the Universe . . .'[45] Godbole refused to commit himself to saying that the Marabar expedition had been unsuccessful.[46]

Mrs Moore and Adela have been visited by their dismal experience not because they have committed any great sin in the

Christian sense but because, according to the Neo-Platonic scheme, their souls have gone into division in the mere fact of exercising perception and so 'take in much that clashes with their nature and brings distress and trouble since the object of their concern is partial, deficient . . .'[47] In exercising perception the women have permitted themselves to fall under a spell which deludes them, they have been deceived by a magic which pervades the entire universe. Plotinus specifically mentions caring for children and planning marriage (precisely what has brought both Mrs Moore and Adela to India)[48] as activities which lead away from the inward contemplation which alone can realise Vision.[49] Even before going into the caves, Mrs Moore, in a general, and therefore impersonal,[50] and Adela, in a personal,[51] way have begun to doubt the efficacy of these activities. While they land themselves in what appears to be a greater evil, yet it works to a greater good: by the end of the Marabar trial, Adela has experienced a vision and Mrs Moore become a minor goddess.

Given Forster's concurrence with a philosophy which regards action as a weakened form of contemplation (in *Aspects of the Novel* Forster laments that a novel has to tell a story),[52] the part played by Godbole and the Hindus in the earlier stages of the novel takes on a significance in inverse proportion to their share in the action. Godbole's strange song has, in fact, been a call to the slumbering spirit, registering only the distinction between pleasure and pain, to break out, in the image of Psyche as butterfly, from its cocoon of self-enthralment and social endeavour.[53] It is after hearing Godbole's song that Mrs Moore and Adela begin to experience a dissatisfaction with their way of life. Adela later acknowledges this,[54] while Mrs Moore feels her disillusionment in the form of a person trying to take hold of her hand,[55] possibly a covert reference to Godbole, within whose consciousness at Mau she will be further compelled to the place where completeness is found.[56]

Fielding, likewise, may be subject to Godbole's prompting ('it was as if someone had told him there was such a moment') but he wholly misses his chance of vision (significantly, the Marabars transformed) just after he has asserted the innocence of Aziz.[57] The fact is that the very best sort of humanism ('good will plus culture and intelligence')[58] which Fielding represents is found to be inadequate to the task of sustaining a single friendship, let alone the whole world. He is an atheist and, according to Plotinus, the question of vision cannot even be discussed with those who have 'drifted far from God'.[59] The very purpose of Fielding's life is to teach 'people to be individuals, and to understand other in-dividuals'.[60] It is basic to the *Enneads* that the individual in any form, while 'more readily accessible to our cognizance', does not in fact exist.[61] On this account, Fielding, even more than Adela, remains a dwarf without the apparatus for judging whether or not the hundred Indias are One,[62] his marriage determines he is no longer even the holy man minus the holiness he once described himself as being[63] and by the end Aziz has become 'a memento', separated from him in terms of both space ('not there') and time ('not yet').[64] The significance, though not the recollection, of Godbole's song eludes him to the end.[65]

The invisible forces which determine the course of events in the novel manifest themselves by way of sights and sounds almost too delicate for the ordinary senses. The novelist, like the philosopher, has to resort to the sensible if he wishes to image the Intellectual. Plotinus, though he uses the imagery of sight, prefers that of sound and asks us to think of a soul as 'a sound passing through the air and carrying a word' liable to strike any ear receptive to it.[66] Since the Neo-Platonists regard the whole universe as ensouled, they, like the Vedantins, have a concept of an all-inclusive Cosmic Sound, the property of the all-encompassing Aether. This is of considerable importance to the novel, though by its nature it can be made known only by the slightest suggestion and only to those who, in Plotinian phrase, let the hearings of the senses (and the echoes) go by and listen for the desired voice.[67] Ordinary sound can come close to this invisible power only in what Plotinus terms 'the tune of an incantation, a significant cry' which has 'a natural leading power over the soul'.[68] The chanting by the Hindus of Mrs Moore's name not only helps her to deification and Adela to vision but ensures that Aziz will always be helped to a more harmonious frame of mind. The emotionalism of Aziz leads him to build his life on a mistake[69] but, as Forster says, it may also bear him to an anchorage no less than carry him across it to the rocks.[70] His belief in ghosts leaves him open to intimations from the Unseen which cause him to love in an Impersonal way: the chant of the Hindu crowd at Mau, which Forster pointedly relates to that of the crowd outside the court at Chandrapore and which combines the two names, Radha and Krishna, that remained separate in Godbole's original song, leads him to revise his attitude to Ralph Moore[71] and, unlike Fielding, he is responsive to the prompting—this time 'not a sight, but a sound'—which flits past him and causes him to promise Adela he will associate her thereafter with the irreproachable Mrs Moore.[72]

The whole festival at Mau may be read in terms of a single paragraph from Plotinus where he explains how the soul obtains its vision of The Good. The soul is stirred towards Intellectual Beings for the radiance about them 'just as earthly love is not for the material form but for the Beauty manifested upon it . . . The soul taking that outflow from the divine is stirred; seized with a Bacchic passion, goaded by these goads, it becomes Love.'[73] Forster describes the festival as an orgy not of the body but of the spirit,[74] and his sentiment as well as his terminology is particularly close to that of the *Enneads* in his description of the Hindu villagers as they glimpse the image of Krishna: 'A most beautiful and radiant expression came into their faces, a beauty in which there was nothing personal, for it caused them all to resemble one another during the moment of its indwelling, and only when it was withdrawn did they revert to individual clods.'[75] Plotinus says that if the soul remains in the Intellectual-Principle the vision is not complete: 'The face it sees is beautiful no doubt but not of power to hold its gaze because lacking in the radiant grace which is the bloom upon beauty.'[76] Earlier, he has spoken of Vision (of which the beauty and radiance are a manifestation) as pertaining to 'the self-indwelling Soul'.[77] In the light of Plotinus, Forster's passage may be read to suggest that in so far as any onlooker can ever know, the villagers have become Love and do enjoy the Mystic Vision. That is, until they fall under 'the rules of time' and revert to 'individual clods': 'Individuals have their separate entities, but are at one in the [total] unity.'[78]

Professor Godbole is the Hindu through whom we can particularly trace the path to the Love, both Impersonal and Infinite, which annihilates, in a way which seemed impossible to Fielding,[79] all the sorrow that exists on the face of the earth.[80] His soul is 'a tiny reverberation', part of 'the chain of sacred sounds' which evoke Vision. At Mau certain definite images impinge on his memory until he is returned to his immediate environment by the stone which, we are told, he had been wrong to attempt, having been seduced by logic and conscious effort.[81] What had gone wrong? In a central passage on the One Life, Plotinus tells us that at the stage of the Intellectual-Principle, Vision is still multiple if indivisible, every item distinct, though not to the point of separation. But association of 'item after item' is not identity[82] and the soul must speed to 'something greater to its memory' where it acts not by seeing and knowing but by loving, the lover elaborating for himself 'an immaterial image'.[83] The trouble for Godbole is that he became distracted by the external: the need for a new hymn and the readjustment of his pince-nez.[84] Plotinus writes: 'In the looking, beware of throwing outward.'[85] It is precisely the tiny fragments of Godbole's consciousness that attend to 'outside things' which permit 'tiny splinters of detail', distinct images, to emerge from the Imageless Vision, 'the universal warmth'. Thereafter, item can follow item, however affirmative the understanding, and Chance come into play.[86]

Plotinus had posed the question as to whether the stones had life, a question already taken up by Forster outside the Marabar caves,[87] and if it is stone which proves resistant to Godbole's vision, it is because mineral, of all creation, is the form most obviously resistant to any state of consciousness short of the Ultimate Vision. There is, however, a further reason why Godbole had been wrong to attempt the stone. At one point, Plotinus actually tries to explain the One by using stone as a contrast: 'It is not like a stone, some vast block lying where it lies, covering the space of its own extension, held within its own limits, having a fixed quantity of mass and of assigned stone-power.'[88] The One is wholly free of such limitations, which are secondary. In choosing stone for this contrast, Plotinus not only sees it as the visible form least receptive to Vision; he also points out that there is a fallacy in conceiving of the metaphysical in terms of the physical. Spirit operates by way of all conceivable principles but lies outside them and encompasses them all. For this reason Plotinus says: 'Seeking Him, seek nothing of Him outside: within is to be sought what follows upon Him; Himself do not attempt.'[89] Godbole should not have attempted stone, not only because stone is the physical ultimately most resistant to absorption into the metaphysical but because the metaphysical Ultimate, which alone could absorb it, should not be attempted. The Ultimate Vision will not be achieved by conscious effort any more than by logic: it will come, beyond image and idea, at that point where there can be no perception of, but only the existence of, Infinite Love. It was for this reason that Godbole, for all his spirituality, was initially 'silenced' by mention of the Marabar caves[90] and avoided either talking about them or visiting them.

This mystical experience is the passage to India or, in the words of Whitman's poem, the passage to more than India.[91] Forster says that it is 'a passage not easy, not now, not here, not to be

apprehended except when it is unattainable'.[92] Plotinus, referring
to the nature of Unity, is pertinent: 'No wonder that to state it is not
easy; even Being and Form are not easy, though we have a way, an
approach through the Ideas.'[93] The difficulty for the soul is that the
nature of what it is trying to grasp (the Formless) and its own means
of grasping it (assimilation to it by means of identity) preclude
knowledge of attainment: 'In seeking thus to know the Unity it is
prevented by that very unification from recognizing that it has
found; it cannot distinguish itself from the object of this
intuition . . . Our way then takes us beyond knowing . . . knowing
and knowable must all be left aside; every object of thought, even
the highest, we must pass by . . .'[94] If the passage is not to be
apprehended except when it is unattainable, then it is not to be
attained except when it is inapprehensible.

This is why Forster is not being sceptical of the Neo-Platonist
position but absolutely consistent with it when he says it is
impossible to tell whether the Mystic Vision has succeeded. It
cannot be expressed in anything but itself – neither in literature nor
in philosophy, both of which it flings down no less than science or
history.[95] The highest to which art can attain is the Intellectual-
Principle – images indivisible but nonetheless multiple. If the adept
in the Mysteries thinks he has been with God his thought falls under
the rules of time. Of such adepts Plotinus writes: 'It is that they see
God still and always, and that as long as they see, they cannot tell
themselves they have had the vision; such reminiscence is for souls
that have lost it.'[96]

Few and inconclusive as these references are, they do raise the
possibility that Forster was heir to an old tradition, itself Platonic,
which has made the passage to India by way of Platonism. Yet the
fact that there are passages in the later volumes of MacKenna's
translation from which Forster would seem to, but could not, have
borrowed even the phraseology may serve to remind us that the
attraction of Neo-Platonism for the artist is that it is an intellectual
tradition which makes an imaginative act the precondition for its
apprehension, its re-creation, like that of the phoenix, dependent on
its own destruction. Ever since the time when Alexander, at the
limit of his world conquest, was confronted by Brahmin philosophers who queried whether he had conquered himself, his city,
Alexandria, has been a critical point of embarkation for India. It
was in Alexandria that a character in one of Lucian's dialogues
relinquished all his money before going off to join the Brahmins;[97] in

the time of Plotinus himself, not only did Alexandria provide first evidence that Buddha's name was known in the West[98] but the first record of an Indian cave and its sculpture was immediately incorporated into an Alexandrian novel.[99] If India is symbolic of a passage beyond Alexandria it is perhaps because, to the mind of the Hellenist, it is a place, as remote in space as Classical Athens is in time, which has given, and been known to give, to mystical experience a central importance which becomes increasingly peripheral the farther West one comes. In quoting Plotinus to that effect by way of epigraph to *Alexandria*, Forster recognises that to any vision must be brought an eye adapted to what is to be seen. It may be that we can never see more of India than was seen in Alexandria, albeit Alexandria itself might see there was more to India than meets even the Alexandrian eye. As Forster discovered in his novel, so abstract is the image of India that it is not even the promise that he had earlier supposed, but only an appeal.[100]

10 Forster and Dewas

J. Birje-Patil

Miles and miles of flat green fields and then Dewas. Rising sheer above it like a huge fist clenched at the top is Devi. A town lost in its own legends, ignored by gypsies. The giant lorries rolling along the Bombay-Agra Road scarcely noticed it a few years ago. Indeed no one would have noticed it if E. M. Forster had not decided to pay a second visit to it in 1921. Perhaps he had to go back to see if it really existed. It could have been an image that had lingered after an evening at Sadlers Wells. During his first visit it had the appearance of a Gilbert and Sullivan[1] kingdom.

The dichotomy of flat land and hill is remarkable. Since the earth has heaved itself up so high, one expects a valley on the other side. Devi is almost at a right angle from the land with the sky as hypotenuse. And the lights of Dewas have a way of coming to life that would distract fireflies.

So much dust has settled over the place that when a figure detaches itself from a peeling wall one is surprised to see it move. The highway which had ignored the town for a long time has now spawned, on its outskirts, brand-new factories gleaming with affluence where the trucks which had formerly rumbled past indifferently toward Bombay grind to a halt, emitting smoke of fuel collected from distant parts. Within its own old limits the town continues to decay to the tune of raucous film songs hurled at it by the ubiquitous transistors crackling in wayside hotels swarming with flies. This crumbling affair of mortar and wood, menaced by the streamlined angular structures rearing their snouts in the starlit Malwa skies, spells to the young the dawn of a new era and to the old the eclipse of their civilisation.

But surely, even by the standards of the princely states during the first decade of this century, the Dewas of Forster's day had been something of an anachronism. H.H.'s[2] attempts to modernise Dewas were epitomised by the new palace outside the town. The new palace, complete with an English Secretary and equipped with gadgets that rarely, if ever, worked, seemed to be in a good state of repair. But it was the old palace, with a quality described by Forster as 'numinous', that retained possession over the lesser ruins and like a haunted homestead continued to pull H.H. back to itself. There 'lurked the proud ancestral servants'[3] as they do now. Within the walls of the old palace stalks the spirit of H.H.: his presence comes alive there during the festival of Krishna's birth, which is celebrated, if less ostentatiously, as vigorously as when H.H. lived in Dewas. It was the fulcrum of intrigue and ritual. Today only the local Deuteronomy, nostalgically viewing the place from the top of the hill, can tell where it stands. The red glow emanating from its tower proclaimed its presence once. Today a mute unilluminated patch at the heart of a town which is glittering with light indicates its location. It must have looked utterly ridiculous during the Raj, when it was little more than a town from the fables where lived a king who had incurred divine wrath. There was a king in Buckingham Palace and a King in the old palace in Dewas. Was there a congruence somewhere? Only the haunting sense of orphanage informing the town perhaps justifies Forster's splendid epithet. 'Some will rejoice that it has vanished. Others will feel that something precious has been thrown away amongst the rubbish – something which might have been saved.'[4]

The Hill of Devi has perhaps become a classic in its own right but the offspring of those whose paths crossed Forster's half a century ago and those younger men and women of today who stand at the crossroads of Dewas's manifest destiny generally have to strain hard to produce a few well-worn titbits of Forsteriana in the context of Dewas. Some offer exotically misguided versions at the mention of the name. Dewas has built no memorial to its most celebrated visitor. There are no 'Here slept Forster' plaques nor a pigeon-tormented statue of a bookish Englishman with a donnish stoop. Conversely, Forster himself never strayed much beyond the palace grounds. Besides the courtiers and a few servants, the general citizenry was a vague mass of humanity heaving outside the old palace. First there was the language problem; and secondly, all the significant life splashed around the two palaces. That's where the 'action' was, so to speak. But even there one searches in vain for a cherished aphorism or a typically Forsteresque turn of phrase preserved by a close friend. H.H.'s second wife, that gracious lady called BaiSaheb in *The Hill of Devi*, is eighty-four. Forster tells us how much he admired her and how they sometimes played a game of cards together with friends. 'He never discussed politics or the court', BaiSaheb says haltingly. It is obvious that although she recalls Forster vividly and talks about him with genuine affection, it is the Darlings who matter to her most. Only Mr Bidwai, who died a few years ago, once said emphatically that Forster had been an avid reader of Gibbon's *Decline and Fall of the Roman Empire*. Mr Bidwai, who was the chief minister of the state, recalled going for long walks with Forster. And one wonders what happened to the paper on Dostoevsky read by Forster to the Dewas Literary Society? It would be interesting to locate the script, which is probably yellow with age if it still exists and if the white ants have not yet devoured it. Where the number of people who had known him personally has dwindled to half a dozen or less and whose knowledge about Forster's literary work is at best vague, any attempt to locate the script of the paper on Dostoevsky is literally like hunting for a needle in a haystack.

But the community of interests which Forster shared with H.H. during his short stay proved to be remarkably fecund. Dewas spoke to Forster through H.H., and even a brief visit to Dewas after a careful perusal of *The Hill of Devi* reveals the extent to which Forster drew upon his experience of the place while writing the Temple section of *A Passage to India*. Dewas was small, dull and even ugly, but it was also a place where the Krishna cult flourished with a saturnalian gusto quite unlike anything he had known before, corresponding to something which was fast disappearing from Europe. The terminal notes to *Maurice* reveal Forster's deep nostalgia for such a haven. 'Our greenwood ended catastrophically and inevitably. Two great wars demanded and bequeathed regimentation which the public service adopted and extended, science lent her aid, and the wildness of an island never extensive was stamped upon and built over and patrolled in no time.'[5]

His second visit to Dewas occurred after he had completed *Maurice*. His creativity was at its peak and his personal crisis was growing more acute day by day. The Temple section of *A Passage to India* was thus born of a need to impose order on a rage that his Western Puritan heritage could neither contain nor appease. His contact with a Prince who performed a Dionysian dance before his God, the Krishna cult reminiscent of the 'Adonis festival, where the God is born and dies, and is carried to the water, all in a short time',[6] and the women who taunted strangers with a provocative savagery as part of their fertility ritual as women had done in Ancient Greece, perhaps seemed to be essential parts of an unfamiliar but tantalisingly liberal social order where, as in 'the greenwood' it was possible 'neither to reform nor corrupt . . . but to be left alone'.[7]

Everything about India suggested formlessness. This catalysed a rage for chaos that beat against his soul. The draft of *A Passage to India* had got stuck in one of the caves. The chaotic life swirling within this odd place seemed perhaps to call forth a rage of his own that he had struggled a little too hard to suppress. Dewas did not actually shrug off his uranian escapades casually – it is doubtful if anyone besides H.H. actually had any knowledge of them – but it seemed to provide a matrix which accommodated a large variety of human folly. It was just possible that this order which seemed liberal to the point of anarchy and which expressed itself through the saturnalian rituals surrounding Krishna's birth might perhaps accommodate his deviation as a variant of folly. In Dewas, the greenwood might still flourish. If occasionally he grew impatient with the pointless intrigues and inane rituals of court and town, the good-humoured acceptance of folly soothed his mind tormented by a corrosive sense of guilt. The younger son of H.H., Mr Bhojraj Pawar, who teaches English at the local college in Dewas, has a theory that his father was perhaps aware of his friend's problem but might have accepted it as evidence of the eccentric ways of 'Saheb Log'. Perhaps it reminded him of similar idiosyncracies of his princely colleagues in the neighbouring states.[8x]

The rationale was provided by the Krishna cult of 'Bhakti' or 'Devotion' for the deity, whom one thought of as a beloved. 'Dolly', the tiny image of Lord Krishna in the old palace, was not meant to be installed in a temple as big as the one where it is to be found today. The spaciousness of the temple on the ground floor facing the courtyard shrinks 'Dolly' even further by contrast. Dolly was the chief among H.H.'s household gods at Supa in Maharashtra and had lived there peacefully among many other gods and goddesses of its size in a carved wooden cabinet designed like a miniature temple. As the first-born he had the right to carry it away with him when he went to Dewas after he was adopted by the Dewas family. Normally, in a temple the size of the present one at Dewas, the image would be made either of marble or some special wood, and would be at least two to three feet tall. It would not be smothered out of sight by a few flowers. Dolly's present residence therefore is a king's tribute to an ancestral god who catapulted him into kingship from the position of an upper-middle-class country gentleman's son.

The Temple section of *A Passage to India* is Dewas-oriented to a much greater degree than has been noticed hitherto. There are various theories about which of Forster's Indian acquaintances could have served as a model for Godbole. Godbole's evocation of Tukaram suggests closer affinities with H.H. himself, whose dancing and singing before Krishna is still talked about in Dewas. Also there is a reference to the Junior Rani in Chapter XXXV of *A Passage to India* which is equally puzzling. There is no official record suggesting bifurcation of Mau into Senior and Junior. The *chattri* (canopy) with the squatting statue of the king's father 'made to imitate life at enormous expense'[9] is not unlike the one located in the Royal Tombs at Dewas overlooking the lake. There are two statues there representing the king's father and mother. Although the lake described in *A Passage to India*, in which the village of Gokul is immersed, was obviously suggested by the bigger one at Mau, the route of the procession and the final scenes leading to the immersion of the clay model of Gokul are obviously based on the festival he witnessed at Dewas. The lake, the statues and the temple have more than a mere geographical significance for the last sections of the novel. Despite the strangeness of the rituals he witnessed, Forster always managed to find certain familiar symbolic patterns behind them. The festival of Krishna's birth obviously bewildered him, especially the fatuousness of some of the rituals. However, it was precisely the pranks which legend attributes to Krishna, enacted by his devotees with childlike candour, which intensified his awareness of a basic lack of liberalism in Christanity as he knew it. As he says in *The Hill of Devi*, he was 'left, too, aware of a gap in Christanity: the canonical gospels do not record that Christ laughed or played. Can a man be perfect if he never laughs or plays?'[10]

One wonders whether Forster would have gained this insight into the true nature of the Krishna cult had he not at this time been yearning for a spiritual order that would accommodate his uranian impulses without trivialising itself. Perhaps his association with H.H., who as an exponent of the Bhakti cult wooed his beloved Krishna through his songs, dances and short religious couplets (composed by him and now collected in a book of religious verse), enabled him to perceive in the cult a moral order which sustained him when his sense of guilt became corrosive.

It would indeed be perverse to say that the Krishna cult encourages deviant behaviour. Nevertheless at least one aspect of the cult and a very significant aspect, one that accounts for its popularity and its endurance in folk art and culture, celebrates that phase in Krishna's legendary life which was devoted to a sort of divine philandering. Krishna is there viewed as a heterosexual 'Puck' or 'Ariel' figure. His many seductions or near-seductions stand for his pervasive divine penetration of the human consciousness. In these cases the husbands are generally depicted as crude, overbearing, money-grubbing non-believers who have to be brought to their senses.

But Krishna also has male admirers who cast him in the role of a beloved. They implore him to 'come'. But he doesn't 'come'. H.H.'s hymns depict him in a role similar to a 'milkmaiden' stricken with deep longing for a glimpse of her beloved Krishna. This subtle combination of the religious and erotic would certainly fascinate someone in search of an order which would allow rationalisation of impulses whose very existence was an affront to the social order which he had inherited.

On the other hand the Middle Ages had not only ritualised life at the level of ordinary existence, they had also developed elaborate spiritual games which enabled the community to exorcise folly collectively. During the renaissance Rabelais and Erasmus had stressed the significance of 'folly' in relation to life in general. The recognition and acceptance of it could be regarded as primary conditions for initiating the process of regeneration, as in *King Lear*.

'A queer impressive story of a Holy Man who died about 50 years ago' is mentioned in *The Hill of Devi*. This man was reportedly 'dressed in women's garments to be the bride of God and adorned with Tulsi plant, and he was encased in a beautiful box to float down the Ganges.[11]

Would it be far-fetched to imagine that Krishna's Brindaban garden where, according to the legend, he lived in a state of pastoral polygamy, served as a 'substitute greenwood'? The Alecs and Maurices were expelled from their greenwood in England and they found in Dewas a place of refuge which lacked some features of the original yet satisfied their basic needs. When, overcome by his sense of isolation, Maurice calls Alec, the word that leaps out is Godbole's 'come'. 'Whom had he called? He had been thinking of nothing and the word had leapt out . . . He wasn't alone.'[12]

The amused acceptance of human imperfections implied in the Erasmian concept of 'folly', the games devotees play even today during Easter at the Cathedral at Seville, offer him Western analogues for the spirit of 'merriment' informing the festival of

Krishna's birth. As Forster concludes in the Temple section of *A Passage to India* it was this absence of 'merriment' from Puritan Christianity that made it exclusive, leaving no room for human imperfections without which no human being is completely human.

The forces that destroyed the greenwood in Europe and Dewas were similar. It was the 'wheels of Western righteousness'[13] which flattened it in both places. Although he was not blii ' ɔ the fact that the society at Dewas was decadent Forster found in it something worth cherishing. What that something was is not made very clear in *The Hill of Devi*. It was perhaps a combination of metaphysics and merriment and a capacity for spontaneous friendship and warmth and the genuinely liberal spirit informing the cult of Krishna which touched life at several levels – something that is summed up with the characteristic candour informing *The Hill of Devi*: 'Affection, or the possibility of it, quivered through everything, from Gokul Ashtami down to daily human relationships.'[14]

11 Life's Walking Shadows in *A Passage to India*

V. A. Shahane

The moment I had been looking forward to for weeks approached and at 12.30 p.m. on Wednesday, 18 May 1966, I entered Forster's rooms in King's at Cambridge. I found Forster seated on the same sofa on which I had seen him several times a decade ago. As soon as Forster saw me, he got up and embraced me in the Indian style and I was overwhelmed by this affectionate gesture. We talked about our previous meetings and the letters we had exchanged.

One of the aims of my interview was to trace 'life's walking shadows' in *A Passage to India*, to inquire into the genesis of some of the important characters. We talked about Syed Ross Masood, Forster's most intimate Indian friend, about whom he wrote in 1937:

> My own debt to him is incalculable. He woke me up out of my suburban and academic life, showed me new horizons and a new civilisation and helped me towards the understanding of a continent. Until I met him, India was a vague jumble of rajahs, sahibs, babus, and elephants, and I was not interested in such a jumble: who could be? He made everything real and exciting as soon as he began to talk, and seventeen years later when I wrote *A Passage to India* I dedicated it to him out of gratitude as well as out of love, for it would never have been written without him.[1]

We also talked about Forster's other distinguished friends in Hyderabad – Haroon Khan Sherwani, Saeed Yar Jung, Sajjad Mirza and Ali Akbar – and also of his Indian visits.

'Do you recall Chandrapore in *A Passage to India?*' [I asked.]

'Yes, of course, it's Bankipore, the cantonment town near Patna. Masood and I spent a good deal of time there together.'

'Is Aziz close to Masood or Saeed or any other person whom you have met?'

'Not quite. Aziz is a mixture of many traits derived from different individuals. This is equally true of Godbole. No single individual is involved as a specific model in either case. However, I am naturally influenced by people whom I have met. . . .'

'Where did you get the songs which Godbole recites in the novel?'

There are two songs. The Marathi song about Tukaram was given to me by a friend at Dewas. Since you know Marathi well, you can grasp what it means. The other song about *gopis* is partly an invention and partly derived from the Bhakti cult prayers. . . .'

At this point I was reminded of Kacheshwar's *aaratis* (prayers) of Tukaram, the Marathi saint poet. Lunch arrived, however, and the discussion about Godbole was interrupted.

2

The source of Godbole (if any) has always puzzled me. The genesis of Aziz is equally enigmatic, since there seem to be several sources that Forster made use of in the making of this character. Forster is reported to have said during a conversation in June 1962 to K. Natwar-Singh:

> Aziz is modeled on Masood, my greatest Indian friend. To him I dedicated *A Passage to India*. Godbole is also modeled on a friend. But I think of them – of Aziz and Godbole – as people and not as religious types.[2]

The men and events in *A Passage to India* do not quite support this view, however. Forster's 'Indian Entries',[3] part of his Indian diary, gives a number of clues to the 'raw material', the experiences at Dewas and Aurangabad which went into the creation of *A Passage to India*. There are several correspondences between events described in "Indian Entries", *Goldsworthy Lowes Dickinson, The Hill of Devi*, and incidents in *A Passage to India*. For instance, the man who pulled the punkah – 'Almost naked, and splendidly formed, he sat on a raised platform . . . and he seemed to control the proceedings'[4] – corresponds to an actual event: 'punkah boy, seated at end of table, had the impassivity of Atropos.'[5] Forster stayed at Aurangabad in Saeed's (Saeed Yar Jung's) house in 'a lovely wooden hall: two rows of triple arches which, like the internal pavilions, were painted blue'.[6] Fielding's room in Chandrapore in *A Passage to India* is like a replica of Saeed's house in Aurangabad. Many qualities of Saeed seem to have been re-created in Aziz's character. During the sightseeing tour in Aurangabad, Saeed, says Forster, 'would guard and order me and invent imaginary perils of beast and reptile'.[7] Mrs Moore is warned by Aziz in a similar tone as she walks alone to the mosque: 'I think you ought not to walk at night alone, Mrs Moore. There are bad characters about and leopards may come across from the Marabar Hills. Snakes also' (PI ii, 15). The textual evidence in *A Passage to India* suggests a close resemblance between Saeed and Aziz, and the latter seems a fictional re-creation of the former. Saeed is described in the 'Entries' as a 'remnant' of the 'vanished Moghal Empire', which Aziz indeed appears to be. Saeed has 'more charm than swagger', and Aziz seems an equally charming character. Saeed is an 'amiable show-off' and a 'reckless talker', qualities which can be attributed to Aziz as well. Forster's conversation with Saeed about debts, generosity, extravagance, girls, marriage, etc., might well have formed part of an exchange between Fielding and Aziz. Saeed's outburst against the English – 'It may be 50 or 500 years but we shall turn you out' ('Entries', p. 26) – is similar in tone and spirit to Aziz's onslaught on the English in the last scene of *A Passage to India*. 'Clear out, all you Turtons and Burtons. . . . Clear out, clear out I say. . . . Down with the English anyhow' (xxxvii, 311–12). Saeed hates the English as rulers and is a reckless talker; Aziz is in no way different. Saeed says to Forster that 'the accounts of friends are written in the heart' ('Entries', p. 27); the primary characteristic of Aziz's personality is indicated in the key phrase, 'the secret understanding of the heart'.

About five years ago, when I met Saeed Yar Jung in his home in Hyderabad, he was nostalgic and warm-hearted about Forster, but was evasive over his part in the creation of Aziz. In the light of all these facts, the statement in Natwar-Singh's recorded interview that 'Aziz is modelled on Masood' needs further critical scrutiny. In his tribute to Ross Masood, Forster writes:

Masood was essentially an artist. Those who knew him as an official may be surprised at this statement, but though his career was of a practical character his temperament was aesthetic. He lived by his emotions and instincts, and his standards were those of good taste. 'Don't be so damned inartistic' he would say if he wanted to criticise my conduct. For logic, and for ethical consistency, he had very little use. He had an artist's recklessness over money; he was fantastically generous, incredibly hospitable, and always happiest when he was giving something away.[8]

Aziz can by no means be described as an artist or a person of aesthetic temper, though he talks to Mrs Moore at Fielding's tea of the beauties of his host's room: 'See those curves at the bottom of the arches. What delicacy! It is the architecture of Question and Answer' (PI vii, 63). It is true that Aziz, like Masood, lives by his 'emotions and instincts'; he has no use for logic and is extremely reckless over money; but the points of resemblance between the two, Masood and Aziz, disappear into disparities rather too quickly. Whereas Masood 'handled the English splendidly', Aziz is at sea when confronted by the insolence of the English bureaucracy in India. Major Callendar's note disturbs him and he repairs to his house only to be snubbed by his boss's total indifference. Mrs Lesley and Mrs Callendar take away his carriage and he smiles helplessly; it is this obsequiousness to the British, this total lack of self-respect that makes Nirad Chaudhuri say that Aziz is a 'pest' and that he 'would not have been allowed to cross my threshold'.[9] As against this servility of Aziz, Masood in real life was a person of scrupulous self-respect and personal dignity. If anyone intruded on his freedom he was a great fighter. Forster writes:

> There is a story that he was once involved in a 'railway-carriage' incident. He was stretched full-length in an empty compartment when a British officer bounced in and said 'Come on! get out of this.' Masood looked up quietly and said, 'D' you want your head knocked off?', whereupon the officer exclaimed, 'I say, I'm awfully sorry, I didn't know you were that sort of person,' and they became excellent friends.[10]

It is obvious that Aziz and Masood are in many ways poles apart. Forster may have compounded the elements of character of not only Saeed and Masood but of other Muslim friends such as Haroon

Khan Sherwani, Rasheed, Sajjad Mirza, Ali Akbar and others. Many 'walking shadows', derived from actual experience of individuals, must have contributed to that charming person – Aziz.

Aziz is a person in his own right, however, and not just a type. He is a strange blend of many paradoxes – grave and gay, magnanimous and ridiculous, large-hearted and narrow-minded, charming and crude at the same time. Forster's characters have a way of emerging from 'life's walking shadows', from the fitful moments of experience, into larger realms. Mrs Moore and Godbole are such characters, puny in their physical impression but magnificent in their inner life and their spiritual dimensions. They rise from the titbits of the novelist's actual experience, and become mysterious as they grow in his created world, which neither reason nor metaphysics can truly fathom.

3

Perhaps it is more difficult to trace 'life's walking shadows' in Professor Narayan Godbole's character than in that of Aziz. What indeed could have been the 'original' of this mystifying character? Forster's own view, expressed in a meeting with G. K. Das ('I never met anyone like him. Godbole was mainly constructed by me. He was to a large extent a created character.'), rings true. However, G. K. Das, in a perceptive analysis, has outlined three possible sources of Godbole (*The Review of English Studies*, February 1977, XXVIII, 56). The question whether Forster met a real person called Godbole or not must remain ambiguous. G. K. Das quotes P. N. Furbank's discovery that Forster, during his visit to Lahore in 1912–13, attended a Brahmo-Samaj party and met a man named Godbole. They are said to have strolled in a garden where Godbole sang songs and also commented upon aspects of Indian music. Mr Furbank had told me in London in 1971 about Forster's 'scribbled entries' on the back of the invitation card of the Brahmo-Samaj gathering. This is indeed a valuable clue to the role of 'life's walking shadows' in Godbole's making; the shadows are far wider and deeper, however, than what emerges from this chance encounter in Lahore.

A short reference to the Maharaj in 'Indian Entries' for instance, offers another clue.

Maharaj sang Hindi love-songs to us in the Indra Sabha cave – Indra, said S. (Saeed), was fond of music.[11]

This 'Maharaj', of course, is very different from Godbole. I was told that Godbole was indeed the name of an education minister in an Indian state in Madhya Bharat whom Forster might have met in Dewas. Undoubtedly, many qualities of Sir Tukoji, the Maharajah of Dewas, and the Maharajah of Chhatarpur are compounded in Godbole's personality. Forster had 'a Krishna conversation' with the 'fantastic and poetical Maharajah of Chhatarpur' and the latter told him:

> . . . I can meditate on love, for love is the only power that can keep thought out. I try to meditate on Krishna. I do not know that he is a God, but I love Love and Beauty and Wisdom, and I find them in his history. I worship and adore him as a man.[12]

Both the Maharajahs, of Dewas and Chhatarpur, seem to converge in the 'adoration of Krishna'; their religious temper must be one of the main constituents in the genesis of Godbole. In a letter to Mrs Aylward, dated 6 March 1913, Forster describes the spiritual attitudes of Sir Tukoji III, the Maharajah of Dewas, especially his 'belief in a being who, though omnipresent, is personal, and whom he calls Krishna'.[13] Such a faith is also the primary quality of Godbole. He embodies the Maharajah's devotion to the *bhakti* cult and his attitudes to food and fasts; he also projects powerfully Tukoji's intense belief in universal love, a love which 'can keep thought out', reaching the edge of transcendental meditation. Godbole is, of course, a Chitpavan Brahmin, but his connection with the great tradition of the rebellious Tilak or of the moderate Gokhale, as suggested by G. K. Das, needs further interpretation. The Brahmin-Kshatriya or Brahmin-Maratha differences are as old as the Maratha power itself, but in my view, these have only a limited relevance to Godbole's mind and personality. Godbole the educator or education minister is as disappointing as Sir Tukoji III is as the ruler of Dewas State Senior. Their greatness and magnificence lies in their inner life, which is beautifully evoked in *A Passage to India* as well as in *The Hill of Devi*.

The Dewas dynasty, like Professor Godbole, sing passionately of Tukaram, the eminent Maharashtrian saint and poet. Forster writes: '"Tukaram, Tukaram, thou art my father and my mother and all things," we would sing, time after time, until we seemed to be worshipping a poet' (HD(1953) 117). In *A Passage to India* Godbole and his choir sing: 'Tukaram, Tukaram, Thou art my father and mother and everybody' (xxxiii, 275). I believe that this couplet is the English version of a Marathi prayer and the poet probably derives from Kacheshwar's *aaratis* of Tukaram. The original Marathi version, which I once read to Forster, seems like this:

Tukarām, Tukarām, tunchi māza baap, tunchi māzi maya,
Tukarām, Tukarām, tunchi sarwaswa māze . . .

Perhaps there are two Godboles, not one, in *A Passage to India*. The somewhat insubstantial and ambiguous figure in 'Mosque' and 'Caves' is matched in 'Temple' by the potent, subtle, deeply knowledgeable person, exercising a benign influence and charting out his own course of universal love, and becoming, later still, the embodiment of the Forsterian voice. The Godbole whom we meet at Fielding's tea is a quiet Deccani Brahmin, who speaks very little and perhaps conceals more than he reveals. He is an embodiment of harmony, a synthesis of east and west and a genuine and true friend. In 'Caves' he seems to be a sort of philosopher who talks about the Hindu view of God, of good and evil and a godly or godless universe. At Fielding's, he sings a song invoking Lord Krishna, 'Come, come, come.' In contrast to this small and limited social world, he is seen in 'Temple' dancing on a strip of red carpet 'in the presence of God' – which is indeed a soul's long journey from the mundane into a totally different, spiritual world.

Whether there is one Godbole, a 'round' character, or two Godboles may always remain a controversial issue. Certainly more than one individual in real life served as 'source material' for Forster's re-creation of this enigmatic character. A reading of R. D. Ranade's excellent study, *Mysticism in Maharashtra*, for example,[14] provides a very meaningful background to his religious temper. An eminent scholar in Poona (a cultural centre of Maharashtra), Professor Sonopant Dandekar (1895–1968), was known for his devotion to Tukaram and every year he led a choir and danced before Vithoba at Pandharpur. The genesis of Godbole was thus complex and the 'walking shadows' which finally merge into his personality are marked by both variety and heterogeneity.

Godbole is, in my view, the subtlest embodiment of the Forsterian Voice, the expression of an all-inclusive vision of love. Mrs Moore's vision – or antivision – too, merges into Godbole's vision of an all-comprehensive reality. In a mystical state he remembers Mrs

Moore and impels her imaginatively to that place 'where completeness can be found'. Mrs Moore dies; her body is lowered into 'another India', but her spirit continues its journey to India, allegorically through Ralph and Stella, and mystically through her reappearance in Godbole's visionary moment. 'In his culminating view of India', writes J. B. Beer with great perception, 'Forster thus achieves his greatest fusion of vision and realism.'[15] This fusion is at the heart of Godbole's ecstasy and mystical realisation of the divine.

In its projection of human relations, *A Passage to India* reflects a total engagement of Forster's creative genius with the Indian universe. To observe the transformation of some momentary contacts with actual persons and events in India into the substantial and lasting characters and episodes of his novel is to appreciate and admire the subtlety of his art.

12 Promise and Withdrawal in *A Passage to India*

John Colmer

In all Forster's fiction there is a characteristic pattern of promise and withdrawal. It is there in the visionary short stories and Italian novels, it becomes more marked in *The Longest Journey*, *Howards End* and *Maurice*, and finally achieves definitive expression in *A Passage to India*. That it had its roots partly in the author's earliest response to experience is clear from Marianne Thornton's account of the infant Forster.

> One thing I don't believe any body makes allowance enough for, & that is his intense enjoyment of this world & all it contains & his proportionate misery when anything is withheld from him.[1]

Illuminating as his great-aunt's observation may be, in the light of his subsequent development as a writer, it is not sufficient to account for the persistence of the pattern nor its representative quality and expressive power. To explain this it may be useful to consider aspects of Forster's political and intellectual milieu, to analyse what Lucien Goldmann or Lukács might call his world-view. Thus the following account of *A Passage to India* draws lightly and somewhat eccentrically on genetic structuralism to illuminate the pattern and to rebut some of the charges brought against Forster for failing to grasp the political realities in India.

At the outset it is worth recalling that genetic structuralism is a form of criticism that seeks to explain literary works by reference to social and political structures. The approach rests on the assumption that common mental categories underlie both literary works and social forms, or at least that there is a homologous relationship between the two. The relationship need not be one of identity; but,

whatever it is, it will be a significant one, especially in the case of
major works. It is unnecessary to suppose that the writer is fully aware
of the internal contradictions of his class and its world-view, but it is
a characteristic of great writers, suggests Goldmann, that they
reflect the totality of the situation through drawing on the
unconscious and the collective consciousness, as well as the personal
consciousness. The critic's task is therefore to discover the underlying mental structures that link the literary work and society, that
will account for the whole of the text, from its large-scale plot to the
grammatical structure and rhythms of the individual sentences. A
formidable task, indeed; and even with a team of collaborators
working on a single text, Genet's *Les Nègres*, progress was 'extremely
slow', Goldmann reports in a late essay, 'The Sociology of
Literature: Status and Problems of Method'.[2] From the individual
critic all that one can reasonably expect, especially in a brief essay,
are a few significant examples of the 'model' at different levels of
imaginative organisation.

What sort of statements do novels make? And how do they make
them? Clearly our answers to these two questions will depend to
some extent on the actual examples we consider. Yet no matter how
different in intention and form the novels may be, there are solid
grounds for believing that few novels make simple statements about
life. Ultimately the meaning is something that we grasp imaginatively. We apprehend it only after we have responded as
sensitively as we can to the interplay of plot, character and
language, to the underlying structures that regulate and control this
precise interplay. This proposition may be tested by applying it
tentatively to Forster's *A Passage to India*.

A special reason for adopting this approach with *A Passage to India*
is that it may offer an answer to those critics who have complained
that Forster overlooks larger political and ideological issues in the
novel. It may also reveal that the much-praised aesthetic design is
more integral to the deeper meanings of the novel than has been
supposed. It is perhaps natural for Indian writers to be especially
critical of Forster's alleged political deficiencies. In a well-known
1954 *Encounter* article, Nirad Chaudhuri condemned the novel for
containing 'nothing of the conflict between Indian nationalists and
the British Administration', for making both groups of Indians,
Hindu and Moslem, insignificant and despicable, for assuming that
Indo-British relations presented a problem of personal behaviour
and could be tackled on a personal plane (which they could not), for

showing a 'great imperial system at its worst, not as diabolically evil but as drab and asinine', and for depriving 'our suffering under British rule' of 'all dignity'.[3x] Many of Forster's English critics, including the Marxist D. S. Savage, have voiced similar complaints. In his chapter on the novel in *E. M. Forster: The Perils of Humanism*, F. C. Crews says that it seems to him 'that Lionel Trilling comes closest to the truth when he says that *A Passage to India*, rather than telling us what is to be done, simply restates the familiar political and social dilemmas in the light of the total situation.'[4] Behind this unconscious tribute to the 'totality' and the typical representativeness lies the twofold assumption that novels make statements and when they touch on political issues they should tell us what to do next. Both assumptions are questionable.

What I should like to suggest is an alternative view, that in *A Passage to India* Forster has created a coherent fictional universe that faithfully embodies the internal contradictions of a social class and of a number of traditions, more especially the tradition of Romantic liberalism and the tradition of British Imperialism. At this stage in his career, Forster was ideally placed to present these contradictions, since his attitude towards them was critical without being utterly unsympathetic. An inheritor of the romantic liberal tradition and a bourgeois beneficiary of British imperialism, clearly he could not be totally unsympathetic to either. But growing awareness of the limitations of each, and extensive experience of other traditions which he gained from foreign travel, gave him the necessary critical standpoint. Moreover, a deep and almost mystic insight into irrational and unconscious modes of being allowed him to escape the narrow bounds of western rationalism.

In *A Passage to India*, I suggest, there is a dominant pattern which not only gives order and coherence to the disparate elements but which is related to and is an expression of mental structures that underlie the whole intellectual and political life of Forster's society. The pattern in the novel is ultimately a simple one. It consists of expectation and promise, followed by disappointment and withdrawal. This pattern appears in the novel at four distinct but related levels: it is embodied in the plot, the visionary descriptive passages, the dialogue, and the grammar, tone and rhythm of the individual sentences. That it affects both the large-scale structure of events in the plot and the detailed texture of the language suggests that it is a structural principle of the first importance. Goldmann, it will be recalled, insists that a valid structural reading should be able to account for the whole text, down to the individual sentence or phrase.

Before proceeding to examine the four levels at which the pattern of promise and withdrawal is embodied, it is necessary to establish that the pattern has a homologous relation with internal contradictions in the English liberal tradition and the tradition of British imperialism. It will be convenient to take the liberal tradition first. Based on a faith in individualism, it believed that the individual possessed the power to impose order on experience and invest the universe with meaning. A secular world-view, it attributed quasi-divine powers to the human mind. According to one branch of the tradition, that which sprang from John Stuart Mill, it was the unfettered reason of the individual that possessed this power. According to the other branch, that which sprang from the Romantics, it was imagination that bestowed order and significance. For neither branch was the promise fulfilled. Keats's line 'Fled is that Vision – Do I wake or sleep?' poignantly records the romantic dilemma, as the closing lines of 'Dover Beach' record the Victorians' faith in personal relations as a substitute for God. Much nineteenth and twentieth-century fiction presents a pattern of expectation and promise followed by disappointment and withdrawal. George Eliot's idealistic heroines, Dorothea Brooke, for instance, pass through stages of bleak disenchantment before settling for something less than their visionary dreams. Forster, it is clear, in *A Passage to India* explores both the paths of reason and imagination, the first through the commonsense Adela and the rational educator, Fielding, the second through Mrs Moore, Aziz and Professor Godbole. Whichever path the characters pursue they are involved in a similar pattern of promise and withdrawal.

The political tradition of British imperialism may be subsumed within the same pattern. It had, as Forster noted in an unpublished essay called 'In the Early Years of this Century', its idealistic and its darker side. Its ideal was to bring freedom and the benefits of Western civilisation to all the peoples of the world. In this tradition the quasi-divine role is attributed to a nation, not to a function of the human mind, as in the liberal tradition. The expectations aroused by early British imperialism were great; the promise seemed infinite; but, from the Boer War onwards, historical events marked a series of disappointments and withdrawals. Moreover, the whole movement contained within itself an internal contradiction. It purported to bring freedom, but actually enforced economic and political dependence. It promised justice but produced the comic pantomime of the Trial at Chandrapore. As with the liberal intellectual tradition, a noble idealism disguised a selfish materialism. In the unpublished essay alluded to above, Forster remarked: 'Many of us soon saw that this crude imperialism had an economic side and we were put off.'[5]

In *A Passage to India*, the pattern of promise and withdrawal is more prominent in the first half of the novel than in the second. All the early details look forward to and prepare us for the nihilistic anti-vision in the Marabar Caves, when the cave in which Mrs Moore is crushed seems to murmur 'Pathos, piety, courage – they exist, but are identical, and so is filth. Everything exists, nothing has value.' This anti-vision expresses the failure of the human mind to encompass negation, its incapacity to invest what is alien to itself with beauty and significance. Once the reader has experienced withdrawal in its most absolute form, there is less need for frequent reminders of the informing structural principle. In the final section of the novel, set in the independent state of Mau, Forster reaffirms the pattern with great delicacy and suggestive power, but now the emphasis falls on muted promise, muddled revelation and harmony, not on withdrawal, anti-vision and negation. Yet even so the qualification and reservations are considerable, as the climax of the ceremonies at Mau make clear.

> That was the climax, as far as India admits of one. The rain settled in steadily to its job of wetting everybody and everything through, and soon spoiled the cloth of gold on the palanquin and the costly disc-shaped banners. Some of the torches went out, fireworks didn't catch, there began to be less singing, and the tray returned to Professor Godbole, who picked up a fragment of the mud adhering and smeared it on his forehead without much ceremony. Whatever had happened had happened. . . . Looking back at the great blur of the last twenty-four hours, no man could say where was the emotional centre of it, any more than he could locate the heart of a cloud.   (xxxvi, 305–6)

The pattern of promise and withdrawal is embodied in the plot in a great variety of ways, most basically of all in the invitation to Adela to visit India and the promise that the visit seems to hold for a happy marriage with Ronny and for the opportunity to see 'the real India'. The latter is an arbitrary abstraction of her rationalising intellect and therefore a false promise bound to be withheld. In fact, both major promises remain unfulfilled. Moreover, during her stay in India, Adela experiences a recurrent pattern of promise and withdrawal, marked out by her response to the Indian landscape and its peoples and also in her changing relations to Ronny. But there is a significant contrast between the sudden mysterious withdrawals that suffuse the novel, expressive of all that cannot be contained within the framework of western rationalism, and Adela's abrupt withdrawal of her charge against Dr Aziz. 'It was in hard prosaic tones that she said, "I withdraw everything." '[6]

The first event in the plot that suggests the main structural pattern is the invitation issued by Mrs Bhattacharya at Turton's unsuccessful party to bridge the gulf between the English and the Indians. For Adela and Mrs Moore, who do not understand that for some Indians it is more painful to cause displeasure than to tell a lie, who do not realise that the invitation was a gesture of friendship not to be taken too literally, the incident creates a pattern of high promise followed by puzzled disappointment. The same pattern is also apparent at Fielding's tea-party, but on that occasion even Ronny's peremptory rudeness does not entirely dispel the promise of greater friendship between Indians and English. The visit to the Marabar Caves begins in an excited mood of high promise for Aziz, but his hopes are dashed when Fielding misses the train. ' "Mrs Moore, Miss Quested, our expedition is a ruin." He swung himself along the footboard, almost in tears.'[7] His friendship with Fielding ultimately leads to a double accusation of desertion, first at the railway station when Aziz is arrested, and later after the trial: ' "Cyril, Cyril, don't leave me," called the shattered voice of Aziz.'[8] Promise of friendship apparently leads to the withdrawal of the cherished friend. And in the final reconciliation on the last page of the novel, the reader is perhaps more aware of the surging tides of disappointment and natural obstacles than of renewed friendship. Thus it can be seen that in the plot both the major action and many of the minor incidents are all in some way connected with the pattern that I am analysing.

It is when we turn to the great visionary passages in the novel that the full significance of the pattern becomes apparent. Often the sense of withdrawal is linked with the idea of an endlessly vanishing sense of infinity, symbolised by the sky, as in the climax of the long discussion between Mrs Moore and her son on the Englishman's role in India, at the end of chapter five.

Mrs Moore felt that she had made a mistake in mentioning God, but she found him increasingly difficult to avoid as she grew older, and he had been constantly in her thoughts since she entered India, though oddly enough he satisfied her less. She must needs pronounce his name frequently, as the greatest she knew, yet she had never found it less efficacious. Outside the arch there seemed always an arch, beyond the remotest echo a silence. (v, 45–6)

Clearly the justly famous description of Professor Godbole's song at the end of Fielding's tea-party dramatises the contrast between Western and Eastern attitudes towards expectation and promise: withdrawal and negation.

'I will explain in detail. It was a religious song. I placed myself in the position of a milkmaiden. I say to Shri Krishna, "Come! come to me only." The god refuses to come. I grow humble and say: "Do not come to me only. Multiply yourself into a hundred Krishnas, and let one go to each of my hundred companions, but one, O Lord of the Universe, come to me." He refuses to come. This is repeated several times. The song is composed in a raga appropriate to the present hour, which is the evening.'

'But He comes in some other song, I hope?' said Mrs Moore gently.

'Oh, no, He refuses to come,' repeated Godbole, perhaps not understanding her question. 'I say to Him, Come, come, come, come, come, come. He neglects to come.'

Ronny's steps had died away, and there was a moment of absolute silence. No ripple disturbed the water, no leaf stirred.

(vii, 72)

Mrs Moore's gentle 'But He comes in some other song, I hope?' expresses the inability of the Western mind to accommodate withdrawal, absence and negation within its world-view, while Godbole's patient, reiterated invitations to the divine express the ability of the Eastern mind to accept absence as well as presence as an aspect of the divine.

One of the most striking descriptive passages is the evocation of the false dawn, a passage that prepares the reader for the nihilistic message of the Marabar Caves. It represents a vast expansion of Forster's vision, as may be seen if it is compared with the limited false dawn of the 'Open Road', experienced by Leonard Bast in *Howards End*. As Adela spoke,

> the sky to the left turned angry orange. Colour throbbed and mounted behind a pattern of trees, grew in intensity, was yet brighter, incredibly brighter, strained from without against the globe of the air. They awaited the miracle. But at the supreme moment, when night should have died and day lived, nothing occurred. It was as if virtue had failed in the celestial fount. The hues in the east decayed, the hills seemed dimmer though in fact better lit, and a profound disappointment entered with the morning breeze. Why, when the chamber was prepared, did the bridegroom not enter with trumpets and shawms, as humanity expects? The sun rose without splendour. He was presently observed trailing yellowish behind the trees, or against insipid sky, and touching the bodies already at work in the fields.

(xiv, 129)

Here the whole paragraph builds up a poignant sense of the disparity between promise and fulfilment, and the language effortlessly extends the details of nature to the moral and spiritual life: 'They awaited the miracle. But at the supreme moment, when night should have died and day lived, nothing occurred. It was as if virtue had failed in the celestial fount.' Later, the Biblical allusion, 'Why, when the chamber was prepared, did the bridegroom not enter with trumpets and shawms, as humanity expects?', establishes the obvious equation between the Sun and the absent Divine Spirit, the Spirit that withdraws its presence at the awaited and prayed-for moment. A similar passage occurs after Fielding's high-principled resignation from the English club, 'lovely, exquisite moment – but passing the Englishman with averted face and on swift wings.' The vision, enjoyed by the reader alone, tells him that neither imperial club-rule nor heroic gestures can disguise the moral vacuum in India. '"A creditable achievement"', Fielding thinks to himself, 'but as the moment passed, he felt he ought to have been working at something else the whole time – he didn't know at what, never would know, never could know, and that was why he felt sad.'[9] Few novelists have caught so exactly the internal contradictions of the liberal-minded Englishman, his impotence as the promises of reason and vision pass him by.

It might be thought that the combination of good will, reason and a shared culture would bring about complete understanding and therefore friendship between two people. Yet, when Fielding and Adela earnestly analyse past events, the promise of perfect understanding remains unfulfilled. The visionary passage that describes them as dwarfs shaking hands conforms to the basic structure that informs the whole novel.

> They spoke the same language, and held the same opinions, and the variety of age and sex did not divide them. Yet they were dissatisfied. When they agreed, 'I want to go on living a bit', or, 'I don't believe in God', the words were followed by a curious backwash as though the universe had displaced itself to fill up a tiny void, or as though they had seen their own gestures from an immense height – dwarfs talking, shaking hands and assuring each other that they stood on the same footing of insight. They did not think they were wrong, because as soon as honest people think they are wrong instability sets up. Not for them was an infinite goal behind the stars, and they never sought it. But wistfulness descended on them now, as on other occasions; the shadow of the shadow of a dream fell over their clear-cut interests, and objects never seen again seemed messages from another world.   (xxix, 252)

This is a strangely moving passage. It communicates precisely the haunting pattern of promise and withdrawal that dominates the novel.

Dialogue, as well as plot and visionary description, serves to develop the pattern. In the passage quoted above the phrases of reported speech bestow a special authenticity. Elsewhere in the novel Forster employs direct speech to suggest how the promise of friendship and racial unity is withdrawn at the very moment it seems about to be achieved. The comic misunderstandings arising from differences of idiom, which are dramatised in the dialogue, express the gap between promise and fulfilment. The dialogue about Aziz's collar-stud, Post-Impressionism, and Fielding's 'I don't believe in God' to the Indians at Aziz's bedside, is not only a source of rich humour, it also exposes a void that neither tolerance nor goodwill can bridge. Over these and many other snatches of conversation there hangs a wistfulness, an indefinable sadness, which springs from the withdrawal of some special essence at the critical moment, felt most deeply in the conversation between Aziz and Fielding on the rooftop after the victory of the trial. The use of dialogue in an earlier incident is of special interest. At the end of the chapter describing Fielding's visit to Aziz's house, one of the Indians tries to soothe Fielding's obvious disappointment by saying 'Aziz has a high opinion of you, he only did not speak because of his illness.' The chapter then ends:

> 'I quite understand,' said Fielding, who was rather disappointed with his call. The Club comment, 'making himself cheap as usual', passed through his mind. He couldn't even get his horse brought up. He had liked Aziz so much at their first meeting, and had hoped for developments.   (ix, 104)

But in this case developments do follow. Fielding hears Aziz call and returns to the house. In the ensuing scene affection triumphs and, through the display of the photograph of Aziz's dead wife, the two men become brothers. This incident is a reminder that affection may revive good states of mind, either forgotten or driven out by suspicion, irritation or hostility.

The reversal of the dominant pattern is once beautifully suggested through the nuances of language. Few critics have noticed that early on in the novel Aziz at first disavows the most memorable experience of his life, 'the secret understanding of the heart', reached with Mrs Moore in the moonlit mosque. Irritated by Fielding's apparent snub about Post-Impressionism, he says:

> 'I do not consider Mrs Moore my friend, I only met her accidentally in my mosque,' and was adding 'a single meeting is too short to make a friend,' but before he could finish the sentence the stiffness vanished from it, because he felt Fielding's fundamental goodwill.   (vii, 60)

Here, the movement of a single sentence captures the creative power of affection to restore the promise that had been disavowed or withdrawn. And at Fielding's tea-party, Aziz now refers to *our* mosque, not *my* mosque as when he momentarily felt the need to exile Mrs Moore from the shared moment of unity.[10] In the later stages of the novel, the elusive but pervasive memory of Mrs Moore's affection brings about similar restorations of harmony and goodwill. Thus we see that the pattern is reversible: the withdrawal may be only temporary, the promise may return.

The last example has already illustrated that a single sentence may embody the large-scale pattern that gives structural coherence to the novel and which is homologous with the internal contradictions of Forster and his social class. In a great variety of ways the particular grammar, tone, rhythm and images of single sentences conform to and embody the pattern of promise and disappointment. The underlying mental structure accounts for some of the smallest verbal units in the novel. In complexity this ranges from the simple contrast enforced in the sentence describing Aziz's oscillations of mood, 'Wings bore him up, and flagging would deposit him', to the complex statement about Aziz's wavering faith:

> God's unity was indubitable and indubitably announced, but on all other points he wavered like the average Christian; his belief in the life to come would pale to a hope, vanish, reappear, all in a single sentence or a dozen heart-beats, so that the corpuscles of his blood rather than he seemed to decide which opinion he should hold, and for how long. (vi, 49)

From the opening of the novel, 'Except for the Marabar Caves', to its close, ' "No, not yet," and the sky said, "No, not there",' every positive has its counterbalancing negative or qualifying phrase.

It should now be clear that *A Passage to India* makes no simple statements about friendship or political rule in India, but rather communicates a pattern of experience that bears a homologous relationship to the internal contradictions of liberalism and of British imperialism, to the high promise of each and their disappointing failures. This pattern, it has emerged, regulates the precise interplay of the various elements in the novel and is embodied in the plot, the visionary passages, the dialogue, and the detailed texture and structure of the individual sentences. Only a novelist who was deeply aware of the internal contradictions of his own class and who possessed an intuitive insight into the contradictions inherent in the historic situation that produced the bankruptcy of liberalism and imperialism could have produced such a complex and finely organised work of art. As an autonomous work of art it is true to the laws of its own being. As an expression of social and political values it is true to the dense ambiguity of motive and consequence. Clear-sighted and sceptical in its estimate of the extravagant claims made on behalf of liberal rationalism and imperialism, it neither evades political issues nor offers the creed of personal relations as a simple solution to political problems, but explores life at a deeper level than admitted by such a distinction.

To claim that it is imperfect or untruthful because it ignores topical issues or because Hindus and Moslems no longer behave as they do in *A Passage to India* is singularly wide of the mark. It is a mistake that arises from confusing the difference between the facts of history and the truths of art, which depend on the justness and appropriateness of structure and form. In *A Passage to India* the three-part symphonic form finally reconciles the opposites of promise and withdrawal. At the end of the novel we realise that true wisdom comes from acceptance of absence as well as presence. The novel communicates no simple political message, rather it expands our vision of life by bringing East and West into a new and significant relationship. It is the only great novel of the twentieth century to embrace the declining civilisations of East and West in unified vision.

13 *A Passage to India:* Epitaph or Manifesto?

Benita Parry

(i)

The symmetrical design and integrative symbolism of *A Passage to India* confirm Forster's wish to make a coherent statement about human realities through art – for him the one internally harmonious, material entity in the universe, creating order from the chaos of a permanently disarranged planet[1x] – while the deeper structure to the novel holds open-ended, paradoxical and multivalent meanings, discharging ideas and images which cannot be contained within the confines of the formal pattern. In a text consisting of a political fiction, an allegory, a philosophical novel, a social tragedy and a metaphysical drama, both centrifugal and centripetal forces are at work: the themes diverge from the axis and realign, the literary forms radiate and join, the ostensibly poised whole emitting ambiguity, dissonance and contradiction which are ultimately repossessed and transfigured in an affirmative if allusive coda. The novel's mythopoeic mode strains after models of universal and ahistorical order, composing an archetypal symbolism intimating that there exists a metaphysical wholeness of all the antinomies in physical reality, social formations and the psyche. Countermanding this vision of total connection is a pessimistic realism which perceives a universe apparently random and inhospitable to habitation, a disjunctive historical situation and the human mind divided against itself. The one orientation points towards an escape from the dislocations in the material world to the timeless womb of myth, the other confronts the present disarray in all its specificity and contingency. But finally, in the 'not now, not here', 'not yet, not there' (xxxvi, 304; xxxvii, 312), another direction is indicated, one which forecasts that the visionary and the secular will be reconciled. This anticipation of a future still to emerge, a tomorrow radically different from what exists, is rooted in the belief that institutions are not inviolable nor consciousness fixed; with this hope, the novel merges metaphor with realism, establishes that the flight into emblematic resolutions has been abandoned, and reaffirms history.

Forster's nonconformity was evident in his distance from both the orthodoxies and heresies of British society. Though he shared the ideology of the middle-class milieu to which he was born, he was at crucial points disengaged from it, was a part of Bloomsbury yet apart, a socialist without doctrine, a reverent humanist reassured by the sanity of rationalism and the sanctity of individual relationships, who came to speculate on the satisfactions of sacred bewilderment and the dissolution of self in a transcendent other. With the accelerated disintegration of the old order after 1914, Forster's refuge in liberal-humanism, never wholly proof against the elements, was drastically damaged. Confronted by the breakdown in established values, the ravages of European competition, intensified class conflict within British society and growing disaffection amongst the colonial peoples, he looked outside England for a focus on this multiple disorder and, in choosing a route which passed from fiction centred on the condition of England to the global context created by imperialism, initiated a meeting with one of the defining realities of his times.

Forster has written of his visits to India in 1912 and 1921 as transforming experiences. For a small but significant number of English writers, brought through circumstance or choice into contact with the colonised world, the encounter exposed their consciousness to rival conceptions of civilisation, culture and community, to cosmologies postulating variant orderings to the universe, other definitions of the human condition and alternative versions of personality structure. In negotiating the contrary modes of awareness, the divergent precepts and goals devised by the west and by India, Forster produced a novel which neither fully accepts nor entirely repudiates the standards and usages of either. The text deliberately reveals the crisis of liberal-humanist ideology – its impotence as a code in an embattled social situation where moderation and compromise are not possible, its inadequacy as an explanation of a universe more extensive than the environment made by human intervention, and the insufficiency of its insights into a psyche whose experiential range exceeds ratiocination and sensory cognition. Nevertheless, although the work ventures no affirmation of its creed, it is the product of an intelligence and sensibility nurtured within the cultural and intellectual context of liberal-humanism. It is because the novel is mediated through this world-view and returns there for repose, that the advance into new and profoundly astonishing perceptions is accompanied by retreats to the confines of known sterilities. The narrative voice oscillates between faith and disbelief in the validity of humanist mores, observing that within an India divided into cultural groups not always sympathetic towards each other and ruled over by aliens hostile to all, community is both a refuge and a laager, that if immersion in mysticism wastes secular proficiency, then adherence to rationalism atrophies other possible facets of personality, that whereas empiricism can provide a rigorous arrangement of appearances, it misses essences, and if exclusion and definition lead to functional and aesthetic excellence, it is the suspension of discrimination and the abolition of barriers which makes for the unbroken circle.

To these polarities no resolution is suggested, yet because *A Passage to India* calls on resources outside the norms and priorities of western societies, summoning other social configurations, ethical codes and philosophical systems, evaluations which have been made of Forster's 'medium mind' and his imprisonment within a superannuated system of ideas and values should be rephrased, for this novel both articulates in ontological and moral terms a radical dissent from the conventions and aspirations of the late bourgeois world, and omits to make the critical connection between these and the social and political structures they accompanied and sustained. Because of this, there is a vacuum at the core of the political fiction. Forster, always a cultural relativist, was amused at the rhetoric of a 'high imperial vision' and came to applaud the colonial people kicking against imperialist hegemony,[2] but just as liberalism was unable to produce a fundamental critique of western colonialism, so is a consciousness of imperialism's historical dimensions absent from *A Passage to India*. Imperialism, the expression as well as the negation of modern Europe's values, inflicted a catastrophic dislocation on the worlds it conquered and colonised, generated new forms of tension within the metropolitan countries and brought the west into a condition of permanent conflict with other civilisations. Yet about this very epitome of the contemporary chaos, the novel is evasive;

neither origins nor motives are rendered and the concept of exploitation is notably absent.

But if such elisions tend to disembody the critique, suggesting an evaluation of a superstructure uprooted from its base, the British-Indian connection is nevertheless composed as the paradigmatic situation of irreconcilable conflict, and the relationships brought into being by imperialism are perceived as grotesque parodies of human encounters. The chilly English circulate like an ice-stream through a land they feel to be poisonous and intending evil against them; British domination rests on force, fear and racism, generating enmity in articulate Indians sustained by memories of past opposition to conquest and mobilised by prospects of the independence to be regained. Here the novel asserts the confrontation of opposites as the essential reality of the social world. It is the politically innocent Mrs Moore who challenges her son's brutal pragmatism with an appeal for love and kindness, a gesture towards humanising an inhuman situation, which is repudiated in the novel's recognition that hostilities will increase as Indian resistance grows (a process to which passing references are made) and British determination to retain power hardens. Aziz, the Moslem descended from Moghul warriors, and the Brahmin Godbole, whose ancestors were the militant Mahrattas, may have conflicting recollections of an independent Deccan resisting British conquest, but they are united by their distinctively expressed disinclination to participate in their own subjugation, a shared refusal which culminates in a Hindu-Moslem entente. On the other side, the British make up their differences and close ranks, with even Fielding throwing in his lot with Anglo-India and so betraying his ideals.

The effeteness of liberal codes in a situation such as that of imperialism is established in the novel by the catastrophic failure of British and Indian to sustain personal relations. The friendship between Fielding and Aziz, disturbed throughout by differences in standards and tastes, is finally ruptured when each withdraws, as he inevitably must, within the boundaries of the embattled communities, and it is Forster's consciousness that social connections will fail which sends him in pursuit of spiritual communion between Mrs Moore and both Aziz and Godbole. But perhaps the most eloquent demonstration of liberalism's impotence is its inability to offer any opposition to the enemies of its values. The obtuse, coarse, arrogant and bellicose deportment of Anglo-Indians, as realised in the novel, is the very negation of those decencies defined through

Fielding: 'The world, he believed, is a globe of men who are trying to reach one another and can best do so by the help of good will plus culture and intelligence' (vii, 56). When Fielding, after his courageous stand against his countrymen and women, aligns himself with the rulers of India, he is submitting to the fact of imperialism, deferring to a mode of behaviour and feeling made and needed by an aggressive political system and conceding that his liberal principles and hopes of doing good in India exist only by favour of a Ronny Heaslop. Forster's tone can be mild, but the integrity and toughness of his pessimistic acknowledgement that here there is no middle way to compromise and reconciliation marks a break with his previous, though increasingly hesitant, appeals to rapprochement between contending social forces.

(ii)

In an essentially speculative novel, intimating a universe which is not human-centred and departing from the romantic humanism of his earlier works, Forster—without relinquishing reason—deviates from the dogmatic rationalist's scepticism about the numinous. The liberation to ecstasy and terror of the psychic energies subdued by modern industrialised societies, as invented in *A Passage to India*, is significantly different from Forster's former domesticated exhortations to connect the outer and inner life, the prose with the poetry, for the sublime now contemplated has heights and depths never discerned in dearest Grasmere or artistic Hampstead, and recognition of this augurs existential possibilities still to be assimilated by the west. 'Inside its cocoon of work or social obligation, the human spirit slumbers for the most part, registering the distinction between pleasure and pain, but not nearly as alert as we pretend' (xiv, 125). The awakenings of two Englishwomen in India to what seems a surge from the deep and ancient centre in the universe takes cataclysmic form and results in derangement and delusion, the one mimicking in her feelings and behaviour the ascetic stance of isolation from the world but misunderstanding its meanings as meaninglessness, the other assailed by knowledge of sexuality and misinterpreting this as a sexual assault. When the urbane Fielding has intuitions of a universe he has missed or rejected, of that 'something else' he is unable to know; when he and Adela Quested (a devotee of common sense) speculate on the possibility of worlds beyond those available to their consciousness, they are not yielding to concepts of heaven or hell, but admitting that some essential part to their beings is undeveloped.

What the novel creates in its transmutations of the numinous are dimensions to experience which are authenticated by their psychological truthfulness alone—expressing a hunger for perfection, a discontent with the limitations of the present and an aspiration to possess the future. The need for the unattainable Friend 'who never comes yet is not entirely disproved' (ix, 97), the yearning after the 'infinite goal beyond the stars' (xxix, 252), the longing for 'the eternal promise, the never withdrawn suggestion that haunts our consciousness' (x, 106), these are signs of that permanent hope which will persist 'despite fulfilment' (xxxvi, 294), just as the images, substitutions, imitations, scapegoats and husks used in religious ritual are figures of 'a passage not easy, not now, not here, not to be apprehended except when it is unattainable' (xxxvi, 304). Significantly *A Passage to India* is a novel from which God, though addressed in multiple ways, is always absent – necessarily excluded from the Caves of the atheist Jains, and failing to come when invoked in the form of the Hindu Krishna or the Moslem's Friend – the Persian expression for God.[3x] As invented in the novel, the numinous is not divinely inspired nor does it emanate from arcane sources; it needs no religion and meets with no God. Forster's disbelief in the power of the human spirit to 'ravish the unknown' informs his transfigurations of the mystical aspiration:

> Did it succeed? Books written afterwards say 'Yes'. But how, if there is such an event, can it be remembered afterwards? How can it be expressed in anything but itself? Not only from the unbeliever are mysteries hid, but the adept himself cannot retain them. He may think, if he chooses, that he has been with God, but as soon as he thinks it, it becomes history, and falls under the rules of time.   (xxxiii, 278)

What Forster does acknowledge is that faith confers grace on the believer during 'the moment of its indwelling' (xxxiii, 275), and he affirms the gravity of religion's concerns, the fruitful discontent it speaks and the longings it makes known: 'There is something in religion that may not be true, but has not yet been sung . . . Something that the Hindus have perhaps found' (xxxi, 265). This paradox signifies the meanings which Forster assigns the institutionalised routes to an understanding and changing of human nature and existence devised by India's religious traditions.

(iii)

Theme and symbol in the novel's component texts converge on India. It is interesting that Forster's perceptions are in the tradition of Walt Whitman and Edward Carpenter, the one a passionate believer in popular democracy, the other a romantic socialist, both mystics and homosexuals disassociated by temparament and conviction from the conventions of their respective societies. Instead of the bizarre, exotic and perverse world made out of India by western writers in the late nineteenth and early twentieth centuries, a compilation serving to confirm the normality and excellence of their own systems, Whitman and in his wake Carpenter found in that distant and antique civilisation expressions of transcendent aspects to experience and access to gnosis, predicting that, when connected with the secular, these would open up new vistas to democratic emancipation, international fellowship and progress.[4x] But if Forster's India does have affinities with these poetic evocations, the perspectives in *A Passage to India* are informed by enquiry into, rather than new-found belief in, alternative ways of seeing, and the altogether more complex configuration centres on the polarities of division and cohesion, separation and coalescence, the allegory pursuing the dialectical process from disjunction and fracture to a total, all-containing wholeness, while the realist mode composes a version of an internally splintered social formation moving towards solidarity against the outside source of conflict.

It is as if the defining concepts of the major Indian cosmologies are objectified in the landscape made by the novel, and this presents to the alien a new awareness that humanity's place is within a chain of being linking it with monkeys, jackals, squirrels, vultures, wasps and flies, and on a continuum of existence extending to oranges, cactuses, crystals, bacteria, mud and stones. Drawing on Indian traditions, the text constructs an ontological scale situating the species in a universe indifferent to human purpose and intent, contiguous to an unconcerned inarticulate world, planted on a neutral earth and beneath an impartial sky. It is a position which seems to reduce existence to a respite between two epochs of dust, inducing a view of people as moving mud and contesting the centrality of human aspiration and endeavour. The Marabars, as a figure of eternity, and the distance behind the stars, as the sign to infinity, create mythological time-space, challenging the myopia of empirical observation and measurement. In the environs of the Marabars, where hills move, fields jump, stones and boulders declare themselves alive and plants exercise choice, hylozoistic notions formulated by archaic philosophies and congenial to the traditional Indian mind are confirmed. To the rationalist this failure to delineate and define, this obliteration of distinctions, spells disorientation and chaos; to the metaphysician it speaks of a continuous series accommodating disparate modes of being within one coherent structure.

It is this organisation of reality that is produced through the multiplex metaphor of India: an India which with its various cultures, religions, sects and classes, is difficult, arbitrary, intricate and equivocal, a microcosm of the 'echoing, contradictory world' (xi, 108), and an India which is the emblem of an intrinsic and deep harmony, an all-including unity accommodating paradox, anomaly and antinomy. For if 'no one is India' (vii, 65) and 'Nothing embraces the whole of India' (xiv, 136), it may all the same be the case that 'the hundred Indias which fuss and squabble so tiresomely are one, and the universe they mirror is one' (xxix, 251). This possibility is translated in the gravitation of Aziz and Godbole towards a united front. Aziz attempts consciously to identify with India – 'I am an Indian at last' (xxxiv, 284) – and unwittingly becomes absorbed, as had his ancestors, in India; Godbole, while continuing to live obediently within the sects and castes of Hinduism, assists Aziz in moving to a Hindu princely state and declares himself his true friend. But it is in the Hindus' ritual celebration of the entire universe of living beings, matter, objects and spirit taken into the divine embrace, that the conception of a dynamic blending of opposites is symbolically enacted, that enigmas and contradictions are ceremonially resolved and fusion is abstractly attained.

Although he was not a scholar of Indian metaphysics, Forster was familiar with the myths, epics and iconography of the country and found their innately dialectical style congenial. On rereading the *Bhagavad-Gita* in 1912 before his first visit to India, he noted that he now thought he had got hold of it: 'Its division of states into Harmony Motion Inertia (Purity Passion Darkness).'[5] These three qualities, constituting in the classical Indian view the very substance of the universe,[6] are permuted in *A Passage to India* as Mosque

Caves and Temple, a sequence with multiple meanings—one of which is the ontological and psychological significance pertaining to three major Indian philosophical-religious systems: they are figures, respectively, of consciousness and the present, the unconscious and the past, and the emergent metaconsciousness and the future. The novel offers this triad as the form of paradoxical differences contained within the unbroken whole: incorporated in the enclosing frame is the gracious culture of Islam in India, a society where personal relations amongst Moslems do flourish; the unpeopled Jain caves, place of the ascetic renunciation of the world; and the buoyant religious community of the Hindus, internally divided and internally cohesive. The approach to the component meanings of these systems is, however, profoundly ambiguous, moving between responsiveness and rejection, making the myth and subverting it.

Mystical Sufi tendencies are invented by the novel in the unmistakably Indian incarnation of Islam, a monotheistic and historically recent religion, dually committed to the mundane and the sacred. But having confronted the more ambitious theories of older India Forster now relegates Islam's consummation of the prose-poetry connection as too symmetrical, shallow and easy. With Caves, the novel passes back to the world-rejecting atheist tradition of the Jains,[7] a post-Vedic heterodoxy of the fifth century B.C. but, like Buddhism—with which it has historical and theoretical affinities—rooted in the ancient, aboriginal metaphysics of primal, Dravidian India. Here the novel produces a version of this uncompromisingly pessimistic outlook, one which disparages bondage to the phenomenal universe as the source of pain and suffering, and pursues liberation from all involvement with matter. The contemplation of negatives and Nothing within the text culminates in the transfiguration of the ascetic world-view, and if 'Everything exists, nothing has value' (xiv, 140) is a statement of nihilism, it has an alternative meaning, one which acknowledges the material world as verifiable but assigns significance only to Nothing, to complete detachment: 'Nothing is inside them, they were sealed up before the creation of pestilence or treasure; if mankind grew curious and excavated, nothing, nothing would be added to the sum of good and evil' (xii, 118).

There is a striking ambivalence to the imagery of the Caves; their 'internal perfection' is evoked through crystalline figures of pure emptiness:

There is little to see, and no eye to see it, until the visitor arrives for his five minutes, and strikes a match. Immediately another flame rises in the depths of the rock and moves towards the surface like an imprisoned spirit: the walls of the circular chamber have been most marvellously polished. The two flames approach and strive to unite, but cannot, because one of them breathes air, the other stone. A mirror inlaid with lovely colours divides the lovers, delicate stars of pink and grey interpose, exquisite nebulae, shadings fainter than the tail of a comet or the midday moon, all the evanescent life of the granite, only here visible. Fists and fingers thrust above the advancing soil – here at last is their skin, finer than any covering acquired by the animals, smoother than windless water, more voluptuous than love.   (xii, 117–18)

But competing with and countermanding the delicate transparency of their interiors is the opaque menace of their external form:

There is something unspeakable in these outposts. They are like nothing else in the world and a glimpse of them makes the breath catch. They rise abruptly, insanely, without the proportion that is kept by the wildest hills elsewhere, they bear no relation to anything dreamt or seen. To call them 'uncanny' suggests ghosts, and they are older than all spirit.   (xii, 116–17)

This speaks of the formless, primordial abyss before time and space, threatening to overwhelm consciousness; and the awesome possibility that the secret of the cosmos is not pristine order but ancient chaos is translated in the disasters which emanate from Caves.

Moving forward to the Hinduism of India's Aryan invaders, the novel creates that tradition's ecstatic affirmation of the entire world, the ceremonial celebration of all matter and spirit as originating from and sharing in the Lord of the Universe. But if the text participates in the ambition of Hinduism – itself compounded over aeons through the assimilation and reworking of many other existing beliefs – to tie, weld, fuse and join all the disparate elements of being and existence in a complete union, it withdraws from the incalculable and unassimilable enormity of the enterprise. While *A Passage to India* applauds the refusal of the present as it is, the wish to supersede all obstacles in the way of wholeness, it rejects emblematic resolutions. The impulse to the ceremonies is shown as magnificent:

Infinite Love took upon itself the form of SHRI KRISHNA, and saved the world. All sorrow was annihilated, not only for Indians, but for foreigners, birds, caves, railways, and the stars; all became joy, all laughter; there had never been disease nor doubt, misunderstanding, cruelty, fear. (xxxiii, 278)

But when the celebrations end, the divisions and confusions of daily life return. Just as consciousness of political conflict and social divergence transgresses against the will to union, so is there here a humanist's repudiation of symbolic concord. The allegory is over before the novel ends, the aesthetic wholeness dismembered by the fissures and tensions of the disjoint, prosaic world that the novel invents; the permanent is dissolved in the acid of contingency. In the last pages emblems of reconciliation and synthesis compete with their opposites: 'the scenery, though it smiled, fell like a gravestone on any human hope' (xxxvii, 311). The illimitable aspiration is not consummated: ' a compromise had been made between destiny and desire, and even the heart of man acquiesced' (xxxvi, 297).

In retrospect it is apparent that the authority of the allegory is throughout seriously undermined by other modes within the text; as each positing of universal abstractions is countermanded by perceptions of the specifics in the human condition, so the cosmic is cut down to size by the comic – the squeals of a squirrel, though 'in tune with the infinite, no doubt' (x, 105), are not attractive except to other squirrels; trees of poor quality in an inferior landscape call in vain on the absolute for there is not enough God to go round; there are Gods so universal in their attributes that they 'owned numerous cows, and all the betel-leaf industry, besides having shares in the Asirgarh motor omnibus' (xxxv, 289), and a God whose love of the world had impelled him to take monkey flesh upon himself. From the infinite the novel returns to the ordinary, from eternity there is a bridge back to the mundane. The worth of human effort, ingenuity and creativity is restored in the view Mrs Moore has on her last journey across India:

She watched the indestructible life of man and his changing faces, and the houses he had built for himself and God . . . She would never visit Asirgarh or the other untouched places; neither Delhi nor Agra nor the Rajputana cities nor Kashmir, nor the obscurer marvels that had sometimes shone through men's speech: the bilingual rock of Girnar, the statue of Shri Belgola, the ruins of

Manu and Hampi, temples of Khajraha, gardens of Shalimar.
(xxiii, 199)

The balance is redressed, and in the retreat to the Mediterranean it
is overturned in favour of the secular and the 'normal'. The relief
and pleasure known by both Adela Quested and Fielding on their
return voyages from India is shared by Forster, whose paean to
Venice is eloquent of a deep ambivalence towards the alternatives
he had so courageously posed:

> the harmony between the works of man and the earth that
> upholds them, the civilisation that has escaped muddle, the spirit
> in a reasonable form . . . The Mediterranean is the human
> norm. When men leave that exquisite lake, whether through the
> Bosphorus or the Pillars of Hercules, they approach the mons-
> trous and the extraordinary; and the southern exit leads to the
> strangest experience of all.   (xxxii, 270–1)

Forster's knowledge, feelings and experiences outside this putative
standard cannot stem the flood of his response nor discompose the
peace it offers.

But neither this tenuous repose nor the symbolic solutions, neither
the inevitability of compromise nor the permanence of conflict is the
final word, for these are superseded by the generation of hope in a
future when the obstacles the novel has confronted will have been
overcome in history. On their last ride together, Aziz and Fielding,
after misunderstanding, bitterness and separation, are friends again
'yet aware that they could meet no more' (xxxvii, 307), that
'socially they had no meeting place' (xxxvii, 309). But Aziz,
anticipating the time of freedom from imperialist rule, promises
'and then . . . you and I shall be friends' (xxxvii, 312); and when
Fielding asks why this cannot be now, earth, creatures and artefacts
intercede to reject the possibility: 'they didn't want it, they said in
their hundred voices, "No, not yet," and the sky said, "No, not
there."'

A Passage to India is Forster's epitaph to liberal-humanism; in
search of alternatives he had turned to other traditions only to
withdraw, and had looked beyond the bleak present towards a
transfigured tomorrow. He was at the height of his powers and he
wrote no more novels; as fascism, war, the death-camps and the
repression of the colonial struggles brought force, violence and

chaos near and made the 'not yet' seem more distant, Forster retired to essays, criticism, biography and broadcasts, forms through which it was still possible to state belief in liberal values, in full knowledge that the ideology sustaining these had been drained of vitality and was without relevance to the changing historical situation. Conscious of new threats, he had the independence and courage in 1935 to attend the International Association of Writers for the Defence of Culture in Paris, and before a largely communist audience reiterated his creed of individuality, personal decency, tolerance, justice, culture and liberty;[8] with Aldous Huxley, he was the only British writer to sign the Manifesto of that Congress. Forster needed no critics to tell him of the ambiguities and contradictions in his vision of life; he saw his faith crumbling and could find no other.[9x]

14 Language and Silence in *A Passage to India*

Michael Orange

Wovon man nicht sprechen kann, darüber muss man schweigen.

Wittgenstein, Tractatus

I

Forster's delicacy of style in the novels that precede *A Passage to India* almost guarantees the rectitude of his attempt to understand the alien worlds of Islam, Hinduism and 'British India'. Elements of potential condescension or of patronising naïveté in the class attitudes of some of the characters of *Howards End* are carefully noted by the novelist, a useful starting-point for one whose last-written novel will share their position of attempted understanding.[1x] Over fifty years after the first publication of *A Passage to India* it is possible to measure the success of that book in the context of renewed attempts at discovering the relevance for the industrialised nations of cultures whose assumptions have been so different. Forster goes incomparably further than the instinctive refusal to articulate that has often accompanied the quest. Yet *A Passage to India* justifies this disengagement with language. More, it explains, while enacting, the strategy behind such refusals to communicate.

'The Ganges happens not to be holy here' (PI i, 2). The novel's third sentence thus quietly registers and assimilates a phenomenon unfamiliar except in classical mythology to Western readers. The concept that a river may be 'holy' coincides, however, with the further understanding that in India, apparently, the same river is, in different locations, religiously speaking 'neutral'. Yet the phrase's undemonstratively parenthetical tone insinuates that this is not remarkable. The sense of wonder will be exercised more fully later. In the scale *A Passage to India* plays upon, such differentiation from Western values is scarcely noticed. None the less, it is crucial. As an index of the gap between Oriental and Western culture the phrase asserts, quite literally, a world of difference: wholly divergent concepts of the universe.

However, even with this abyss confronting Western consciousness so early in the novel, a converging movement can be detected. Classical mythology and Forster's unemphatic tone combine to imply that such an alien world-view may be assimilated at least conceptually. In the act of reading a bridge of some kind has been thrown across. By the third section of the novel, when this continual verbal oscillation between alien and familiar has become a conditioning medium of response, Forster can spin the coin almost carelessly to reveal the common metal on which two different cultures are stamped:

> a Brahman brought forth a model of the village of Gokul (the Bethlehem in that nebulous story) and placed it in front of the altar . . . Here, upon a chair too small for him and with a head too large, sat King Kansa, who is Herod, directing the murder of some Innocents, and in a corner, similarly proportioned, stood the father and mother of the Lord, warned to depart in a dream.
>
> (xxxiii, 277–8)

But this is the limit to Forster's cultural parallelism. For *A Passage to India* continually asserts, despite some initiation into concepts of unity, that the images are firmly embedded in history; that the coin is diamond-faceted; and that language itself is powerless to convey the central experience to which the novel leads.

The success of *A Passage to India* depends acutely upon its pervasive sensitivity to its own verbal medium. In this novel the language of cognition, as the expression of thought and feeling in hierarchy subject to ordering by time, is avowedly insufficient as a means of incarnating mystical experience which exists outside time and is subversive of hierarchical order. In translating private, inward experience into public, shared understanding, the writer commits himself to materials crudely subject to history, hierarchy and consciousness. Where language encounters the silence beyond 'liberal humanism' or conceptualisation itself, it must settle for being sign-post rather than analogue. At the point of silence the alternatives for the artist are to retreat into the crudity of words again, or to fail to create at all. Forster's interest in musical expression underlines the point.[2] The conclusion to the biography of Dickinson provides an interesting commentary on the problem, which has special relevance to *A Passage to India*:

> He was an indescribably rare being, he was rare without being enigmatic, he was rare in the only direction which seems to be infinite: the direction of the Chorus Mysticus. He did not merely increase our experience: he left us more alert for what has not yet been experienced and more hopeful about other men because he had lived. And a biography of him, if it succeeded, would resemble him; it would achieve the unattainable, express the inexpressible, turn the passing into the everlasting. Have I done that? *Das Unbeschreibliche hier ist's getan?* No. And perhaps it only could be done through music. But that is what has lured me on.[3]

Such contemporary examples as Eliot's choice of ending for *The Waste Land* and the experimental fictions of Virginia Woolf, Gertrude Stein and Aldous Huxley illuminate Forster's patient understanding of his craft. His achievement in *A Passage to India* is measured in part by his considerable success in transcending those limitations while preserving fidelity to traditional means of expression: the passage is to India, but the importance of the return ticket is not minimised. While the novel is a supremely graceful farewell to Forster's art, it is by no means a leave-taking imposed by insufficiency in his manipulation of the form, which proves flexible enough to focus both on the mystery of the tunnel of the stars and on the rigours of 'Cousin Kate' as performed in Central India.

This flexibility is paramount in the novel. Forster quietly but insistently induces belief in his verbal structures while disavowing their efficacy. The persistent muting of his ironic tones disinfects the prose of any trace of self-seeking virtuosity and directs attention outwards to the ostensible subject-matter – which necessarily resides, of course, within the words themselves. This controlling irony at the expense of the fiction itself functions as a continual reminder that any commitment to values expressed through words and based upon the hierarchies that they express must contend with functional limitations. Much experience is resolutely non-verbal. Non-verbal values become progressively and necessarily more remote in proportion to the persuasiveness of the language employed to embody them. The more felicitously they are expressed, the more readily they induce assent to propositions they set out to counter. This fundamental paradox is the source of the novel's classic consequent tension. While language eternally asserts its own reality, one of hierarchy, reason, time, and the logic of emotion, India itself represents a mysterious, sempiternal, mystical reality. Joseph Campbell makes this general point about Eastern culture:

> Throughout the Orient the idea prevails that the ultimate ground of being transcends thought, imaging, and definition. It cannot be qualified. Hence, to argue that God, Man, or Nature is good, just, merciful, or benign, is to fall short of the question. One could as appropriately – or inappropriately – have argued, evil, unjust, merciless, or malignant. All such anthropomorphic predications screen or mask the actual enigma, which is absolutely beyond rational consideration; and yet, according to this view, precisely that enigma is the ultimate ground of being of each and every one of us – and of all things.

> Prayers and chants, images, temples, gods, sages, definitions, and cosmologies are but ferries to a shore of experience beyond the categories of thought, to be abandoned on arrival.[4]

The resolution of the dichotomy between language and enigma represents the most complex aspect of Forster's success in the novel. He reconciles an adept manipulation of his verbal structures to the complete insufficiency of language itself, without finding it necessary to rely upon crudity of utterance to make the crucial disavowal of literary expression's congruence to mystical experience. This confident belief in the elastic power of his medium to work in opposed directions at the same time is the hallmark of *A Passage to India*. (It is pertinent to recall in this context that the British established their hegemony in India largely through the imposition of their language.) The power to reconcile disparity, to unify without sacrificing particularity, which the sensitive manipulation of language can command, establishes *A Passage to India*'s status as a still-breathing masterpiece, rather than as a sad but exquisite register of failures.

II

The conflict dramatised and partly resolved in *Howards End*, between the worlds of 'telegrams and anger' represented by the Wilcox family and that of sensitive personal relationships incarnated by the Schlegels, is considerably more complicated in *A Passage to India*. The simple plea 'only connect' is applicable fundamentally to the abyss between the efficient English and the sensitive Indians they govern. None the less, Aziz's sensitivity is matched (despite the latter's evident limitations) by Fielding. British devotion to rigid class distinction is more than echoed in the triumph of caste represented by the Nawab Bahadur (cf. iv, 30–1). Aziz, despite his eventual decision to reside in a Hindu native state, is dismayed to find that after all he feels closer to Fielding than to Professor Godbole. Evidently the precarious bridge thrown across to an alien realm of experience by Margaret Schlegel is metaphorically insufficient to the complexity of *A Passage to India*. The very idea is ridiculed in the unsuccessful 'Bridge Party' convened to cater to Miss Quested's desire to know the 'real' India: 'a party to bridge the gulf between East and West; the expression was [the Collector's] own invention, and amused all who heard it' (iii, 222). At the end of the novel there is no 'marriage' between Aziz and Fielding. Forster's ironic tones, which effectively qualify the sense of kinship expressed in the banter at the Club, hint at the necessity of acknowledging such reservation. It appears that the sole means of attempting to communicate securely with others takes place from within the solipsistic shell of the individual personality. Mrs Moore is no befuddled sentimentalist, but because of, rather than despite her sharpness, is sufficiently sure of herself to reach out to Aziz.

On the level of plot, too, as well as of language, this kind of irony is maintained. The subaltern who baits Fielding for his championship of Aziz (xx, 177–8) unknowingly uses the example of his own brief meeting with Aziz to censure the latter's typical presumption (xx, 175). This restates in slightly different fashion Heaslop's mistaken initial pleasure and subsequent shock at his mother's first encounter at the mosque with the Indian. Yet the subaltern's earlier meeting with Aziz on the Maidan is the most graceful bridging of the racial abyss that the novel offers:

> They reined up again, the fire of good fellowship in their eyes. But it cooled with their bodies, for athletics can only raise a temporary glow. Nationality was returning, but before it could exert its poison they parted, saluting each other. 'If only they were all like that,' each thought.   (vi, 51–2)

It is an episode whose comprehensive irony only becomes apparent at the novel's close. Aziz's and Fielding's last ride together painfully echoes this earlier one but expresses no more, despite all their efforts. Guarded friendliness, goodwill allied to circumspection remain after the vistas of instinctive communication and reciprocal affection close off. It seems scant reward.

The language which describes the polo-practice on the Maidan is crisply adequate to its purpose. The metaphors of temperature neatly register both exercise and passion, while the placing and choice of 'poison' conveys the disquietingly jarring note which characterises the relationship between the different races implicit in the scene, assimilated at the same time to the placid rhythm of the sentence which acknowledges the weary normalcy of such diseased relations. The passion for clarity and dispassionate observation harmonises with sensitivity to the subtleties of relationships: metaphor and plain-speaking cohere in this unemphatic idiom. Yet the ironies created by the tone of the narration tend disquietingly to subvert the assurance derived from any sense of confederacy with the latter's congenially sceptical outlook. For example, the Nawab Bahadur's social distance from his co-religionists (iv, 30–1) partly endorses the toughly self-protective realism of the general British aloofness from the natives. Switching to the missionaries Graysford and Sorley, this attitude is more directly, if regretfully, sponsored: 'perhaps it is futile for men to initiate their own unity, they do but widen the gulfs between them by the attempt' (iv, 32). In following the quotation through to the animal, insect and bacteriological kingdoms, the narrator's tone becomes gradually less respectful, more sardonic:

> Consider, with all reverence, the monkeys. May there not be a mansion for the monkeys also? Old Mr Graysford said No, but young Mr Sorley, who was advanced, said Yes; he saw no reason why monkeys should not have their collateral share of bliss, and he had sympathetic discussions about them with his Hindu friends.

The culmination of the enquiry is as brutally full of good sense as the rulers at the Club, and the narration mimics their voice:

> And oranges, cactuses, crystals and mud? and the bacteria inside Mr Sorley? No, no, this is going too far. We must exclude

someone from our gathering, or we shall be left with nothing.
(iv, 32)

It is, however, only much later in the novel, at Mau, that it appears possible that these tones, for all their practical good sense, are themselves subject to contextual irony. Mr Sorley joins Mrs Moore and Ralph with Professor Godbole, possessors of some fundamental knowledge or instinct which renders Fielding and Miss Quested liable to seem as crass as the Collector.

The very success of Forster's presentation of the two latter demonstrates both the shortcomings of language as an instrument fit to enact religious revelation and of the development of a civilisation whose achievement is consonant with verbal expression. The unobtrusive confidence of the account of Aziz's encounter in the Maidan with the subaltern attends the presentation of the schoolmaster and the young woman. The reasoned good sense of the narration is wholly appropriate to these vintage liberal humanists. Like the narrator, Miss Quested understands clearly, if not at first her own limitations, at least those attendant on marriage to Heaslop and the British in India: 'she would see India always as a frieze, never as a spirit, and she assumed that it was a spirit of which Mrs Moore had had a glimpse' (v, 41). This elusive 'spirit' holds her interest, as it does the narrator's, and alienates her from her compatriots. Yet her charity and sympathy draw her back to them. In announcing to Heaslop that they are not to be married, her intellectual and morally scrupulous nature is infused with the flow of feeling:

> She felt ashamed. How decent he was! He might force his opinions down her throat, but did not press her to an 'engagement', because he believed, like herself, in the sanctity of personal relationships. (viii, 76)

> . . . a wave of relief passed through them both, and then transformed itself into a wave of tenderness, and passed back. They were softened by their own honesty, and began to feel lonely and unwise. (viii, 77)

The explicit metaphor is appropriate to the conceptions that Miss Quested and Heaslop entertain of themselves, in which personal relations, work, religious feeling and duty are readily understood as separate entities, and personality conceived in terms of 'dryness' or 'damp' does not necessarily appear ludicrous. Characteristically, the narrator, by drawing attention to the apparently irrelevant detail of the Indian bird that they see, disclaims their typical ordering of experience in this fashion, without insisting on its insufficiency. 'Nothing in India is identifiable, the mere asking of a question causes it to disappear or to merge in something else' (viii, 78): the comment reflects as much upon the genesis of *A Passage to India* as upon the characters it describes. Miss Quested's dissatisfied longing for a verbal absolute – ' "Mrs Moore, if one isn't absolutely honest, what is the use of existing?" ' (viii, 89) – is similarly pertinent to the novelist's sense of his vocation and the problems posed by the subject-matter of India.

Fielding, while less naïve than Miss Quested, shares her limitations as well as her virtues. The latter include most obviously an attempt to ignore the racial barrier: 'the world, he believed, is a globe of men who are trying to reach one another and can best do so by the help of good will plus culture and intelligence' (vii, 56). Once again the aspiration's Schlegelian overtones reveal in how close a relationship this character stands to Forster's central preoccupations as a novelist, while the critique of his shortcomings shows the direction in which this novel develops by comparison with the rest of Forster's fiction.

Forster defined the humanist as possessing 'four leading characteristics – curiosity, a free mind, belief in good taste, and belief in the human race',[5] characteristics which Fielding shares. His humanism derives from personal conviction without philosophical or religious sanction. His disavowal of religious conviction scandalises his Moslem friends, but Forster admires the 'zeal for honesty' (ix, 102) that inspires his plain-speaking and his refusal to indulge in the easy, acceptable answers. Yet as the novel proceeds, Fielding's lack of spiritual development is shown as a disabling limitation. It accompanies a circumscription of spontaneous feeling similar to Miss Quested's: 'he felt old. He wished that he too could be carried away on waves of emotion' (xi, 109). Fielding's honesty has its price: 'experience can do much, and all that he had learnt in England and Europe was an assistance to him, and helped him towards clarity, but clarity prevented him from experiencing something else' (ibid.). The virtues of clarity and honesty do not compensate for the fundamental commitment to instinct crucial to an understanding of Aziz, nor are they adequate to a concept as far beyond their range as the sense of evil:

> He felt that a mass of madness had arisen and tried to overwhelm them all; it had to be shoved back into its pit somehow, and he didn't know how to do it, because he did not understand madness: he had always gone about sensibly and quietly until a difficulty came right. (xvii, 154)

The metaphor of the pit dramatises the separation of conscious volition, which exercises the capacity for integrity and directness of address, from the unconscious, which prompts the entrapping of Aziz and the subsequent drama of Miss Quested's accusation and retraction: the latter demands response from a different source than that which regulates conduct, morality and justice. It is to Fielding's great credit (and a tribute to Forster's faith in the profundity of instincts for truth and decency) that he instinctively believes in Aziz, despite a personal philosophy which repudiates faith. The insistently spiritual context of the novel forces the realisation that this belief in Aziz is a quasi-religious affirmation:

> Fielding, too, had his anxieties . . . but he relegated them to the edge of his mind, and forbade them to infect its core. Aziz *was* innocent, and all action must be based on that, and the people who said he was guilty were wrong, and it was hopeless to try to propitiate them. (xix, 164)

Yet despite the instinctive quality of Fielding's avowal, it rests on experience and the capacity to form workable judgements of people. Fielding's knowledge of his man is at stake, his sense of outrage located in the same area drawn upon by the novelist who offers an understanding of 'character'. Fielding's sense of limitation bears directly upon Forster's struggle with his art in *A Passage to India*. He reaches towards new understanding similar to that undertaken by the novelist, but unlike Forster it appears to elude him. At the moment of his great triumph over himself, when his dignified championship of Aziz withstands the insult of the Club's sneering disparagement, Fielding becomes aware of dimensions of experience foreign to his doggedly decent mentality. The Marabar Hills 'leap into beauty', but the mythical associations (Monsalvat, Walhalla) conjured by the novelist do not touch the schoolmaster.

Legal justice, due process of law, the bricks and mortar of civilisation occupy his interest: 'who was the guide, and had he been found yet? What was the "echo" of which the girl complained? He did not know, but presently he would know. Great is information, and she shall prevail.' Forster, by confronting justice with beauty, denies Fielding the enjoyment of his dignified triumph over pettiness and malice. While the latter has fought with great moral courage, it appears that he was entered in the wrong lists. His sense of discouragement derives not from the degrading spectacle of the British herding together under a banner that parodies his own, nor from the regrettable insult to Heaslop, but from an apprehension of inadequacy that short-circuits his usual channels of communication with himself. Justice, morality and decency at their best ignore too much of human aspiration and potential, and of forms of being that transcend the merely human. This central, beautifully controlled passage deserves full quotation:

> It was the last moment of the light, and as he gazed at the Marabar Hills they seemed to move graciously towards him like a queen, and their charm became the sky's. At the moment they vanished they were everywhere, the cool benediction of the night descended, the stars sparkled, and the whole universe was a hill. Lovely, exquisite moment – but passing the Englishman with averted face and on swift wings. He experienced nothing himself; it was as if someone had told him there was such a moment, and he was obliged to believe. And he felt dubious and discontented suddenly, and wondered whether he was really and truly successful as a human being. After forty years' experience, he had learnt to manage his life and make the best of it on advanced European lines, had developed his personality, explored his limitations, controlled his passions – and he had done it all without becoming either pedantic or worldly. A creditable achievement, but as the moment passed, he felt he ought to have been working at something else the whole time, – he didn't know at what, never would know, never could know, and that was why he felt sad. (xx, 181)

The centre of experience appears to be mystical rather than ethical. Forster's prose contrives unemphatically the oppositions between the majesty of hills, starlight and universe, and the restrained evocation of Fielding's decency and self-dissatisfaction. The silence is felt, not remarked. The description indicates its presence in the phrase 'lovely, exquisite moment' without allowing it to expand, because Fielding fills it with words directed inwards. Unlike Godbole later, he does not resist the impulse to conceptualise: the difference is stressed by the comparison 'as if someone had *told* him'. Silence, *A Passage to India* insists, must be felt. The superb, gently deflating phrase 'wondered whether he was really and truly successful as a human being' rings achingly hollow in this context of physical beauty, mythology and eternity. Despite his concern for the oppressed, the wrongfully accused, despite even his awareness of his own circumscription, Fielding at such a moment is locked within the prison of the self. And despite her hostility towards him at this point in the novel, Miss Quested shares Fielding's nihilistic dissatisfaction, pointed by the quasi-religious context of her statement to Heaslop:

> 'How can one repay when one has nothing to give? What is the use of personal relationships when everyone brings less and less to them? I feel we ought all to go back into the desert for centuries and try and get good. I want to begin at the beginning. All the things I thought I'd learnt are just a hindrance, they're not knowledge at all. I'm not fit for personal relationships.'
>
> (xx, 188)

By this recognition of their limitations, both Fielding and Miss Quested begin in some degree to 'inhabit the desert', to withdraw from their compatriots and from intercourse itself into inner contemplative silence. But although they can go so far, they are incapable of greater self-transcendence. Miss Quested's resumption of her 'morning kneel to Christianity . . . the shortest and easiest cut to the unseen' (xxiv, 201) is the product of temporary distress rather than a sign of new understanding. She confesses wryly to Fielding her own sense of the shortcomings of honesty as a code (xxvi, 228–9), which parallels his own dissatisfaction. Immediately afterwards, however, they reassert their religious scepticism, explicitly disavowing any belief in an after-life: 'there was a moment's silence, such as often follows the triumph of rationalism' (xxvi, 229). This silence differs qualitatively from that experienced and then consciously sought by Mrs Moore, Aziz and Godbole. The sceptics' is, rather, a spiritual emptiness, the internal desert which clears the path to spiritual understanding but should never be confused with it. Hamidullah's lack of sympathy with Miss Quested after the trial examines the latter's valuable personal qualities in the light of a culture whose central emphases differ fundamentally:

> her behaviour rested on cold justice and honesty; she had felt, while she recanted, no passion of love for those whom she had wronged. Truth is not truth in that exacting land unless there go with it kindness and more kindness and kindness again, unless the Word that was with God also is God. (xxvi, 233)

Miss Quested's triumph over herself by sticking to her principles in preference to not letting down her friends remains insufficient even judged from the standpoint of her own culture, as the culminating phrases of this description insinuate. Integrity and fairmindedness are shown to be just the rump of religion, admirable qualities indeed but spiritually speaking negligible. At the end of this scene at the College, when Miss Quested's lodging after the trial has been under consideration, Fielding in weariness is visited once again by the displacing vision of love crucial to Hamidullah's philosophy:

> fatigued by the merciless and enormous day, he lost his usual sane view of human intercourse, and felt that we exist not in ourselves, but in terms of each others' minds – a notion for which logic offers no support and which had attacked him only once before, the evening after the catastrophe, when from the verandah of the club he saw the fists and fingers of the Marabar swell until they included the whole night sky. (xxvi, 237)

Once again the insufficiency of developing personality, exploring limitation and controlling passion (xx, 181) as a goal of the whole man (rather than the civilised social being) has become apparent. Hamidullah's tone is taken up by the narration, when Fielding and Miss Quested offer their inadequate explanations of the experience in the cave and of Mrs Moore's intuitive understanding: 'they had not the apparatus for judging' (xxix, 251). In condemning the inadequacy of their prose world, the narration adopts for purposes of judgement the idiom of Professor Godbole:

> When they agreed, 'I want to go on living a bit,' or, 'I don't believe in God,' the words were followed by a curious backwash as though the universe had displaced itself to fill up a tiny void, or

as though they had seen their own gestures from an immense height – dwarfs talking, shaking hands and assuring each other that they stood on the same footing of insight . . . Not for them was an infinite goal behind the stars, and they never sought it.

(xxix, 252)

At the end of the novel, Fielding's slightly regretful curiosity about Hindu religion confirms this Godbolian deployment of phrase, as he attempts to question Aziz about Ralph's and Stella's affinity (obviously transmitted by Mrs Moore) with Hinduism. Aziz is silent. The silence is entirely consonant with the subject that occasions it, as Mrs Moore has demonstrated earlier: ' "Say, say, say," said the old lady bitterly. "As if anything can be said! I have spent my life in saying or in listening to sayings: I have listened too much. It is time I was left in peace" ' (xxii, 190–1). The explicit attack upon language from Mrs Moore becomes vicious in its rejection of the novel's sole form of expression: ' "Oh, how tedious . . . trivial . . . " . . . "Was he in the cave and were you in the cave and on and on . . . and Unto us a Son is born, unto us a Child is given . . ." ' This develops more explicitly than the example cited earlier into a questioning of the idea of 'character' as customarily understood by the novelist: ' "One knows people's characters, as you call them," she retorted disdainfully, as if she really knew more than character but could not impart it' (xxii, 196). The 'character' of Aziz only becomes available as we understand the silences of his religion and poetry. The narrator partly explains Mrs Moore's disillusion and feeling of displacement in the chapter which follows, but her own refusal to trust words is more significant as evidence of her capacity for in-dwelling, in such contrast to the eternally public world of the Club, and particularly of Fielding's and Miss Quested's best efforts.

The blend of sympathy and irony with which Aziz is presented illuminates the status of the latter tone in the novel. Irony in an important sense is equivalent to silence because it represents an implicit rather than externalised attitude to its subject. Yet irony is insufficient to Forster's purposes in presenting Aziz, who will increasingly command the narrator's sympathy as the novel progresses. In order to encompass the alien quality of this man's culture, Forster adopts a more tentative idiom than that used to portray the British: 'Here was Islam, his own country, more than a Faith, more than a battle-cry, more, much more . . . Islam, an attitude towards life both exquisite and durable, where his body and his thoughts found their home' (ii, 13). Lionel Trilling remarks that 'so far as the old Mediterranean deities of wise impulse and loving intelligence can go in India, Forster is at home; he thinks they can go far but not all the way, and a certain retraction of the intimacy of his style reflects his uncertainty. The acts of imagination by which Forster conveys the sense of the Indian gods are truly wonderful; they are, nevertheless, the acts of imagination not of a master of the truth but of an intelligent neophyte, still baffled.'[6] However, it might be argued against this view that the narration's faltering into silence in the preceding quotation matches precisely the inarticulate nature of Aziz's own indefinite aspiration. Moreover, this willingness to trust to silence rather than more direct expression marks a primary strategy in Forster's attempt to penetrate Eastern culture. The phrase 'Islam, an attitude towards life both exquisite and durable' slackly generalises a sensation that exists in the blank space preceding it. Unless the reader links these words to the description of the mosque open to the moonlight, to the aspiration of Aziz which transcends patriotism, religion and valour, and then attempts to empathise with the silent crescendo of longing, the comment on Islam remains meaningless. In the description of the Bridge Party, for the most part incisively rendered in tones of English social comedy, the language again retreats from arenas to which speech is inappropriate. The contrast with the prevailing idiom in that scene makes the insufficiency of verbalisation quite overt:

> There was a silence when he had finished speaking, on both sides of the court; at least, more ladies joined the English group, but their words seemed to die as soon as uttered. Some kites hovered overhead, impartial, over the kites passed the mass of a vulture, and with an impartiality exceeding all, the sky, not deeply coloured but translucent, poured light from its whole circumference. It seemed unlikely that the series stopped here. Beyond the sky must not there be something that overarches all the skies, more impartial even than they? Beyond which again . . .
> They spoke of *Cousin Kate*.   (v, 34)

As the novel progresses, the distrust of verbalisation becomes absolute. Fielding refuses to point out to Aziz that water will not run uphill: 'he had dulled his craving for verbal truth and cared chiefly for truth of mood' (vii, 65). Mrs Moore refuses to accept her son's words alone as an unimpeachable index of his state of mind and feeling: 'his words without his voice might have impressed her' (v, 44). Her own invocation of the deity is subject to the same qualification: 'She must needs pronounce his name frequently, as the greatest she knew, yet she had never found it less efficacious. Outside the arch there seemed always an arch, beyond the remotest echo a silence' (v, 45–6). And this point of view is enlarged on at the Caves in the reference to 'poor little talkative Christianity' (xiv, 141). None the less, Aziz's susceptibility to the poetry of religion fails to exempt his feelings from the strictures made by silence on words. Aziz's religion is scarcely closer to that reality than Fielding's ethical philosophy: ' "there is no God but God" doesn't carry us far through the complexities of matter and spirit; it is only a game with words, really, a religious pun, not a religious truth' (xxxi, 264).

The clarity of Forster's probing analysis of the interaction between matter in the shape of language and the elusive spirit is a gauge of his own sensitivity to what his medium can, and, more importantly, cannot perform. The nagging uncertainty about the significance of the 'echo' in the Caves measures the novelist's refusal to accede to his form's propensity for continual explication. Only by attending to the breakdown of language accompanying the presentation of Godbole and the Hindu religion does the echo release its (strictly incomprehensible) 'meaning'. To begin with, Godbole refuses to 'explain' the secret of the caves to Aziz and the English ladies: 'the comparatively simple mind of the Mohammedan was encountering Ancient Night' (vii, 68). Godbole preserves the enigma. Yet his singing transcends the petty temper which accompanies the ending of Fielding's tea-party. The explanation of the song of the milkmaiden to Shri Krishna insinuates a possible reconciliation of eternity to time, by drawing futurity into the present:

> 'But He comes in some other song, I hope?' said Mrs Moore gently.
> 'Oh no, he refuses to come,' repeated Godbole, perhaps not understanding her question. 'I say to Him, Come, come, come, come, come, come. He neglects to come.'   (vii, 72)

Expectancy has been celebrated. This heralds the crucial understanding that the moment itself (rather than the structures of potential realisation and futurity built upon it), when prolonged, absorbs eternity. Significance resides in waiting. That is the condition on which insight and understanding become available.

Yet the point is not made explicit, because Godbole initiates his audience into participation rather than partial understanding. With the departure of the intrusive Heaslop the meaning of the song infuses the entire scene: 'Ronny's steps had died away, and there was a moment of absolute silence. No ripple disturbed the water, no leaf stirred' (vii, 72). Forster finishes the chapter on this (non) note of silence, prolonging its effect without attempting explanation. The words do not approach enactment but figure as sign-posts to a condition of feeling that is the antithesis of ratiocination, and therefore of language.

At the Caves, Godbole's absence forms part of the atmosphere of doom that attends the expedition: 'a new quality occurred, a spiritual silence which invaded more senses than the ear' (xiv, 132). Aziz's inadequacy to interpret the Caves is related to the Hindu: 'he had no notion how to treat this particular aspect of India; he was lost in it without Professor Godbole' (xiv, 133). Mrs Moore, shattered by the experience of the Caves, can only respond to her feelings with direct honesty. She is unable to assimilate silence in Godbole's manner, to accept it fully. But she does register the totality of the silence and the apprehension of eternity:

> . . . the echo began in some indescribable way to undermine her hold on life. Coming at a moment when she chanced to be fatigued, it had managed to murmur, 'Pathos, piety, courage – they exist, but are identical, and so is filth. Everything exists, nothing has value.' If one had spoken vileness in that place, or quoted lofty poetry, the comment would have been the same – 'ou-boum'. If one had spoken with the tongues of angels and pleaded for all the unhappiness and misunderstanding in the world, past, present, and to come, for all the misery men must undergo whatever their opinion and position, and however much they dodge or bluff – it would amount to the same . . .
> . . . suddenly, at the edge of her mind, Religion appeared, poor little talkative Christianity, and she knew that all its divine words from 'Let there be Light' to 'It is finished' only amounted to 'boum'. Then she was terrified over an area larger than usual; the universe, never comprehensible to her intellect, offered no repose to her soul, the mood of the last two months took definite form at last, and she realized that she didn't want to write to her children,

didn't want to communicate with anyone, not even with God.
(xiv, 140–1)

Where Mrs Moore approaches the obliteration of mental,
spiritual and emotional distinctiveness that preludes the experience
of totality or oneness, Godbole's culture, typically, enables him to
make the necessary lesser distinctions between suffering and evil.
His religious philosophy embodies acceptance, totality, reconciliation. His explanation to Fielding of Hindu concepts of good and
evil strains Forster's prose style with its unwonted abstraction:

> 'Good and evil are different, as their names imply. But, in my own
> humble opinion, they are both of them aspects of my Lord. He is
> present in the one, absent in the other, and the difference between
> presence and absence is great, as great as my feeble mind can
> grasp. Yet absence implies presence, absence is not non-existence,
> and we are therefore entitled to repeat, "Come, come, come,
> come."'   (xix, 169)

This difficult explanation of Hindu morality opposes Fielding's
ethical philosophy, which remains determinedly secular. The
certainty of Godbole's faith dissolves the sort of self-doubt to which
Fielding is liable. Nevertheless, a noticeable feature of Godbole's
explanation is Forster's satirical framing of it by Fielding's im-
patience, tiredness and boredom, and – to be anachronistic – the
insistence on Godbole's Peter Sellers brand of near-fatuity and
inconsequentiality. The result is not, of course, to deprecate the
Hindu's faith, but the process of explanation itself. The enactment
at Mau is accorded almost sacred respect.[7x]
To convey the intricate feeling of the Shri Krishna ceremonies,
Forster stands his language on its head:

> . . . Professor Narayan Godbole stands in the presence of God.
> God is not born yet – that will occur at midnight – but He has also
> been born centuries ago, nor can He ever be born, because He is
> the Lord of the Universe, who transcends human processes. He is,
> was not, is not, was. He and Professor Godbole stood at opposite
> ends of the same strip of carpet.   (xxxiii, 274)

'Stands' in the course of three sentences becomes 'stood'. The
change of tense indicates the co-presence of time and eternity. The

antitheses 'is, was not, is not, was', which further interfuse history and the present, are syntactically without meaning: Forster has exchanged the prose of reason and understanding for language as mystery, which modulates naturally into chant, '"Tukaram, Tukaram"'. 'Nonsense' becomes truth that lies beyond sense. Yet the language which is so effective at creating Fielding and Miss Quested is also capable of registering a range of feeling which is impossible to recreate more directly:

> When the villagers broke cordon for a glimpse of the silver image, a most beautiful and radiant expression came into their faces, a beauty in which there was nothing personal, for it caused them all to resemble one another during the moment of its indwelling, and only when it was withdrawn did they revert to individual clods.
>
> (xxxiii, 275)

The sign of divine presence and the language which records it are both inadequate to the state of feeling created by the ceremony, a failure transmitted again by Forster's ironic tones: 'the God to be born was largely a silver image the size of a teaspoon' (xxxiii, 274). Yet his sign partakes, like the Cross, of the reality it represents, is, more properly, the symbol of 'God Himself' (xxxiii, 275). Likewise, language transcends sign in the act of reading and becomes itself symbol, the chant:

> 'Tukaram, Tukaram,
> Thou art my father and mother and everybody.' (xxxiii, 275)

The necessary shortcomings of language, insisted upon throughout the novel, are transcended by the spirit of Hinduism which fleetingly gathers all mortal expression into a single communion: 'God si Love' (xxxiii, 276). The fractured proclamation of Mrs Moore's hesitant insight much earlier in the novel (v, 45), now repeated in a significant but unimportant abuse of language, heralds the spirit's attempt by 'a desperate contortion to ravish the unknown' (xxxiii, 278).

Yet afterwards language once again must submit to its syntactical, hierarchical, time-ridden status:

> how, if there is such an event, can it be remembered afterwards? How can it be expressed in anything but itself? Not only from the

unbeliever are mysteries hid, but the adept himself cannot retain them. He may think, if he chooses, that he has been with God, but as soon as he thinks it, it becomes history, and falls under the rules of time.   (xxxiii, 278)

The clash of rowing-boats and the dialectical exchange between Fielding and Aziz prevent a simplistic reading of the closing Hindu section as any kind of solution for problems of mortality, separation, racialism, or straightforward human cross-purposes. At the novel's end, the syntax recovers its confident tones confronting a reality to which it is fully adequate, and bangs shut like a gate: 'no, not yet . . . no, not there' (xxxvii, 312).

Forster's language makes no pretence of dissolving the intractable difficulties it has created. Yet while it imposes its linear conception of time and its rational order upon the timeless, chaotic diversity of experience, language itself strives also to accommodate the twin sensations of flux and stasis. It forms a central communication with both aspects of our experience. Forster's language in *A Passage to India* possesses an essentially moral dimension – the only morality of art apart from subject, as Conrad avowed[8]– manifest in the scrupulosity it consistently displays towards its own status even as it shows a willingness to trust to experience beyond language. As such, rather than further perpetrate problems of inevitable alienation, Forster's stylistic delicacy recreates the complex interaction between certain individual, social and spiritual conditions of being in permanent but fluid form.

15 Forster and 'Bloomsbury' Prose

P. N. Furbank

When, in writing about the Brownings, Virginia Woolf takes as her hero a spaniel, and when, to write about Keats, Forster assumes the standpoint of his unscrupulous guardian Mr Abbey (not even naming the poet till the last paragraph),[1] we recognise a likeness and say to ourselves, here is a 'Bloomsbury' trick, here is 'Bloomsbury' writing. How shall we define the quality? Perhaps, 'cultivated perversity'? In neither writer is the trick or invention a pointless whimsicality; and Forster's essay, though it verges on over-playfulness, makes its point, a novelist's point, very brilliantly. Nevertheless, this obliqueness and teasing refusal of the high road is a distinctively Bloomsbury trait. Indeed, come to think of it, such a devious approach to hallowed subjects is central to Bloomsbury's appointed task, the dismantling of Victorianism. It is the technique prescribed by Lytton Strachey in the Preface to *Eminent Victorians*:

> It is not by the direct method of a scrupulous narration that the explorer of the past can hope to depict that singular epoch. If he is wise, he will adopt a subtler strategy. He will attack his subject in unexpected places; he will fall upon the flank, or the rear; he will shoot a sudden, revealing searchlight into obscure recesses, hitherto undivined. He will row out over that great ocean of material, and lower down into it, here and there, a little bucket. . .

Bloomsbury writing, to speak more generally, aims at a beautiful amusingness. It is not the implacable, systematic spoofing of Max Beerbohm, which has shades in it still of art-for-art's sake and the nineties; it is not the tragic lightness of Ronald Firbank, which lies closer to 'modernism'. It is a more enjoying, more sociable lightness; there is a holiday feeling about it, as there is about Bloomsbury painting. 'Amusing' it must however, inexorably, be. Leonard Woolf recalled once, in a paper to the Memoir Club:[2]

> Just as one hesitated in Moore's rooms in Cambridge to say anything amusing which was not also profound and true, so in Bloomsbury one hesitated to say anything true or profound unless it was also amusing.

In its prose, as in its conversation, Bloomsbury followed the jets, the freaks, the vagaries of the mind; it prized spontaneity – the bubble blown, the fantasy constructed, upon the instant. Bloomsbury prose-style says, 'Having throw off corsets and crinolines, see how very nimbly I can move.'

As for 'perversity', the word of course cannot but have its sexual overtones. What Virginia Woolf is conveying in the hero/heroine of *Orlando*, what David Garnett is conveying in *Lady into Fox*, is some message about homosexuality and feminism. 'If it is possible for a husband to remain in *rapport* with a wife even after she has become a fox, then how much easier the task of an ordinary husband – yet the Victorians failed in it'; such is the message, or part of the message, of David Garnett's neo-Victorian fable.[3x] And in *Orlando*, of course, such thoughts become more explicit. These are light jokes about a theme – the need to understand and enter into the other sex's experience – which almost constituted modernity, and which received directer treatment in *Women in Love* and *The Waste Land*. (Edward Carpenter thought that the 'Uranian', being supposedly especially adept in such understanding, might be Nietzsche's true Superman.)[4x]

The lightness was Bloomsbury's chosen instrument, as it was sometimes its weakness. And Forster's lightness of touch – the informality, the cattiness, the demure and deflating good sense – can be thought of as 'feminine'. Equally that mixture in him (so disconcerting) of lightness and earnestness can, if you like, be thought of as a reconciling of 'femine' and 'masculine' qualities. But one does not need to think of this in biographical terms. The *Zeitgeist* recommended such a reconciling. Modernism and anti-Victorianism lay precisely in that direction, the assumption or resumption of feminine characteristics by men.

Let me now quote the opening of an essay I much admire, Forster's 'A Letter to Madan Blanchard':

The London Library,
St James's Square,
London.

April, 1931.

MY DEAR MADAN,—

Captain Wilson keeps telling me about you, and I feel I should like to write you a line. I shall send it by air mail to Paris, but from Paris to Genoa in a pre-war express. At Genoa the confusion will begin. Owing to the infancy of Mussolini the steam-packet will not start on time, and will frequently put in for repairs. So slow is the progress that the Suez Canal may close before it can be opened, and my letter be constrained to cross Egypt by the overland route. Suez is full of white sails. One of them, tacking southwards, will make India at last, another bring tidings of Napoleonic wars on a following breeze. Smaller boats, duskier crews. Brighter dawns? Quieter nights anyhow. The world is unwinding. What of Macao, where no news follows at all? What of the final transhipment? The last little vessel scarcely moves as she touches the Pelews, the waves scarcely break, just one tiny ripple survives to float my envelope into your hand. As the tide turns, I reach you. You open my letter a hundred and fifty years before it is written, and you read the words "My Dear Madan".[5]

Here, I would say, we have the quintessence of Bloomsbury prose. And how close in some ways it is to Virginia Woolf (who indeed published the essay as a Hogarth Press pamphlet in 1931). As an invention (and it is a lovely invention) this prose enactment of the unwinding of time and history could so easily, one feels, have found its place in *Orlando*. In texture and tone, though, it is not quite Virginia Woolf, and is indeed pure Forster. How characteristic is that progression: 'Suez is full of white sails. One of them, tacking southwards, will make India at last . . .' Forster, as often, surprises by his sense of reality. We read 'full of white sails' lazily, as piece of conventional scene-painting, and then, with a tiny jolt, we are reminded of the function of sails. How typical, and admirable, again is: 'Smaller boats, duskier crews. Brighter dawns? Quieter nights anyhow. The world is unwinding.' Prose could hardly be more nimble and disencumbered or more rich in *nuances*. And then, with what beauty, what 'amusingness' raised to high art, the sentences lengthen again and mime in their arrangement the turning of a tide.

This kind of prose is somewhat out of fashion, for good and for bad reasons. It was even, in a sense, out of fashion at the time that it was written. For Woolf and Forster (like Yeats) had a 'style'; and it was characteristic of serious artists in the 1920s to have gone beyond 'style', to practice a hundred styles and no style, to create a new style for each work. But if Woolf and Forster had a style, they had one with a difference. Forster's ease and informality gave him a quite new flexibility. In his novels he is in a sense more Victorian than the Victorians in that he is always conversing with the reader, buttonholing him, telling him what to think. The difference is, he is better at it than they. Or rather that, whilst they did it only some of the time, he is doing it all the time: it is always the one voice, though endlessly modified, and we notice no hiatus or change of gear in passing from light witticism to compelling eloquence. As for Virginia Woolf, we feel the existence of a style which is her very self, the expression of her inmost being; and in her novels the deeper she delves into her characters, the more they speak with this voice and begin to sound like herself. But she is far from always using this voice. She also plays with 'style', in an extravagant way. *Orlando* is full of rather unplaceable games with style, which you cannot call 'parody' or 'pastiche'. Sometimes it even falls into concealed doggerel. And altogether it represents a curious new attitude to 'style', peculiar to its author. We may think, too, of Lytton Strachey. One tends to assume that he had, very unmistakably, a 'style', but this may be an over-simplification. In looking through *Lady Ottoline's Album*, the collection of Ottoline Morrell's snapshots published in 1977, it struck me how Augustus John always looked exactly like himself, whereas Lytton Strachey looked like all sorts of different people: he would look hunnish, like Count von X of the Prussian Foreign Office; or aspiring, like the young Robert Elsmere; or exotic and criminal, like Fagin. The impression agrees with what Max Beerbohm said, very perceptively, in his 1943 RedeLecture on Strachey:

> His manner is infinitely flexible, in accord to every variation of whatever his theme may be. Consider the differences between his ways of writing about Lord Melbourne, Lord Palmerston, Mr. Disraeli, and Mr. Gladstone. His manner seems to bring us into the very presence of these widely disparate Premiers. Note the

mellow and leisurely benignity of the cadences in which he writes
of Lord Melbourne – 'the autumn rose' as he called him. Note the
sharp brisk straightforward buoyancy of the writing whenever
Lord Palmerston appears; and the elaborate Oriental richness of
manner when Mr. Disraeli is on the scene.[6]

The 'Madan Blanchard' passage leads me to my second theme,
Forster's prose not in its 'Bloomsbury' aspect but in its own right.
One of the things that one notices about Forster's prose is that he
always 'realises' or follows through his metaphors. Having said that,
like a rat, he has deserted the ship of fiction, he continues 'and *swum*
towards biography'. This fidelity to his metaphors is one source of
his wit – as when, speaking in 'Ibsen the Romantic' of the influence
of mountains upon Ibsen and Wordsworth, he writes: 'Wordsworth
fell into the residential fallacy; he continued to look at his gods
direct, and to pin with decreasing success his precepts to the flanks of
Helvellyn.'[7] (The final clause is almost a Beerbohm cartoon.) This
same fidelity also rewards him with thoughts of extreme originality,
as when, in 'Forrest Reid', he writes:

> He [Reid's hero Denis Bracknell] has reached squalor through
> beauty. It is as if, in the world beyond daily life, there was no
> moral full-stop: it is as if the scale of ecstasy might there rise until
> it has traversed the entire circle of its dial, and, passing the zero,
> indicate a state far lower than that from which it started.[8]

Indeed this characteristic leads us to the heart of Forster's beliefs.
He trusted metaphor to lead him where it would because he
believed 'things' contained the truth, albeit a truth probably very
different from men's presuppositions. Though a rationalist and a
humanist, he was neither a materialist nor a solipsist. Schoolmasters
and men of good will, he wrote once (in 'The Game of Life') were
keen to tell us what Life is. 'Once started on the subject of Life they
lose all diffidence, because to them it is ethical. They love discussing
what we ought to be instead of what we have to face – reams about
conduct and nothing about those agitating apparitions that rise
from the ground, or fall from the sky.'[9] He refused to assign those
'agitating apparitions' to any traditional category – such, for
instance, as 'the supernatural'. For him the truth about them was
that they could come in any form, and in any context – in the visible

scene or in human relationships, in the bed or the temple or at the tea-table. Accordingly, though he gave them a large role in all his writing, he assigned them only the status of an 'as if'. He wrote often *as if* inanimate things had wills and purposes of their own. At the end of *Where Angels Fear to Tread* it is as if the train deliberately shakes Phillip towards Miss Abbott and then away from her. At the end of *A Passage to India* it is as if the horses, the earth, the temple, the tank and the jail want to part Fielding and Aziz. He restricted such notions to metaphor; they pervade *A Passage to India*; and they have the force that they do because of his habitual respect for, and faithfulness in 'realising', metaphors.

And a further aspect may be perceived to his respect for 'the truth of things'. He was, as his scene-descriptions show, fascinated by topography. And, by extension, he looked at human life itself in a topographical fashion. He was a master of *angle*. There was such-and-such a fact, such-and-such a truth, that one could see, in any situation, and others that were concealed by the lie of the land. Of course, one could change one's viewpoint . . . Nothing is more striking in his masterpiece *A Passage to India* than the continual, and sometimes dizzying, shift of viewpoint, so that at one moment we are *tête-à-tête* with his characters, and the next moment viewing them from the ends of the universe.

16 E. M. Forster's Travelogue from the Hill of Devi to the Bayreuth Festival

Evelyne Hanquart[1]

As John Sayre Martin has recently pointed out,[2] travel, as an allegorical theme, is all-pervasive in E. M. Forster's fiction. Highly significant for the characters' potential development, it provides them with the opportunity to see and make a symbolical choice between two orders of experience. They may either remain deaf and blind to what is different from their customary behaviour and mentality, or they may open themselves to the new, unexpected, sometimes *a priori* strange ways of the foreign countries they visit, and – further – accept these ways. If they accept them, they enrich their own personalities and become more complete human beings.

So the Forsterian quest for humanism – the word is used here essentially with Renaissance overtones, not those of the nineteenth-century thought – goes heartily enough through 'the wide-open world',[3x] because travelling is *per se* – in this context – a move towards the Other Man, a willingness to meet. It brings out the natural brotherhood of man and the richness of life in its diversity, and makes them enjoyable over a wider range. Thus it appears in E. M. Forster's fiction, and thus it was in his own experience from the very beginning.

Forster was able to visit Austria, Italy and Greece for a few months shortly after he went down from Cambridge. This was his own variant of the traditional Grand Tour. The vital importance of this tour, which broadened his vision of the world and his human experience, and also nourished his creativity as a writer, can be seen from his long-lasting gratitude to his great-aunt, Marianne Thornton, which found expression many years later in his biography of her.[4]

Forster's Florentine, Roman and Sicilian letters to his Cambridge friends Nathaniel Wedd, E. J. Dent and G. L. Dickinson show the genesis of his first serious attempt at novel-writing, triggered off by his daily experience of *pension* life among the British tourists wintering in Italy, and his own longing for a more personal discovery of the 'beautiful country where they say "yes" . . . where people respond . . . where things happen', as one of his early characters says.[5] The 'Lucy Novel', which after several years and ample revisions, would become *A Room with a View*, is, in this respect, a faithful reflection of the young traveller's mood during this first significant continental journey. Many of its phrases echo Forster's correspondence to his friends at home in a very straightforward manner, as shown by this example:

Letter to G. L. Dickinson, March 25, 1902, Naples	'Old Lucy Novel'
'Oh what a view point is the English hotel or Pension. Our life is where we sleep and eat, and the glimpses of Italy that I get are only accidents.'[6]	'It was for this that she [Lucy] had given up her home . . . that she might sit with a party of English ladies who seemed even duller than ladies in England. This was Florence, but her life would be where she ate and slept.'

Indeed, the relationships between Forster's private life and his literary one were always close, though elusive, and pervade his fictional work. Not only did he tend to invest one of the characters with some of his own traits and preoccupations, as he openly admitted in the case of Philip Herriton,[7x] but he would also use incidents of his life to enrich the development of the plot. Though neither *Where Angels Fear to Tread* nor *A Room with a View* are autobiographical in a strict sense, they offer glimpses of their author's outer and inner life which appear explicitly in his letters to his friends: a fund-raising concert organised by the English hotel-population in Cortina d'Ampezzo while the Forsters were there in the summer of 1902[8] becomes the focus of the action in the earliest version of the 'Lucy Novel', originally indeed entitled 'The Concert', and reappears as a side incident in 'The Eternal Moment', a story dating from the same period.

Thus the most vivid examples of Forster's receptiveness to the countries he visited are to be found in his early short stories and in the 'Italian novels'. Literary creation might start with a stroke of inspiration on a particular spot;[9x] reminiscences were often intensified through the magnifying glass of time and distance once he was back in England.

The case of India is, however, much more striking – 'The East has spoiled Europe for me, though not England' he once wrote to a friend – and a parallel reading of the letters he chose to print as *The Hill of Devi* and of *A Passage to India* proves rewarding to those interested in the transformation of 'life' into 'art'. Much of the substance and background of the novel can be extracted from the diary Forster kept during his 1912–13 Indian tour, an emended version of which appeared as 'Indian Entries' in *Encounter*, January 1962, and from his letters home, principally to his mother and to Malcolm Darling,[10x] the nucleus of *The Hill of Devi*. Both texts, meant for 'private consumption', are fresh, lively and witty as well as informative. The letters indeed correspond to what the novelist was later to call his 'travelogue lines . . . all about what has just been passed'.[11] Through the pleasure, surprise, and genuine amusement, devoid of any condescension, which permeate them, the recipient was led to an imaginary retrospective participation in noteworthy events of this incursion into Oriental life, such as 'Gokul Ashtami', a festival which aesthetically plays a central part in the last section of the novel.[12x] The description of this celebration appears in a more detailed and vivid way in the series of letters Forster wrote home towards the end of August 1921.[13] The hysterical atmosphere at the Club after Adela's assault recalls his description of the Anglo-Indians after the bombing of the vice-regal procession which took place in Delhi just before Christmas 1912.

But the most interesting debt of *A Passage to India* to Forster's correspondence takes a rather surprising form, as the novel seems to owe its completion to a later exchange of letters rather than to his original epistolary snapshots. Thanks to Forster's influence, his new friend, Joe Ackerley,[14x] went to Chhatarpur in 1923 in the capacity of Private Secretary to the Maharajah, the very position held by Forster in Dewas two years earlier. It was Ackerley's turn, now, to send regular travelogues home. At that time Forster was painfully resuming his work on his Indian novel, which had gone stale at an early stage in 1913 and which even his stay in Dewas had failed to revive in a satisfactory way:

. . . As soon as [the opening chapters] were confronted with the country they purported to describe, they seemed to wilt and go dead and I could do nothing with them. I used to look at them of an evening in my room at Dewas, and felt only distaste and despair.[15]

Ackerley's letters rekindled Forster's memories and triggered his imagination, and – being a loyal Cambridge student – he received this further Indian experience as it were 'by proxy', thus enabling himself to shape what was to be his masterpiece in a much more 'inspired' way:

> 29.1.24 [place unknown]
> My dear Joe,
> Have had two letters from you and must get off a line this mail. . . . Your letters were a godsend to my etiolated novel. I copied in passages and it became ripe for publication. . . .

After months of a slow, painful and fruitless work, this new rejuvenating intake of Indian anecdotes led the novel to the completion already perceptible in January:

> 1.4.24   Weybridge
> [. . .]
> My MS is with the printers' [*sic*], but I hope to piddle a little urine over the proofs.

A Passage to India came out on 4 June 1924. It is interesting to note how much this work, so elaborate and so enthusiastically received by the general public, owes to the mere fact of letter-writing on a very personal, private basis, without pretence at literary excellence in spite of the intrinsic quality of the subject matter.

As a man, though, Forster did not cease to experience the excitement and joys of travelling after the publication of his novel in 1924. Even if distant journeys and meeting with new shades of civilisation were no longer a source from which sprang fictional writing, they always remained for him an incentive to go on living and developing.

These later experiences, numerous and varied, continued to take place until a very advanced age. They did not give rise to literary treatment as such but they are vividly recorded in his correspondence–Forster was an indefatigable letter-writer[16x]–and in some of his later contributions to periodicals such as the *Listener* and the *Spectator*. They all testify to his permanent humanistic concern and enjoyment of life throughout this long span of years, and take us to countries unvisited by his fiction.

During the First World War Forster had discovered Africa under the mildly exotic form of Alexandria and Egypt. This long stay, which was decisive in his personal life, nourished his literary achievement in two ways generally connected with such events: journalism and guidebook-writing. And the tone of his articles is to be felt again, perhaps in a more familiar and unrestrained way, in his letters to Bertrand Russell and R. C. Trevelyan, the poet, who seemed to have been among his chief correspondents during this period spent in a totally different atmosphere both intellectually and otherwise. But he had had no first-hand experience of 'Black Africa' until 1928, when George Barger, who had been his contemporary at King's, suggested that he might join his wife, Florence, and himself in their forthcoming visit to South Africa. This idea was most welcome. The Bargers were family friends by now, and Forster took eagerly to the plan, saving 'every penny' for months.

Their fabulous cruise started in June 1929, from Tilbury on board the s.s. *Llandovery Castle*. Ackerley was to be his principal correspondent. The first impression of the traveller between Tilbury and Dover was similar to his early feelings during his passage to India in 1912 with G. L. Dickinson and R. C. Trevelyan, when they found themselves alienated from the other passengers' mode of living.

> The voyage does not promise too well. A raging band at meals, but my cabin mate is innocuous – young and gentlemanly, cleanshaven, tennis-racket on bed.[17x]

The travelogue as such only begins several days later, when the ship had already called at Ascension, 'all red extinct craters and black lava flows, with one hill going green at the top because of its height'. Off the African coast new people, new landscapes, are in sight, at least in prospect, and the tone formerly dyspeptic, faintly bored or disappointed, has turned lively and alert to any stimulus: 'the size of the earth excites me in a way it doesn't Lady Bailey or you, perhaps new stars, occasional fish, the Doldrums . . . '[18x] The traveller was enjoying his experience and looking forward to an exciting, animated prospect of human intercourse. The least of this was certainly not for him the promise made by a fellow-traveller, who ran a mission for natives in South Africa, to show him 'something of their life'. Saint Helena was next visited with enthusiasm, not indeed for its Napoleonic associations but for the beauty and mildness of its 'loveable loving' inhabitants 'all hu _ ˰om coffee to ink, and as gentle as their climate', for its luxuriant flora and fauna whose sight enchanted him.

During his stay in Africa, Forster continued to write letters which echo his preoccupations and beautifully reflect, at times, the various facets of an attentive vision. But the only published aftermath of this cruise is the rather disappointing 'Luncheon at Pretoria', oddly included in *Two Cheers for Democracy*, whose main interest lies in the rather vague evocation of the city with its Union Buildings:

> Pretoria turned out to be a dear little place with the touch of two civilisations upon it. . . . Up the hill was a fine imperial effort: Union Buildings, with its pavilions, its long terraces, its two domes. An agreeable morning was spent, the sights were indicated and viewed with complaisance.

When he wrote this article for *The Abinger Chronicle* in 1940, Forster's memories may have been dimmed and softened by the passing of time. His letters are more vivid, revealing much stronger reactions to the South African scene. In 1924, the moderate Afrikander Party had been defeated by the Nationalists, who gradually increased their racial segregationist policy until they enforced apartheid throughout the country in 1948. At the time of Forster's visit it was already active in parts of the Union and his horrified dismay is perceptible under the neutral informative tone:

> You cannot imagine what things are like out here. India gives no idea. In the Transvaal and Orange Free State it is now illegal for black and white to marry, or even to live together; the present (Herzog) govt. aims at the complete separation of the two races.[19]

The vague sketch of Pretoria, with its rather flatly appreciative mention of the Union Buildings as 'a fine imperial effort', has replaced the grandeur and pathos evoked by the letter:

I *was* moved – tears coming – by the nobility of the new Union Govt Buildings at Pretoria: such a splendid gesture, English and Dutch participating, and such an empty gesture, for beneath and beyond both English and Dutch are these millions of blacks whom one never speaks to and whose existence one assumes as one does electric bells'. That was why I nearly cried at Pretoria. It is Valhalla, and the dwarfs haven't been paid.

Instead of the farcical anecdote of the article, the letters describe much more typical or humanly interesting episodes, such as Forster's visit to the 'slums and mine compounds of Johannesburg' thanks to the missionary whom he had met on the boat and who had kept his promise. Though Forster deplored the fact that he was only '*seeing*' a great deal of native life, whereas he would have liked to take part in it as he had done in India, we feel his curiosity and sympathy for the miners. This did not prevent him however from expressing his feelings without sentimentality, indeed even with some humour:

All the miners live in dormitories, by tribes, and grinning at them was pleasant and easy. They are well fed, and happy, and their bathing halls would have ravished you, and incidentally caused them not to smell. That – I must say in passing – is one of the reasons why the natives of S. Africa are so remote. They usually smell like high roast turkeys. The dusky youth as he approaches down the lonely narrow path knocks you over in more senses than one. There is not much water in S. Africa, and what there is doesn't get much used. They are made to wash in the mine compounds. Do read a story (called Ula Masonga) in W. Plomer's *I Speak to Africa*[20x]. It isn't bad; but life in the gold mines is better now than he describes: the owners find it pays to treat the chaps well. I have been down a gold mine (3000 feet), but it's the compounds that are really worth seeing: every race of the South and East runs grinning at you, and *playing* upon musical instruments to you.

By early August, South Africa was left behind, the journey northwards which was to take them along the eastern coast of Africa, visiting Rhodesia, Zanzibar, Aden, and Egypt, had begun. This way homeward was still full of exciting prospects of both discovery and reunion. Forster had long wished to visit Africa and

those three months proved at once a valuable experience and a
disheartening one: it revealed to him indigenous aspects of a culture
he was not acquainted with, but it also renewed his former concern
with the evils of colonialism which he had already pointed out in *A
Passage to India* and which he now saw at work on another continent.
His Coleridgean descriptions of the Victoria Falls[21x] or of the Nile
coming out of the Victoria Nyanza are marred for him by 'all the
horrors of the European impact':

> corrugated iron, filthy clothes. Most of the African peoples seem
> simply heart-broken, they wander about as if their lives were lost,
> trade and Christianity together have done them in. Zanzibar,
> Aden and the northern parts have been saved by Islam.[22]

It is fascinating to note that this latter theme already plays a central
part in 'The Life to Come', one of Forster's posthumously published
short stories, whose conception Oliver Stallybrass dates from 1922
or so.[23]

When they reached Egypt, the novelist could not resist the call of
friendship. Leaving his travelling companions, he looked up many
of the friends whom he had not seen since his call in 1921 on his way
back from India. He was eager to meet them again, longing for
warmer, closer human relationships than those provided by the
chance encounters of his travelling life. 'Egypt revisited' proved
satisfactory, and Forster's delight in re-establishing his connections
with the country that had been dear to him ten years earlier enlivens
the last letter of this voyage, though it never found expression in a
published form:

> I was 250 years old a fortnight back, and now you can knock off
> the naught. Egypt after the British Empire is more wonderful,
> beautiful, and amusing than can well be described.[24x] It began at
> Aden . . . Then Port Sudan, and Portissimo Said, and the Canal,
> and the Mummied Cat room in the Cairo Museum – too purely
> comic as must perhaps be expected of Cats – and how the Air
> Force entertained the Tanks, and the Egyptian Army me, and
> the Greek himself, as must perhaps be expected for Greeks[25x]. I
> never saw such a place.

The end of the cruise, marked by a number of friendly reunions,
took place in France, where the novelist managed to meet the

dedicatee of *A Passage to India*, Syed Ross Masood, in Marseilles before going to stay with the Maurons in Provence. Charles Mauron had just translated *A Passage to India* into French, as he was later to do for Forster's other novels. Charles and his wife Marie, whom Forster had met through Roger Fry and Bloomsbury early in the twenties, were to remain lifelong friends. Loaded with colourful reminiscences and friendly memories, Forster returned to the chilly atmosphere of an English autumn, and to his sedate Abinger life, by early October 1929.

This tour, the longest and most exotic of Forster's travels since his 1921 stay in India, had revealed to him the natural beauties of the African continent which he had been so eager to discover and to which he reacted enthusiastically. But beyond those landscapes and picturesque sights, the travelling humanist had been in search of human relationships. The glory of his vision had been sullied by the interference of racism and colonialism, preventing any new straightforward reaching of the Other Man. The glamour had only been recovered in Egypt where his former friendships had been rejuvenated and strengthened by his visit.

The 'human element' of the tour aroused an ambiguous feeling in Forster's sensibility: sadness and disillusion at the colonial be-haviour of the Europeans on one hand, warmth and personal happiness born of the friendly reunions on the other. It remains nevertheless at the heart of his concern as well as of his love of travel. A reading of his correspondence to Ackerley at the time also shows that it was an infinitely richer experience than its single public record would lead us to believe.

This attitude towards travelling colours the next trip with bright-er shades, both in his correspondence with Ackerley and in the two articles which sprang from it after his return: 'The Eyes of Sibiu' and 'Chess at Cracow'. Three years later, in May-June 1932, Forster visited Romania, or rather visited some friends stationed there, the Randalls. Alec Randall and his family had been Weybridge neighbours around 1922. As a diplomat, Alec (later Sir Alec) Randall had previously served at the Holy See and was then First Secretary at the British Legation to the court of King Carol.[26x] Besides Romania, the trip took him through the major cities of Central Europe: Vienna and Budapest, then Cracow, where he attended the strange, Alice-in-Wonderland game of chess described in his article, and Berlin, which he had known since 1905 when he stayed at Nassenheide with the Count and Countess von Arnim.[27]

Bucharest he did not like: he found it 'quite appalling, and too large to be a joke for its area is equal to Paris', which it was indeed, as confirmed by the *Times Atlas* of this period. If one adds that Bucharest's population was then a tenth of Paris's (i.e. about 500,000 inhabitants), the impression produced must indeed have been awkward. The image of Romania he wished to convey to the English readers was not, as a consequence, that of the capital. For his *Spectator* essay, he chose to introduce them to Sibiu, which was with Cluj – the famous University and fourteenth-century cathedral town of the country – the only Romanian city he really enjoyed. Both places are in Transylvania and were parts of Hungary before the First World War. Sibiu, of Germanic tradition, charmed Forster for the loveliness of its architecture and clothes and set his fancy going. In the delightfully fresh and naïve atmosphere evoked by the article, legendary and descriptive elements intermingle very pleasingly:

> It had never occurred to me that when the Pied Piper of Hamelin led his little charges through the mountain they would emerge in Roumania. . . . But here they were, his fair-haired and blue-eyed German children, clean, friendly and a little dull, and here they grew into broad-shouldered men, and here behind them, were the crinkled green hills, antimacassared with trees and picked out here and there with white threads of snow. . . . This was one of their towns, Sibiu which they called Hermannstadt, and standing in its lovely square I thought. . . . It was a most lovely square and what so took me were the elongated eye-shaped openings in the roofs of the houses. It was as if the heavy dark red tiles had parted to produce a wink. And this fancy can be substantiated for (a) the openings were the exact shape of eyes, this lay beyond argument; (b) in the centre of each was a window resembling a retina; (c) a pigeon . . . would frequently perch in the window and, glancing this way and that act the part of a pupil. . . . The broad lines of the scheme were admirable, and watched by these amiable flickering eyes the great square slumbered in the sun.[28x]

The correspondence also shows the impact of another aspect of Romania associated with romance, folklore and fairyland. His description of the bucolic, picturesque outing he had in the Carpathians is so vivid that we feel he is still paganly revelling in the delight of his recollections, relishing the very sonorities of the words he uses to describe it. No ambiguous feeling here, but only pleasure to be alive, exhilaration to meet new, simple people, and enjoyment in sharing with them the magic of the day:

> The scenery, the gorgeous rough costumes, the peasants and workmen sprawling in the brilliant sun, the wolves, bears and boars lurking to pounce upon them from the beeches, birches, larches and spruces and to dapple with their rich gore their couches of pansies and thyme . . . . The Carpathians, in other words, *can* be all one dreams and the beauties of their inmates indescribable, . . . what lovely things I ate in the forester's verandah – beginning with a log of wood which was unlaced and full of sheep's cheese, then speckled trout, meat pancakes swimming in soup, chickens that go without saying, nut pastry, piles of wild strawberries and cream, they go without saying in this country too, also liqueur made from plums,[29x] and strong white wine and stronger Turkish coffee, but the air was stronger still so that I leapt up when the meal was over and ran hither and thither among the recumbent peasants until it was imperative to return.

The magic atmosphere of this unsophisticated day, so youthfully and so spontaneously lived, crowns Forster's visit to Central Europe and also marks the end of an era. The coming years were to be coloured with more sombre hues, first in his personal life by G. L. Dickinson's death a few months later, then in the international sphere by the rise of Nazism and the Spanish tragedy, and later still by the war itself, which embittered his faith in human nature for a while, and put an end to the incursions into unfamiliar ways of life which had enhanced his perception and enjoyment of the world.

Once the cataclysm was over, Forster's first major expedition into the newly-reopened world took him back to India. His connection with this country had not been interrupted by the war, since he had been one of the major contributors to the BBC Eastern programme 'We Speak to India'. At the end of 1945 – shortly after his mother's death – he revisited the subcontinent in the capacity of an official literary guest. Although he wrote to Ackerley during this trip, none of these letters can rank as an interesting 'travelogue'. Whether there were indeed no such letters or whether they were not preserved, we are in no position to tell. He 'was back to the country

[he] loved, after an absence of twenty-five years', however, and the two extensive BBC talks on 'India after Twenty-Five Years' which he gave when he came back, and which were later reprinted in *Two Cheers for Democracy* as 'India Again', give a detailed account of the Indian intelligentsia and cultural life after the British Raj which goes beyond an immediate documentary interest by its personal note of love and concern. Both as humanist and friend he was watching the youthful country's efforts towards a modern literary life, independent, fruitful and diversified. The strong sympathy felt by Forster, who was again trying to bridge the gap of misunderstanding between the British and the newly-independent India, does not however conceal from him certain dangerously fanatical trends to be sensed in the various cultural manifestations he attended. These two texts are to a certain degree travelogues, but they also convey a deeper note, and end with a humanistic appeal of universal significance much in keeping with the part played by Forster as a public figure in our modern City (to use a Platonic expression), since the Second World War:

> I do pray that young English people who like Indians and want to be with them will be encouraged to go to their country. Goodwill is not enough. Of that I am too sadly convinced. In fact, at the present moment goodwill out there is no use at all. The reactions to it are instantly cynical. The only thing that cuts a little ice is affection or the possibility of affection. . . . But it must be genuine affection and liking. It must not be exercised with any ulterior motive. It must be an expression of the common humanity which in India and England and all the world over has been so thwarted of late, and so despised.

The man who 'spoke to India' all through the war was now addressing the Home audience with the same message of human relationships, 'the holiness of the heart's affection', which had been his creed since his Cambridge days and which gives to his enjoyment of life and travel its unique flavour.

Forster's discovery of the New World, at the age of 68, originated as a kind of 'business trip'. Early in 1947, he had been invited by Harvard University to deliver a talk 'on criticism at a Musical Conference . . . On May 1st'.[30] Though he felt apprehensive about the task he knew '[he] want[ed] to visit America and this [was] probably [his] only chance'. So, a series of lectures was organised for him by his American publisher. Spring and early summer 1947 saw him travelling in North America far and wide. As usual, what had started as the official visit of a famous lecturer became a gladly-renewed pilgrimage into the world of friendship, both tightening former links and creating fresh ones with his usual generosity and open-mindedness. At Harvard he saw an associate of his early Cambridge days, the philosopher A. N. Whitehead, then he discovered the West Coast as 'the guest of an acquaintance made casually in England: a young man who has an equally nice Jugoslav wife'.[31x] The wide range of his 'American' friends also included Gerald Heard and Christopher Isherwood, both of them by now American citizens. After his much enjoyed mule ride and trip in the Grand Canyon described in the *Listener*[32x], which met his longing for 'gigantic' scenery, he went back eastwards, gladly snatching even the slightest opportunity of enjoyment and human intercourse:

> I am on my way from San Francisco to Chicago on the 'Feather River Route'. It passes the Feather River in the dark, and the view from the window is the Californian desert mistaken by me for the Nevadan. . . . I have had breakfast with a negro sergeant major from Japan, and have listened to the negro Pullman attendant ticking off a white G.I. for washing in too smart a lavatory. 'Gee I'm surprised at you fellows.' The G.I. hung his sprotty [sic] head.[33x]
> I enjoy the charm and friendliness of America. What a contrast to malnourished disgruntled England! One is never snubbed, and sometimes the contrary. I sat for half-an-hour in Arizona on a wall which a Mexican was cementing for his mother, and a correspondence had resulted. Do you remember a Canadian airman I contacted? Very nice letter from him too, and I am nerving myself to dash from Chicago to see him and the Niagara Falls. I have only just found out that they are close together. . . . Then to New York . . . Paul Cadmus has lent me his flat.[34x] It is in deepest Greenwich village – very sympathetic.[35]

His 'Impressions of the United States', delivered in August 1947, convey feelings very similar to those expressed in his letters. 'My visit was a complete success from my own point of view', the broadcaster publicly acknowledged, in unison with the man's warmth and pleasure perceptible in the private impressions gathered from his long-awaited discovery of the New World.

Through the invitation of Harvard University, music had been the excuse and the prime mover of Forster's crossing of the Atlantic. Music, again, was the incentive of the next trip, this time on a private basis. At 75, Forster, a lifelong Wagnerian, was induced to attend the Bayreuth festival. That was to be the last journey recorded as a travelogue. However, the letters describing the main lines of the elderly expedition display the same openness, blended with a touch of mild, good-tempered humour towards what was offered him, the same power to enjoy the multiple gifts of a travelling life, however modest, that we have perceived earlier on. It is indeed fascinating to watch the old man's fresh outlook and his readiness to live fully, though sedately and rather contemplatively, the natural pleasures of this expedition, to see the keenness of his perceptions and the total absence of any *blasé* attitude. Obviously, for him the dynamics of the humanistic quest might have lost of its vital urgency with the passing of time, but it never lost any of its attraction.

The Controller of the Third Programme had asked Forster to give a talk on the Festival, which he did the following autumn.[36] Although the broadcast lays more emphasis on the artistic side of the trip – it is essentially a critical appreciation of the festival's atmosphere, singing and performance – it also conveys the traveller's simple, good-tempered attitude revealed in the letters. Indeed, as in the case of the Italian letters and novel quoted at the beginning of this paper, in 'Revolution at Bayreuth' Forster used several phrases which had already appeared in his correspondence:

Letters to Ackerley, 3 and 13 August 1954[37x]	'Revolution at Bayreuth'
But I must say it too (['Hitler's'] the Autobahn) is good: rural or mountainous scenery all the way, no poles, wires or adverts. One rushes along through greenness and under blueness quite unexpected. This afternoon . . . I wandered through the meadows up into the woods. As England was before its ruin-	I stayed not in the town but fifteen miles out in a tiny country hamlet. There I could walk in any direction through meadows and cornfields and up into woods. There were streams and familiar flowers. There were no poles, no wires, no aeroplanes, no advertisements, and I was reminded of what the English countryside used to be before it

ation[38] . . . It is a little guesthouse attached to a little brewery squashed in a little village with a pumpkin-topped church tower, . . . about 15 miles from Bayreuth. We drive in to the performances. . . .

The Wagner here is odd. Lovely music, productions which are often conceited, but sometimes come off. We have been stumbling about in the orchestra and over the stage today – the latter particularly perilous. There's a huge muffin filling it, five feet thick and I should guess 200 feet across, and tilted sharply towards the audience. On this the singers manouvre [*sic*], jamming themselves into their toes or against their heels at every step, or, should they fall prone with passion wobbling on their bellies and bums. This muffin is for the Ring. Parsifal has a crumpet, laid flatter.

was ruined. . . . From this homely paradise I drove in of an afternoon to Bayreuth. . . . The famous theatre disconcerted me. It is an odd shape outside. . . . I shall not be speaking about the music, so let me here emphasize how magnificently it sounded, how finely the orchestra played and most of the singers sang. . . . Bayreuth hates light, hates colours, mistrusts movement, and identifies mysticism with mist. It is trying to get away from . . . realism. . . . [For *Parsifal*] In the centre of the stage was a round raised area resembling a crumpet . . . . Odd as the scenery looked, it was odder still when one was on the stage with it. One morning I had the chance of going behind the scene – a fascinating tour, though beset by many physical perils. . . . It [the stage] was occupied by a large round object, shaped like a muffin, six feet thick . . . and about 25 feet across, and tilted sharply towards the auditorium. . . . Here Brunehilde had been laid to sleep and Siegfried had awakened her at his own risk.

This parallel account of Forster's stay in Bavaria ends the travelogue proper. But the old man had not renounced travelling yet. No further broadcast or article intended to share his pleasures and experiences with the general public has come to light. However, the correspondence to Ackerley gives evidence of

Forster's mobility in spite of the increasing difficulties brought by age. There is no longer any exploration, but returns to places which he loved and where he had formerly been happy, discovered attractive aspects of life and made friends in the long-distant past. Austria was revisited in the summer of 1957, the trip 'culminating in a wonderful Vienna . . . and a beautiful flight over sun-lit spread out Europe';[39] then Italy, in a semi-official capacity, where he delivered, to a Roman audience, a lecture on 'Three Countries' (Italy, England, and India) which had 'influenced and helped [him] as a writer', and modestly acknowledged his taste for travelling:

> I like to see the face of the world and to think about it. I enjoy travelling and am indeed a confirmed globe-trotter, though a trotter upon a rather quiet globe, none of my travels having been adventurous.[40]

The final series of foreign journeys took the familial form of summer holidays in Provence in the welcoming atmosphere of Charles Mauron's home,[41] testifying, up to the end of a 'not too ungrateful life' – as he once styled it – to his constant and warm curiosity for his fellow-beings, his never-ending delight in human intercourse, and his sensitiveness to beauty in its simplest and most natural manifestations, even if the human richness brought along by travelling remained an ideal not always attainable in the world of his novels.

17 Some Reminiscences

May Buckingham

I first met Morgan in his flat in Brunswick Square in 1931 and was with him when he died in our house in Coventry in 1970.

Over the years our relationship changed and developed, passing through many stormy passages to a close, loving understanding.

To him I owe a great debt of gratitude. For his widening of horizons, by meeting his friends, by travel, but mostly by his talk.

I am by nature bossy, as he claimed all women are, especially nurses. He helped me to realise this and try to be less so. I was then a 23 year old night sister in a maternity hospital knowing almost nothing outside nursing.

I now know that he was in love with Robert and therefore critical and jealous of me and our early years were very stormy, mostly because he had not the faintest idea of the pattern of our lives and was determined that Robert should not be engulfed in domesticity.

Over the years he changed us both and he and I came to love one another, able to share the joys and sorrows that came.

Our son had the names Robert Morgan and his eldest son Clive Morgan and this meant a lot to Morgan. The Battersea Rise nursery table that he inherited and wrote about he left to Clive because he liked to think how nice it would be for his children to sit at as Marianne had. The continuity pleased him however vague it may seem to others.

We were gently guided and educated by loans and gifts of books. When his Mother died in 1945 I feel that in some ways I took her place. He always came to stay with us whenever he was unwell from then on and always spent his birthday with us. His birthday was very important to him, partly I think because it fell on January 1st. He never wanted a large party, he only wanted specially loved friends. When we lived in London this always included Florence Barger and Joe Ackerley. We all signed his birthday book which had been made by the children at Abinger Hammer school, signed by each child and given him when he left West Hackhurst. Later, when we were in Coventry our grandsons before they could write made their mark in it. He also made up his diary on New Year's Eve.

Because of Robert's work we had to move to Coventry in 1952 which greatly upset both Morgan and I. He never did get to like the city but I did. It was not as convenient for him to get to. The cross-country train journey from Cambridge is uncomfortable and difficult. There still is not a concert hall and at that time the only theatre never put on plays.

He visited frequently and as time went on had to stay for quite long periods when some structural alterations were being made in King's and his rooms were in danger of collapse.

From 1955 he felt he ought not to travel abroad alone and we went with him, mostly touring in France, always going to St Remy in Provence to visit Charles Mauron. Twice we went to Greece with the Hellenic Society. He never missed an expedition ashore. In 1958 he insisted upon climbing to the stadium at Delphi because he had recently read an ode by Pindar about it. He always did his homework for these holidays, knew where he wanted to go and what he wanted to see. He was an excellent map-reader, keeping to minor roads and finding us simple accommodation.

After 1965 his health was failing, so we didn't go abroad again but continued to go to the Aldeburgh Festival where he could meet so many friends.

He had many young friends, and was not critical of the young; he declared that the elders had said much the same things about his generation, criticising their clothes and behaviour, and said that it is not easy to be young now, the world is too complex.

The simplest machine defeated him. It took years to persuade him to have an electric gramophone and he had the greatest difficulty with tin openers, partly because of lack of strength. We were always buying him new ones to try.

When in Coventry he insisted upon our going for a walk each day, as had been his habit all through his life. Only ice stopped him, but as we couldn't go far afield it meant going every day through the same monotonous suburban streets.

He never complained, said how lucky he had been, especially in his friends. He played the gramophone a great deal, mostly Beethoven, Bach, Brahms, Mozart and Haydn, waiting for Robert to come home. I read to him when his sight deteriorated, and wrote his letters. It must have been especially hard for him whose whole life had been reading and writing, but he insisted that he was so lucky to have us to be with and King's to go to when fit enough.

We were pleased when any friends could come to help amuse him and there were several who came frequently.

He often said that he had lived too long, was aware of failing faculties. We often discussed death, especially after the death of our son, deciding there was no reason to fear it and that under certain circumstances it was to be welcomed.

Because he was president of the Cambridge Humanist Society he didn't want any religious ceremony at all, not even a memorial service, so there was a concert in Hall at King's. He did greatly care for the chapel though; it just was that he felt he must not let the Humanists down.

On 27th May 1970 we went to Cambridge to get him for the last time. He had been unable to get up from the table in Hall and was assisted to his rooms. With help he had been able to get up and potter in his room but a day or two later he collapsed and crawled to the door for help. He never walked again but his mind was perfectly clear and he was cheerful. The young resident artist Mark Lancaster helped Robert to carry him down 'A' staircase to the car and we managed to carry him up to bed in Coventry laughing and joking. Usually when ill he had a bed downstairs but he asked to be taken up to the bedroom.

On the 30th our very dear friends Audrey and Eric Fletcher came unexpectedly and stopped to supper. It became a jolly party, we took our coffee up to his room.

That was the last time he fed himself. Next morning he was weaker and this progressed each day.

On Sunday June 7th he died at 2.40 a.m. His ashes mingle with Robert's in a rose bed at the crematorium overlooking Warwick University.

So ended a long life which has enriched mine so.

18 Forster on Lawrence

C. E. Baron

Lawrence first read Forster in 1911, and Forster must have read Lawrence at about that time or shortly thereafter. They met in 1915, and for the remainder of Lawrence's life, despite some sharp criticisms each made of the other, each had considerable respect for the other's – alien – work. They wrote of course out of very different temperaments and outlooks on life.

Intimate acquaintance with a respected but somewhat anti-pathetic contemporary's evolving work has often created the conditions favourable for the production of genuine criticism, and this seems to me the case with the mutual criticisms of these two authors. On the occasion of Lawrence's death in 1930 Forster put himself firmly and challengingly on the record as believing Lawrence to be 'the greatest imaginative novelist of our generation'.[1] This judgement has frequently been saluted. However, lying side-by-side with it is a thought which appears virtually to have escaped attention: '*The Plumed Serpent* blares out explicitly what the snowdrops in *The White Peacock* shyly hinted at . . . In a sense he never developed . . .' This thought might prove critically fruitful if teased out into greater explicitness.

It may at first appear that Forster cited *The Plumed Serpent* together with *The White Peacock* because he was expressing a comprehensive verdict on all Lawrence's novels by naming the first and last, at a time when the final novel, *Lady Chatterley's Lover*, which followed *The Plumed Serpent*, was not in general circulation. However, Forster nowhere traced any continuities through Lawrence's work and therefore whether or not he noted in detail that Lawrence steadily turned up the volume, as it were, with each novel that he wrote, cannot now be determined. On the other hand there are clues that he judged *The White Peacock* and *The Plumed Serpent* to be in certain respects specially linked. In his BBC broadcast about Lawrence of 16 April 1930 Forster spoke at greater

length and more enthusiastically about *The Plumed Serpent* than
about any other work by Lawrence. He concluded his admiring
though also qualified account: '. . . the general effect has been
superb, we have assisted at a great mystical ceremony, and all the
Mexican landscape has come alive.'[2] The words 'mystical ceremony' and Forster's exclusive concentration in his account of the
novel on its religious subject-matter rather than the characters
conforms with and so confirms the discovery of what it was he found
hinted at in *The White Peacock*.

The fuller context of Forster's critical comment reads:

> He was both preacher and poet, and some people, myself
> included, do not sympathise with the preaching. Yet I feel that
> without the preaching the poetry could not exist. With some
> writers one can disentangle the two, with him they were
> inseparable. As he grew older, he became more didactic and
> mannered, and, if one differed from him, more tiresome; but the
> poetry, also, was increasing in strength. *The Plumed Serpent* blares
> out explicitly what the snowdrops in *The White Peacock* shyly
> hinted at, yet, exquisite as were those early woodlands, they
> droop towards unreality beneath the sunlight of Mexico. In a
> sense he never developed. One can hear from the first what he is
> going to say, but one never knows what his own message will
> evoke in him, and although I cannot believe in it, I believe it was
> the mainspring of his greatness.

By making 'blares out' co-operate with 'increasing' and 'became',
Forster indicates a development in intensity on Lawrence's part
rather than any linear development in direction. The puzzling
sentence is the one where Forster names the novels, for he appears to
make three different ideas overlap. Two of the ideas can be
identified as a continuation of the dualistic argument already set
out. The 'message' which was hinted at in *The White Peacock* is blared
out in *The Plumed Serpent* (although Forster does not describe that
'message'); on the other hand the woodlands of the earlier novel,
although exquisite, are unreal in comparison with the descriptions
of Mexico (Forster seems almost to equate 'poetry' with the
evocation of landscape). The third – perhaps intentionally cryptic,
perhaps not fully controlled – idea is intimated by the use of the
word *snowdrops*. Why does Forster choose to describe the 'message'
as voiced by the snowdrops? By the ensuing phrase '*yet* exquisite as

were *those* early woodlands', Forster appears to link the hitherto
distinct 'message' and 'poetry'; and if he did, consciously or
unconsciously, thereby make the woodlands a metaphor for the
message, is he also implying that the message was more acceptable
when hinted at in *The White Peacock* than when exposed to the full
glare of the Mexican sun? Does the message droop towards unreality
when made fully explicit?

It seems that despite the clear-cut antithetical argument of this
paragraph, Forster blurred the clarity when, focusing for the
moment on these two novels, he intruded the word *snowdrops*
because of what he had in the corner of his mind as Lawrence's
message.

Although snowdrops figure at a few points throughout the novel,
there is an episode in which Lawrence did make them hint, and this is
almost certainly the passage which lodged in Forster's mind:

Other flower companies are glad; stately barbaric hordes of
bluebells, merry-headed cowslip groups, even light, tossing
wood-anemones; but snowdrops are sad and mysterious. We have
lost their meaning. They do not belong to us, who ravish them.
The girls bent among them, touching them with their fingers, and
symbolising the yearning which I felt. Folded in the twilight,
these conquered flowerets are sad like forlorn little friends of
dryads.

'What do they mean, do you think?' said Lettie in a low voice,
as her white fingers touched the flowers, and her black furs fell on
them.

'There are not so many this year,' said Leslie.

'They remind me of mistletoe, which is never ours, though we
wear it,' said Emily to me.

'What do you think they say—what do they make you think,
Cyril?' Lettie repeated.

'I don't know. Emily says they belong to some old wild lost
religion. They were the symbol of tears, perhaps, to some strange-
hearted Druid folk before us.'

'More than tears,' said Lettie. 'More than tears, they are so
still. Something out of an old religion, that we have lost. They
make me feel afraid.'

'What should you have to fear?' asked Leslie.

'If I knew I shouldn't fear,' she answered. 'Look at all the
snowdrops'—they hung in dim, strange flecks among the dusky

leaves—'look at them—closed up, retreating, powerless. They belong to some knowledge we have lost, that I have lost and that I need. I feel afraid. They seem like something in fate. Do you think, Cyril, we can lose things off the earth—like mastodons, and those old monstrosities—but things that matter—wisdom?'

'It is against my creed,' said I.

'I believe I have lost something,' said she.

'Come,' said Leslie, 'don't trouble with fancies. Come with me to the bottom of this cup, and see how strange it will be, with the sky marked with branches like a filigree lid.'

She rose and followed him down the steep side of the pit, crying, 'Ah, you are treading on the flowers.'

'No,' said he, 'I am being very careful.'

They sat down together on a fallen tree at the bottom. She leaned forward, her fingers wandering white among the shadowed grey spaces of leaves, plucking, as if it were a rite, flowers here and there. He could not see her face.

'Don't you care for me?' he asked softly.

'You?'—she sat up and looked at him, and laughed strangely. 'You do not seem real to me,' she replied, in a strange voice.

For some time they sat thus, both bowed and silent. Birds 'skirred' off from the bushes, and Emily looked up with a great start as a quiet, sardonic voice said above us:

'A dove-cot, my eyes if it ain't! It struck me I 'eered a cooin', an' 'ere's th' birds. Come on, sweethearts, it's th' wrong place for billin' an' cooin', in th' middle o' these 'ere snowdrops. Let's 'ave yer names, come on.'

'Clear off, you fool!' answered Leslie from below, jumping up in anger.

We all four turned and looked at the keeper. He stood in the rim of light, darkly; fine, powerful form, menacing us. He did not move, but like some malicious Pan looked down on us and said:

'Very pretty—pretty! Two—and two makes four. 'Tis true, two and two makes four. Come on, come on out o' this 'ere bridal bed, an' let's 'ave a look at yer.'

'Can't you use your eyes, you fool,'·replied Leslie, standing up and helping Lettie with her furs. 'At any rate you can see there are ladies here.'

'Very sorry, Sir! You can't tell a lady from a woman at this distance at dusk. Who may you be, Sir?'

'Clear out! Come along, Lettie, you can't stay here now.'

> They climbed into the light.
>
> 'Oh, very sorry, Mr Tempest—when yer look down on a man he never looks the same. I thought it was some young fools come here dallyin'——'
>
> 'Damn you—shut up!' exclaimed Leslie—'I beg your pardon, Lettie. Will you have my arm?'
>
> They looked very elegant, the pair of them. Lettie was wearing a long coat which fitted close; she had a small hat whose feathers flushed straight back with her hair.
>
> The keeper looked at them. Then, smiling, he went down the dell with great strides, and returned, saying, 'Well, the lady might as well take her gloves.'
>
> She took them from him, shrinking to Leslie. Then she started, and said:
>
> 'Let me fetch my flowers.'
>
> She ran for the handful of snowdrops that lay among the roots of the trees. We all watched her.[3x]

Forster says little but he implies a good deal. Can we, by looking at this snowdrops episode, see what he may have had in mind? And can we also, by taking his tip of comparing the novels in the light of this passage, discover further connections?

In *The White Peacock* Lawrence organised his material by deploying elaborate codes of flower and animal symbolism, literary and cultural allusions, and name-games, which overlaid and perhaps at points interpenetrated the novel like an almost Joycean network of cross-reference; and these were techniques which facilitated the introduction and partial expression of certain compelling preoccupations. Later on in his novel-writing career, he was able to move straight to the kind of material which flower and other symbolism had obliquely introduced in that first novel.

The snowdrops simultaneously comprise a natural symbol and a self-consciously discussed symbol. The characters in the novel are actually made by the author to discuss the flowers as symbols, and at the same time the independent life of the flowers in this episode invests them with a representative naturalness by contrast with which the characters themselves are made to seem artificial or over-cultivated.

The discussion of the snowdrops' symbolism opens the topic of old lost religion. This is the central theme of *The Plumed Serpent*, and as is usual in Lawrence's novels, the highly conscious characters themselves discuss the theme. Ramon, for example, in explaining why he wants to revive the ancient Mexican religion, draws on the very same thoughts which the snowdrops have hinted at:

> So if I want Mexicans to learn the name of Quetzalcoatl, it is because I want them to speak with the tongues of their own blood. I wish the Teutonic world would once more think in terms of Thor and Wotan, and the tree Igdrasil. And I wish the Druidic world would see, honestly, that in the mistletoe is their mystery, and that they themselves are the Tuatha De Danaan, alive, but submerged.[4]

One can say that Ramon's gropings here gesture towards those alternatives to either Christianity or the variety of modern beliefs or non-beliefs which not only *The Plumed Serpent* itself but also, for example, *Etruscan Places*, *The Man Who Died*, and *Apocalypse* were Lawrence's attempts to explore. Forster's description of *The Plumed Serpent* in terms of this theme may well indicate that this was one of the things he had in mind when referring to the snowdrops.

Lettie's gathering a bunch of snowdrops simultaneously enacts her state of being cut off from natural life and her yearning to repossess it. But the subtler evocation of the possibilities of human nature lost to modern men and women is effected not through the snowdrops' symbolic associations but by the dramatic confrontation with the man who lives in the woods. The furs and feathers which (rather than, say, wool and silks) Lettie wears, as an elegant modern lady, enact the same artificiality and yearning for wild naturalness as her bunch of snowdrops, which becomes a final memento of her foray into nature; and the contrast is underlined by the gamekeeper's presence, in his own natural associations with fur and feathers, and his explicit sardonic distinction between lady and woman.

Both before this episode and subsequent to it, the keeper, Annable, has associated with him the words 'demon' and 'devil', which belong to Lawrence's cluster of thoughts about Pan, a god, though a god to be respected more than admired. Annable is later specifically designated 'a devil of the woods', and has already been vividly presented:

> 'Damned brute!' I ejaculated, bruising my knuckles against the fellow's jaw. Then I too found myself sitting dazedly on the

grass, watching the great skirts of his velveteens flinging round him as if he had been a demon, as he strode away.[5]

The heart of Lawrence's embryonic thought is given in the word Pan. In *The White Peacock* Annable is a multiple creation. Lawrence hasn't tried to make the idea of Pan and the figure of the gamekeeper one and the same, but 'Pan' has crept into his conception of this character. Annable in many ways seems outside Lawrence's control, although Lawrence got a lot into him and indeed probably got more into him than he would have if he had had him fully under imaginative control. The mystery of Lawrence's characteristic mode of creation is that he seemed to sink into the depths of his novel as he wrote and lose contact with its surface, and so find words for the unconscious impulses that were coming to him. *The White Peacock* is the work of a young genius who feels far greater pressure of material within him than he has capacity to create an adequate and proportionate vehicle for. His thoughts about Pan are still in embryo, and yet it is possible to see that when he comes fully to work them out and articulate them in 'Pan in America'[6] (January, 1926), they are essentially the same as in *The White Peacock*.

The contrast that we see in *The White Peacock* between Annable and the refined youngsters is the same contrast that is writ large in *The Plumed Serpent* between Mexico City (the representative of modern Mexican life) and the returning gods (in Mexico's equivalent of the woodlands). Forster's own sense of the denaturing effects of modern urban civilised life led him in his 1930 broadcast to identify the contrast in *The Plumed Serpent*:

> We begin in the filth and meanness of Mexico City, which seems to represent the whole country; then there is the hint of something else, of an inland lake of sweet waters, where the filth and meanness are not so much washed away as recomposed; and behind the lake, above the thunderclouds of horror and splendour, rise the shapes of the returning religion.

And further it may be that it was Forster's interest in the mythology of Pan that led him to juxtapose *The Plumed Serpent* and *The White Peacock*, so that following his hint we can see the parallels in the confrontation between the representative of Pan and representatives of modern civilised life, and the representatives of the old

Mexican religion and modern Mexico. And indeed the Indian Cipriano, the living manifestation of the ancient Mexican god Huitzilopochtli, has 'the face at once of a god and a devil, the undying Pan face'. Cipriano is a growth of the central embryonic features of Annable:

> As he sat in silence, casting the old, twilit Pan-power over her, she felt herself submitting, succumbing. He was once more the old dominant male, shadowy, intangible, looming suddenly tall, and covering the sky, making a darkness that was himself and nothing but himself, the Pan male. And she was swooned prone beneath, perfect in her proneness.
>
> It was the ancient phallic mystery, the ancient god-devil of the male Pan. Cipriano unyielding forever, in the ancient twilight, keeping the ancient twilight around him. She understood now his power with his soldiers. He had the old gift of demon-power.[7]

This quotation compels us to recollect that Lawrence's Pan figures cannot simply be considered on their own, and if we were to explore fully the connection Forster perceived we should need to examine the distinctive and strange marital history Lawrence (one wants to say) felt compelled to endow the gamekeeper with; and the ways in which Cipriano's marriage to Kate is a greatly transposed reworking of the same basic material. It would carry the present discussion inappropriately far from Forster's perception to take up the question why Lawrence wrote of Annable in this way, but we may extract from *The White Peacock* the narrator's significant confession: 'He treated me as an affectionate father treats a delicate son',[8] and juxtapose with it a paragraph from the sketch *Adolf*:

> But sometimes [my father] was happy, because of his long walk through the dewy fields in the first daybreak. He loved the open morning, the crystal and the space, after a night down pit. He watched every bird, every stir in the trembling grass, answered the whinnying of the pewits and tweeted to the wrens. If he could, he also would have whinnied and tweeted and whistled in a native language that was not human. He liked non-human things best.[9]

Finally we may gather into this context Jessie Chambers's striking comment on *The Plumed Serpent* made in 1933:

Lawrence did put something of himself into every character. I was particularly struck by this in the case of Kate in *The Plumed Serpent*. Obviously the figure is that of his wife, but every word she utters might have fallen from his own lips, and a good proportion of them from his mother's.[10]

Forster's vision has focused on a part of *The White Peacock* which is clearly a seed-bed for those later developments which are writ particularly large in *The Plumed Serpent*. It seems to me that Forster was justified in his cautious phrase 'in a sense he never developed', because he thereby draws attention to the fundamental and continuing problems on which Lawrence exercised his art, though it may also be that the defensive aspect of 'in a sense' concedes that Lawrence's drawing into consciousness, refocusing, and complete rearrangement of the proportions of his material might constitute something that could legitimately be called development. Without those little clues of language to which Forster has drawn our attention, we might easily not have identified the possibility that the Annable–Lady Crystabel and the Cipriano–Kate marriage are alternative handlings of the same basic material.

It is striking that Forster, alone of Lawrence's serious critics, judged *The Plumed Serpent* to be Lawrence's finest novel, and it may be that the reason can be unearthed by culling from Lawrence's letters two brief comments that he made about *A Passage to India*. He first read Forster's novel when he had half-drafted the first version of *The Plumed Serpent*:

> [23 July 1924] Am reading Passage to India. It's good, but makes one wish a bomb would fall and end everything. Life is more interesting in its undercurrents than in its obvious; and E. M. does see people, people and nothing but people: ad nauseam.[11]

And he was still speaking of the novel with enthusiasm some months later when he was on the point of returning to Mexico to complete his own novel in the winter of 1924–5:

> [3 Oct. 1924] I'm glad you like the Hopi Dance article. All races have one root, once one gets there. Many stems from one root: the stems never to commingle or 'understand' one another. I agree Forster doesn't 'understand' his Hindu. And India to him is just negative: because he doesn't go down to the root to meet it. But

the *Passage to India* interested me very much. At least the repudiation of our white bunk is genuine, sincere, and pretty thorough, it seems to me. Negative, yes. But King Charles *must* have his head off. Homage to the headsman.[12]

Forster's effort to handle the intermingling European and non-European consciousnesses in India may have clarified for Lawrence his problem of handling comparably different modes of consciousness in Mexico. And finally it may be that it was as a result of his creative labour in writing *A Passage to India* that Forster was enabled especially to appreciate Lawrence's.

19 The Naturalisation of Eden

Alan Wilde

Pan pandemic: not simply figured in Forster's work but, at least until his final disappearance, submerged throughout, visible in his effects. Variously a symbol, an emblem, presence or force, Pan is, as he begins his career in *The Celestial Omnibus*, above all an *idea* – the abstraction of desire, an urgency made conformable to the demands of consciousness. So it is, most notably, in 'The Curate's Friend'. That the relationship described in the story is homosexual seems to me even more likely today than it did when I first suggested it some fifteen years ago.[1] The clues, indeed, are everywhere: in the Faun's central act, which brings the curate to self-knowledge and thus to conversion and redemption by saving him from marriage; in the figure of the Faun himself, a peculiarly domestic creature, whom the curate, when he first sees him, takes for a man and who, when last referred to, is described as 'sitting before the beech copse as a man sits before his house';[2] and most of all, of course, in the curate's deliberate indirection, his resort, as he puts it, to 'the unworthy medium of a narrative': 'For if I breathed one word of that,' he explains, 'my present life . . . would come to an end . . . [and] I might find myself an expense to the nation' (p. 124). Shades of the poorhouse, or the madhouse? Certainly. But of the prison-house too. The year is 1907, the atmosphere still very much that of 'the love that dare not speak its name'. Homosexuality, however, is not the main point. The most revealing aspect of the story lies in the more general nature of the sexuality—or, rather, the lack of it—implied by the description of the curate's life. Briefly, what we are presented with is Forster's idea of homosexual love, an image of unconsummated perfection, of perfect innocence, of 'the comradeship, not passionate' that he was later to celebrate so passionately in *Howards End* (xxxiii, 265). We are, in other words, in Forster's oddly

theoretical and platonic version of Eden, where such accommodation as is achieved between the ideal and the real is made
possible by a process of exclusion. If sexuality is implied at all, it
must be seen as hovering over the curate and the Faun, disembodied
but somehow productive – productive because disembodied. But
it's probably more accurate to say that desire has been effectively
pre-empted by the consciousness of desire. Whatever else Forster's
tale disguises, its ideal of friendship is authentic; and along with the
values that ideal implies – awareness, stability, continuity, and
duration – it will continue to resonate through his work, though
more feebly as time passes, until the last page of *A Passage to India*.

The familial love of Margaret and Helen Schlegel apart, 'The
Curate's Friend' is probably the least compromised, that is, the most
idealised, expression of such a relationship in Forster's work. But if
we are to understand completely how Forster manages through his
Pan figures to intimate sexuality (largely, though by no means
exclusively, homosexuality) and at the same time to desexualise it,
we need to look to a different kind of relationship and to a different
sort of Pan: the disruptive figure who presides over 'The Story of a
Panic'. Despite Patricia Merivale's insistence, in her authoritative
study of the goat-god through the ages, on maintaining a 'rigorous
separation of fauns from Pans',[3x] it seems clear that the two are
second-cousins at least, implicated alike in the network of values
that determine the satiric perspective of *The Celestial Omnibus* and
spill over into the more ironic pre-war novels. But this is not to deny
differences. Forster's Faun is Arcadian and Orphic and, except for
one passing reference ('The great pagan figure of the Faun towered
insolently above them' [p. 121]), an altogether benign presence.
Generally, though, Pan and the forces cognate with him are, to use
Merivale's terms, less benevolent and more sinister. So, in 'The
Story of a Panic', the god reveals himself as an explosive force, a
sudden impact and violence, an astonishment. To Forster's villains,
he comes as a terrible vengeance, a rending of the accustomed social
fabric, but the terror, though intense, passes; convention and
restraint, temporarily shattered, reassemble untransformed. But for
those, like Eustace, who can hold their ground and absorb his
revelation, he erupts from the depths of a heretofore unknown and
mysterious world, calling forth from the depths of the self a response
not only to neglected nature but to a more radically neglected
desire. Whether or not, as at least one critic has suggested,
something homosexual attaches to Eustace's relationship with

Gennaro,[4x] this much can be said: the outward dispersal of the other characters in the story is matched by a far more profound, inward dispersal of Eustace's very being. Confronted by Pan's allness, the boy undergoes what we have to recognise as a psychic disintegration and a subsequent reintegration, from which he emerges, literally, remade; as, years later, Maurice hopes to be when he longs 'for the [hypnotic] trance, wherein his personality would melt and be subtly reformed' (M 209). And if Eustace's experience prefigures that of Forster's first overtly homosexual hero, it anticipates too that still later time when, the Edenic vision of allness lost, panic leads only to the scattering of the self's energies and beliefs and not to their reunification. But more of that later.

The most significant aspect of Eustace's encounter is that, in any real sense—and allowing for the fact that we are in the precincts of fantasy—it leads nowhere. The anomaly of 'The Curate's Friend' among the early stories is that it contrives an image of relationship achieved in this world.[5x] Except for 'The Road from Colonus', which records a defeat for its protagonist, the remaining tales end with their heroes and heroines in heaven, that is to say, in one or the other of those heterocosmic enclaves, the other kingdoms, that recurrently and paradoxically embody Forster's primitivist vision of natural and spontaneous feeling. Eustace, to be sure, is, as we last hear of him, only in flight, but no reader of *The Celestial Omnibus* can doubt his destination. Salvation is at hand, and one can hardly help noticing that the world, unchanged and presumably unchangeable, has been left all too emphatically behind. However we define the alteration in Eustace, then, whether in terms of sexuality or homosexuality, or, more generally, as the creation and release of compelling emotion, clearly Forster has once again elected to go the way of abstraction, providing his readers with no more than the blueprint of desire. Consequently, though so much more vital and energetic in spirit and conception than 'The Curate's Friend', 'The Story of a Panic' effectively, if unintentionally, makes the same point. If, through the agency of the Faun, relationship is spiritualised, through Pan's it is evaded altogether; and it may not be irrelevant to note that less violence attends the ambiguously related curate than does the solitary boy, for it seems to be the case that the more implicit the desire—the more disembodied and incapable of realisation—the more explosively Forster's imagination responds. In any case, whatever the difference in emotional resonance, both stories are dream work, longings of various but related kinds suspended in the conceptual embrace of consciousness.

It is Forster's fantasy that makes more or less acceptable the generally rather bloodless visions of relationship the stories project. The novels demand at least an effort to touch earth. How successfully is another matter. All of the aspects of Pan I've glanced at so far recur in the novels, most especially as they manifest themselves in the theme of friendship (Pan under the guise of the Faun) and in the disruptive impact of panic. Naturally enough, there are changes: friendship becomes, paradoxically, both more socially acceptable and demonstrable, and, for the reasons I've just suggested, more sexually charged; while the psychic dispersals of the theoretically stable self threaten ever greater visions of chaos, as they do, for example, to Helen Schlegel, whose panicky sexual en- counters, those 'chance collisions' and 'electrical discharge[s]' (HE iv, 22–3), stir her so deeply, briefly, and destructively. But as Helen's development makes clear, the Arcadian and Orphic Pan, pastoral god and emblem of the unity of all things, continues to hold an increasingly uncertain sway throughout the pre-war fiction. For Helen's moments of abandon, or rather the impulse behind them, are, however intense at the time, finally stilled in the all-resolving scene that concludes *Howards End* – the point being that, whatever else he may and does represent, Pan persists, even beyond *Howards End*, as Forster's symbol or myth of connection and co-ordination: the potential for harmony, integrity, and coherence in a disordered world. To be sure, this ultimately benign Pan is, with the passage of time, increasingly besieged by other, more vehement and sinister aspects of his ambiguous godhead. But at no little cost to the integrity of the novels, Forster maintains his allegiance; and until *A Passage to India*, Pan continues to function as the sign of that ideal and temperate world whose presence, substance, and significance Forster, with visibly increasing discomfort, hectically continues to affirm.

It would be supererogatory to pursue every goat-track in the fiction. Forster's readers and critics are familiar with Pan, and there's no need to do more than register the trajectory of his career. In *A Room with a View*, he appears twice, initially as 'the little god Pan' (vii, 69), who presides over Lucy's first kiss, and then, as the force behind the bathing scene, as something more like, if not quite, the great god. Pan's panics occur in Forster's fiction most often at picnics and outings but, in any case, at times when characters are freed from their accustomed settings; and it says something significant that the second outing is the more spontaneous and irregular of the two. Presumably, the novel's happy ending implies not only relationship but sexuality. The implication, however, is weak, and the mood of the book remains that of other kingdom: fantasy transformed here into fairytale. Odd though the connection sounds, Lucy and George resemble no two characters so much as they do the curate and his friend. Which is not to say that we are dealing again with covert homosexuality but to recognise that Forster's heterosexual relationships are at least congruous with and perhaps derive from his conception of homosexuality. As a preamble to the eventual marriage, Mr Emerson's windy discourse on love, comradeship, the body, and 'the holiness of direct desire' (xix, 204) serves only to present desire once more as something indirect and spiritual. Not passion but connection is the point: a static connection that is, for that very reason – and herein lies its value for Forster – enduring. By contrast, a dynamic and vital spirit informs the bathing scene,[6x] and if, as Forster says, its 'influence did not pass' (xii, 133), it is because the event itself does. Lucy and George, then, represent an ideal of coherence prescribed by consciousness; the bathers, an ideal of desire inscribed in memory, an ideal arrested, made eternal, like so many Forsterian moments, by the intensity of the feeling it generates. In either case, passion is cheated, thinned into friendship or disembodied in the abstraction of 'influence'.

Nevertheless, passion has been announced, however obliquely, and in *Where Angels Fear to Tread* and *The Longest Journey* its presence, if at certain levels still only implied, becomes more tangible. But this is perhaps to construe the matter too narrowly. In a broader sense, passionate living provides the theme, or rather the countertheme, of all three early novels. Besides lurking among Italian hills and English pinewoods in *A Room with a View*, Pan takes up residence, as it were, in Gino Carella and Stephen Wonham, bodying forth in them Forster's primitivist values: instinct, directness, involvement in life, and a rooted connection with the land. Stephen's association with Pan and panic is made overtly but, no less than he, Gino presents to Forster's protagonists – and to other characters in the novels – a vision of what they themselves are not. Philip and Rickie suffer from what I've called elsewhere the aesthetic view of life. (In the other novel the role devolves to Cecil Vyse.) Too conscious or ironic, seeing as from a distance all of life's intricate complexities, they stand on life's sidelines, imposing a spurious order on what they can neither control nor embrace. But at this point something odd becomes apparent. Both Stephen and Gino are filled with vitality and even, at times, with a kind of violent brutality, but neither in any way suggests sexuality. And yet the books resonate with sexual feelings of various kinds. Caroline's love for Gino, Agnes's for Gerald (that parody of Pan, for whom she confusedly mistakes Stephen at one point), and, at more submerged levels, Philip's and Rickie's for Gino and Stephen, all attest to the presence of desire in the two novels: desire thwarted or submerged. *A Room with a View* gives us our paradigm. In the bathing scene feeling flows, one-sidedly, from Mr Beebe to George, though George, like Eustace, is the one transformed by the dispersal of his gloomy silence. We are meant, of course, to focus on young Emerson's pursuit of Lucy, but in this scene at least, he serves as the *object* of desire. In the other two novels, the dynamics of unreciprocated feeling are clearer still. Gino and Stephen are, quite simply, the unmoved movers of the novels' heterosexual narratives (compare Stephen's shadowy wife) and of their homosexual sub-texts as well. Feeling, then, again travels in one direction, and, as it does so, it also moves away from the accustomed and familiar. Apart from Lucy and George, who seek an equality of character, a static union of two similar and like-minded people, Forster's characters increasingly search, even if their motivations remain unacknowledged, for what they are not, and if they are more than half in love with Pan, it is because he is, above all, *other*. More and more, they – and Forster with them – seek relationships that are unequal, indeed abrasive, as Pan, henceforth more sexual, alien, and terrifying, promises (as I've already suggested apropos of Maurice) nothing less, in the defeat of consciousness and self-consciousness, than a new self.

The most heartfelt wish in the three early novels may be Rickie's, when he longs for 'a kind of friendship office, where the marriage of true minds could be registered' (LJ (WC) vii, 74). At this point, he is thinking of his Cambridge friends, and the model is, in a manner of speaking, that of the curate and his Faun. Rickie's deluded and then miserable marriage to Agnes illustrates the Forsterian fatality of combining sex and love and, still more, of committing oneself to a continuing relationship. Only his love for Stephen—friendship invested with and thus subverted by sexual feeling—seems to promise that radical release from the confines of selfhood toward which Forster's panics seem, from the start, to gesture. Rickie fails (for reasons we needn't go into here), but the possibilities his career projects are explored – with his marriage replaced by Maurice's

response to society's expectations and pressures – in Forster's homosexual novel. Because *Maurice* presents Forster's polarities in an
almost schematic fashion and because I've recently written about
them,[7] I want to be brief here. The first relationship the book
describes, however homosexual in provenance, falls under the
heading of friendship, loving friendship perhaps, but hardly more
sexual than the curate's. Assuming an equality between the two
boys, it bases itself on such values as consistency, permanence,
affection, and calm. Thanks to Clive, it is controlled by consciousness and directed toward the goal of harmony. Thanks to Clive too,
it does not last; and however glowing Forster's dramatisation of it, at
least in its early stages, he is no longer willing to settle for platonic
raptures. And so Maurice's symbolic dream of 'a voice say[ing],
"That is your friend"' gives way, in the person of Clive's
gamekeeper, Alec Scudder, to his other dream of 'a nondescript
whose existence he resented' (M 22) – and to a relationship
motivated by inequality and opposition, difference and even
antagonism, struggle and finally psychic fusion. 'Physical love',
Forster writes in the wake of their most savage encounter, 'means
reaction, being panic in essence' (M 226). The remark is crucial to
an understanding of Maurice's development. Coming as it does
after the two men have slept together but before Maurice has
accepted not only Alec but himself, his homosexuality, and his
estrangement from society and its notion of class, it points directly to
Pan as the pivot of his relationship with Alec. If it was not clear
before, it is now, that panic means the disequilibriating of the
psyche, the scattering of consciousness and order, the opening of the
self to mystery and terror and to disruptive forces which begin but
do not end in sexuality. We have come, then, in many ways to a
climax, to a turning-point that seems to leave far behind the curate
and his Faun: the ideals and forms of friendship. But not quite. The
flight to the greenwood has to be read as Forster's final attempt to
bring together Maurice's two dreams, a stilling or eternalising of
sexual energy in yet another other kingdom. One last time desire
floats free of the earth. Something more is required to complete the
naturalisation of Pan and his panics.

That something more erupts in *A Passage to India*, though hints of
it are to be found in *Howards End*. Helen's awareness of panic and
emptiness follows hard on the first of her 'chance collisions': the brief
moment with Paul Wilcox, which fulfils for Helen 'that abandon-
ment of personality that is a possible prelude to love' (HE iv, 21). It

is Helen, of all the characters in the novel, who, through her night with Leonard, learns what 'panic in essence' means; but, as I've already suggested, the earlier, pastoral and primitivist Pan, though Forster nominally dismisses him ('Of Pan and the elemental forces the public has heard a little too much' [xiii, 106]), wins out over his more sinister brother and, in Margaret's vision of comradeship and connection, brings *Howards End* to a close that is about as convincing as *Maurice*'s in the greenwood. *Howards End* is, in other words, nearer in spirit and design to Forster's homosexual than to his Indian novel, and we may leave it to pursue panic and emptiness into the caves of *A Passage to India*, where they are ultimately raised to the level of metaphysical desolation. Adela's vision, to be sure, is not that profound, though it is destructive enough as its after-effects ramify through the Anglo-Indian community, causing a panic of a particularly ugly and nasty kind. Adela herself speaks primarily to the new urgency of physical love as reaction. Obviously, we are expected to recognise her experience as a response both to the 'spurious unity' (PI viii, 80) of her consciousness-dominated relationship with Ronny and to the presence of the more energetic and sexual Aziz. No longer the sign of connection, Pan has become a more exigent god, and Adela, incapable either of acknowledging desire or, apparently, of suppressing it altogether, gives in to her shattering fantasy of rape: Pan's vengeance on her habitual presumption of reasonable control. Mrs Moore, however, violates none of the god's injunctions, unless we are to believe that even the most flexible and comprehensive ordering of the world presumes against this new Pan's power to undermine the illusion of coherence. And apparently that is so, for Mrs Moore's vision is by far the more corrosive of the two. In apprehending Pan—and probably she sees him more directly than any of Forster's characters—she experiences his symbolic allness not as coherence but as chaos. Viewed metaphysically, Pan becomes the principle of an inclusiveness so total and so terrible that in it all meaning and all relationship are swallowed up. In the abyss of the caves and equally, though in a different way, in the Hindu ceremony, the classical, humanistic contours of Pan simply dissolve: the agent of dispersal is himself dispersed into the merely contiguous fragments of a universe in which 'Everything exists, nothing has value' (xiv, 140).

Against this ominous background the friendship of Fielding and Aziz is played out; and, as might be expected, the relationship differs as much from its remote progenitor in *The Celestial Ominibus* as the novel's panics do from their distant original in the same volume. As in *Maurice*, if I can make the comparison without intimating homosexuality, the attempt is to endow a relationship based on radical difference with a continuity Forster's universe will no longer sustain. Toward the end of 'Caves', during a conversation that, for the narrator as well as for the two men, turns on the question of friendship, Aziz refers to 'The Friend: a Persian expression for God' (xxxi, 265), and in doing so he foregrounds one of the novel's most suggestive 'rhythms'. Earlier, the sun, God's emblem, is described as 'not the unattainable friend . . . [but] merely a creature, like the rest, and so debarred from glory' (x, 106). Backward and forward, the comment throws a grim irony over the notion of friendship in the novel; but earlier still, another remark indicates specifically the nature of that irony. Speaking of a poem Aziz has just recited, the narrator says: 'it voiced our lone-liness . . . our isolation, our need for the Friend who never comes yet is not entirely disproved' (ix, 97). The structure of the final clause, the balanced poise of an unresolvable paradox, is our clue: first to the friendship, which if it does not altogether fail, yet cannot succeed—attainable, at best, 'not yet' and 'not there' (xxxvii, 312); and second to the vision of the novel itself. For if *A Passage to India* resists collapse under the pressure of the caves' awesome revelations, it is because Forster transforms the problematics of his novel into its aesthetic form. In other words, metaphysical panic generates in *A Passage to India* a formal perfection that arrests, even as it reveals, the novel's tensions and contradictory impulses. Distant as he has never before been, Forster neutralises the panic he means to explore, subsuming the paradoxes of the book to an irony so absolute as to direct the reader's attention, finally, away from mimetic depth and toward artistic surface in a triumph of reflexive design. But in the aesthetic coldness of Forster's gaze, Pan receives a mortal blow. Arcadian or Orphic, the Pan of friendship or of sexuality and desire conceived *sub specie amicitiae*, all are swallowed up by a panic that has become too sinister, too disruptive – disruptive, that is, in its power to disassemble the order that the earlier fiction demands. Henceforth, Forster looks to the discrete intensities of an incoherent world: the great God Pan is dead.

But in fact there is one instance of panic, referred to as such (LTC 164), among Forster's last stories in *The Life to Come*; and though it – or its cause – proves mortally destructive to the story's villain, Perpetua, the *virgo victrix* of 'The Torque', it is generative and redemptive for the rest of her family. Indeed, the farm over which she has held her increasingly sour sway becomes, after her death, 'a charmed spot' (p. 165), fecund, prosperous, and happy: altogether a more earthy, sexual, uninhibited vision than one finds in the other kingdoms of *The Celestial Omnibus*. But though the scene is in some sense a pastoral one again, it is not Pan, son of Hermes (*The Collected Tales* are dedicated to Hermes), who presides over the clucking, copulating animals and the hardly less sexually active Marcian, but a new god in Forster's pantheon.[8x] Behind the panic glows the mysterious torque, prolific and erotic, icon of Priapus, son of Dionysus, who gives life to the landscapes of *The Life to Come*. More or less directly, the stories pay repeated tribute to the Priapic symbol: the frequently self-sufficient and anonymous phallus that figures variously as the torque or the obelisk and at times appears more directly still as the sailor Tiny or, most notably, as the enlarging member of the statue in 'The Classical Annex'. In that minor and not altogether pleasant fantasy, a nude statue, 'a worthless late Roman work . . . represent[ing] an athlete or gladiator of the non-intellectual type' (p. 147)—or so he appears to the museum's curator—undergoes 'an obscene change' (p.148), which fashions him into the image of a Priapus; and as such, now strangely come alive, he rapes, or at any rate seduces, the curator's son. But that is not all. Later, making a timely sign of the cross, the curator freezes the Priapic gladiator and, inadvertently, his son back into a piece of statuary, which, under the name of 'The Wrestling Lesson', provides, inadvertently, a synthesising image for Forster's homosexual stories: an image of desire frozen into the simulacrum of passion, movement made irretrievably static.

As I've suggested in other essays, the homosexual stories of *The Life to Come*—or at any rate those in which desire is unimpeded by additional hungerings after love—celebrate sex for its own sake, dramatising a series of unconnected, virtually anonymous encounters: the electrical discharges of *Howards End* characterised approvingly here as 'the smaller pleasures of life' (p. 103).[9x] Thus, as Pan makes way for Priapus, there is a transformation in the nature of Forster's heroes—a reduction or minimalisation of what is individual in character; the long hoped-for remaking of the self attained at last. And there is, as well, a shift in the way they respond to experience. Count Waghaghren, the villain of 'What Does it Matter?', is a man 'unaccustomed to incidents without consequence' (p. 132), and the description hints obliquely at the

Priapic ethos of the sexual tales. For Forster's late figures are men unconcerned with consequences; and the stories explore and celebrate, precisely, a world without causality or sequence or depth. Unlike Pan, Priapus is not the means to achieving salvation but purely a force of intensification: the condition and justification of experience as an end in itself. Pan, as we've seen, disintegrates consciousness so as to reintegrate into its still controlling circumference the arc of desire. Priapus, on the other hand, concentrates desire to a burning point, heedless of what else, outside its narrow limits, is consumed in the flames. The naturalisation of other kingdom—of Eden or Arcadia—produces, then, a world of random, multiple, and fractured incidents: Mrs Moore's vision accepted and, more, celebrated. In the landscape of unmediated desire, everything exists, and though it is not true that nothing has value, still value is now a function of a Priapic assent to disconnection and to the unrelated, intermittent, and isolated pleasures it entails.

An odd and unexpected conclusion: to find emerging from the harsh and barren vision of the caves the careless, hectic figure of Priapus; to see materialising out of absence a presence so unforeseen. And odder still to see figured in the two gods a relation of apparently complete opposition—total innocence replaced by total experience, platonic love by unobstructed and fulfilled desire. This is to simplify, of course. I've tried to indicate throughout the ambiguous nature of Pan: disruption (panic) threatening the hegemony of consciousness and coherence (all). But even if we restrict ourselves to the extremes of Forster's career, it becomes clear that the conclusion is premature, that in the balancing of Pan and Priapus similarities in fact take precedence over differences. So, to return to a point I made earlier and to enlarge its scope: if the early stories express the need for love, the later ones for sex, still what is central to both is the idea: the *idea* of love, the *idea* of sexuality—'Maîtresses de l'âme, Idées'.[10] Confessedly auto-erotic, Forster's late stories, for all their often attractive exuberance, are curiously theoretical: amusing schemata of passion, which, because of their abstractness, qualify, in their comparatively decorous way, as at least quasi-pornographic. Furthermore, the early and late stores alike achieve their ends by a process of exclusion or substitution. Their apparently pulsing, sexual energy notwithstanding, the stories of *The Life to Come* are, in the final analysis, as reductive, static, and spatial in their conceptions as those earlier tales that hypostatise fantastic other kingdoms. In both cases, a world of insupportable density and facticity has been replaced by a more manageable, which is to say, a more abstract version of it. If Pan fails, it is because, at the last, he coerces into a supposititious coherence the energies he is meant to release; and if the landscape of Priapus disappoints, it is not because of the sexual activities of its inhabitants but because of their bloodless, unresonant twitchings. Forster's Pan and Priapus are, after all, brothers in deprivation: half-lives pretending pathetically to wholeness.

I don't mean, in tying together the ends of Forster's literary career, to deny change and development. But I do mean to stress an underlying continuity. Consciousness and desire, love and sexuality, the platonic and the violent – each half, though more or less separated out in the two collections of stories I've discussed, represents a strand of what Forster attempted, repeatedly but never with complete success, to entwine in the longer fiction. All the more ironic, then, that in a recent novel Forster is invoked to exemplify the oppressive continuation into the present of an earlier generation's certainties. 'There they all are, however', says the narrator of Renata Adler's *Speedboat*, 'the great dead men with their injunctions. Make it new. Only connect.'[11] But Forster is the novelist of connection sought, not achieved; and in that sense the spirit of Pan informs all of his work, even, by its absence, *The Life to Come*. For Priapus is, in one respect, no more than the looking-glass image of Pan: consciousness masquerading as desire, perfervidly seeking its own obliteration and, in the process, announcing its continued life. On the other side of panic, Forster's earthly paradise speaks of acceptance and assent, of passion, vigour, and sexuality, but the thinness of the dream belies its reality—if not the longing for it. Among the scattered bits of Forster's disconnected world, Pan is no longer a power making for connection, but he is, as the residual energy of the Priapic panic, a presence—a reminder that the meaning of Forster's work lies not in its unstable resolutions but in the intensity of its desperate search.

20 E. M. Forster, T. S. Eliot, and the 'Hymn Before Action'

G. K. Das

'Do you know anything about this Krishna business? . . . What I want to discover is its spiritual side, if it has one.'   (Fielding in *A Passage to India*)[1]

'I sometimes wonder if that is what Krishna meant . . .'
(T. S. Eliot, 'The Dry Salvages', III)

E. M. Forster and T. S. Eliot were both drawn to the Indian spiritual tradition, for both were concerned, against a background of the collapse of Christianity and the horror of the First World War, with a spiritual search drawing inspiration from other ancient sources of wisdom. If the teachings of Buddha and the *Upanishads* offered possibilities of meaningful life to the poet of *The Waste Land*, it was a vision of Krishna's birth that stimulated Forster to bring about a resolution of the horror and negation in *A Passage to India*.[2]

Some correspondences between *The Waste Land* and *A Passage to India* are indeed of a fundamental nature. The decay of western civilisation is at the basis of both works, and their common concern is with sterile human relations and the impossibility of fruitful action. Nothing fructifies in the Waste Land, where

> April is the cruellest month, breeding
> Lilacs out of the dead land . . .

and where one sees only sterile lust, the burning sun, and 'mountains of rock without water'. A picture of sterility also dominates the central part of *A Passage to India*. As a prelude to the crucial Marabar episode, where the moral undertone resembles that of 'The Fire Sermon' in *The Waste Land*,[3x] similar notes of aridity and horror are struck:

> April, herald of horrors, is at hand. The sun was returning to his kingdom with power but without beauty – that was the sinister feature. If only there had been beauty! His cruelty would have been tolerable then . . .   (x, 106)

In the Waste Land human relations are without roots, and take the shape of a meaningless encounter between the protagonist and Stetson, or an equally meaningless affair between a girl typist and a house agent's clerk; the atmosphere is one of nightmare, loneliness, loveless lust, and a haunting sense of futility. It will be seen that the atmosphere which domineers over the Europeans in *A Passage to India* is essentially similar. It is an atmosphere in which nothing materialises:

> Life went on as usual, but had no consequences, that is to say, sounds did not echo or thoughts develop. Everything seemed cut off at its root, and therefore infected with illusion . . . (xiv, 132)

Mrs Moore, Adela, Fielding – all experience an oppressive sense of nullity as they pursue their 'grail quest', and the expedition to the Marabar caves, like the journey to the Chapel Perilous, reveals nothing to the explorers but a terrifying echo and self-delusion. They, like the Wastelander amidst 'a heap of broken images', are struck by a sense of disharmony with the universe and their quest for a form and purpose in life is defeated by their Indian experience:

> . . . India fails to accommodate them. The annual helter-skelter of April, when irritability and lust spread like a canker, is one of her comments on the orderly hopes of humanity. Fish manage better: fish, as the tanks dry, wriggle into the mud and wait for the rains to uncake them. But men try to be harmonious all the year round and the results are occasionally disastrous. The triumphant machine of civilization may suddenly hitch and be immobilized into a car of stone, and at such moments the destiny of the English seems to resemble their predecessors', who also entered the country with intent to refashion it, but were in the end worked into its pattern and covered with its dust.(xxiv, 201)

A question of central importance which is asked in *The Waste Land* as well as *A Passage to India* is: how is one to act in a situation where all action seems fruitless, where, to use Forster's words, in a state of 'spiritual muddledom . . . we can neither act nor refrain from action'? (xxiii, 198) 'Shall I at least set my lands in order?' wonders the protagonist of *The Waste Land*, contemplating as it were the injuctions of the prophet Isaiah and also of Buddha,[4x] and he thinks that the course before him lies through ascetic self-control and through self-cultivation by acts of genuine kindness and sympathy: 'give, sympathise, control'. In visualising such a spiritual course Eliot was influenced partly by Buddha's doctrine of the eight-fold path,[5x] which advocates 'right effort towards self-control', and also partly by the thought of the *Brihadaranyaka Upanishad*, which, like Buddha's doctrine, pleads for enlightened self-control and sacrifice. As for Forster, there is similarly an attempt in *A Passage to India* to find answers to the question of right action in terms of Indian thought, but his attitude to Buddhist and Hindu doctrines as such remains, unlike Eliot's, essentially ambivalent. Faced with the impossible situation created by racial conflict and irrationality in Anglo-India, Mrs Moore is at one stage inclined to take the Buddhist position of a detached renouncer – 'I'll retire then into a cave of my own . . .' she says, 'Why has anything to be done . . . Why all this marriage, marriage? . . . The human race would have become a single person centuries ago if marriage was any use. And all this rubbish about love, love in a church, love in a cave, as if there is the least difference . . .' (xxii, 191–2). But Mrs Moore's is not the final word in the novel; her search for detachment and renunciation is juxtaposed with Fielding's desire for affection and passionate friendship – which, he believes, can destroy ir-rational barriers and fill the void in personal life. 'Why can't we be friends now?' he asks Aziz, holding him affectionately, 'It's what I want. It's what you want.' (xxxvii, 312) Against the notions of detachment and renunciation, Fielding's argument is for affirmation of spontaneous emotion and for action.

In their approaches to the Indian doctrine of action Forster and Eliot differ in two significant ways. First, although the philosophy of action is welcome to Forster in general, he is sceptical of disinteres-ted action, the central teaching of the *Bhagavad Gita* – a doctrine which is of fundamental importance to Eliot – and he sees that disinterested action can have little value without personal vision. Secondly, he is out of sympathy with Eliot's adherence to the

Buddhist (as well as Christian) belief in the relation between action and suffering – '. . . action is suffering/And suffering action';[6] 'Our only health is the disease . . . to be restored, our sickness must grow worse.'[7] Commenting on the Eliot of 'Little Gidding' he remarked: 'How I dislike his homage to pain! . . . It is here that Eliot becomes unsatisfactory as a seer, as Coventry does as a shrine.'[8]

To elucidate Forster's point concerning the relationship between action and vision one should look at his essay 'Hymn Before Action' (1912)[9] and in the light of it, analyse the theme with reference to some of the novels. The 'Hymn' is his own rendering of the dialogue between Krishna and Arjuna in the *Bhagavad Gita* on the question of right action. Different in outlook from Kipling's poem 'Hymn Before Action' (1896), which is only a spirited exhortation to imperial Britain to battle and a prayer for divine mercy and strength, Forster's piece emphasises the fact that, however strong the argument in favour of action as duty, it is impossible to act sensibly unless one is inspired by a personal vision. He analyses the situation in which Arjuna finds himself on the battleground of Kurukshetra in the *Mahabharata*. The battle is to be between kinsmen on either side; Arjuna stays his chariot in hesitation and despondency, unwilling to fight, and asks Krishna, his charioteer, 'Why should we not refrain?' Krishna gives him the reasons why he must fight, namely: (i) he should not hesitate to kill, because death is negligible, being merely a passage from one life to another; (ii) as a soldier it is his duty to fight; and (iii) what he should renounce is not action, but thoughts on the fruit of action. Krishna's argument, as abridged by Forster, is:

> The saint may renounce action, but the soldier, the citizen, the practical man generally – they should renounce not action, but its fruits. It is wrong for them to be idle; it is equally wrong to desire a reward for industry. It is wrong to shirk destroying civilization and one's kindred and friends, and equally wrong to hope for dominion afterwards. When all such hopes and desires are dead fear dies also, and freed from all attachments the 'dweller in the body' will remain calm while the body performs its daily duty, and will be unstained by sin, as is the lotus leaf by the water of the tank. It will attain to the eternal peace that is offered to the practical man as well as to the devotee.[10]

Forster sees that in the *Bhagavad Gita* Krishna's argument for disinterested action is necessarily followed by a vision which reveals to Arjuna, before he can actually proceed to action, the real glory and mystery of the universe embodied in Krishna. 'I have heard thy words of truth, but my soul is yearning to see: to see thy form as God of this all'[11] – pleads Arjuna, and it is only when he has a personal vision of universal reality and mystery that his delusion is over and he is inspired to act. Thus what Forster's 'Hymn Before Action' suggests is, I think, the importance of vision as an essential precondition to meaningful action.

Forster complained that Eliot in *The Waste Land* lacked a 'further vision' beyond horror. He remarked that Dostoievsky and Blake possessed such a vision, but Eliot, 'their equal in sensitiveness . . . is not a mystic . . . what he seeks is not revelation, but stability. Hence his approval of institutions deeply rooted in the State, such as the Anglican Church, hence the high premium he places upon statesmanship.'[12] In this context one can see why the doctrinal rather than the individualistic aspect of Hindu thought should have had more relevance for Eliot, while Forster looked for what lay behind doctrine, i.e. the individual vision and direct sense of the unseen in the Hindu way of life. Two years after 'Hymn Before Action' was written he turned to the subject once more to remark:

> The Hindu is concerned not with conduct, but with vision. To realise what God is seems more important than to do what God wants. He has a constant sense of the unseen – of the powers around if he is a peasant, of the power behind if he is a philosopher, and he feels that this tangible world, with its chatter of right and wrong, subserves the intangible. He can point to a Heaven where virtue is rewarded, and to a Hell where vice is punished, but he points without enthusiasm; to realise or not to realise, that is the question that interests him. Hinduism can pull itself to supply the human demand for Morality just as Protestantism at a pinch can meet the human desire for the infinite and the incomprehensible. But the effort is in neither case congenial.[13]

Following such a line of enquiry Forster comes to portray Hinduism under a more congenial aspect in *A Passage to India*, where one of his major aims is to express the futility of mindless action and to search for a meaningful vision of the life of the spirit. The Anglo-Indians ruling India live a life dedicated to work – 'I am out here to work . . .' says Ronny Heaslop (v, 44) – and Forster, in fact, while generally registering the collapse of the whole work ethic behind the Empire, portrays the City Magistrate's life of disinterested action rather sympathetically:

> He spoke sincerely. Every day he worked hard in the court trying to decide which of two untrue accounts was the less untrue, trying to dispense justice fearlessly, to protect the weak against the less weak, the incoherent against the plausible, surrounded by lies and flattery. That morning he had convicted a railway clerk of overcharging pilgrims for their tickets, and a Pathan of attempted rape. He expected no gratitude, no recognition for this, and both clerk and Pathan might appeal, bribe their witnesses more effectually in the interval, and get their sentences reversed. It was his duty . . .   (v, 44)

There is however a wider concern in the novel, which is to affirm, in terms of personal vision, a way of life more meaningful than mindless dedication to action. It is to introduce the spiritually impoverished Westerner, living inside the 'cocoon of work or social obligation' (xiv, 125), not to an Indian gospel, as Eliot does in *The Dry Salvages* ('I sometimes wonder if that is what Krishna meant/ . . . that is the one action . . . / Which shall fructify in the lives of others/And do not think of the fruit of action/Fare forward.') but to moments of self-releasing vision inspired by the Indian universe. Adela Quested has such an experience when at the time of her trial she sees in the Court the vision of the punkah-puller, 'the beautiful naked god', which enlarges her mind and enables her to perceive the truth. When she is asked whether Dr Aziz had actually followed her into one of the caves, her answer is delivered to her by way of an epiphany:

> Her vision was of several caves. She saw herself in one, and she was also outside it, watching its entrance, for Aziz to pass in. She failed to locate him. It was the doubt that had often visited her, but solid and attractive, like the hills, "I am not – " Speech was more difficult than vision. "I am not quite sure."   (xxiv, 217)

Similar moments of vision illumine the way for Fielding when shadows fall in his life. He worked for the good of Indians and Anglo-Indians, believing in education and without minding whom he taught: public school boys, mental defectives, policemen, Europeans and Indians. He was a success with his pupils, but the idea that the world 'is a globe of men who are trying to reach one another and can best do so by the help of good will plus culture and intelligence' (vii, 56) which inspired his social spirit, was 'a creed ill suited to Chandrapore'. The Marabar incident and the blind racial tensions that followed brought him to a point of crisis. He was haunted by a sense of the futility of all his actions and wondered in loneliness 'whether he was really and truly successful as a human being'. At this stage his mind is nourished momentarily into health by a vision of the Marabar Hills:

> . . . to cool himself and regain mental balance he went on to the upper verandah for a moment, where the first object he saw was the Marabar Hills. At this distance and hour they leapt into beauty; they were Monsalvat, Walhalla, the towers of a cathedral, peopled with saints and heroes, and covered with flowers . . . It was the last moment of the light, and as he gazed at the Marabar Hills they seemed to move graciously towards him like a queen, and their charm became the sky's. At the moment they vanished they were everywhere, the cool benediction of the night descended, the stars sparkled, and the whole universe was a hill . . . (xx, 181)

Forster's emphasis on the need for vision is a seminal point in his earlier work also. It appears in his use of fantasy in the short stories; *Where Angels Fear to Tread* (the very title is suggestive) is an indictment of mindless action; Rickie Elliot's tragedy in *The Longest Journey* is his failure to resolve the conflict between his own predisposition to vision and his admiration of men and women of practical action ('Who wants visions in a world that has Agnes and Gerald?')[14]; in *Howards End*, the need to connect outer with inner life is the central issue. The need for vision, as a spiritual need, is nowhere, however, presented more searchingly than in *A Passage to India*, where Forster's perception of the horror and the void in personal life is at its sharpest.

As I indicated at the beginning of this essay, both Eliot and Forster were trying to communicate that horror, and its possible resolutions, in terms of their discovery of India. In Eliot's case India was not a direct experience and its interest for him remained a matter of the intellect. But for Forster it was a revelation of the most profound kind. Eliot was particularly attracted by one aspect of the wisdom of its seers of the past, namely, the wisdom of 'action'. To Forster India unfolded actual visions of darkness (as did the Congo to Conrad) and of light, as was revealed to Arjuna by Krishna on the battlefield of Kurukshetra. It gave him vivid glimpses of the unseen, which the symbolism in the 'Temple' section of *A Passage to India* so powerfully captures; it also reinforced his belief in the value of 'seeing' – particularly when the mind acts foolishly, or is unable to act.

21 Forster and Virginia Woolf: the Critical Friends

H. K. Trivedi

In terms of personal relationship, E. M. Forster was probably closer to Virginia Woolf than to any other contemporary novelist of comparable stature. His friendship with her spanned just over three decades, from about 1910 to the suicide of Virginia Woolf in 1941, and the congeniality and affection which existed between them is vividly suggested by a number of little incidents described in the autobiographical or biographical publications relating to them which have been appearing recently.[1x] For instance, on a visit to Cambridge in 1915, Virginia Woolf found Forster spending his time in 'rowing old ladies upon the river' (Bell II, 29) and somewhat solicitously associated this with the fact that he was not able to get on with his novel (eventually *A Passage to India*). In 1919, on being asked to come down to the Woolfs' cottage in Sussex for a weekend, Forster candidly explained, according to her (Diary I, 295), that he would do so if they paid his fare, for he had at the time only £26 left in the bank. When he did pay this visit a month later, the indigent Forster sold to Virginia Woolf a page from his manuscript of 'Old Lucy', an earlier version of *A Room with a View*, for the sum of 2s. 6d. (Incidentally, this page was recently re-sold at Sotheby's for over a thousand times the original price.[2]) In 1928, again during a weekend visit by Forster to the Woolfs in Sussex, 'we got drunk and talked of sodomy and sapphism, with emotion – so much so that next day he [Forster] said he had been drunk' (Bell II, 138). And again at the same house, in 1940, Forster got his trousers burnt one freezing winter night by getting too close to the 'Cosy Stove' in his bedroom, and promptly wrote a little poem to celebrate the incident: 'O hearth benign! O decent glow! . . . ' etc. (Bell II, 213n.).

Such warm intimacy between Forster and Virginia Woolf existed, of course, within the context of a larger circle of common friends, the Bloomsbury Group. In fact, Forster came to Virginia Woolf through his induction into Bloomsbury, and to Bloomsbury through 'the Apostles', a secret and select society at Cambridge to which he had been admitted in 1899, and of which nearly all the young men who later with Vanessa and Virginia Stephen formed the nucleus of Bloomsbury had also been members. Thus it was that Forster's friendship with Virginia Woolf's husband, Leonard, was at least as close as with her and even older, for they had been Apostles together at Cambridge long before Forster, or for that matter Leonard, had met Virginia.

On the other hand, a special bond that existed only between Virginia Woolf and Forster among all the variously talented members of the Bloomsbury Group was that they were fellow-novelists. Indeed, in her vivid recollection of Forster's entry into Bloomsbury in the year 1910, Virginia Woolf referred to the fact of his being a novelist as a major cause of her immediate fascination with him:

> And once at least Morgan flitted through Bloomsbury lodging for a moment in Fitzroy Square on his way even then to catch a train. . . . I felt as if a butterfly – by preference a pale blue butterfly – had settled on the sofa: if one raised a finger or made a movement the butterfly would be off. He talked of Italy and the Working Men's College. And I listened – with the deepest curiosity, for he was the only novelist I knew – except Henry James and George Meredith; the only one anyhow who wrote about people like ourselves. But I was too much afraid of raising my hand and making the butterfly fly away to say much.
>
> (*Moments* 176)

This initial impression of Virginia Woolf that Forster was like a butterfly – as attractive and as elusive – in fact became a recurrent image in her descriptions of him, coming to symbolise for her the essence of his personality. 'I met Morgan Forster on the platform at Waterloo yesterday,' she recorded on 12 July 1919, 'a man physically resembling a blue butterfly – I mean by that to describe his transparency and lightness. . . . I like Forster very much . . . ' (*Diary* I 291). And again, when Forster came to dinner with her about a fortnight later, she wrote:

> He is an unworldly, transparent character, whimsical &

detached. . . . He is fantastic & very sensitive; an attractive character to me, though from his very qualities it takes as long to know him as it used to take to put one's gallipot over a humming bird moth.[3x] More truly, he resembles a vaguely rambling butterfly; since there is no intensity or rapidity about him.

(Diary I, 294)

Forster seems in turn to have had his own image for Virginia Woolf. Oliver Stallybrass, editor of the Abinger Edition of Forster, tells me that during December 1929 or January 1930 he wrote in his Commonplace Book:

Visit to Virginia, prospects of, not wholly pleasurable. I shall watch her curiosity and flattery exhaust themselves in turn. Nor does it do to rally the Pythoness.[4]

In his regard for Virginia Woolf, apparently, Forster conformed to her expectation of him as somebody who, while reciprocating a feeling of attraction and affection, would at the same time be more at his ease keeping a little distance from her. It was not only that Forster himself was by temperament 'strange, elusive, evasive', with 'something flitting and discontinuous about him';[5] he probably found Virginia Woolf to be a formidable and somewhat daunting person in her own right, a Delphic priestess rather than the kind of young woman he would have felt most comfortable with. 'I don't think that she cared for most people', he was later to tell Virginia Woolf's biographer, Quentin Bell. 'She was always very sweet to me, but I don't think she was particularly fond of me, if that's the word' (Bell II, 133). His caution at the time of publication of *Aspects of the Novel* is betrayed in a letter of 2 September 1927 to his editor at Edward Arnold, Brian Fagan, in which he records his decision

not to send Mrs Woolf the uncorrected proofs for a small private reason; they contain a criticism of her own work which I have modified in the revise!!   (Introd., AN p. xiii)

For her own part, Virginia Woolf pointed to another fundamental difference between them when she recorded in her diary in 1919: ' . . . I always feel him shrinking sensitively from me, as a woman, a clever woman, an up to date woman' (Diary I, 262). Forster was, indeed, generally happier with his own sex, even as many of the closest friends of Virginia Woolf throughout her life were women, for example Madge Vaughan, Violet Dickinson, Katherine Mansfield, Ethel Smythe, and last but not least, Vita Sackville-West. Virginia Woolf's pronounced feminism would have only further aggravated Forster's unease.

Thus, while Virginia Woolf rightly had the feeling that if she as much as moved a finger, the butterfly that was Forster would be off, Forster, too, had reason to shrink away from her and her ensnaring gallipot. A strong and instinctive attraction towards the other, tempered by a constant wariness of each other, seems to have been the emotional keynote of their relationship.

II

When they came to know each other in 1910, Forster already had four novels behind him, while Virginia Woolf had barely begun her first. She naturally looked up to him, therefore, as a wise elder, an attitude which later made her hang on with some anxiety and enormous respect to whatever verdict he let fall on each of her books as they appeared. Even when he was the only one among her friends to give an adverse judgement on her second novel, *Night and Day* (1919), she acknowledged that she 'value[d] Morgan's opinion as much as anybodies (*sic*)' (Diary I, 307). When, a few days later, she had clarified with Forster precisely what he found to be wrong with the book, she generously added:

> Morgan has the artist's mind; he says the simple things that clever people don't say: I find him the best of critics for that reason.
> (Diary I, 310–11)

He remained the one friend whose opinion of each of her successive books she most keenly awaited, dreading his censure as much as she cherished his praise. Upon the publication of her next novel, *Jacob's Room* (1922), 'the letter I've liked most of all' was from Forster (AWD, 54), and when he wrote admiring *Mrs Dalloway* (1925), it was 'a weight off my mind' (AWD, 77). It was 'a little ominous' that Forster would not review her feminist book *A Room of One's Own* (1929) (AWD, 148), but his letter about *The Waves* (1931) pleased Virginia Woolf so much that she even copied out a few lines from it in her diary, and added:

I daresay that gives me more substantial pleasure than any letter
I've had about any book. Yes, I think it does, coming from
Morgan.   (AWD 176)

Later in the 1930s, when severely attacked by the *Scrutiny* and
Wyndham Lewis and others, she could 'balance' the criticism by
pitting against it the praise conferred by Yeats and Lowes Dickinson
and Forster (AWD, 231). In 1936, when driven to despair by her
intractable next novel *The Years* (1937), and assailed by serious
doubts whether it was even worth publishing, she somehow carried
on with it, telling herself: 'when it is done, we can always ask
Morgan' (AWD, 272).

But the dread anxiety with which she awaited Forster's verdict on
her books throughout her life is most acutely illustrated in her diary
entries relating to *Roger Fry* (1940), the last of her books to be
published in her lifetime. On 25 July 1940, the day of the
publication, she wrote: 'I shall be relieved if Morgan approves.
That I suppose I shall know tomorrow.' But the next day, she found
'No Morgan'. A week later, 'No review by Morgan: no review at all.
No letter.' She suspected he had refused to review the book, 'finding
it unpalatable'. Ten days after publication, all the friends and
reviewers had given their opinions: 'now only Morgan remains.'
Finally, six days later, Forster's review did appear. 'And then,
Morgan slightly damped me' (AWD, 339–41).

All this seems fully to bear out not only Quentin Bell's
observation that 'Forster was the English contemporary for whom
she had most respect' (Bell II, 132–3), but also the rather more
acutely worded impression of Forster's biographer, P. N. Furbank,
that 'she feared and respected his literary judgment more than
anyone else's.'[6]

Forster, on the other hand, had not much to fear at the hands of
Virginia Woolf if only for the fact already noted that four out of the
five novels of his published in his lifetime had already appeared
when he came to know her. However, the regard in which he held
both Virginia and Leonard Woolf, and the trust which he reposed in
their literary judgement, are evident from the fact that during the
long years when *A Passage to India* hung fire, he shared his problems
with them (see Diary I, 311), as he presumably did not with many
others. And, in January 1924, it was Virginia Woolf whom he
informed before he did any one else that he had at last finished this
book, a distinction by which she was suitably touched (Bell II, 133).

III

Apart from what they had to say about each other's works privately in letters and diaries, both Forster and Virginia Woolf had several occasions to appraise the other in public. To take first Virginia Woolf's published criticism of Forster, she had already reviewed, anonymously in the *Times Literary Supplement*, his third novel, *A Room with a View* (1908), before she knew him personally. Compared to her two later essays on Forster, this review is somewhat perfunctory and uninspired, though, interestingly, it arrives at a verdict quite similar to that expressed in her later, longer essays on him. While she recognised in this novel 'that odd sense of freedom which books give us when they seem to represent the world as we see it, . . . the sense that one sees truth from falsehood', and while she spoke admiringly of 'the cleverness, the sheer fun, the occasional beauty' of the book, she was in the end 'conscious of some disappointment'. For all its 'originality and observation', the novel somehow did not seem to her to fulfil its promise: 'the view is smaller than we expected.'[7]

Notwithstanding her partial disappointment with him here, Virginia Woolf made significant mention of Forster some years later in perhaps the most important and best-known of all her discussions of contemporary fiction, 'Mr. Bennett and Mrs. Brown' (1924). Counting him as one of her allies, she lined him up alongside D. H. Lawrence, Lytton Strachey, James Joyce, T. S. Eliot, and (implicitly) herself, as the 'Georgian' writers, whom she saw as challenging and demolishing the conventional vision and moribund techniques of the preceding generation, labelled by her the 'Edwardians', of whom she named H. G. Wells, Arnold Bennett, and John Galsworthy as the most important. However, while she went on later in this essay to comment at some length on the works of Strachey, Joyce and Eliot, she referred to Forster (as to Lawrence) only once more, and that to say that both had 'spoilt their early work because, instead of throwing away those [i.e., the 'Edwardian'] tools, they tried to use them. They tried to compromise' (Essays I, 333).

But the fullest statement of Virginia Woolf's views on Forster is to be found in two essays on him which she published within a month of each other three years later, in 1927. The occasion for these seems to have been the appearance of *Aspects of the Novel*, delivered as the Clark lectures at Cambridge in the Spring of 1927, and published on

20 October the same year. The first of Virginia Woolf's two essays was, in fact, a review of *Aspects*, the second a retrospective survey of all his fiction published to date.

In both these essays, Virginia Woolf's evaluation of Forster was distinctly critical. Indeed, some of her observations here led to an exchange of fairly sharply worded letters between them, in which both seem to have discovered that their differences were hardly reconcilable, and which concluded with Virginia Woolf fearing that she had 'hurt or annoyed' Forster (Bell II, 135) – as she had, at the beginning of one of these essays, 'The Novels of E. M. Forster', suspected she might (Essays I, 342).

The main thrust of Virginia Woolf's criticism in this essay was that Forster had in his novels attempted to blend two fundamentally different ways of perceiving and depicting reality, and had failed. Throughout her essay, Virginia Woolf described this unresolved duality in various terms and from many angles, but, basically, the 'ambiguity' to which she was here pointing may be summed up as that between the naturalistic and the symbolic modes of representing reality. On the one hand, she said, Forster was a comic satirist and 'among the descendants of Jane Austen and Peacock'; his old maids and clerical characters were, indeed, 'the most life-like we have had since Jane Austen laid down the pen'. Thus, social historians of the future were likely to find his earlier novels 'full of illuminating information' about such matters as precisely when young women began to ride bicycles, or how regularly maids cleaned drawing-rooms in the year 1905, or the manner in which they took off their gloves. Beyond the originality and cleverness of such observation, however, there was also something finer and more spiritual in Forster's fiction. The mass of keenly observed realistic details had a 'burning core', she said: 'It is the soul; it is reality; it is truth; it is poetry; it is love . . . ' Always in his novels, therefore, the immediate had a counterpoint in the remote, the appearance in the truth, the prosaic in the poetic. 'Sawston implies Italy; timidity, wildness; convention, freedom; unreality, reality' (Essays I, 342–4).

This 'double vision' (Essays I, 351) had come about, Virginia Woolf explained, because Forster's numerous gifts as a novelist were not mutually subservient and harmonious but, rather, a 'contradictory assortment' (Essays I, 348). His greatest problem as an artist seemed to her to be to fuse together the various contrary elements of his temperament: 'satire and sympathy; fantasy and fact; poetry and a prim moral sense.' Forster himself seemed fully aware, she noted, of this rift and of the need to close it, when he spoke of the desirability of the 'rainbow bridge that should connect the prose in us with the passion' (quoted by her, Essays I, 344).

But in Virginia Woolf's final judgement this discord at the centre of Forster's fiction remained unresolved, and his attempt to bridge the various sets of opposites enumerated by her was a failure. In his first three novels the resultant discrepancies were obvious and sharp, and his attempts at reconciling them crude and unconvincing. In *Howards End* and *A Passage to India*, however, it seemed as if Forster had at last chosen to write of subjects which lent themselves to his dualistic treatment. But even here, she thought, he had failed to achieve perfect harmony. She granted that he had now relaxed his constant care to place his characters within a rigid framework, and that it had helped him to move away from Sawston and 'beyond the influence of Cambridge' to a 'bigger and more sinister background' in *A Passage to India*. But there still persisted in this last novel 'moments of imperfect symbolism, [and] a greater accumulation of facts than the imagination is able to deal with', so that while the double vision of the earlier novels was now 'in the process of becoming single', it had not yet become so. In conclusion, Virginia Woolf said that the fact that Forster had 'almost achieved' the great feat of illuminating 'this dense, compact body of observations with a spiritual light' made one wonder: 'What will he write next?' (Essays I, 350–1).

Virginia Woolf's speculative question remained, of course, unanswered, for Forster published no more novels. By implication, therefore, Forster's career as a novelist seems to have come to an end just at the point when Virginia Woolf had begun to see great possibilities in him. Her last word on him was typically of guarded optimism, rather than indicative of any personal affinity or even acclaim.

More significant than what Virginia Woolf directly said about Forster in this essay, however – and also more derogatory to him from her own point of view – is a series of images which she repeatedly used to describe his fiction, in the impressionistic manner which is characteristic of her criticism generally. It is remarkable that she described the predominant 'realism' of Forster here in precisely the same images which she had earlier used to debunk the 'materialism' of her chief adversary among the 'Edwardian' novelists, Arnold Bennett, that is, in terms of bricks and mortar. In her analysis (in 'Mr. Bennett and Mrs. Brown') of Bennett's characteristic mode of writing fiction, Virginia Woolf had taken up the first few pages of his novel *Hilda Lessways* to demonstrate how heavily he relied on bricks and mortar in order to achieve a semblance of reality in his created world. The opening pages of this novel, she had said, constantly dinned into the reader the impression that Hilda, the heroine, 'not only looked at houses, and thought of houses, [but also] . . . lived in a house'! Virginia Woolf had gone on to allege that Bennett was here 'trying to hypnotize us into the belief that, because he has made a house, there must be a person living there' (Essays I, 329–30).

This same preoccupation with houses, in the sense of concrete external shells which had little to do with the inner truth of human beings, she also found in Forster. There was less of fantasy in Forster's second novel, *The Longest Journey*, than in the first, *Where Angels Fear to Tread*, she adjudged, because in the former Forster had built 'his Sawston of thicker bricks' (Essays I, 344). Similarly, the rainbow bridge by which Forster sought to connect the prose with the passion was desirable because his true business, Virginia Woolf felt, was not 'to build in brick and mortar, but to draw together the seen and the unseen' (Essays I, 345). Yet, even though Forster seemed to believe that it was the soul that mattered, the soul remained in his novels 'caged in a solid villa of red brick somewhere in the suburbs of London' (Essays I, 346). If Forster was to succeed in conveying to us his vision it was necessary, Virginia Woolf prescribed, that 'his reality must at certain points become irradiated; his brick must be lit up; we must see the whole building saturated with light' (Essays I, 346). But this Forster had failed to do, 'chiefly because that admirable gift of his for observation has served him too well. He has recorded too much, and too literally' (Essays I, 347). Even in his last novel, *A Passage to India*, the same method predominated. Here, too, Virginia Woolf found,

> The attitude is precisely the same four-square attitude which walks up to life as if it were a house with a front door, puts its hat on the table in the hall, and proceeds to visit all the rooms in an orderly manner. (Essays I, 350)

It would appear, then, that though Virginia Woolf had enlisted Forster among fellow-'Georgians', she in fact found him to be a bird of the same feather as the arch-'Edwardian', Arnold Bennett. The whole crux of Virginia Woolf's criticism of Forster as a novelist can be seen, in fact, to relate directly to the broader discussion of the 'materialist' and the 'spiritual' modes of writing fiction which she had put at the centre of her polemical essay 'Mr. Bennett and Mrs. Brown'.

Not surprisingly, some of the same issues came up again in Virginia Woolf's review of *Aspects of the Novel*, and in the private correspondence between Forster and herself which followed it. In her opinion, Forster had in *Aspects* laid too great an emphasis on something he called 'life', and grossly neglected to consider some other, higher 'aesthetic functions' of the novel (Essays II, 54). In his 'notably harsh judgement' of Henry James, for instance, Forster had undervalued the virtues of 'pattern' in his novels, denounced 'pattern' as being inimical to humanity, and had even proceeded to declare that '[m]ost of human life has to disappear before he [James] can do us a novel.' Controverting this, Virginia Woolf asked Forster: 'what is this "life" . . . ? Why is it absent in a pattern and present in a tea-party?' Why was the pleasure that a reader derived from the pattern of *The Golden Bowl* 'less valuable', she asked, than the pleasure he derived from Trollope's description of a tea-party in a parsonage? 'Surely the definition of life is too arbitrary', she suggested to Forster, 'and requires to be expanded' (Essays II, 53). Besides, there was also the crucial question of precisely how 'life', whatever its definition, was best depicted in novels. Forster, she said, regarded fiction as 'a parasite which draws sustenance from life and must in gratitude resemble life or perish.' According to him, she mocked, novelists 'must first and foremost hold themselves at the service of the tea-pot and the pug-dog' (Essays II, 54).

A direct resemblance between Virginia Woolf's remarks here and her criticism of the 'Edwardians' in her essays 'Modern Fiction' and 'Mr. Bennett and Mrs. Brown' can again be clearly perceived. Just as she challenged Forster's 'definition of life' here, she had earlier demanded of the 'Edwardians', 'Is life like this? Must novels be like this?', and proceeded to show them an utterly different and finer perception of life: 'Look within, and life, it seems, is very far from being "like this"' (Essays II, 106). Forster, as well as the 'Edwardians', appeared to her to share the assumption that a realistic depiction of life had somehow a greater element of humanity in it than any more sophisticated or less direct method, such as that of Henry James. He seemed to think that Trollope had more 'life' than James; Arnold Bennett, similarly, had claimed – or so Virginia Woolf alleged – that he 'possess[ed] more "life"' than she did (AWD 161). To persuade the reader of the truth of their characters, the 'Edwardian' novelists, she had said, described in minute detail the material appurtenances of those characters: their houses, their servants, their hot-water bottles (Essays I, 333). Forster's deference to the tea-pot and the pug-dog was of the same order in her eyes, evidently.

IV

All this serves merely to strengthen the suspicion that, though Virginia Woolf had named Forster as one of the 'Georgians' when marshalling the combatants in 'Mr. Bennett and Mrs. Brown', her detailed analysis of his works makes him out to be really more of an 'Edwardian', both in practice and in precept. This considerable divergence of creed between them is equally reflected, in fact, in the many reservations which Forster, on his part, felt about both the method and the achievement of Virginia Woolf as a novelist. But before turning to the two essays which Forster published on Virginia Woolf (besides less significant reviews of four of her minor works), it may be appropriate to look briefly at his comments on her in *Aspects of the Novel*, which, though sketchy, have had a notable influence on the later criticism of her fiction.

In the first 'Introductory' chapter of *Aspects*, Forster brilliantly juxtaposed short passages from three pairs of novelists – Richardson and James, Dickens and Wells, and Sterne and Virginia Woolf – to prove his point that writers vastly distant from each other in time may still look at life from broadly the same point of view. (Incidentally, in her review of *Aspects*, Virginia Woolf had commented on the yoking together of Richardson with James and of Dickens with Wells, but had refrained from mentioning Forster's third pair with a scrupulousness which seems as self-conscious as it must have been modest.) The original critical insight which Forster displayed here in comparing Virginia Woolf to Sterne has been followed up by some more recent critics, notably Walter Allen and Robert Curtis Brown, not only to elucidate the stream-of-consciousness technique as Virginia Woolf used it but also, retrospectively, to illuminate Sterne's method as a novelist.[8x]

Elsewhere, however, Forster seemed to perceive less acutely the peculiar qualities of Virginia Woolf as a novelist. In both his essays on her, the first published in 1925 and the second delivered as the Rede lecture in Cambridge a few months after her death in 1941, he offered carefully qualified praise and seemed unwilling to confront some of the major aspects of her work at all. At the beginning of his first essay, he made much of the fact that his pen had disappeared when he had sat down to write about her. He himself thought it 'profoundly characteristic of the art of Virginia Woolf': 'So near, and yet so far!' (AH (1936) 104). One may also, perhaps, think it symptomatic in a Freudian way of his reluctance to write about her. In any case, even when Forster was reunited with his pen, he did not, in the judgement of one of his more sympathetic critics, Lionel Trilling, 'succeed in bringing the art of Virginia Woolf nearer'. In his other, final estimate of Virginia Woolf, which was virtually an obituary tribute, Forster, as an old friend, could have been expected to err on the side of generosity, yet the main strength of his criticism here, again according to Trilling, is that 'it does not try to praise too much.'[9]

In this long essay, Forster devoted no less attention and space to Virginia Woolf's 'problems' and 'dangers' than he did to her achievement. She had 'all the aesthete's characteristics', but had somehow just escaped her obvious and calamitous pitfall – 'the Palace of Art, . . . that bottomless chasm of dullness, . . . really a dreadful hole into which the unwary aesthete may tumble, to be seen no more' (TCD 240). Yet, in the end, Forster found in her books both an ornate preciousness and a lack of stature: 'it is as a row of little silver cups that I see her work gleaming' (TCD 252).[10x] He talked at some length, and with patent distaste, of her feminism, holding it 'responsible for the worst of her books – the cantankerous *Three Guineas*' (TCD 249); he also pointed out that she was 'not only a woman but a lady' and that the consciousness of this fact on her part had given 'a further twist to her social outlook' (TCD 251). As for her novels, he disposed of the whole development of Virginia Woolf in her nine novels from *The Voyage Out* (1915) to *Between the Acts* (1941) in the space of just over two pages in an essay which runs (in the Abinger edition) to fifteen. Later, as if he were happier doodling in the margin than concentrating squarely on the central preoccupations of her work, he expatiated for over a page on the passages in Virginia Woolf's novels in which she describes food. 'They are invariably good', he said unstintingly (TCD 246), but just how relevant this eulogy was to the strictly literary merits of Virginia Woolf's works is perhaps indicated by the fact that this passage was later culled from Forster's essay and reprinted under the title 'Virginia Woolf's Enlightened Greediness' in the trade magazine *Wine and Food* (spring 1943, 60–1)!

As for her fiction, Forster described the first short stories in her experimental method, 'Kew Gardens' and 'The Mark on the Wall', as 'lovely little things' which, however, 'seemed to lead nowhere', and *Mrs. Dalloway* as 'a civilized book . . . written from personal experience'. This may be construed as an uncharitable suggestion if, besides the primary reference to Virginia Woolf's personal experiences of madness described in this book, an identification is also implied between the snobbish and somewhat shallow Clarissa Dalloway and her authoress. *To the Lighthouse*, however, was 'a much greater achievement' and his own personal favourite among her novels, he said, not so much because of its symbolism or remarkable structure, which he does not seem to have particularly noticed, but 'partly because the chief characters in it, Mr. and Mrs. Ramsay, are so interesting' (TCD 242-3).

It was in his comments on *The Waves*, the most experimental as well as perhaps the most quintessential of all Virginia Woolf's novels, that Forster again underlined the basic differences between himself and her. Reviving a term which had been at the centre of their quarrel following her review of *Aspects of the Novel*, Forster now rather pointedly observed: 'Pattern here is supreme – indeed, it is italicised.' (It will be recalled that at the beginning of each of the sections in *The Waves*, there are brief descriptions of the various stages in the progress of a single day, which run broadly parallel to the course of the lives of the central characters in this novel; these are all printed in italics.) *The Waves*, Forster added, was 'an extraordinary achievement, an immense extension of the possibilities of *Kew Gardens* and *Jacob's Room*', but it was also 'trembling on the edge' of the aesthete's treacherous abyss, and barely saved from being 'dull and arty'. After all this, Forster went on to conclude that it was Virginia Woolf's 'greatest book' (TCD 243)—just as earlier, upon its first publication, he had written to her of his sense of having 'encountered a classic' (quoted in AWD, 176). But he himself seems to have provided, unwittingly, enough evidence here to lend conviction to P. N. Furbank's suspicion that 'Forster's praise of *The Waves* was not altogether sincere.'[11] In acclaiming as Virginia Woolf's 'greatest book' a work which he himself had found all but 'dull and arty', Forster would appear either to have been acquiescing uneasily in the common critical opinion or to have allowed some personal and pious considerations to muffle an honest critical reaction.

V

These substantial and radical criticisms of each other's works by Virginia Woolf and Forster seem further to reinforce the impression that, as novelists, they could hardly have been any less disparate than Virginia Woolf and the 'Edwardians', for example. In a narrow and mainly technical sense, this would be true, but such a verdict would also ignore some other large areas of affinity and common beliefs. Even if they did not agree on how 'life' was best represented in fiction, or how important it was as an element of the novel, they did share many basic attitudes and values which have been described as 'Bloomsbury' and which deeply permeated both their personalities and their works. Both believed that personal relationships were of the utmost importance, both shared a profound sense of life as being (in a word that recurs frequently in Virginia Woolf's diary) a mystery or (in Forster's favourite formulation) a muddle. This spiritual obscurity at the centre of existence was illuminated only in those rare moments when some visionary character, such as Helen or Mrs Moore, in Forster's fiction, or Mrs Ramsay or Isa in Virginia Woolf's, achieved either an intuitive insight into the nature of things, or a brief understanding and harmony with another person. Both Forster and Virginia Woolf also shared a similar, and perhaps peculiarly 'Bloomsbury', conception of culture and civilisation. Not many people beyond the immediate circle in which they both moved would have quite mourned Roger Fry's death as 'a definite loss to civilization', yet Forster made this statement (AH (1936) 39), and Virginia Woolf, fully agreeing, quoted it in her life of Fry.[12]

Even as novelists, Forster and Virginia Woolf both reflected in their works the finer, idealistic vision, as well as the ineffectual disabilities of the liberal humanist, as C. B. Cox has argued.[13] The scope and the nature of their understanding of, and sympathy with, the world around them were similarly determined by their broadly common environment and congeneric sensibility. Both were at their natural best when depicting 'the liberal culture of the middle class'[14], but in the face of a wider and more unfamiliar reality, both retreated – Forster to his 'islands of quiet tolerance', and Virginia Woolf to an even more remote 'solitude'.[15]

In the end, however, there seems to be no escape from the conclusion that in the battle between the 'Edwardians' and the 'Georgians', which provided the perspective for at least Virginia

Woolf's appraisal of all contemporary writers and which has also influenced the terms in which much of the critical discussion of the English novel in this century has taken place, Forster and Virginia Woolf were not in the same camp. Their public position as fellow-members of the Bloomsbury Group, their long and close personal friendship with each other, their solicitous regard for each other even in their published writings—sometimes at the expense of their honest opinions— and the greatest possible goodwill between them generally, have all served to obfuscate this fact. But there are also one or two scattered and seemingly casual remarks by each in which they betrayed their different colours. Once, at least, Virginia Woolf did mention Forster's name in the same breath as those of her adversaries the 'Edwardians'. The characters in a Hugh Walpole novel, she said, belonged to 'that composite group of English families created by Mr. Galsworthy, Mr. Arnold Bennett, and Mr. E. M. Forster'.[16x]

Forster, too, made his own allegiance plain when, discussing Henry James in *Aspects of the Novel*, he quoted H. G. Wells' notorious attack in *Boon* with evident relish, and went on to declare unambiguously enough that '[m]y own prejudices are with Wells' (AN viii, 112). Later, in his final estimate of Virginia Woolf, he found, as Arnold Bennett had done earlier, that 'her problem's centre', 'her great difficulty', was that she could not get her characters to live. Virginia Woolf had earlier proclaimed Forster the novelist a descendant of Jane Austen. Now Forster judged her by comparison not only with Jane Austen but also with her own *bête noire*, Arnold Bennett, and found her wanting:

> Life on the page she could give; . . . [but] Life eternal she could seldom give; she could seldom so portray a character that it was remembered afterwards on its own account, as Emma is remembered, for instance, or Dorothea Casaubon, or Sophia and Constance in [Bennett's] *The Old Wives' Tale*.　　(TCD 245.)

22 Two Anonymous Writers, E. M. Forster and Anton Chekhov

James McConkey

E. M. Forster requires in his readers a greater personal stability than do many writers, for he appeals even in his youthful fiction to our inclination to reflect on our own experiences as well as to our wish for wholeness and wisdom. I know I didn't discover him until I was grown-up, or thought myself so; until I was back from service in the Second World War, beginning a career, and feeling more secure in my sexual and spiritual nature than I had as an adolescent or soldier. What I found in him were a number of qualities I had responded to in my childhood and adolescent reading – fantasy, humour, compassion, a loneliness connected with both a sense of foreign places and a desire for something beyond one's apparent grasp – all of these qualities transformed or given perspective by an authorial presence that, while it forbade the self-indulgence of my adolescent responses, permitted an understanding of the failings of specific human beings as well as of the limitations of the human condition itself. I first read Forster in my mid-twenties, a period in which a certain kind of imaginative literature can influence us for the rest of our lives; to a considerable extent the authorial presence in his fiction became (to misuse the common definition of the phrase) *my* second self, and so it has remained to the present day.

In reading the recently-published first volume of P. N. Furbank's projected two-volume biography of Forster,[1] I found myself as fascinated by it as I had been by the books of my childhood; I read it with a kind of wonder at the distance separating the details and anxieties of the life from the knowledge found in the fiction. Forster was frank and honest about himself in his personal notations, which is as admirable as it is uncommon; but the biography, dependent as it is on its subject's candour, manages to be, like Alice's rabbit-hole, a means of enchanted diminution. The Cambridge of the *Life* is a tinier place than is the Cambridge of *The Longest Journey*; the Italy of the *Life* is far more confining than is the Italy of *Where Angels Fear to Tread* and *A Room with a View*, the intimacy with specific Italians in the *Life* apparently being limited to lessons with a language teacher. How lonely, how unfulfilled, Forster must have been – later, in England – to seek out male companionship in various disagreeable locales! As we journey through the *Life*, the Baedeker we require to point out the spirit of Forster – to define the inner life, to provide stars for the grand vistas – consists of the novels and stories and essays he wrote.

The publication in England of this first volume of the *Life*, coming in advance of the hundredth anniversary of his birth and after the appearance of the homosexual fiction, will inevitably bring about the demand for a re-evaluation of Forster from a variety of psychological perspectives. Attempts in this direction are bound to be reductive even as they celebrate complexity. Forster himself knew better than to rely on the methods of any science of the mind for an understanding of who and what we are. His own best characters are simple but not flat, for he seeks the depths rather than the intricacies; his fiction is remarkably free of the more popular terms of psychology, even in defining a character so vulnerable to them as Adela Quested. In *Aspects of the Novel*, while discussing the qualities of Melville's mind, Forster writes, 'What one notices in him is that his apprehensions are free from personal worry, so that we become bigger, not smaller, after sharing them';[2] and, in general, the comment is applicable to Forster himself, to the presence inhabiting his fiction. The major exception is *Maurice*. In that novel, the presence, while there, is muted for the sake of the argument. If allowed its normal play, that presence would have implied a base in Maurice deeper than his homosexuality, and would have severely undercut the intention to give him happiness once he had openly accepted his sexual nature—much as it undercuts conscious intentions, thereby preventing them from becoming sentimental, in most of the other novels.

But of course 'authorial presence' is too restrictive a term to describe what we respond to in Forster's writing, as we listen to whatever it is that lies behind the character and between the words and the structural blocks. It used to bother me when I was younger that my favourite author, whose accents were so familiar to me that

I felt him to be my friend, would subscribe to the notion of anonymity in literature – a notion quite fashionable in the forties and fifties, for it was in keeping with the views of the New Criticism. His remarks in 'Anonymity: An Enquiry' bothered me because I wasn't attending to them properly; words so simply put have to be felt in our entire psyche, not just in the reasoning part. What he was saying in that essay I had to discover for myself, as a truth about my own nature, though his words are so clear a child *should*, by natural right, be able to understand them:

> Just as words have two functions—information and creation—so each human mind has two personalities, one on the surface, one deeper down. The upper personality has a name. It is called S. T. Coleridge, or William Shakespeare, or Mrs. Humphry Ward. It is conscious and alert, it does things like dining out, answering letters, etc., and it differs vividly and amusingly from other personalities. The lower personality is a very queer affair. In many ways it is a perfect fool, but without it there is no literature, because unless a man dips a bucket down into it occasionally he cannot produce first-class work. There is something general about it. Although it is inside S. T. Coleridge, it cannot be labelled with his name. It has something in common with all other deeper personalities, and the mystic will assert that the common quality is God, and that here, in the obscure recesses of our being, we near the gates of the Divine. It is in any case the force that makes for anonymity. As it came from the depths, so it soars to the heights, out of local questionings; as it is general to all men, so the works it inspires have something general about them, namely beauty.[3]

Later in this lucid essay – one that moves me as much as do the finest passages in his novels – Forster makes some comments that ought to be read by any reader of *E. M. Forster: A Life*:

> The personality of a writer does become important after we have read his book and begin to study it. When the glamour of creation ceases, when the leaves of the divine tree are silent, when the co-partnership [between reader and writer] is over, then a book changes its nature, and we can ask ourselves questions about it such as 'What is the author's name?' 'Where did he live?' 'Was he married?' and 'Which was his favourite flower?' Then we are

no longer reading the book, we are studying it and making it subserve our desire for information. 'Study' has a very solemn sound. 'I am studying Dante' sounds much more than 'I am reading Dante.' It is really much less. Study is only a serious form of gossip. It teaches us everything about the book except the central thing, and between that and us it raises a circular barrier which only the wings of the spirit can cross.[4]

As for the passage about the two personalities upon which this second quotation depends—either we understand it fully, or we don't understand it at all. In rereading 'Anonymity' some twenty years after I'd last read it, I was surprised, disconcerted, and finally delighted to find the attitudes towards the acts of reading and writing that I had been slowly developing over the years, as well as the two critical terms that had become of crucial importance to me in explaining those attitudes to others, actually had their specific origins in this essay and their general origins in Forster's fiction and other writings. What is *tone*, after all, but the attitudes communicated to us by the upper personality? What is *voice* but our apprehension of the lower? We can say that 'authorial presence' accommodates both tone and voice, but only if we are willing to admit that the latter term is subversive. In *Aspects of the Novel*, Forster refers to prophecy as a quality of voice.[5] Prophecy is a consequence of the power of voice to invoke the general and universal at the expense of the personal and idiosyncratic; tone, as I would use the word, belongs to the realm of the personal and idiosyncratic.

Two questions are apt to trouble the reader of 'Anonymity' who does not immediately accede to the truth it contains. The first, which is easier to meet, has to do with the somewhat guarded nature of its comments on mysticism. Isn't Forster at once appealing to our acceptance of the mystic truth at the heart of any number of religions (' . . . the mystic will assert that the common quality is God') *and* sidestepping his own acceptance of such truth? Between the two passages I have quoted, and as part of his bridge between them, Forster speaks regretfully of the loss of the old theories of composition that permitted literature to be 'not an expression but a discovery, and was sometimes supposed to have been shown to the poet by God'.[6]

The first question, then, takes on the form of 'How serious is Forster? Does he really believe what he says?' The answer, of course, is that he is wholly serious, that he does believe in something called the 'soul' or the 'spirit' of man; that, in speaking of 'a circular barrier which only the wings of the spirit can cross' he is not speaking sentimentally or decoratively. Few humans – certainly none of those engaged in the acts of reading and writing – are simple receptacles to be filled up with the divine message; we are not the bucket itself. And yet individually we do possess a lower personality: it is what we have in common. His fiction everywhere depends on the assumptions of 'Anonymity', as does all literature that relies on heightened moments in which the self or the individual consciousness recedes or pales before an apprehension of unity.

The second question, which I once asked and which some critics of Forster still are asking, seems to involve us in a paradox. The question is: 'If the greatest literature is that in which the author most closely approximates anonymity, if in it the writer moves himself or herself and us toward the extinction of "presence", of individual ego, why is it that in that literature we hear certain distinct and unique accents and thus can clearly distinguish those of Melville from those, say, of Dostoevsky or Emily Brontë – something that we can't do for any number of lesser writers?'

'Anonymity' can answer this question, too. The movement toward anonymity through the lower personality *does* provide a closer relationship between reader and writer than is possible without it; they are drawn together at the level that truly matters, the level beneath differences of race, nationality, sex, politics, culture, and quirky individualism. Sometimes ideas are so simple it takes us half a century to comprehend them; they are the sort of ideas once accepted without much thought and sometimes without much comprehension as belonging to the matrix of the religious doctrines of the age. The value of struggling for them without the benefit of creed and orthodoxy is that one can finally get to them without their robes on, can see them in their elemental form. It took me nearly five decades to realise that the personality – the separate identity – I prize in others and in myself would be devoid of meaning or value did I not somehow *know* that a point exists in which all these diverse selves merge, become one. What significance (we must stand outside of our private lives and the world we subjectively create to ask this question) could there possibly be in our separate opinions, our lonely desires, the glint of intelligence in our eyes, the very pattern of our thumbprints, without such a point? And isn't it obvious that all writers who find their essential interest in a person or persons and not in the relationship of individuals to human institutions accept, whether they are conscious of the fact or not, this final point of convergence?

Our lower personality – the writer's voice – acknowledges such a point; and, by giving us in the process our common value, makes meaningful communication at least a possibility. Our higher personality – the writer's tone – can think and talk (usually unsuccessfully) about that point beyond words, is consciously affected or unconsciously influenced by it in varying degrees even as it is engaged in classifying, declaring one thing or idea better than another, or performing the mundane activities that Forster ascribes to it.

It is true, I feel, that the lower personality would, if left unchecked, lose itself wholly in that silence that for Augustine is the voice of God. Writers of fiction, however, work of necessity with human beings, and such a concern serves – as did the example of Christ for Augustine – to pull even the most prophetic of them back to Earth. In the writing in which we are most aware of such a dual allegiance, the characters ultimately are defined not in social or material terms but in spiritual ones.

Here is Forster's younger contemporary and friend, Virginia Woolf, on a writer whose name for a moment will remain, fittingly enough, anonymous:

> We have to cast about in order to discover where the emphasis in these strange stories rightly comes. X's own words give us a lead in the right direction. ' . . . such a conversation as this between us,' he says, 'would have been unthinkable for our parents. At night they did not talk, but slept sound; we, our generation, sleep badly, are restless, but talk a great deal, and are always trying to settle whether we are right or not.' Our literature of social satire and psychological finesse both sprang from that restless sleep, that incessant talking; but, after all, there is an enormous difference between X and Henry James, between X and Bernard Shaw. Obviously—but where does it arise? X, too, is aware of the evils and injustices of the social state; the condition of the peasants appals him, but the reformer's zeal is not his—that is not the signal for us to stop. The mind interests him enormously; he is a most subtle and delicate analyst of human relations. But again, no; the end is not there. Is it that he is primarily interested not in the soul's relation with other souls, but with the soul's

relation to health—with the soul's relation to goodness? These stories are always showing us some affectation, pose, insincerity. Some woman has got into a false relation; some man has been perverted by the inhumanity of his circumstances. The soul is ill; the soul is cured; the soul is not cured. Those are the emphatic points in his stories.[7]

Such a description—except for the quotation, which tells us that X simply has to be Russian: the English never generalise so freely about their spiritual complaints—could easily be of Forster's fiction, but Woolf is speaking of Chekhov.

In his letters, Chekhov talks readily enough about his personal feelings, but in his fiction his characters rather than he are open. He tries always in his stories to be impersonal, objective, though he does generalise about man's relationship with the universe, about the vastness of space and the loneliness and ephemerality of the human condition—those generalisations that Forster in *Aspects of the Novel* approves of, partly, I suspect, because they have their source in the lower personality.[8] Chekhov, though, does construct characters that represent the elements of his own nature.

In this regard, no more telling story exists than 'Gusev', a brief piece of fiction that Woolf praises in her essay 'Modern Fiction'.[9] It is the account of two men who die as a ship slowly makes its homeward way to Russia. Gusev himself is simple, accepting everything and everybody in his world but the Chinese. He makes no intellectual distinctions, no moral categories; folk tales and myths, no matter how superstitious, satisfy his need for explanation. He may be, from the rationalist's point of view (and that is the viewpoint of the other character) a perfect fool, but he is also soul, the lower personality—without ever becoming a symbol. The other dying man, Pavel Ivanych, is constantly aware of classes, divisions – and of himself. He is outraged at human injustice, but not because he is compassionate – rather, because he sees it in reference to his personal suffering. He too is not a symbol, he is a particular man, Pavel Ivanych. He is also (in contrast to soul) body, which reason serves for body's own ends; he is the higher personality untouched by any knowledge of the lower.

The deaths of both men are described in the most laconic and objective of terms, as is Gusev's sea burial. The only intrusions Chekhov permits himself come at the very end, as he describes what would be a physical impossibility for any human to see: the depths and the heights. He employs a kind of double vision, that is, to capture the realms of both water and sky – the substance and soul of a natural universe totally oblivious of any such division in it. Below, a shrouded body is sinking deeper and deeper into subterranean darkness, followed by pilot fish and a shark that finally rips the shroud; above, the clouds over the ocean are illuminated to a transcendent beauty by the light of the setting sun. The verbal intrusions, such as they are, consist of the attempt to give human emotions to the fish and ocean and to see the clouds as representations of familiar objects—a triumphal arch, a lion, something so homely as a pair of scissors. The attempt, in short, is to make the pathetic fallacy *work*, to impose as much human meaning as is possible upon an indifferent natural world in which men as diverse as Gusev and Pavel Ivanych are treated exactly alike, in the fact of their dying; but the final emphasis is on a beauty and truth beyond words or human encompassment—even though there is one final attempt to describe nature as if it were man. 'Looking at this magnificent enchanting sky'—so goes the last sentence—'the ocean frowns at first, but soon it, too, takes on tender, joyous, passionate colours for which it is hard to find a name in the language of man.'[10]

If I were to meet in person one of those people who sometimes grumble in print about *A Passage to India* – those who feel it to be an expression of fatigue, or who do not understand the importance of both the old fool Godbole and the rational but discontented Fielding, or who declare that since not even Godbole can encompass stone in his quest for unity the book is a novel of despair and nothing more—I would give that person this little Chekhov story to read in solitude, trusting to his or her own psyche to make the necessary connections. I wish Woolf had re-read 'Gusev' before she composed her often perceptive, but sometimes condescending, essay on Forster's novels.[11]

No 'name in the language of man' exists, of course, for that ultimate point of convergence, for the unifying Beauty or Truth beyond human consciousness; and both Forster and Chekhov disclaim knowledge of 'Truth'. Both of them have more sceptical intelligences than most prophetic writers do; like some writers of the eighteenth century, their very emphasis on reason makes them aware of its limits. The care with which they construct their sentences, with which they give structure to their works, is a sign of intelligence paying homage to a beauty beyond it and separates them from those who rely with more singleness of intent on the lower personality.

For most of his novelistic career – up to *A Passage to India* – Forster believed the greater unity beyond consciousness could at least be sensed through the natural flux, through a person's spiritual kinship with place, and that such an awareness could lead to a true connection among men. That this Wordsworthian view was for him an intellectual conviction or nostalgic desire merely, not the knowledge of the lower personality, is obvious in the disparity between what all the earlier novels say and what they imply – the disparity between tone and voice. It is possible that Forster's homosexuality – which, whatever his efforts, set him apart and gave him an immense need for a connection to be achieved with our bodies, on this Earth – accounts for such a thematic conviction; it is likely also that his English reasonableness for a long time demanded something tangible, something to be looked at and touched, as proof of what the lower personality already knew. In a similar way, Augustine's rationality caused him for some years to believe that God somehow must be an object, a material substance however diaphanous or permeable—or how else can we approach and love Him?

Unlike Forster, Chekhov never proposed nature as a solution for our spiritual cravings. The appeal to him of sky and steppe, of the immense landscapes of his native land, simply is in keeping with his impulse toward anonymity. In his stories, this impulse is reflected in his efforts to be as objective as possible. In his life, it is reflected in his continual desire for freedom, to escape from labels, social categories, political distinctions—and from pettiness and all the other imprisoning tendencies of his own ego. It is, we could say, the lower personality rebelling from the upper—the simple Gusev seeking freedom from that irksome Pavel Ivanych.

And yet that part of him which urges him toward an overcoming of self – which tells him of a unity beyond consciousness – that part of him permits, as it does with Forster, the moral concern: what finally matters is 'the soul's relation to health . . . the soul's relation to goodness', with health and goodness always connected to what unifies us, as a community of human beings. The enemy – the evil – is that which is self-centred and self-seeking, arrogant, petty, divisive. The enemy can be any social force, any political or religious orthodoxy, that does injury to the person, that denies the implicit value of the individual for the sake of class or category or ideology; and it equally can be any imprisoning force within that individual.

As a young man I wrote a book about Forster's novels – it was my doctoral dissertation – that he liked enough to write me a letter expressing his appreciation for the copy I had sent him. What he apparently liked most were the comments on *A Passage to India*. He took exception to my calling Stephen Wonham of *The Longest Journey* a minor character, for that was not what he had wanted Stephen to be – though he recognised that he had not shown, other than through Stephen's talk with Ansell, what he should have about him. In a postscript, he called attention to my error in referring to Eleanor Lavish of *A Room with a View* as Lydia: 'Eleanor Lavish, not Lydia – but she would be too delighted to be mentioned at all to mind'; and in a second postscript he wrote—in reference to my wish in the letter accompanying the book— 'Yes—I hope we meet some day.'[12]

If my one meeting with Forster, which finally took place in July 1963, when he was eighty-four, was not the disaster it might have been, the credit must go to his tolerance and kindness. In the note he had sent me in Paris, where I was spending the year with my family, he said King's would be deserted for the vacation, and gave me the simple directions for finding his rooms. I suppose the emptiness of the courtyard, lending the buildings a loveliness that belonged to the past, had something to do with my conversational ineptness. Also, upon climbing the stairs, I saw the faded paint of Forster's name on the door and it immediately made me remember one of the many tokens of mutability in *The Longest Journey* – the fact that underneath Rickie Elliot's name on *his* door at that college lay the ghost of an earlier one. At any rate, Forster, upon answering my knock, looked to me so frail and elderly – he was recuperating from a heart attack—that my eyes filled with tears and I was even more incoherent than an educated Englishman expects the average American to be. Almost at once, I blurted out what I fear I said too often during my hour or so with him (and what these present recollections disprove somewhat): I said I came neither as scholar nor critic, not for any *use* to which the meeting could be put, but simply to tell him his books had been one of the crucial influences upon my life.

He smiled and set about putting me at ease. He made tea – drawing water for the kettle, if I remember correctly, from the taps of an old-fashioned bathtub – and produced a cake. And, wanting to show an interest in me, he asked about my own writing – for surely the book about him could be but a small part of my literary efforts. Since at the time it constituted my chief writing accomplishment, the subject was quickly exhausted. For the sake of talk, he asked me which city I preferred – London or Paris. I said quickly, 'Paris', for I knew it better and found a greater aesthetic delight both in its buildings and in its river; he told me he had such a distaste for Paris – for the rudeness of its citizens – that he bypassed it on all his trips to the south of France. His current writing struck me as possibly a more profitable topic, so I asked him about it. He said he no longer was doing anything creative; his time now was taken up in going through all his papers and destroying everything he didn't want to linger after his death. I wanted to know what future he had in mind for the unpublished novel about homosexuality I had heard so much about. Quite firmly he said he had decided never to have it published; written primarily to protest attitudes that now had altered, the novel was both old-fashioned and lacking social justification.

For the greater part of our meeting, we talked about novels we both liked and novels he thought I would like, such as Mrs Gaskell's *Wives and Daughters*. He expressed his low opinion of motion pictures generally but of his liking for the theatre. Santha Rama Rau's stage adaptation of *A Passage to India* had pleased him. Toward the end of our conversation, and without connection with anything that had preceded it, he told me that as a young man he had made one major mistake. Of course I asked him what that mistake had been; his reply, the only one I can remember accurately enough to put quotation marks around it, was, 'I trusted people too much.'

He waited for my response. Why was it that such a statement would shock and even embarrass me into silence? Why wasn't I wise or Russian enough to answer, at least to reveal something about myself? Instead I passed off what he had said as best I could, saying something about how *A Passage to India* reminded me of the late quartets of Beethoven: I meant such a comparison to imply that I understood what he had said but that I was unable to cope directly with it. Actually, I had understood it only in my mind. My feelings told me I hadn't wanted an elderly man whom I had always admired to tell me anything like that; my feelings told me – wrongly – that it negated the importance of human relationships, including the one I had hoped to establish with him. He said at once he much preferred the early Beethoven to the late; my response clearly had been inadequate, and we were back to our original positions. As I prepared to leave, he said he would accompany me to the gate. Too solicitous, perhaps, of his health, I suggested he needn't do that. Almost acidly he said that he owed it to me, for my book.

And so he saw me down the stairs, over the uneven cobblestones of the courtyard where I feared he might fall, and over too an odd plank at the bottom of the open gate. I thanked him for his hospitality as he stood beside the ornate mail collection box—a reminder of the Victorian age, with the initials V. R. central to its iron embellishments. Because I didn't want to say goodbye, partly because something had gone wrong that still might be saved, I said what I felt at that instant. I said, 'I like that mail box', meaning I liked seeing him there beside it. He said that he had always liked that pillar-box too; and he smiled warmly, as if in my departure we might yet be affectionate.

So much for the gossip of information that perhaps tells more about me than the ostensible subject. But as the years have passed I have often thought of his phrase, *I trusted people too much*. For a time I was able to convince myself that it was intended only as a kindly warning to me, the naïve young American; and doubtless that was at least part of its intention. Those words most recently came to my mind in reading the first volume of Furbank's biography. Had Forster been remembering the trust he had placed as a young man in Hugh Meredith and Syed Ross Masood and their betrayal of it?

But one doesn't really need biographical details to understand such a remark by a truthful elderly man. All of us would, if we could, impart to the familiar world and to those whom we love the constancy and wholeness lying beyond the grasp of our consciousness. Chekhov's characters, struggling for an unobtainable happiness, lie again and again about the nature of that happiness, about themselves, and about those whom they would love: their self-deceptions prevent the degree of happiness that otherwise would be possible. In a somewhat similar fashion, Rickie Elliot, Forster's most autobiographical character, places a burden of trust on Agnes and particularly on Stephen that no human can bear. The seen and the unseen, the prose and the poetry, the upper personality and the lower, the body and the soul, remain separate.

Although in his major essays Forster makes no reference to Chekhov, he did write a review in 1915 of two collections of Chekhov stories – a fact brought to my attention by Frederick P. W.

McDowell, compiler of the recent annotated bibliography of writings on Forster, when he learned of my interest in discussing the two writers. In his review, Forster is wary of the reason – the English want all the information they can get about the national spirit of their wartime ally – for the sudden interest in Chekhov and other Russian writers. Chekhov provides no such information; he is concerned not with generalisations about the Russian people but with specific individuals and subjects. Chekhov is 'both realist and poet. With one hand he collects facts; with the other he arranges them and sets them flowing.'[13] (Woolf later was to criticise that kind of ambidexterity in Forster's fiction, for she preferred fewer bricks and a more constant flowing.) Forster gives the following quotation from a Chekhov story to illustrate what he means:

'In which country are the birds most at home, in ours or over there?' Savka asked.

'In ours, of course. They are hatched here, and here they raise their young. This is their native land, and they only fly away to escape being frozen to death.'

'How strange!' he sighed, stretching. 'One can't talk of anything but what is strange. Take that shouting bird over there, take people, take this little stone—there's a meaning in everything. Oh, if I had only known you were going to be here this evening, sir, I wouldn't have told that woman to come. She asked if she might.'

'These affairs of yours with women will end badly some day,' I said sadly.

'Never mind.'

Then, after a moment's reflection, Savka added:

'So I have told the women, but they won't listen; the idiots don't care.'

Silence fell. The shadows deepened, the outlines of all objects faded into the darkness. The streak of light behind the hill was altogether extinguished, and the stars shone ever brighter and brighter. The mournful, monotonous chirping of the crickets, the calling of the rail-bird, and the whistling of the quail seemed not to break the nocturnal silence, but rather to add to it a still greater depth. It was as if the stars, and not the birds and insects, were singing softly, and charming our ears as they looked down from heaven.

Savka broke silence first. He slowly turned his regard to me, and said, 'This is tedious for you, sir, I can see. Let's have supper.'[14]

I find echoes of this scene in *A Passage to India*; indeed, part of its resonance for me comes from my knowledge of that novel. Effects somewhat similar to those found in this quotation—effects gained by the movement from the specific to the general or universal and then quickly back—can be found throughout Forster's fiction. But the affinities are probably more the result of spiritual kinship than of influence. Certainly it is the attraction of what lies beyond self, the attraction of an encompassing and holy silence, that gives to both Chekhov and Forster an elusiveness. I know that Forster led me to Chekhov and that Chekhov led me back to Forster. The process is similar to that in learning a foreign language: the study of it informs us of the workings of our native tongue by making accessible those crucial parts that both languages have in common. The voice in Forster and Chekhov alike is a mediator between seemingly irreconcilable elements, giving us what solace it can, reminding us of our likenesses, and telling us that oneness exists – but not now, not here.

23 'The Last Englishman': Lawrence's appreciation of Forster

John Beer

In his book *Thought, Words and Creativity*, F. R. Leavis ends a discussion of Lawrence's greatness by quoting two remarks of his concerning Forster. On 23 July 1924 he wrote to Secker,

> Am reading *Passage to India*. It's good, but makes one wish a bomb would fall and end everything. Life is more interesting in its undercurrents than in its obvious; and E. M. does see people, people and nothing but people ad nauseam.

A year later, on 13 August 1925, he wrote to him again:

> *St Mawr* a bit disappointing. The Bloomsbury highbrows hated it. Glad they did. Don't send any more of my books to E. M. Forster – done with him as with most people. Vogue la galère.[1]

Taken in isolation these quotations might suggest that Lawrence's attitude to Forster was always, and primarily, hostile; and many modern readers would no doubt accept the implication without question. There is at first sight such a marked contrast between the whimsical, understating, ironic Forster and the vivid, forthright, combative Lawrence that one would hardly expect to find either liking the other. Yet even the comments just quoted may be seen, on scrutiny, to be gesturing in another direction as well. *A Passage to India* is, after all, being described as 'good'; and if Secker is not to send any more of Lawrence's books to Forster, this shows that he has, for some reason, been encouraged to do so in the past. Examination of Lawrence's comments at the time modifies further the impression of hostility. The first quotation represents what is in many respects a first judgement of *A Passage to India*, which he had not yet finished reading. On the day when he did finish it he wrote to Forster himself, offering a more extended critique (as we shall see later); a fortnight later, asking Carlo Linati if he had read it, he expressed the opinion that Forster was 'about the best of my contemporaries in England.'[2]

Dr Leavis himself, some years ago, paid a memorable, if guarded, tribute to Forster, in which he acknowledged a possible kinship between the two men. Forster's 'radical dissatisfaction with modern civilization', he said, 'prompts references to D. H. Lawrence rather than to Jane Austen.' (Later in the essay, admittedly, he warned his reader that this was an 'over-emphasis'.)[3] Other critics, including Frank Kermode and Wilfred Stone, have drawn attention to specific points of comparison.[4] It is only with the availability of their writings in completer form, however, that it has become possible to explore the full extent of the relationship, both in literature and in life.

There are some things which can be discerned (and perhaps more clearly) without such apparatus. Surveying the novels of both men side by side, one is struck by a common curve in their careers. Each wrote an important early novel around the theme of an attractive young girl faced with a choice between two suitors, one of whom is acceptable by the standards of her own society, the other 'unsuitable' but more deeply attractive to her physically; in each case the novel proved difficult to work. The 'Lucy novel' took various forms in Forster's mind before it was published as *A Room with a View* in 1908; Lawrence's *The White Peacock*, similarly, went through various changes before its final version of January 1911.[5]

As one compares these two novels, on the other hand, certain resemblances and differences between the two writers begin to define themselves. In *A Room with a View*, the heroine's choice is between Cecil Vyse, a cultivated and witty but enclosed young man on the one hand and George Emerson, an open-minded impulsive young man on the other. In the course of the novel she learns to trust the wholeness of her instinct towards George rather than the attractive aestheticism of Cecil. The choice is presented ultimately as one between enclosure and freedom: life in a succession of rooms with Cecil Vyse or life with an outward view, as offered by George.

By comparison Lettie Beardsall, the heroine of *The White Peacock*, seems more like a woman of the world. Her problem is something of the same, however; to choose the man who will respond to her own deepest instincts: the open bucolic George Saxton or the thriving young industrialist Leslie Tempest. It is in her own moments of self-examination that Lawrence's advance shows itself. For Forster's Lucy the question is simply one of self-liberation, of accepting the possibilities of the body and so discovering the full nature of love. At that level Lawrence's Lettie has no problem; her problem is rather that the physical George is also turgid, needing some further quickening if he is to flower into true humanity. There can be no doubt of George Saxton's general attractiveness, but he lacks delicacy of intuition. Lettie gropes to define her situation to him in a long speech which includes the observation:

> You never grow up, like bulbs which spend all summer getting fat and fleshy, but never wakening the germ of a flower. As for me, the flower is born in me, but it wants bringing forth. Things don't flower if they're overfed.

Both writers use flower imagery centrally, but the difference between Forster's Lucy and Lawrence's Lettie further defines itself in terms of the straightforwardly positive and sensuous role of the violets in *A Room with a View*, by comparison with the mysterious 'otherness' of snowdrops in *The White Peacock* (as discussed by Carl Baron in his essay).[6]

Each writer, similarly, wrote a pivotal early novel involving detailed examination of elements in his own personality. In *The Longest Journey* Forster invented a crippled version of himself who shared his idealisms and who like him wrote short stories with a mythological content, but who lacked his own sense of other actualities.[7] Lawrence's Paul Morel, in *Sons and Lovers*, is closer to his author (for a reduced version on the lines of Rickie we should look rather at Cyril Beardsall, the narrator of *The White Peacock*) yet the novel as a whole is, like Forster's, an occasion for oblique self-examination.

In the case of each writer, also, his career pivots on two long novels, the first conceived positively, the second negatively. Forster's *Howards End*, when set at the side of *The Rainbow*, produces some revealing comparisons, particularly between the respective quests of the heroines, Margaret Schlegel and Ursula Brangwen. At the end, Margaret, looking across the fields by her house, sees a 'red rust', the creeping line of buildings that marks the encroachment of

London, and feels it as a threat. She can still hope, however (almost against hope) that the current civilisation of motion will eventually be replaced by a civilisation that will 'rest on the earth'.[8] At the end of *The Rainbow*, Ursula Brangwen looks out from her window to see 'the hard, cutting edges of the new houses, which seemed to spread over the hillside in their insentient triumph', but is relieved by the sense that life continues in all human beings ('the rainbow was arched in their blood and would quiver to life in their spirit'); in that fact she can descry 'the earth's new architecture'.[9] As usual, Lawrence's vision is the more extreme, but the recognised predicament is strikingly similar.

Convergences of theme and organisation may further be traced between *Women in Love* and *A Passage to India*. Both novels carry, as a main element in their plots, the attempt by one man to reach a fruitful relationship with another. At the end of Lawrence's novel, Rupert Birkin is left contemplating Gerald Crich's death and his failure to build with him a friendship which might have complemented, at a less intimate level, his love for Ursula. Forster's novel, similarly, concludes with the recognition between Fielding and Aziz that in the conditions of British India, a full friendship between two men of the different cultures involved is not possible. And where *Howards End* and *The Rainbow* had both ended on a note of tentative affirmation, these two later novels conclude by stressing the theme of separateness; they also—as Mohammed Shaheen and P. N. Furbank have above pointed out in Forster's case—betray greater readiness to make play with the 'shifting point of view'. Since Forster's death, finally, the publication of further work has made possible a comparison between his later fictions, many of which embody homosexual themes, and Lawrence's later tales. Both, despite marked differences of subject-matter, convey a similar sardonic note, often pressing a particular sexual theme to a point of intensity which may resolve itself into either tragedy or laughter.

The possibility of direct influences throughout their careers is not to be ruled out. Lawrence may have read *A Room with a View* during the last stages of writing *The White Peacock*, or *The Longest Journey* before writing *Sons and Lovers*, though it seems more likely that he read much of Forster's early work together in 1915.[10x] We know, certainly, that he had read *Howards End* in 1911, well before he began *The Rainbow*;[11x] it is possible that Forster, in turn, read *Women in Love* before writing *A Passage to India*. Lawrence certainly knew *A*

Passage to India when he wrote 'St Mawr', and M. L. Raina has demonstrated some close verbal parallels in Lawrence's novella which seem to involve reminiscences (conscious or otherwise) from Forster's novel.[12] 'St Mawr', in turn, was sent to Forster and might have helped fuel his move to the sardonic mode in some later short stories.

These questions of possible influence, however, are less important than a common pattern which moves through the parallels as a whole. The point which one notices again and again is that the two writers are handling similar themes, with Lawrence in each case one stage further along the road.

The respective differences of the men define themselves well in their respective relationships to the Bloomsbury Group. Lawrence, as is well known, criticised some of the members, particularly after his visit to Cambridge in 1915. He distrusted their ethos and assumptions and described them generally as 'done for'.[13] Forster's relationship to the group, on the other hand, was more equivocal. He knew many of its members well, and P. N. Furbank, in his contribution to this volume, has pointed to some features of his writing which identify him with it. Yet he always remained somewhat on the edge of their society. Many of the most cutting things said about Forster emanate from Bloomsbury figures; in their more charitable moments they nicknamed him 'Taupe' from his habit of burrowing away during a conversation and then re-emerging into it later 'with some subtle observation or delicate quip'.[14] Sometimes he mystified them, as with *A Passage to India*. 'What happened in the cave?', they asked him—as ingenuously as any 'ordinary reader'.[15x]

Other elements in Forster which caused him to draw back from Bloomsbury, standing at an angle to it as he did to many human societies, link him with Lawrence. One might instance their common liking for Hardy. Forster, who actually knew Hardy, could not give him the highest honours of all in *Aspects of the Novel*, but indicated the nature of his feeling for him when, comparing him with Meredith, he remarked 'the work of Hardy is my home and that of Meredith cannot be.'[16] Lawrence, who was fascinated by his works, made him the focusing point for a long and important essay.[17] The point which drew both men, it might be argued, was the 'passional' note in his writing – the preoccupation with feelings and drives that subsist below the surface of normal human behaviour, creating private dramas which may move at variance with patterns of social behaviour, or set up desires which conventional society cannot satisfy.

In Hardy's novels, however, the dominant note had been that of inevitability. His characters were to be seen as acting out age-old dramas that could be traced back into Greek tragedy or ancient English ritual. An intervening generation had become fascinated with the dynamic element in earlier mythologies, looking to the possibility that they reflected powers which might still survive more positively in human beings.

Various writers, such as Arthur Machen and James Stephens, had explored the theme, but normally with some kind of self-distancing. One may instance the writings of Kenneth Grahame, best known for his book *The Wind in the Willows*, in which waterside animals act out a drama cast partly in human terms. At the centre of the book there is a curious chapter entitled 'The Piper at the Gates of Dawn', in which two of the animals are driven by an urge which they are powerless to resist on a journey which brings them to the vision of a sleeping Pan, who is found guarding a baby otter who has been lost.

This vision of Pan the keeper of the flocks, uneasily obtrusive to many readers, is more understandable when one looks at some of the work that Grahame published earlier, notably a collection of essays entitled *Pagan Papers*, which includes three pieces entitled respectively 'The Rural Pan', 'The Lost Centaur' and 'Orion'. It is not clear whether Lawrence ever saw the book, but there is one (admittedly tenuous) piece of evidence which suggests that he might have done. The group of young people with whom he associated in Nottinghamshire during his college days were, according to one of their associates, called 'the Pagans' and, although paganism generally was a theme in literature of the time, it is not easy to discover another source for such a name which would be so direct.[18x] In Forster's case it is more likely that he knew the book, since it helps to explain a small mystery associated with his writing. In his novel *The Longest Journey*, the hero Rickie Elliot from time to time turns to the constellation Orion, which he uses as a point of reference for the nobility of mankind.[19] The same constellation figures in two of Forster's short stories, 'The Point of It' and 'The Machine Stops'. The hero of the former story shows us more of its significance:

. . . even when he was thinking of other matters, as looking at

Orion perhaps in the cold winter evenings, a pang of joy, too sweet for description, would thrill him, and he would feel sure that our highest impulses have some eternal value, and will be completed hereafter.[20]

Although the figure of Orion the mighty hunter is familiar enough in mythology, it has not hitherto been clear how Forster arrived at his more idealised version. The missing link, I believe, is to be found at the end of Kenneth Grahame's essay, 'Orion', where the constellation Orion is set in contrast to that of the Plough, which symbolises for him the modern civilisation of work. The Hunter he thinks of as corresponding to a 'drop of primal quicksilver in the blood', preserved in every human being but expressed mainly by children and perhaps destined to come into his own when the civilisation of the Plough collapses:

> But for the Hunter—there he rises—couchant no more. Nay, flung full stretch on the blue, he blazes, he dominates, he appals! Will his turn, then, really come at last? After some Armageddon of cataclysmal ruin, all levelling, whelming the County Council- lor with the Music-hall artiste, obliterating the very furrows of the Plough, shall the skin-clad nomad string his bow once more, and once more loose the whistling shaft? Wildly incredible it seems. And yet—look up! Look up and behold him confident, erect, majestic—there on the threshold of the sky![21]

As Peter Green comments in his biography of Grahame, the rhetoric of this passage looks forward to the world of Freud and Lawrence.[22] Grahame, himself, of course, took the theme no further, and would hardly have included it at all had it not been firmly set in a context dominated by whimsical irony. In so far as he did develop the idea, it was by way of idealising childhood as a kind of Golden Age when pagan powers could still express themselves freely—before children were forced into the ranks of what he called the Olympians – the adults who believed themselves to be above such things.[23]

What is written in a context of placing irony may sometimes be read out of it again by an enthusiastic young admirer, however, and I would suspect that the adolescent Forster not only came across it, but was moved to take seriously the point about the 'drop of primal quicksilver in the blood', constructing his own image of Orion in still more splendid terms. Lawrence, as I have pointed out, also had his own 'paganism', whether derived directly from Grahame's book or from the spirit of the age. When he and Forster met, therefore, they had that cognition in common—and in contradistinction to Bloomsbury.

The first meeting took place in 1915, through the hospitality of Lady Ottoline Morrell. This was followed by a visit to the studio of Duncan Grant, where Lawrence delivered an attack on the various pictures that Grant showed him.[24] Shortly afterwards Lawrence invited Forster to come and stay at Pulborough in Sussex, where he and Frieda were living.

That stay was marked (as often with Lawrence's relationships) by restrained tension. Lawrence wrote afterwards that he and Forster had been 'on the edge of a fierce quarrel all the time'.[25x] He long remembered a conversation on the Downs in which, apparently, he warned Forster that he was in danger of 'dying', to be asked in his turn how he knew Forster was not dead—*if* he knew.[26] In a later recollection Forster said, 'Lawrence could be very trying. He spent one whole afternoon condemning my work. At last I asked him if there was anything good in it. "Yes," he said, "Leonard Bast. That was courageous."'[27] Lawrence was then at his fiercest in his rejection of traditional English sensibility, so that the gentler elements in the novel must have irritated him. Nor would he accept the spirit of compromise which could enable Margaret Schlegel to come to terms with the Wilcoxes, with the words 'More and more do I refuse to draw my income, and sneer at those who guarantee it.'[28] Years later he still saw this as a sell-out: 'I think you *did* make a nearly deadly mistake glorifying those *business* people in Howards End. Business is no good.'[29]

The two men discussed religion—naturally enough, since an interest in the 'passional' is always likely to take in the elements in religion that reflect such human needs and desires. Lawrence rejected particular religions in favour of an impersonal striving within the human race. Forster, on the other hand, was more drawn to Eastern religion and evidently discussed, either then or in a subsequent letter, the religion of India (which he had recently visited), for Lawrence reverted to the subject several times. ' . . . Above all,' he wrote, 'don't read the Crown of Hinduism. I can't tell you how I detest things Hindu & Buddhistic—it is all such ineffable self-conceit as to be overwhelming.' The following year he wrote, 'Don't go to India. *All religion is bad.*' Six years after (having visited Ceylon in the meantime) he wrote, 'Frieda spoke of you & Brahma. I didn't care *at all* for Buddha . . .'.[30x]

Lawrence must have made some direct personal judgements of Forster of the kind that he was fond of offering his friends and acquaintances. Forster apparently wrote complaining of his bad manners, but he later acknowledged that he himself had become more outspoken as a result of his 'dressing down' at the Lawrences; in Furbanks's biography, indeed, the visit is seen as something of a turning-point in his whole career.[31x] At the time, Lawrence also told Barbara Low that he got 'a feeling of acute misery' from him, and wrote to Mary Cannan, 'I liked him, but his life is so ridiculously inane, the man is dying of inanition.'[32] To Bertrand Russell he was explicit concerning what he saw as Forster's failings: a man nowadays, he argued, went to women 'not for discovery or new connection or profession' but only 'to repeat upon himself a known reaction':

> When this condition arrives, there is always Sodomy. The man goes to the man to repeat this reaction upon himself. It is a nearer form of masterbation [*sic*]. But still it has some *object*—there are still two bodies instead of one. A man of strong soul has too much honour for the other body—man or woman—to use it as a means of masterbation. So he remains neutral, inactive. That is Forster.[33]

This view was probably not expressed so openly to Forster himself, but it is interesting to set it at the side of P. N. Furbank's account of the latter's sexual life, quoted by Wilfred Stone earlier in this collection:

> He achieved physical sex very late and found it easier with people outside his own social class, and it remained a kind of private magic for him—an almost unobtainable blessing, for which another person was mainly a pretext . . . and by romanticizing them he managed to keep them at a distance.[34]

In one way this is remarkably close to Lawrence's diagnosis. The sense of an unwillingness to enter totally into relationship with another person is abundantly supported. Yet Furbank's account also goes some way towards an enlargement of Forster's point of view, making it clear that Forster's end was not only self-gratification but also enlargement of relationship. Across the barriers that separated him from other individuals there must remain a vision of human connections, fostered rather than negated by the 'private magic' of sexual encounter. Forster was thus able to carry into his later physical relationships something of the 'strong soul' which, as Lawrence saw, inhibited him from undertaking them in his earlier years.

Lawrence's most penetrating criticism of Forster came, however, a little later, when he had read *The Celestial Omnibus*. While Lawrence liked some of the stories in this collection, which corresponded to certain of his own mythological interests, they also helped him to isolate certain points of difference. He found it difficult to accept the extraordinary divide between the conventions of suburban comedy and the rhapsodic note of Pan-worship—which remained, in these stories, hardly bridged. In a critical letter he brought the motto of *Howards End* to bear with telling force:

> I have just read the Story of a Panic. You with your 'Only Connect' motto, I must say that you reach the limit of splitness here. You are bumping your nose on the end of the cul de sac.
>
> My angels & devils are nothing compared with your Pan. Don't you see Pan is the undifferentiated root & stem drawing out of unfathomable darkness, & my Angels & Devils are old-fashioned symbols for the flower into which we strive to burst. Now no plant can live towards the root. That is the most split, perverse thing of all.
>
> You see I know all about your Pan. He is not dead, he is the same forever. But you should not confuse him with universal love, as you tend to do. You are very confused. < You give Pan great attributes of Christ. >
>
> All that dark, concentrated, complete, all-containing surge of which I am the fountain, and of which the well-head is my loins, is urging forward, like a plant to flower or a fountain to its parabola. And my angels and devils are a sort of old-fashioned flowering. I am just in love with mediaeval terms, that is all—& Fra Angelico & Cimabue & the Saints.
>
> But your Pan is a stooping back to the well head, a perverse pushing back the waters to their source, & saying, the source is everything, which is stupid & an annihilation—but very stupid. In these books, these last, you are intentional & perverse & not vitally interesting. One must live from the source, through all the

racings & heats of Pan, and on to my beloved angels & devils, with their aureoles & their feet upon the flowers of light & with their red-mouthed despairs & destructions. However, we wait till you come. Don't be alarmed—I seem to 'stunt' because I use old terms for my feeling, because I am not inventive or creative enough.   auf wiedersehen.[35]

An important point which Lawrence seized upon (and which many of Forster's contemporaries had missed) was that the 'Pan' element in his short stories was fully serious—so that when Helen Schlegel spoke of 'panic and emptiness' she was speaking mythologically as well as directly. How pervasive that mythology was has since been noted by other critics, and is further emphasised by Alan Wilde's essay in this collection, but it has always been easy to be fooled by Forster's manner into believing it less important to him that it actually was. And in one sense such a misreading was justified: unless Forster could find a way of writing about Pan which did not simply set that element in uneasy collocation with a method of whimsical irony, he could not win his way through to a forceful fictional method.

From another point of view, however, Lawrence's critique is at first sight surprising. The great twentieth-century protagonist of the 'dark gods' here describes Forster's devotion to Pan as a 'stooping back to the well-head'. Are we to imagine that Lawrence's own devotion had not yet been formulated in his mind?

In one sense I suspect that we may be. Lawrence, as he himself says, 'knew all about Pan' but Patricia Merivale, who has carried out the most searching investigation of Pan's role in the work of all these writers, has pointed out that while there are stray references to Pan in Lawrence's early work, frequency of reference occurs only in a series of works dating from 1924 to 1926, which she calls his 'Pan cluster' and which takes in work such as 'St Mawr', 'The Last Laugh' and *The Plumed Serpent*.[36] Lawrence had by then turned back from the movement towards flowering consummation which he talked about at the time of *The Rainbow* and towards a greater self-identification with the spirit of Pan.

Lawrence's rediscovery of Pan in those later years went along with a growingly critical attitude to Forster. This was paradoxical, perhaps, but not inexplicable, since he was moved more and more by a rejection of Europe and European values which made him correspondingly more aware of, and hostile towards, the persistent commitment to European liberal values in Forster's work – and particularly the strong emphasis on personal relationships. It was this which tempered his admiration for *A Passage to India* when it arrived in 1924:

> Your book came two days ago, and I have read it and think it very good. The day of our white dominance is over, and no new day can come till this of ours has passed into night. Soit! I accept it. But one must go into the night ahead of it. So there you are. – I don't care about Bou-oum – nor all the universe. Only the dark ahead & the silence into which we haven't yet spoken our impertinent echoes. – You saying human relationships don't matter, then after all hingeing your book on a very unsatisfactory friendship between two men! *Carito!* – After one's primary relation to the X – I don't know what to call it, but not God or the Universe – only human relations matter. But secondarily. There is that religious relationship first—and one is inarticulate about it.[37]

The letter offers one of Lawrence's most open attempts to define the element in human life which he thought most important: something which was to be identified neither with God nor with the Universe, but still as a *relationship* – though a relationship with something not human. He also puts his finger most readily on the points both of resemblance and difference between himself and Lawrence when he argues against Forster's attempts to make his novel hinge on a human relationship: both men ground their ultimate beliefs in relationship, but only Forster in personal relationship. The final point of difference Lawrence sees has to do with the echo in the cave which thwarts all Mrs Moore's attempts to enunciate value against it; his own sense of the cave is as a place for the dark exploration into which he would commit himself adventurously.

The difference between the two men is not, perhaps, so clear-cut as Lawrence thought. Close attention to the novel shows that the echo in the cave is not presented by its author as having the last word. In the end, as Mrs Moore leaves India, India herself, in the form of thousands of palm-trees, derides her acceptance of the echo in the cave as final.[38] But much of the weight of the novel, if one reads it in personal terms, must necessarily fall on Mrs Moore's collapse. This was certainly how Middleton Murry, with his highly developed personal sensibility, had read it, and Murry's review, which Lawrence read before he read the novel itself,[39x] may actually have over-concentrated his attention on that incident.

Shortly after this Lawrence turned against Forster as well.[40x] The reasons are not clear. It is possible that Forster had written about 'St Mawr' in terms which he could not accept, or that some other comment had been reported to him. Or the change may simply have been part of a deepening bitterness towards everything connected with England. Whatever the cause, however, it was in line with a comment which he made about this time concerning 'passional inspiration' in the novel:

> It is such a bore that nearly all great novelists have a didactic purpose, otherwise a philosophy, directly opposite to their passional inspiration. In their passional inspiration, they are all phallic worshippers. From Balzac to Hardy, it is so. Nay, from Apuleius to E. M. Forster. Yet all of them, when it comes to their philosophy, or what they think-they-are, they are crucified Jesuses. What a bore! And what a burden for the novel to carry![41]

The sense that many of his contemporaries had betrayed their passional insights was evidently extending itself in his mind at this time in a way which made it natural for him to concentrate on Forster's failings at the expense of his strengths.

It has to be acknowledged, moreover, that there was a change in Forster himself at this time. After *A Passage to India*, the note of mystery which could still be traced in his fiction up to that point finally dropped away. What one finds instead is a more positive social commentary and a sharper irony. Since they remained embedded in a gentleness of manner, however, Lawrence was not likely to be attracted to either. Re-reading *The Celestial Omnibus* in 1927, he found it 'rather rubbish'; he also said that judging from the notice of Forster's last book – *Aspects of the Novel*, presumably – 'he must be rather a piffler just now.'[42]

When Lawrence wrote those words, he probably did not know of Forster's tribute to him in that book as 'the only living novelist in whom the song predominates, who has the rapt bardic quality, and whom it is idle to criticise.' Forster had expressed dislike of Lawrence's preaching—his 'bullying', as he termed it—but had then continued,

> . . . his greatness lies far, far back, and rests, not like

Dostoyevsky's upon Christianity, not like Melville's upon a contest, but upon something aesthetic. The voice is Balder's voice, though the hands are the hands of Esau. The prophet is irradiating nature from within, so that every colour has a glow and every form a distinctness which could not otherwise be obtained.[43]

Carl Baron's contribution to this collection gives further evidence of Forster's insight into Lawrence's creative processes, which prompted, amongst other things, a gesture for which he has often been praised: the letter to the *Nation and Athenaeum* after Lawrence's death, protesting against the grudging note of many of the obituary notices. After commenting that his character had perhaps not passed 'the test of the Sussex downs', he mentioned that he had heard little from him in after years and went on:

The war tortured him but never paralyzed him; the tremendous nightmare chapter in 'Kangaroo' is sufficient proof of that, and all through his later work the vitality continues. Now he is dead, and the low-brows whom he scandalized have united with the high-brows whom he bored to ignore his greatness. This cannot be helped: no one who alienates both Mrs Grundy and Aspasia can hope for a good obituary Press. All that we can do . . . is to say straight out that he was the greatest imaginative novelist of our generation.[44]

T. S. Eliot, the following week, wrote a critical letter:

I am the last person to wish to disparage the genius of Lawrence, or to disapprove when a writer of the eminence of Mr Forster speaks 'straight out'. But the virtue of speaking straight out is somewhat diminished if what one speaks is not sense. And unless we know exactly what Mr. Forster means by *greatest*, *imaginative*, and *novelist*, I submit that this judgment is meaningless. For there are at least three 'novelists' of 'our generation'—two of whom are living—for whom a similar claim might be made.[45]

To this Forster replied,

Mr T. S. Eliot duly entangles me in his web. He asks what exactly I mean by 'greatest', 'imaginative', and 'novelist', and I cannot say. Worse still, I cannot even say what 'exactly' means – only that there are occasions when I would rather feel like a fly than a spider, and that the death of D. H. Lawrence is one of these.[46]

It is, in most ways that matter, a superb reply – and one which incidentally demonstrates in Forster qualities which Lawrence did not possess. Yet it never does to underestimate Eliot's acumen as a critic, and his probing question may still be acknowledged, in one respect at least, to strike home. Was Lawrence's greatness really, after all, as an *imaginative* novelist? One is drawn back to Forster's phrase in the earlier tribute: 'something aesthetic'; would Lawrence himself have enjoyed being praised in those terms? Does not Eliot's question actually spring from greater awareness of the 'vitality' which Forster praises only in passing—even if he himself tended to see it as no more than insidiously malign, and necessarily to be condemned by the Christianity to which he had now committed himself?

The negative element in Eliot's judgement (though modified many years later) was reinforced shortly afterwards by the appearance of Murry's *Son of Woman* – a persuasive book which seems to have left its mark on Forster as well. Since the personal challenge which Lawrence often offered to those with whom he came in touch had reached its height in the long contentions with Murry, the latter's long account of their relationship was likely to find an echo in the minds of all who had ever suffered from his candour. Forster, who had previously argued that such considerations should be left aside ('If we start resenting or mocking, his treasure disappears as surely as if we started obeying him'[47]) may still have felt a residue of bitterness, or at least unease. Certainly he remained strangely silent concerning Lawrence for many years, apart from a few occasions such as the *Lady Chatterley* trial, when he allowed himself to appear as a witness for the defence.[48x]

In this connection it is worth looking at a lesser-known piece of his writing: his own review of *Son of Woman*.[49] Forster is sharply critical of Murry's book, it is true, but he is not quite as critical as he might have been, and his account suggests that he was partly persuaded by it – that as he turned Murry's pages he was reminded of aspects of Lawrence that he had turned away from in writing his posthumous tribute. Lawrence's hostility towards a belief in personal values and personal relationships – the very beliefs which played a dominant part in Forster's philosophy—was emphasised throughout the book.

In one sense, clearly, Murry had misread the later Lawrence. He had missed the underlying motive power of the vision, the fierce adherence to the life-principle which Lawrence believed to be threatened by the insidious work of modern civilisations, and the concentration upon honest acceptance of the inner processes of physical life as offering the one source of true value. Yet if Murry had missed this it was because he was more aware of other elements in Lawrence's vision, elements which he had tried to cut out of himself in his revulsion against European culture after the death of his mother and the outbreak of war. For Murry those elements had represented the 'true' Lawrence, and his turning away from them a betrayal.

If Forster, in turn, was, as I have suggested, half-persuaded by Murry's argument, that was because he too had registered the existence of this other side to Lawrence's philosophy, carrying on a subterranean existence beneath more overt and hostile utterances. Yet he had also seen it in a more positive light. It enabled him to see behind the apparent brutality of *The Plumed Serpent*, for example:

> He does believe in individuality—his mysticism is not of the Buddhistic, annihilistic sort—and, illogical as it sounds, he even believes in tenderness. I think here that the memory of his mother counts. Theirs was an attachment which cut across all theories, and glorified other relationships when she died. Tenderness is waiting behind the pseudo-scientific jargon of his solar-plexuses and the savagery of his blood-tests. It is his concession to the civilization he would destroy and the flaw in the primitive myths he would re-create. It is the Morning Star, the Lord of Both Ways, the star between day and dark.[50]

When Forster says this he is not, I think, talking about the role of Lawrence's mother in the central evolution of his later philosophy. From that point of view she counted rather as an embodiment of the spark of life that shines and resists death. He is referring rather to the more tender kind of relationship with the mother portrayed in *The White Peacock* and *Sons and Lovers* – a relationship on which Lawrence's hero had turned his back at the end of the latter novel. This strand, which flourished more strongly in Forster himself, enabled him to detect its subterranean presence throughout Lawrence's work.

That presence is less easily perceived by later readers, since the notion of a relationship between mother and son which assists the transmission of a certain kind of spirituality is now so unfashionable as to be almost unthinkable; yet we cannot fully understand the literature of the beginning of the century without paying some attention to that idea, and its origins in the mid-nineteenth century, when it had promised to provide a counterweight to the lack of scope for the 'spiritual' in utilitarian thinking.

Here another nineteenth-century writer calls for attention: John Ruskin, who was, like Hardy, a figure with whom many aspiring young writers found themselves forced to come to terms. Ruskin, whose impact in Victorian times was partly due to his success in the enterprise just mentioned – that of keeping alive a sense of the 'spiritual' while giving full weight to the demands of utilitarian thought – embodied in a more absolute form the strong feeling for the mother that is evident in Forster and the early Lawrence.[51]

A familiar pattern is re-enacted. Where Lawrence comes to reject firmly (at least at the conscious level), Forster remains torn between rival attitudes. We know from Jessie Chambers that Lawrence read Ruskin in his early youth and lent *Sesame and Lilies* to her brother; but by the time he was corresponding with Blanche Jennings (in 1908) he was telling her that while all Ruskinites were not fools the 'deep damnation of self-righteousness' lay 'thick all over them'.[52x] Will Brangwen in *The Rainbow* was a devotee of Ruskin;[53] in Lawrence's critique of him, we are entitled to trace the probing of a phase which he recognised as having taken place in himself. In his famous letter of 1912 discussing the meaning of *Sons and Lovers*, moreover, he talked about the situation which arises when a young man has a mother who 'holds his soul' and is thus inhibited from entering properly into life, claiming that what he has written is 'the tragedy of thousands of young men in England' and goes on 'I think it was Ruskin's, and men like him'.[54x]

Once again, Lawrence's vehemence was not matched by Forster. But there is something not altogether dissimilar in the drafts for *A Room with a View*, where the heroine enters Santa Croce with *Mornings in Florence* – 'that invaluable and exasperating book' – and finds herself bewildered by the forcefulness and self-righteousness of the author; it also emerges in *Howards End*, when Leonard Bast reads *The Stones of Venice*, hoping 'to come to culture suddenly, much as the Revivalist hopes to come to Jesus.'[55x]

A similar ambiguity dogs Forster's attitudes to the mother-son relationship itself. His awareness of the imprisoning power which

the affections of the mother could exert upon the child is expressed
vividly in his short story 'The Machine Stops', where the threat held
over those who try to escape from the machine is that of
'homelessness' and where the tentacles which the machine exudes to
draw back any who do try to escape are like the clutches of
smothering affection. P. N. Furbank's biography makes it clear that
he himself was sometimes irritated by aspects of his mother's
behaviour; yet he went on living with her for the rest of her life. One
key to this devotion may perhaps be sought in a sense that in an age
growingly dominated by scepticism certain of his values were
preserved through the mother-child link.[56x]

What is being suggested here bears on the points made by Wilfred
Stone in his essay above – that in Forster's early fictions love is often
seen as a kind of 'spiritual currency'; and by Richard Parkinson –
that in *Howards End* the dominating question, who shall inherit
England?, is almost identifiable with the question, who has
inherited the spirit of Mrs Wilcox? In *The Longest Journey* a similar
point about the 'currency of the soul' is crucial to the discussion of
the hero, Rickie Elliot. It is central to his tragedy that his sense of his
mother has become hardened into certain fixed ideas which are now
a kind of 'coinage', so that when these images are challenged or
broken he becomes spiritually 'bankrupt'.[57] Even his acceptance of
Stephen Wonham as his half-brother is dominated by the image of
his mother. When Stephen asks him to come away with him, not as a
brother but as a man, he cannot do it. Yet there is one thing in
Stephen's appeal which ensures Rickie's allegiance to him:

> In the voice he had found a surer guarantee. Habits and sex may
> change with the new generation, features may alter with the play
> of a private passion, but a voice is apart from these. It lies nearer
> to the racial essence and perhaps to the divine; it can, at all
> events, overleap one grave.[58]

The final possibility which Forster raises here is also, and
deliberately, a possibility which he chooses to leave open. Rickie
may have bankrupted himself by trusting an image of his mother
which was stamped by him and bore his own superscription, instead
of perceiving that she was in her self-transmitting essence fallible as
well as noble, but there remains a strong suggestion that the deeper
trust of which this was a mistaken form was both valid and central.
And it seems that Forster could not finally reject such a belief. When

he calls *The Longest Journey* his 'preferred' novel,[59] the very impersonality of his chosen term suggests a certain captivity in the judgement – as if while recognising that it is unlikely to be shared by his readers he cannot forfeit it. He could depict Rickie's predicament critically because in some respects he himself had escaped it; yet it was also, at a deep level, his own. He could not but acknowledge the vulnerability of a position which held that the mother-child link might be identifiable with the divine, yet he found it difficult to cut a thread which not only seemed to sustain some of his basic values but also to facilitate his creative gifts.

By the time that he wrote *A Passage to India*, on the other hand, when his former easy fluency had in any case gone, he could handle the question less controversially by centring it mainly in the consciousness of Mrs Moore and keeping her children in the background, at least until the end. In the cave Mrs Moore comes to learn that the validity of the spiritual currency which she has brought to India is not recognised there – still less the secondary bills of exchange ('Let there be light', 'It is finished' and the rest) which pass so easily in her own culture. The discovery bankrupts her spiritually and undermines her hold on life itself; so that she feels herself defeated.[60] Yet once again a door is left open, since something in her spirit has crossed the racial barriers and continues to be recognised, whether by the Indians who chant a ritualised version of her name or by the individuals who remember her.[61] In the closing chapters, likewise, her children, transmitting an outgoing spirit which is recognisably inherited from her, help to heal the breach between Aziz and the English.[62x]

For Lawrence, Mrs Moore's dilemma would have been largely unrecognisable, since he had long before rejected the sense of values on which it was based. For him, therefore, her collapse would not have signalled a spiritual tragedy but would rather have been seen as one aspect of the passing of white dominance.

Yet here again a further depth opens. In Lawrence's later writings the emphasis is always upon the life-force which in retrospect he saw his mother to have embodied: that side of her which had originally responded to his father and which had lent spiritedness to her beliefs. But in another sense he never lost contact with her in her wholeness. Indeed, if it is true that in that tradition the spiritual link with the mother often seemed to assist creative fluency, it could be argued that the underlying ease with which he continued to write had something to do with that former debt. What can in any case, be argued is that that surviving sense of her gentler nature kept alive the note of 'tenderness' which, after *The Plumed Serpent*, he increasingly cultivated.

These are controversial matters, which cannot be pursued further here. It is enough to have indicated the possibility of a mutual recognition, across a gulf as it were, between the sensibility that lived equivocally in Forster and that which, rejected at the creative level in Lawrence, yet survived somewhere in his psyche. And if so, it was that recognition, I would further suggest, which enabled Forster, almost alone among contemporary critics, to discern the element of tenderness in *The Plumed Serpent*, and which caused Lawrence to continue for so long his relationship with Forster in spite of a gentle sensibility in him which he would have reprobated in any other English writer of his time. In the letter that contained his appreciation of *A Passage to India* he stated his position appositely:

> Dear E. M. do you remember asking me, on the Downs in Sussex—how I knew you were not dead—*if* I knew?—Quien sabe! One dies so many deaths, it too ceases to matter.—But there's not a soul in England says a word to me—save your whisper through the willow boughs.[63]

The last words may contain a covert reference to Kenneth Grahame and *The Wind in the Willows*, which would help define the limitations in Lawrence's eyes, of Forster's achievement as a Pan-propitiator. Whatever we make of that, however, he had already, a few months earlier, found phrases with which to indicate still more sharply his view of their respective positions, and of Forster's status as presenting an alternative strongly preferable to mainstream Bloomsbury. The occasion was Forster's sending him his guide to Alexandria, *Pharos and Pharillon*:

> Thank you for Pharos and Pharillon, which I have read. Sad as ever, like a lost soul calling Ichabod. But I prefer the sadness to the Stracheyism. To me you are the last Englishman. And I am the one after that.[64]

In these last phrases, Lawrence formulates, in terms of his own, something of the differences between himself and Forster as they have revealed themselves in this discussion. When he wrote them he had not, of course, received *A Passage to India*, nor could he foresee the long series of essays that Forster would produce in his later years. It is doubtful whether his judgement would have been very much altered by the latter, however, since they belong largely to the 'Bloomsbury' side of Forster, and to that element in him which continued to rejoice in the possibilities of personal relationship between individuals – relationships which he himself had turned away from in favour of those which were 'impersonal'.

For a reader less impatient with Western values, however, Forster's achievements in support of the individual and the personal (the intellectually astringent humaneness that pervades the essays in *Two Cheers for Democracy*, for instance) come into the foreground, making any dismissive elements in Lawrence's comment less persuasive. One may rather set it at the side of some criticisms made by Virginia Woolf in her essay of 1927 (where the note of disparagement has again been eroded by time):

> . . . we have the sense that there is some perversity in Mr Forster's endowment so that his gifts in their variety and number tend to trip each other up. If he were less scrupulous, less just, less sensitively aware of the different aspects of every case, he could, we feel, come down with greater force on one precise point. As it is, the strength of his blow is dissipated. He is like a light sleeper who is always being woken by something in the room. The poet is twitched away by the satirist; the comedian is tapped on the shoulder by the moralist; he never loses himself or forgets himself for long in sheer delight in the beauty or the interest of things as they are.[65]

What Virginia Woolf (and doubtless other critics of her time) would see as a weakness can from a later point of view be regarded as a strength. It shows us Forster trying to remain true to a variety of urges, considerations and roles, each of which works in him equally strongly. Other writers would find their own idiosyncratic paths through the twentieth-century literary jungle; but those who, like Forster, tried to remain true both to the past and to their sense of what was happening in society during their lifetime would be left not with a unified vision but a fragmented one, in which different ways of conceiving the artist's role would pursue one another in quick succession. *A Passage to India*, which Virginia Woolf admired on the grounds that Forster had there 'almost achieved the great feat of animating this compact body of observation with a spiritual light'[66] is, to a later eye, rather a triumph of fragmented vision. Most writers since have felt the need for a more forceful gesture and have (like Lawrence) cut loose from the past – at least in some important respects. Forster, trying to hold on and connect, shows us what they lose when they do so.

Although his own mythological interests gave him an unusual insight into both Lawrence's dark gods and Virginia Woolf's transforming divinity of light, therefore, his urge to inclusiveness precluded him from intense devotion to either. As Judith Herz has perceptively argued, his true god is to be identified neither as Pan nor as Apollo, but as Hermes – who is more intimately concerned than they with human affairs. Hermes is the messenger between the dark and the light but he is also, as Hermes Psychopompus, a less portentous figure: 'machine-breaker and conductor of souls to a not-too-terrible hereafter'.[67] In action he is an unreliable god, perhaps, able to change his shape with bewildering speed and leaving no firm and strong personality for the casual spectator to seize and dwell upon, but in an age which has learned with Lawrence not to look for the 'old stable ego' in fiction[68] his role becomes by the same token more relevant for the writer who is attempting a full exploration of humanity.

And this in turn throws light upon the personality of the novelist himself. Forster was elusive, even to his friends. His interweaving roles as satirist, poet, comedian and moralist were sustained within a personality which burrowed or fluttered away from those who tried to seize hold of it. Yet somewhere in that interplay one glimpses a kind of composite identity, which was trying to remain true to all that it knew – and for which Lawrence's term 'the last Englishman' turns out to have been peculiarly apposite.

Was there also, in spite of their many differences, a place where the two men could recognise a common ground? Perhaps so. When Forster's Fielding passes through Italy on his way back from India, he finds in Venice that he no longer wishes, as formerly, to 'wrap himself up' in St Mark's since he now sees in the city as a whole something 'more precious':

> . . . the harmony between the works of man and the earth that upholds them, the civilization that has escaped muddle, the spirit in a reasonable form, with flesh and blood subsisting.[69]

Lawrence's Aaron Sisson, walking through Florence in the rain, has a similar moment of revelation in the Piazza della Signoria:

> Aaron looked and looked at the three great naked men. David so much white, and standing forward, self-conscious: then at the great splendid front of the Palazzo Vecchio: and at the fountain splashing water upon its wet, wet figures; and the distant equestrian statues; and the stone-flagged space of the grim square. And he felt that he was in one of the world's living centres . . .

If his satisfaction corresponds in one way to Fielding's, however, the quality of his feelings is of a different kind:

> Florence, passionate fearless Florence had spoken herself out. Aaron was fascinated by the Piazza della Signoria. He never went into the town, nor returned to it from his lodging, without contriving to pass through the square. And he never passed through it without satisfaction. Here men had been at their intensest, most naked pitch, here, at the end of the old world and the beginning of the new.[70]

Where Fielding finds himself between two worlds, across the space of the earth, and goes on to recognise the Mediterranean as constituting 'the human norm', Aaron Sisson, who exists rather between two worlds in time, sees Florence as a place where men 'for a moment were themselves, as a plant in flower is for the moment completely itself'.[71] His underlying sense of balance (between the old world and the new) corresponds to Fielding's (between England and India), but the intensity of his feeling in the Piazza looks back rather to the inchoate aspirations there of another of Forster's characters, caught at her moment of growth:

> The great square was in shadow; the sunshine had come too late to strike it. Neptune was already unsubstantial in the twilight, half god, half ghost, and his fountain plashed dreamily to the men and satyrs who idled together on its marge. The Loggia showed as the triple entrance of a cave, wherein dwelt many a deity, shadowy but immortal, looking forth upon the arrivals and departures of mankind. It was the hour of unreality—the hour, that is, when unfamiliar things are real. An older person at such

an hour and in such a place might think that sufficient was happening to him, and rest content. Lucy desired more.[72]

For parallel intensities in *A Passage to India* we would look less to Fielding than to Adela Quested and Professor Godbole. And such moments of aspiration, whenever they occur in his writing, may be seen as offering Forster's own version of the double attitude to life expressed by Lawrence—who could declare, 'My Englishness is my very vision', but who could also write,

> The Englishman, *per se*, is not enough. He has to modify himself to a distant end. He has to balance with something that is not himself.[73]

24 Forster Scholarship and Criticism for the Desert Islander

Frederick P. W. McDowell

E. M. Forster's collected works could conveniently be taken for delight and edification to the proverbial desert island and cause the sojourner-to-be no great physical stress in conveying them there. The collected Forster in the Pocket Edition would bulk not much larger than a collected Shakespeare; and if not so fraught with wisdom and art as Shakespeare's work, still Forster's writings could delight the solitary individual. If by some miracle our traveller could also bring with him a small box containing the best writings on Forster, what should he take? What, in short, are the indispensable books on Forster, and what parts or what aspects of these books would be especially illuminating? And then what articles in books and journals would give our solitary a deeper insight into Forster's mind and art?

Our traveller could omit, I think, the books by Rose Macaulay (*The Writings of E. M. Forster*, 1938) and of Lionel Trilling (*E. M. Forster*, 1943). Valuable as these books were for the recovery of Forster's reputation in the post-World-War-II age, they have now been superseded. For an overview of Forster two other books are more pertinent, both from 1962, K. W. Gransden's *E. M. Forster* and J. B. Beer's *The Achievement of E. M. Forster*. Gransden packs an almost uncanny amount of information and number of illuminating judgements into a small space and is the most reliable of the guides who open up Forster terrain. Beer's *Achievement* is a more extended and relaxed study, containing much plot summary and extended quotation. But these aspects of his book, which could be detrimental to the work of other critics, add authority to his account, which is noteworthy for the acuity of its judgements, for its relating of Forster to the romantic tradition, and for its stimulating and fresh discussion of Forster's symbolism. My Twayne volume, *E. M. Forster* (1969) may also provide an overview, and it relates Forster to the criticism existing on him to the time of publication. Still of great value is James McConkey's *The Novels of E. M. Forster* (1957). McConkey was the first to attempt an extended study of Forster after Trilling's somewhat magisterial book of 1943, and he was among the first to discuss with precision the image patterns, the symbols, and the formal aspects of Forster's work. His high valuation of *A Passage to India* was also instrumental in the upgrading of that novel.

Three other books, in varying degrees controversial, must also be included in any select packet of Forster criticism: Frederick J. Crews's *E. M. Forster: The Perils of Humanism* (1962), Wilfred Stone's *The Cave and the Mountain: A Study of E. M. Forster* (1966), and George H. Thomson's *The Fiction of E. M. Forster* (1967). Crews reveals the merits and defects of a critic who interprets a writer in light of a set thesis. He maintains that Forster found it increasingly difficult to adhere to his humanistic values as the twentieth century advanced and World War I intervened. Crews applies his thesis tactfully and lightly with the result that his book provides a brilliant series of readings of the early fiction but an inadequate reading of *A Passage to India*, though Crews regards it as Forster's greatest work. In my view *A Passage* is not solely a pessimistic novel in which Forster mourns the loss of his humanistic values, but it is also a partially affirmative one, assimilating in its final statement many positive values from Hinduism and other aspects of Indian religion and culture. Thomson rightly sees the novels as being in large part mythical and archetypal, and he is able, therefore, to neutralise many of the strictures which critics, applying standards derived from literary realism, have imposed on them. Though Thomson may underrate in so doing the realistic and comic elements in the novels, his readings of them, as in the case of Crews's book, are brilliant and stimulating. The commentary on *A Passage to India* is especially incisive. Crews's and Thomson's books contain the greatest number of insights per page of any of the books on Forster and are essential texts for any advanced student of Forster and Bloomsbury.

In different ways, the two books are definitive upon Forster's intellectual origins and ambience. This is also the virtue of Stone's monumental book, which is especially excellent on Forster's debt to

Cambridge and to nineteenth-century thought. Stone is temperamentally unsympathetic to Forster's early novels, particularly *Howards End*, and reads them somewhat too rigidly in terms of Forster's own alleged conflicts and confusions and in terms of Freud and Jung. His formulations are not always accurate, since the facts of Forster's homosexuality were not fully known when Stone wrote his book. But when allowances have been made for Stone's approach, his is a book that must be consulted by all Forstereans, for stimulus if not always for agreement; and his reading of *A Passage to India* still seems to me to be the best single essay yet available on the novel, in his skilful relating of it to both British and Indian culture, in his seeing it in archetypal terms, in his defining the dualities and the triadic relationships in it, and in his charting of a dialectical pattern in it between the conscious elements in the psyche and the unconscious.

Some other books should also find a place in our traveller's limited package of writings on Forster. Alan Wilde's *Art and Order: A Study of E. M. Forster* (1964) contains many insights of depth by virtue of the critic's subtle sensibility; and John Colmer's *E. M. Forster: The Personal Voice* (1975) reads the fiction discerningly if somewhat differently from other critics, because he is the first to have written a full-length study since the posthumously published homosexual writings have appeared and because he has also been able to use some of the manuscript materials available in the Forster Archive at King's College, Cambridge. To understand something of Forster's Bloomsbury affiliations, our desert islander would want S. P. Rosenbaum's *The Bloomsbury Group: A Collection of Memoirs, Commentary and Criticism* (1975), with its reprinting of many primary documents previously unpublished or otherwise difficult to secure. Of the essays on Bloomsbury he would find the most valuable to be Geoffrey Moore's 'The Significance of Bloomsbury' (*Kenyon Review*, 17, 1955) and William Van O'Connor's 'Toward a History of Bloomsbury' (*Southwest Review*, 40, 1955). For a listing, accurate, inclusive and informed, of Forster's own work, J. B. Kirkpatrick's *A Bibliography of E. M. Forster* in the Soho series (revised edition, 1968) is standard. Her book documents the fact that Forster continued to be a prolific if somewhat miscellaneous writer after 1924, when he ceased to publish fiction. In order to understand Forster's own intentions, his 1953 *Paris Review* interview ought to be at hand (reprinted in *Writers at Work*, edited by Malcolm Cowley, 1958) and Peter Burra's 'The Novels of E. M. Forster' (*Nineteenth Century and*

After, 116, 1934), which also appeared as the Introduction to the Everyman Edition of *A Passage to India* (1942) and had won by then Forster's approbation for its grasp of his work and purposes.

P. N. Furbank's *E. M. Forster, A Life: The Growth of the Novelist 1879–1914* (1977) is the official biography, a fascinating, informative, and apparently definitive work. It is as sensitive and as imaginative as one had been led to expect from Furbank's shorter pieces in appreciation, 'Tribute to Forster' (*Times*, 28 December 1968) and 'The Personality of E. M. Forster' (*Encounter*, 25, November 1970). Making use of unpublished materials at King's College, Furbank has been able to give exact data concerning many facets of Forster's life: his early discovery of his homosexual inclinations, his realisation as a result in 1911 that he could no longer write about conventional subjects in fiction, his long and ultimately wearying relationship with H. O. Meredith with whom he had some sexual contact, his intense and finally frustrating friendship with Syed Ross Masood, his 'love affair' with his mother but her disheartening pressures on him in his middle years, his abundant exposure to elderly women but his limited contact with younger ones, his expression of passion in his books as contrasted with his outwardly tame existence, his extended career as extension lecturer, his difficulties with his writing after he had acknowledged his homosexuality, and his first Indian visit in 1913 presented in full detail. Our traveller would need to take not only this volume of the biography with him, but the second (not yet available at the time of writing), which deals with the later years.

Forster has also had the advantage of being a major modern author who is being published in an ongoing definitive edition, the Abinger Edition of the Works of E. M. Forster, edited by Oliver Stallybrass. It is reassuring to have textual cruxes resolved by a careful comparison of all known versions of a work from manuscripts through proofs to differing editions. Not only are we experiencing the pleasure of reading Forster in the most accurate text possible, but we have the further satisfaction of encountering in the introductions or appendixes to each volume background information on Forster, some of it previously unpublished and not elsewhere available. Certainly our desert islander would want as the minimum the fiction now printed in this edition if he could make room for the good-sized volumes: *Howards End, A Room with A View, Where Angels Fear to Tread, The Life to Come and Other Stories* and *A Passage to India*. If he had a sizeable enough trunk he would also want *The Manuscripts of Howards End, The Lucy Novels: Early Sketches for 'A Room with A View', Two Cheers for Democracy, Aspects of the Novel, Goldsworthy Lowes Dickinson and Related Writings* and *The Manuscripts of A Passage to India*.

Of the several collections of essays on Forster only two are in the necessary category. *E. M. Forster: A Tribute*, edited by K. Natwar-Singh (1964), communicates a general sense, prevalent among Indian intellectuals, of Forster's importance for them; whereas *Aspects of E. M. Forster*, edited by Oliver Stallybrass (1969), contains many significant essays, some of which I shall note below.

Though the importance of many of the general essays on Forster has diminished with the appearance of the standard books just described, there are at least a dozen that our devotee would wish to have at his disposal in order to reflect upon them. Of first importance is Rex Warner's brief overview of Forster in his *Writers and Their Work* pamphlet (1951, revised in 1960 by John Morris) which, despite its brevity, contains many judgements of value. This pamphlet might well be the first essay for the neophyte to consult and to use, along with Gransden's *E. M. Forster*. Derek A. Traversi on 'The Novels of E. M. Forster' (1937, reprinted in Philip Gardner, editor, *E. M. Forster: The Critical Heritage*, 1973) is the best essay written on Forster before the 1960s. Traversi has a genuine sense of the complexities in Forster, especially of his drive toward unity in his work and of his varying failures to attain it. Virginia Woolf in 'The Novels of E. M. Forster' (1927; reprinted in Gardner) noted the split in Forster between the rationalistic humanist and the poetic visionary and felt that this conflict was essentially unresolved in his fiction. F. R. Leavis independently expressed this same view in an influential essay (1938, reprinted in *The Common Pursuit*, 1952), though he had good words to say for *A Passage to India*. John Crowe Ransom in 'E. M. Forster' (1943, reprinted in Gardner) notes this same collocation of intelligence and vision but does not find it aesthetically detrimental. Ransom also stresses the animating principle of nature in Forster's work and his debt to Meredith. Austin Warren's 'The Novels of E. M. Forster' (1937, revised in *Rage for Order: Essays in Criticism*, 1948) also contains many noteworthy observations. Warren stresses the role for Forster of self-knowledge in human existence, the importance of the realm of values for Forster over the realm of fact, the need for human beings in Forster to attain true proportion, and the crucial role of Mrs Moore in *A Passage to India*. Forster is central to E. K. Brown's

standard *Rhythm in the Novel* (1950) in which he analyses extensively
and with perspicacity the recurring motifs, images, and symbols in
Forster's fiction. His example no doubt encouraged McConkey,
Beer, and others to engage in their further attempts to analyse
Forster's fiction in this manner. Stephen Spender has written twice
on Forster in his books. In 'Personal Relations and Public Powers'
(*The Creative Element*, 1953) he emphasises the complexities of
experience as Forster encountered them, his abrogation of set forms
and perceptions, his high valuation of love and individualism and
personal relationships, and finally his ultimate failure in his fiction
to bridge the personal and the social realms. In 'Elegies for England:
E. M. Forster' (*Love-Hate Relations: English and American Sensibilities*,
1974) Spender demonstrates how the early Forster recorded a
moment in modern history when natural forces could still infuse life
into the culture of a class whose power passed with World War I. A
somewhat similar emphasis occurs in Alwyn Berland's 'James and
Forster: The Morality of Class' (*Cambridge Journal*, 6, 1953). In this
critique Berland maintains that Forster envisions salvation in terms
of pastoral values and emerges as a less convincing mentality,
therefore, than James, who instead stressed the renovating influence
of culture upon the individual's spirit.

A number of important essays date from the 1960s. G. D.
Klingopulos in 'Mr. Forster's Good Influence' (*The Modern Age*,
edited by Boris Ford, 1961) sees Forster as a spiritual leader in
World War II by virtue of his personal example and by virtue of the
strength of his liberal and humanist values, although he also had the
courage to see that the disorder of India was potentially more
creative than the rationalistic humanism which he had embodied in
Cyril Fielding. Stuart Hampshire in 'Two Cheers for Mr. Forster'
(1966, reprinted in *Modern Writers and Other Essays*, 1969) traces the
oppositions in Forster's fiction between a rationalistic liberalism and
a natural order which deflects and transcends such liberalism. In 'A
New Look at E. M. Forster' (1968, reprinted in *The Modern Spirit:
Essays on the Continuity of Nineteenth and Twentieth Century Literature*,
1970) Robert Langbaum contrasts in a brilliant essay the spaciousness of *A Passage to India* with the rather more limited perspectives
found in the earlier fiction, even while he concedes that *Where Angels
Fear to Tread* is a masterpiece. A. Woodward has also written a wide-
ranging article in 'The Humanism of E. M. Forster' (*Theoria*, 20,
1963), in which he explores the tensions in the fiction, particularly in
A Passage, between Forster's agnostic humanism and his sense of a

transcendent reality to be reached through intuition (**Woodward** also comments most acutely on style in *A Passage*). Among **V. S.** Pritchett's many perceptive writings on Forster, a representative essay for our traveller would be 'E. M. Forster at Ninety' (*New York Times Book Review*, 29 December 1968) in which the writer celebrates Forster's leavening influence on the literary and intellectual scene.

At least five essays from *Aspects of E. M. Forster* are of first importance. Elizabeth Bowen in 'A Passage to E. M. Forster' sees the books as having their genesis in conflict and passion, and she engagingly charts her own progress as a Forster devotee. Wilfred Stone in 'Forster on Love and Money' comments acutely on the necessity for Forster of the material but notes his sensitivity also to the limitations it imposes on the spirit. K. Natwar-Singh in 'Only Connect . . . : Forster and India' is standard on Forster's positive influence on Indian intellectuals; and David Garnett in 'Forster and Bloomsbury' defines Forster's firm relationship to Bloomsbury, citing in particular the restraining influence imposed on his vein of fantasy by the rationality of his friends in this group of intellectuals. Malcolm Bradbury's essay on *A Passage to India*, also in *Aspects of E. M. Forster*, I shall mention below.

Three general essays from the 1970s are of first importance for our isolated devotee of Forster. Alan Wilde in 'Depths and Surfaces: Dimensions of Fosterian Irony' (*English Literature in Transition*, 16:4, 1973) traces an alleged advance in Forster to a concern with the depths of experience from an earlier concern with surfaces, and a retreat once again after *A Passage* to a commitment to the surfaces of life. Elizabeth Heine's 'The Significance of Structure in the Novels of E. M. Forster and Virginia Woolf' (*English Literature in Transition*, 16:4, 1973) is controversial but stimulating in arguing that Forster's fiction is more externally wrought and less 'organic' than Virginia Woolf's. In rather abrupt contrast Donald Salter exhaustively studies the pagan aspect of Forster in 'That Is My Ticket: The Homosexual Writings of E. M. Forster' (*London Magazine*, 14, 1975). Salter concludes that Forster failed signally to assimilate this paganism into aesthetically viable and compelling fiction in his posthumously published writings.

Three of the best recent accounts of Forster devolve about some aspect of his political thinking, and this aspect of Forster our islander would wish to come to terms with. Donald Hannah in 'The Limitations of Liberalism in E. M. Forster's Work' (*English*

Miscellany, 13, 1962) rejects as inadequate the programmatic liberalism of *Howards End* in favour of the chastened liberalism that survives more tenuously in *A Passage to India* the challenges that are put to it. C. B. Cox in 'E. M. Forster's Island' (*The Free Spirit: A Study of Liberal Humanism in the Novels of George Eliot, Henry James, E. M. Forster, Virginia Woolf, Angus Wilson*, 1963) stresses the incomplete social commitment of Forster and his characters, and Cox protests the passivity and the escapism which he finds in them. While he overstates his case, there is no question as to his integrity as commentator. In contrast to Cox's view as to Forster's lack of political commitment, Willis H. Truitt in 'Thematic and Symbolic Ideology in the Works of E. M. Forster' (*Journal of Aesthetics and Art Criticism*, 30, 1971) demonstrates a great degree of such commitment in Forster. In a persuasive Marxist reading of the fiction, Truitt sees Forster as a really revolutionary artist. Herbert Howarth in 'E. M. Forster and the Contrite Establishment' (*Journal of General Education*, 17, 1965) reveals how completely Forster embodied in his fiction the liberalism of the Cambridge of his youth and how formative the idealistic approach to politics which he then absorbed was to be upon him later.

Upwards of a dozen essays on *A Passage to India* are first-class, and our hermit would wish to have them at hand to increase his knowledge and understanding of that novel. Earliest to serve as correctives to Trilling's downgrading of the novel were F. R. Leavis's 1938 essay and E. K. Brown's account, both already described. Two essays from the 1950s by Gertrude M. White and Glen O. Allen helped to rehabilitate *Passage*. These accounts are still standard, though each one suffers from some misplaced emphasis. White's '*A Passage to India*: Analysis and Revaluation' (*PMLA*, 68, 1953) offers a Hegelean interpretation of the novel's structure, but it is at its best when analysing characters in relation to theme; whereas Allen's 'Structure, Symbol, and Theme in E. M. Forster's *A Passage to India* (*PMLA*, 70, 1955) is over-schematic in its interpretation of the three divisions of the novel, but it is also greatly suggestive as it relates the novel to oriental religion and to the philosophy of Schopenhauer. Another early essay, D. J. Enright's 'To the Lighthouse or to India?' (*The Apothecary's Shop*, 1957), explicitly takes issue with Trilling's denigration of *A Passage*. In his discussion Enright praises Forster's capacious view of personal relationships and his use of India as the great character of the book. Two of the best early essays comment upon the anthropological, the mythical, the religious, the philosophical, and the metaphysical dimensions of the novel and remain definitive statements: Louise Dauner's 'What Happened in the Cave?' Reflections on *A Passage to India*' (*Modern Fiction Studies*, 7, 1961) and Ellin Horowitz's 'The Communal Ritual and the Dying God in E. M. Forster's *A Passage to India*' (*Criticism*, 6, 1964). Dauner views the caves ambivalently as exemplifying all the elemental dichotomies in human experience and as being, therefore, highly suggestive archetypal symbols; while Horowitz sees Mrs Moore and her fate as an embodiment of primitive fertility rituals wherein a god is thrown into the water and later returns as a spiritual influence to bring fertility and peace to the land. Glenn Pederson in 'Forster's Symbolic Form' (*Kenyon Review*, 21, 1959) is diffuse and somewhat confused perhaps, but he is also most suggestive in regarding Mrs Moore as the spiritual and the structural centre of *A Passage*. Such archetypal aspects of the novel just discussed were to be developed still further in some of the books mentioned earlier as essential for our desert islander to have by him, those by Stone, Wilde, and Thomson.

Most of the best essays on *A Passage to India* in the 1960s and the 1970s follow McConkey and some of the writers just mentioned in positing a Hindu interpretation of the novel or else in suggesting the wide-ranging metaphysical significances to be discovered in it. By his very title Kenneth Burke suggests this kind of reading in 'Social and Cosmic Mystery: *A Passage to India*' (*Language as Symbolic Action*, 1966). In an involuted and convoluted but searching account Burke regards the novel primarily as 'a comedy of ironically sympathetic contemplation' that opens out to suggest universal and cosmic values which are elusive and difficult to define. Michael Spencer in 'Hinduism in E. M. Forster's *A Passage to India*' (*Journal of Asian Studies*, 27, 1968) finds Bhakti Hinduism as central to the comprehensiveness characterising the 'Temple' section, as opposed to the divisiveness and renunciation characterising the 'Caves' section, though Spencer notes that this form of Hinduism may also be too disinterested to have won Forster's entire allegiance as a committed humanist. In a suggestive article, 'An Indian Reading of E. M. Forster's Classic' (*Ibadan Studies in English*, 1, 1969), J. A. Ramsaran finds that the three disparate male characters—Fielding, Aziz, and Godbole—are united by a love of poetry, and he demonstrates that Fielding has possibilities in his nature that take him beyond the rationality of his humanism. Malcolm Bradbury with his 'Two Passages to India: Forster as Victorian and Modern' in *Aspects of*

E. M. Forster (1969) has written one of the most challenging treatments we have of Forster's novel and illustrates how Forster attempted heroically in *A Passage* to unite the opposed strands in his sensibility and mind: rational intelligence with its ironic strength and poetic imagination with its recourse to symbolism to suggest an ineffable reality, at once apocalyptic and unitary, a reality as desirable as it is difficult to attain in this refractory world.

Religious, metaphysical, and philosophical preoccupations also inform some of the other best recent treatments of Forster's novel. S. V. Pradhan in 'A "Song" of Love: Forster's *A Passage to India*' (*Centennial Review*, 17, 1973) breaks some new ground in emphasising the non-Hindu quality of Mrs Moore's vision, in elucidating the Bahkti aspect of Godbole's Hinduism, and in exposing the weaknesses of both Islam and Christianity when they confront the culture of India. And what may be a definitive essay on a difficult subject is Chaman L. Sahni's 'The Marabar Caves in the Light of Indian Thought' (*Focus on Forster's 'A Passage to India'*, edited by V. A. Shahane, 1975), wherein the author sees the Caves as associated, in varying ways, with almost all the forms of Indian metaphysics and religion. In Sahni's view, the Caves portend a superpersonal spiritual reality whereas the Temple portends a personal spiritual reality. Both kinds of reality become aspects of the same Lord, however, (and aspects of the spiritual vision, presumably, informing Forster's book). In contrast to many other discussions of the novel, Hélène L. Webner in 'E. M. Forster's Divine Comedy' (*Renascence*, 23, 1971) convincingly corrects the view that Forster, as an agnostic and devotee of Indian culture and religion, had no concern with Christian values, symbols, and practices. And it is refreshing to have the virtues of Forster's humanism once again extolled by Naomi Lebowitz in '*A Passage to India*: History as Humanist Humor' (*Humanism and the Absurd in the Modern Novel*, 1971). She regards Forster as being aware of the paradoxical (and absurd) nature of reality without at the same time losing his sense of humanistic perspective, thinking of him as a valuable writer because he can give the absurd its due recognition without being thrown off balance by it.

Our traveller's library would be incomplete without access to yet four other accounts of *A Passage*. Benita Parry's *Delusions and Discoveries: Studies on India in the British Imagination 1880–1930* (1972) is a classic book for what she attempts to prove, that Forster can be seen as the humane and sophisticated culmination of a half-century of

Anglo-Indian fiction which tended, most of it, to be superficial and prejudiced. Forster's art and his values, therefore, are largely to be measured in terms of an opposition to the views and the fictional conventions used by the minor novelists and the one major prose artist – Kipling – who had preceded him. Parry then interprets *A Passage* and dwells on how the ethical, philosophical, aesthetic, and religious values dramatised in it relate to the corpus of Indian literature and thought. She stresses the novel's immense scope and notes the paradox, exemplified in Godbole, of India's comprising a static social order yet a dynamic spiritual life. Making use this time of the facts of Indian history and politics in the twentieth century, Jeffrey Meyers in *Fiction and the Colonial Experience* (1973: first appearance of the Forster study, 1971) seems to have been the first commentator to reveal how deeply embedded in *A Passage* were the political events and the political aspirations current in India at the time that Forster wrote it. Though it does not quite meet one's expectations, June Perry Levine's study, *Creation and Criticism: E. M. Forster's 'A Passage to India'* (1971) ought to accompany our traveller. While its overview of Forster scholarship and her own interpretations are disappointing, Levine in her early chapters relates *A Passage* significantly to other accounts of life in India which Forster knew, and she analyses perceptively the manuscripts of the novel. G. K. Das's *E. M. Forster's India* (1977) is a more modest but perhaps more valuable work for our student to possess. Das examines with insight the corpus of Forster's collected and uncollected writing on India, as it helps define Forster's views on the India contemporary with him and as it impinges upon his artistically compelling dramatisation of them in *A Passage to India*.

Though the essays on *Howards End* are fewer and less crucial to our collection of definitive secondary works on Forster, at least five treatments of the novel are first-rate and should form part of our packet of select Forster criticism. James Hall in his deep-probing 'Forster's Family Reunions' (*The Tragic Comedians*, 1963; first appeared 1958) sees the principal conflict and reconciliation in the novel as occurring between Margaret and Helen Schlegel rather than between the Schlegels and the Wilcoxes, and he regards family solidarity as the final value prized in the novel. Cyrus Hoy wrote also a most suggestive essay in 'Forster's Metaphysical Novel' (*PMLA*, 75, 1960), and he defines with precision and originality the numerous dichotomies in the novel, all of which Forster was to transcend in evolving a comprehensive unitary vision. As an essay

which probes deeply into *Howards End* there is Malcolm Bradbury's
'*Howards End*' (1962, revised in *Forster: A Collection of Critical Essays*,
edited by Bradbury, 1966). Persuasively, Bradbury stresses Forster's
own modulation in *Howards End* between a comic mode and a poetic
mode, and a resulting fusion of these modes which enables him to
attain the widest possible significance and the most compelling
unitary vision. Like George H. Thomson, John Edward Hardy
celebrates the visionary aspect of *Howards End* in his '*Howards End*:
The Sacred Center' (*Man in the Modern Novel*, 1964), especially
Forster's healing of divisions and conflict by resort to a fertility
principle in the closing sequence over which Ruth Wilcox in spirit
presides. And that *Howards End*, like *A Passage to India*, is capacious
enough to assimilate specialised interpretations is seen in Paul B.
Armstrong's 'E. M. Forster's *Howards End*: The Existential Crisis of
the Liberal Imagination' (*Mosaic*, 8, 1974). Armstrong sees Forster
as akin to the Swiss existential psychologist Ludwig Binswanger in
the emphasis which the two men place upon the need to attain a
unity of the subjective and the objective. Forster in his novel
dramatises, in short, the difficulties of reaching such unity and such
perspective. Peter Widdowson in his 1977 monograph, *E. M.
Forster's 'Howards End': Fiction as History*, presents in detail the
historical and social circumstances which Forster attempted to
embody in his novel. Widdowson, unlike the other critics mentioned
in this paragraph and like Stone in his *The Cave and the Mountain*,
feels that Forster is relatively unsuccessful in fusing his dichotomies
but argues interestingly that this very failure is in itself a dramatisation of the plight of the Edwardian liberal.

The standard books on Forster – those by Crews, Wilde, Thomson, and Beer, for example – all have stimulating and perceptive
discussions of *The Longest Journey* and may well represent the best
critiques on that novel for our desert islander to peruse. There are
also three essays, however, that call for special mention. John
Harvey in 'Imagination and Moral Theme in E. M. Forster's *The
Longest Journey*' (*Essays in Criticism*, 6, 1956) defines the weaknesses of
the novel in an incisive if severe essay. Some of the blemishes which
he finds are not to be denied, but many of them can also be
construed more positively if the book is read as romance or as
symbolic parable. This is the approach that the best writers of the
book-length studies utilise, and it is also the method of John Magnus
in his masterly 'Ritual Aspects of E. M. Forster's *The Longest Journey*'
(*Modern Fiction Studies*, 13, 1967). This critic defines with commend-

able exactitude the elusive symbols, rituals, and archetypes present in the book and suggests many aspects of this novel that I have not found mentioned elsewhere. Elizabeth Heine in 'Rickie Elliot and the Cow: The Cambridge Apostles and *The Longest Journey*' (*English Literature in Transition*, 15:2, 1972) has analysed the novel in the light of its intellectual origins in McTaggart, Dickinson, G. E. Moore, Russell, and others and has interpreted the characters and the symbols of the novel in terms of the ideas found in these thinkers.

Other Forster novels have more sparingly engaged the writers of journal articles, but *A Room with a View* has, nevertheless, received more attention than the novel more generally recognised as its superior, *Where Angels Fear To Tread*. One fascinating essay as its author comments on the aesthetic and intellectual ambience out of which *A Room with A View* derived is 'Wagner and Forster: *Parsifal* and *A Room with a View*' (*ELH*, 33, 1966) by John Lucas. With resourcefulness and reasonable success Lucas discusses the analogues which he finds in Forster's novel to the characters, situations, and themes found in *Parsifal*. Forster's creative processes as artist have been excitingly traced by Elizabeth Ellem in 'E. M. Forster: The Lucy and New Lucy Novels: Fragments of Early Versions of *A Room with a View*' (*Times Literary Supplement*, 28 May 1971), as she examines in detail the surviving manuscripts and manuscript fragments of this novel. Jeffrey Meyers in ' "Vacant Heart and Hand and Eye": The Homosexual Theme in *A Room with a View*' (*English Literature in Transition*, 13:3, 1970) has found many concealed – and some overt – homosexual elements in what has often been regarded as Forster's only novel that celebrates heterosexual passion (the article was written before the posthumously published work appeared).

A number of general review-essays, inspired by the appearance posthumously of *Maurice* (1971) and *The Life To Come and Other Stories* (1972) have recently appeared, though most are too short and undeveloped to have become standard. One or two of these are of prime importance for our solitary enthusiast, however. Samuel Hynes in 'A Chalice for Youth' (*Times Literary Supplement*, 8 October 1971: reprinted as 'Forster's Cramp' in *Edwardian Occasions*, 1972, and in Gardner) explains much about Forster's total career as he examines the ambience of, the reticences found in, and the passions overtly dramatised in *Maurice*. Hynes's view that Forster had to treat homosexuality indirectly in order to make it artistically viable has by now become a widely held judgement. Another critic who attempted an overview of Forster and who makes some profound observations on him and his work as a result of writing on *Maurice* is George Steiner. In 'Under the Greenwood Tree' (*New Yorker*, 47, 9 October 1971, reprinted in Gardner) Steiner explains how the smugness, cruelty, unimaginativeness, and lack of feeling deplored in *Maurice* were to be given definitive expression in the events connected with the Marabar Caves in *Passage*. Of the reviews on *The Life to Come*, easily the most interesting is that by Eudora Welty, 'A Collection of Old New Stories by E. M. Forster' (*New York Times Book Review*, 13 May 1973), who stresses the integrity of the feeling to be found in these stories and Forster's continuing concern in them with spiritual life as opposed to spiritual death.

Forster scholarship and criticism is distinctive for its quality, its discipline, and its penetration. There are numerous other good essays and reviews that our desert islander could consult with profit, and my overview has been of necessity selective. I would hazard, however, that I have not left very much of the first importance by the wayside. If our student living in his retreat were to be limited to a large knapsack or to a small box, the books and essays that I have singled out would be the indispensable ones for him to have, if he wished to have help in extending his horizons as he read Forster's own works. The secondary works that I have discussed comprise collectively, I think, a lump of pure gold. Forster's cause has been well served by his critics who, seized of his importance, have expressed convincing reasons for his having such importance.

Notes

(The suffix *x* to a note indicator in the text signifies that the note contains extra information, as opposed to simple references and cross-references. Place of publication is London except where otherwise indicated.)

CHAPTER 1 (INTRODUCTION)

1. GLD p. xxii.
2. Letter to Forrest Reid, 1915: M p. viii.
3. AH (1936) 59–63.
4x. See AN i, 4, discussing the *provincialism* of certain English novels.
5. See below, p. 305, note 56x.
6. BBC Interview with Monica Campbell, 1959, quoted by J. S. Martin, *E. M. Forster: The Endless Journey* (Cambridge, 1976) p. 170.
7. Furbank i, 19.
8. Ibid., 37.
9. See below, p. 216.
10x. Furbank ii, 316–7. For examples of his restricted means and lavish giving in earlier years see Furbank, 'The Personality of E. M. Forster', *Encounter* (1970) xxxv, 65.
11. PP (1923) 79.
12. P. N. Furbank, 'The Personality of E. M. Forster', loc. cit., 67.
13. Essays i, 348–9, quoted more fully below, p. 265.
14. Letter to Lady Cynthia Asquith, Jan 1915, *Collected Letters*, ed. H. T. Moore (1962) I, 309.
15. Furbank ii, 308.
16. LJ (WC) xvii, 183.
17x. Furbank I, 55 and 58–9. Furbank's more general account of Cambridge at this time brings out well how some of the most advanced attitudes in England, as instanced by Bertrand Russell, Lytton Strachey and others, were to be found there, against the background of a university which was generally more conservative in its attitudes than the country as a whole.
18. 'G. L. Dickinson: A Tribute', *Spectator* (13 August 1932) reprinted GLD 208 (and cf. pp. 84, 203).
19. 'Epilogue', GLD 201.
20. GLD xi (2), 116.
21. *Listener* (10 September 1953) p. 420 (Cf G. L. Dickinson, *Appearances* (1914) p. 32.
22. P. N. Furbank, 'The Personality of E. M. Forster', loc. cit., 66.
23. See, e.g., Furbank ii, 166–9 and 257.

24. PI xxiii, 200.
25. Furbank II, 297.
26. See, e.g. the essays 'Anonymity: An Enquiry' (1925) and 'The Raison D'Etre of Criticism in the Arts' (1947) in TCD (77–86, 105–16).
27. Furbank II, 175.
28. See G. K. Das, *E. M. Forster's India* (1977) Appendix B, pp. 117–9.
29. Furbank II, 260.
30. See below, p. 69, etc.
31. Letter to *The Guardian*, 29 Dec. 1962.
32x. See especially his 1921 review of G. L. Dickinson's *The Magic Flute* (reprinted GLD 218–20) in which he sets Dickinson's treatment of the theme against Bunyan's and points out that when Tamino reaches the Castle of Sarastro, 'he finds that it is not a haven of attainment, but a record of those who have attained, and that when his name has been entered he must go back to the world.'

CHAPTER 3

1. E. M. Forster, 'Cnidus', AH (1936) 175, 176.
2x. Quoted, Furbank I, 110. I am greatly indebted to Mr Furbank for suggesting that the Hermes I had been seeking was part of the British Museum group: Death, Alcestis, Hermes. The group is reproduced on the dust-jacket to his second volume.
3. Furbank I, 218.
4. *Mythology and Humanism: The Correspondence of Thomas Mann and Karl Kerényi*, translated by A. Gelley (Ithaca, 1975) pp. 9 and 101.
5. Karl Kerényi, 'The Primordial Child in Primordial Times', in Kerényi and C. G. Jung, *Essays on a Science of Mythology* (New York, 1949) p. 73.
6. Kerényi in Paul Radin, *The Trickster: A Study in American Indian Mythology* (New York, 1956) pp. 185 and 189. See also W. Otto, *The Homeric Gods* (Boston, 1964) p. 117, and N. O. Brown, *Hermes the Thief* (Wisconsin, 1947).
7. Patricia Merivale, *Pan The Goat-God: His Myth in Modern Times* (Harvard, 1969) *passim*, especially pp. 180–91.
8. Letter of Thomas Mann to Kerényi (1945), Gelley, p. 126.
9. See Otto, p. 105. The phrase is used in Aristophanes, *Peace*, 1. 394.
10. E. M. Forster, Introduction to *Collected Tales* (New York, 1947). A slightly different version was used as the headnote of *The Eternal Moment* (1928).
11. PP (1926) 98.
12. Kerényi in Radin, p. 190.
13. Henry James, 'The Great Good Place', *The Complete Tales of Henry James*, ed. Leon Edel (Philadelphia, 1962–4), Vol. XI, p. 25; originally published in *Scribner's Magazine*, January 1900, and reprinted in *The Soft Side* (1900).
14. Permission to quote from the unpublished manuscript granted by the Provost and Scholars of King's College, Cambridge.
15. See T. B. Huber, *The Making of a Shropshire Lad: A Manuscript Variorum* (Seattle, 1966) p. 208.
16. Letter to John Middleton Murry, 4 January 1923. This letter is at The Humanities Research Center at The University of Texas at Austin.

17. Furbank I, 195–6.

CHAPTER 4

1x. The real Colonus does not figure in the story. It is in a suburb of Athens, just over a mile and a half from Omonia Square. Now surrounded by a working-class district, it is a raised area of flat rock with a small park adjoining. But Baedeker in his indispensable guide is able to say: 'The view of Athens from the Kolonos is wonderfully beautiful.' See Karl Baedeker, *Greece: Handbook for Travellers* (Leipzig, 1894). All citations are to this edition, the one Forster himself would have used. And all spellings of place-names are based on this edition except those established in the story. 'The Road from Colonus' is included in *Collected Short Stories of E. M. Forster* (1948).

2x. (*a*) Platanos near Olympia is mentioned by Baedeker as on the bridle path from Olympia to Patras via Santameri, route number 46. To judge by Baedeker's detailed map Platanos is just over two miles from Olympia. That distance today has shrunk to one and a half miles. Whether the plane trees have also shrunk with the passage of time, I cannot say. I only know that in this dusty sprawling rural village I could find no sign of them. But the most pressing objection to this location is its closeness to Olympia, which is incompatible not only with the party's view of Plataniste an hour later but with Ethel's concern that they reach Olympia by nightfall.

(*b*) Platanos near Patras is mentioned by Baedeker in his account of route number 47 between Olympia and Patras. The journey from Platanos, which is south and a bit east of Patras, to Olympia would take nearly two days. Objections to this location are: Olympia could not be reached by nightfall, and the travellers would be moving away from Patras, their next objective after Olympia.

(This route is omitted from the 3rd ed. of Baedeker, 1905; all other routes referred to here are included and conditions and times of travel are the same or very little changed. In other words, Forster in 1903 would have found the 1894 Baedeker still generally accurate and relevant.)

(*c*) Platania near the river Neda. North of Kyparissia on the modern coastal road a major highway cuts east and north-east to Tripolis. About a mile along this road one turns north-east at Ano Kopanakion and after passing by or through three villages or hamlets, the first of which is Sidirokastro, and over thirteen miles of rugged winding road, one arrives at Platania. Hugging a steep hillside, overlooking a mountain valley, the hamlet is centred in a tiny square just beyond which the road ends. In the square are three plane trees, one of them large. Water flows from a pipe in the wall backing the square and a stream runs from below the road, which is built up against the steep incline of the mountain. The hamlet is on the east side of a small tributary of the river Neda. The tributary, running north for two miles, joins the river which flows west to the sea. The gorge of the river is so precipitous and wild that for many miles no official road crosses it.

Platania is not on Baedeker's map but it is on or very near the last leg of his route 49 from Kalamata to Phigalia via Pylos. This route, after reaching the coast, goes north just past the mouth of the Kyparissia stream, then north-east through Sidirokastro and thence on to the Neda where a steep path leads to the bed of the river and crosses in the neighbourhood of Phigalia. On the south side of the Neda this path must have been very close to Platania, which is four miles from Phigalia as the crow flies. That Forster's party of travellers should have come this way is not improbable. From Sparta they could go west to Kalamata through the Langada Gorge (Baedeker's route 37), one of the most spectacular sights in all Greece, then to the west coast and up, cutting inland toward Phigalia and thence to Olympia. Platania as the site of the story has the advantage of being in fact in the Province of Messenia, of being exceedingly small, and of having the requisite plane trees and water. Objections are the following: situated as it is on a mountainous decline near the river Neda to which the party must very soon descend, it is improbable that 'the place they had left an hour before suddenly reappeared far below them'; and it is two days' journey from Olympia.

(*d*) Plataniston near Megalopolis is described in Baedeker's route 44 from Megalopolis to Olympia via Phigalia. In not more than one and a half hours after leaving Megalopolis in a westerly direction and after crossing the river Alpheios, one 'approaches the right bank of the little stream of *Gastritzi*, called *Plataniston* in classic times, in reference to the abundant plane-trees which then as now grew near it.' This site, not identified on Baedeker's map, has the advantage of being less a place than a locale, which fits the setting of the story; and the name of the stream is closer in form to that used by Forster. The objections are familiar: it is not in the Province of Messenia; and it is two and a half days from Olympia.

Having completed our tour, we may pause briefly to consider Wilfred Stone's note on Plataniste:

The fictional setting is given as Platiniste, in the Province of Messenia. Since there is no town of that name in Messenia, and since that would be off the travellers' route, the literal setting is probably Platiana, in the Province of Ilia, which is near Mt. Platonos and about fourteen miles from Olympia, the evening destination of the party. (*The Cave and the Mountain*, Stanford, Calif., 1966, p. 145.)

The misspelling Plat*i*niste, the suggestion of Platiana (*plateia*: broad (street); cf. L. *platea*, Fr. *place*), and the injection of Mt Plat*o*nos seem to betray insensitivity to the significance of the name. Platiana is on Baedeker's route 42 from Megalopolis to Olympia via Andritsaena. This route at first runs north from Megalopolis whereas the stream Plataniston lies to the west. According to Baedeker's reckoning the journey from Platiana would take close to six hours, a time just possible for Mr Lucas's party. However, such speculations are by the way since the form Platiana is irrelevant to the story. Finally, the assertion that something (apparently Messenia) is off the route of Mr Lucas and his party is unfounded because there is no clear evidence concerning their route. It is most probable that they are coming from Sparta, in which case Messenia need not be out of their way.

CHAPTER 5

1. Furbank I, 49, 76–7.
2x. The best summary of the cardinal tenets of Moore's ethics is his own: 'That things intrinsically good or bad are many and various; that most of them are "organic unities," in the peculiar and definite sense to which I have confined the term; and that our only means of deciding upon their intrinsic value and its degree, is by carefully distinguishing exactly what the thing is, about which we ask the question, and then looking to see whether it has or has not the unique predicate "good" in any of its various degrees: these are the conclusions, upon the truth of which I desire to insist.' *Principia Ethica* (Cambridge, 1903) p. 223.
3. 'How I Lost My Faith', *The Humanist*, 78 (September 1963) 263.
4x. In response to a question about Moore's influence on his work, Forster replied, 'G. E. Moore was too difficult for me. I'm not a philosopher. I couldn't read him. I got it through the less philosophic minds—H. O. Meredith and A. R. Ainsworth talked to me about it. There was no doubt the thing was filtering through, and affected me in that way.' And in reply to a question about the influence of Proust, Forster said, ' . . . He gave me as much of the modern way as I could take. It was the same as with G. E. Moore; I couldn't read Freud or Jung for myself, it had to be filtered to me.' From an interview with Forster, 6 July 1952, by Ian Watt and P. N. Furbank. Parts of this interview were included in the *Paris Review* interview conducted by P. N. Furbank and F. J. H. Haskell that is reprinted in *Writers at Work: The Paris Review Interviews*, ed. Malcolm Cowley (New York, 1959) pp. 23–35. I am grateful to Professor Watt for allowing me to quote from his notes of the interview.
5. *Beginning Again: An Autobiography of the Years 1911–1918* (1964) p. 24.
6. My Mental Development', *The Philosophy of Bertrand Russell*, ed. P. A. Schilpp (New York, 1963) I, 12.
7. 'Introduction,' LJ (WC).
8. See 'A Book that Influenced Me', TCD 212–15.
9x. Wilfred Stone in *The Cave and the Mountain: A Study of E. M. Forster* (Stanford, California, 1966) points out that Shaw's *Man and Superman* also appears to have influenced Forster when he was writing *The Longest Journey* (p. 199).
10x. The origin of Ansell's name emphasises further the idea of male friendship; Ansell was the name of a garden boy who was Forster's 'first and never to be forgotten friend' (Furbank I, 30). See also the story 'Ansell' in *The Life to Come and Other Stories*.
11. 'The Refutation of Idealism', *Philosophical Studies* (London, 1922) p. 30.
12. Furbank I, 49.
13. *Principia Ethica*, p. 189.
14x. Both Forster and Virginia Woolf use rooms and houses as symbols of consciousness. (Ansell's use of house metaphors in *The Longest Journey* to attack the Idealism of those who believe in the great world is another clear example of this symbolism.) Rickie's words echo E. M. Forster's on the 'message' of *Mrs Dalloway* in 'The Early Novels of Virginia Woolf', AH (1936) 109. I have discussed Forster's recognition of Virginia Woolf's philosophical realism in 'The Philosophical Realism of Virginia Woolf',

English Literature and British Philosophy, ed. S. P. Rosenbaum (Chicago, 1971) p. 331.

15x.   'The Refutation of Idealism', p. 9. The implications of this particular argument upset William Butler Yeats in his discussion of Moore's philosophy with his brother T. Sturge Moore. See *W. B. Yeats and T. Sturge Moore: Their Correspondence, 1901–1937*, ed. Ursula Bridge (New York, 1953) pp. 63 ff., where Yeats argues for the reality of Ruskin's demon cat.

16x.   'The principle of organic unities, like that of combined analysis and synthesis, is mainly used to defend the practice of holding *both* of two contradictory propositions, wherever this may seem convenient. In this, as in other matters, Hegel's main service to philosophy has consisted in giving a name to and erecting into a principle, a type of fallacy to which experience had shown philosophers, along with the rest of mankind, to be addicted. No wonder that he has followers and admirers.' 'The Refutation of Idealism', p. 16.

17.   'The Refutation of Idealism', p. 30.

18x.   Forster may have taken this reversal of Jesus's question from Lytton Strachey, who asked in a review of Blake's poetry published in the *Independent Review* in May 1906, 'What shall it profit a man, one is tempted to exclaim, if he gain his own soul, and lose the whole world?' (reprinted in his *Literary Essays* (1961) p. 147).

19x.   '*Epipsychidion*', ll. 149–59. In using 'world' instead of 'crowd' (l. 151) and 'sad' rather than 'chained' (l. 158), Forster appears to be quoting from an earlier version of the poem—through he does not follow it in another wording that differs from the final text. See the fragments given on p. 426 of *Poetical Works*, ed. Thomas Hutchinson (Oxford, 1968). The earlier words both suit Forster's use of Shelley better than the later ones.

20.   'The Refutation of Idealism', p. 28.

21.   Patrick Wilkinson, 'Forster and King's', *Aspects of E. M. Forster*, ed. Oliver Stallybrass (1969) p. 18, and Furbank I, 77.

22x.   Furbank I, 106. Furbank notes that Sheppard's distinction is not to be taken literally for those at King's and Trinity but rather to represent standpoints characterisitic of each college. Forster's use of Shelley should also be compared to Lytton Strachey's in an Apostle paper he gave a year after Sheppard's paper; Strachey alludes to Shelley and criticises both the monogamous and heterosexual decrees of modern morals. See 'Does Absence Make the Heart Grow Fonder?' in *The Really Interesting Question and Other Papers*, ed. Paul Levy (1972) pp. 102–6.

23x.   Shelley's idea here is similar to Moore's discussion of the value of organic wholes in *Principia Ethica*; Moore shows how the value of the whole, which may be a state of consciousness, 'bears no regular proportion to the sum of the values of its parts' (p. 27).

24x.   Elizabeth Heine, in an article entitled 'Rickie Elliot and the Cow: The Cambridge Apostles and *The Longest Journey*' (*English Literature in Transition*, 15 (Nov 1972) 116–34), also sees Rickie and Ansell as representatives of different Apostolic philosophies, associating Rickie's incipient monism with McTaggart's philosophy and Ansell's ideas with Moore's. The generality of Heine's discussion is indicated by her view of the novel as a Hegelian synthesis.

25. Evelyne Hanquart, 'The Manuscript of Forster's *The Longest Journey*', *Review of English Studies* (1974) XXV, 154.
26x. James McConkey points out that the Orion image is another symbol of continuity in the novel (*The Novels of E. M. Forster* (Ithaca, New York, 1957) pp. 111–12). (See also below, pp. 250–2.)
27. 'An Autobiography', *The Philosophy of G. E. Moore*, ed. P. A. Schilpp (N. Y., 1952) pp. 13–14.
28. Furbank I, 118.
29. 'The Novels of E. M. Forster', (*Essays* I, 344).
30x. The conflict vanishes in Forster's personal re-vision of *The Longest Journey* after he had revisited the Figsbury Rings in 1964. He wrote in his diary, 'I was filled with thankfulness and security and glad that I had given myself so much back. . . . I shall lie in Stephen's arms instead of his child' (Furbank, II, 319).
31. Furbank, I, 119.

CHAPTER 6

1. HE xi, 96. Other references to *Howards End* are indicated by chapter and page numbers in parenthesis in the text of the essay.
2. Cited by Stallybrass in his Introduction to HE, p. xvii.
3. 'E. M. Forster on his Life and his Books.' An interview recorded for television by David Jones. *The Listener*, 1 January, 1959, p. 11.
4. See note 2.
5. 'What I believe', TCD 65.
6. Henry James: *Roderick Hudson*, The Chiltern Library (1947) p. viii.
7. See *The Manuscripts of Howards End*, correlated with Forster's final version by Oliver Stallybrass. Volume 4a of the Abinger Edition, pp. 1 and 2.
8. 'Forster as a Humanist' by W. J. H. Sprott, in *Aspects of E. M. Forster*, ed. Oliver Stallybrass (1969) pp. 75–6.
9. TCD 70.

CHAPTER 7

1. Matt. 16:26; 19:21; 19:24; 22:21.
2x. LJ (WC) xxviii, 264. The passage is echoed again in *Howards End* (xv, 125): ' . . . Miss Schlegel was asked . . . what it would profit Mr. Bast if he gained the whole world and lost his own soul. She answered, Nothing, but he would not gain his soul until and he had gained a little of the world.' See also above, p. 44 and n.
3. 'What I Believe', TCD 72.
4. 'Poverty's Challenge: The Terrible Tolstoy', *The New Leader* (4 Sep 1925) xii, 11.
5. 'Notes on the Way', *Time and Tide* (1934) xv, 696.
6x. Forster seems to have read 'needle' to mean sewing needle instead of the narrow gate adjoining the main gate of an Eastern walled city.
7. Introduction to CSS (1947) p. 6. Quoted Stallybrass, LTC, p. xi.

8x. LTC 63. The apparent absurdity of this answer reminds us of Seymour's answer to Mrs Fedder in J. D. Salinger's story 'Hapworth'. To her question as to what he wants to do after the war, he replies that he wants to be a dead cat since, according to Zen Buddhism, a dead cat is the most valuable thing in the world, because no one can put a price on it. ('Hapworth', *The New Yorker* (19 June 1965) XLI, 36.)

9. Quoted in Jane Lagoudis Pinchin, *Alexandria Still: Forster, Durrell, and Cavafy* (Princeton University Press, 1977) p. 99, from unpublished papers at King's College, Cambridge, dated 28 July 1917.

10. 'The Personality of E. M. Forster', *Encounter* (Nov 1970) XXXV, 62.

CHAPTER 8

1. Forster's situation is best described in the last chapter of Furbank I.
2. 'Higher Aspects', *The Egyptian Mail* (5 May 1918) p. 2.
3. 'A Musician in Egypt', *The Egyptian Mail* (12 May 1918) p. 2.
4. Ibid.
5x. I am aware of Forster's serious attempts on Egyptian affairs (such as on the Suez Canal and the question of the Sudan) but these writings belong to a different period of Forster's life when his eyes turned to the international scene.
6. 'Sunday Music', *The Egyptian Mail* (2 September 1917), p. 2.
7. 'Photographic Egypt', *The Egyptain Mail* (13 January 1918) p. 2.
8. PP (1923) pp. 11–19.
9. Quoted Furbank, I, 259.
10. PP (1923) 75.
11. See chapter iii of *Aspects of the Novel*.
12. *Alexandria: A History and a Guide* (New York, 1961) p. xvi.
13. AHG (1922) 93.
14x. Ibid., p. 60. Forster remarks that Philo's doctrine of the Mediating Logos 'ensured that the deity should be at the same time accessible and inaccessible' (PP (1923) 38).
15. AHG (1922) 66.
16. Ibid., pp. 66–7.
17x. Forster told G. K. Das that Godbole was to a large extent a created character. Das was further informed by Furbank of Forster's remark: 'What a name' when Forster once encountered a Brahman Godbole ('The Genesis of Professor Godbole', *Review of English Studies*, XXVII, 1977, 56–60).

The name of Godbole presumably attracted Forster because of the additional syllable used with the usual monosyllable. This, perhaps, satisfied the idea of the Neo-Platonic Unity of God which Forster found appealing.
18. PI xix, 168–9.
19. PI xxxiii, 274.
20. AN iv (end), 56.
21. Ibid.
22. AHG (1922) 97.
23x. For further information on Forster's life in Alexandria, including his

friendship with Mohammed el Adl, Furbank II should be consulted, especially chapter ii and pp. 103–8.

CHAPTER 9

1. AHG (1922) p. iii; *Plotinus: the Ethical Treatises*, trans. Stephen MacKenna (1917) Vols II–V, containing translations of Enneads II–VI, were published between 1921 and 1930, the final volume with the help of B. S. Page.
2. Ibid., pp. 65–8.
3*x*. Henry More is one of the very few people who have emphasised the central importance of Indian influence on Apollonius (*An Explanation of the Grand Mystery of Godliness* (1660) Book III, pp. 58–9. Cf. also Book IV, pp. 99–136). More's friend and pupil, John Marshall, was the first British collector of Indian antiquities.
4. Strabo, xv. i. 63–5, 68; Arrian's *Anabasis*, VII. ii. 2–4.
5. *Advaita and Neoplatonism* (Madras, 1961).
6. *The Transcendence of the Cave*, (1967) p. 165.
7. *The Eight Volumes of Letters Writ by a Turkish Spy*, G. P. Marana, W. Bradshaw et al. (1694, 8 vols) vol. VI. III. xvii, p. 185.
8*x*. Most successfully in the 'Hymn to Narayena', *Works*, ed. Lord Teignmouth, (1807) vol. XIII, pp. 302–9, and in his essay 'On the Mystical Poetry of the Persians and Hindus', ibid., vol. IV, pp. 211–35. The same approach is evident in the work of Charles Wilkins and Thomas Maurice. It was often assumed at this time, following Apuleius, that Pythagoras had been in India.
9. GLD vii, sect. 2, pp. 35–8; xi, sect. 2, pp. 114–6.
10. Ennead I. v. 10.
11. PI vii, 71.
12. Enn. III. viii. 6.
13. PI vii, 69.
14. Ibid., xix, 167; Enn. VI. ix. 4.
15. PI xxi, 182–3.
16. Ibid., xix, 168–9.
17. Enn. VI. ix. 4.
18. Ibid., VI. v. 12.
19. AHG (1922) 66–7.
20. Ibid., p. 60.
21. PI xii, 116–7.
22. Enn. V. i. 2.
23. Ibid., V. v. 11.
24. Ibid., II. IV. 10–16; II. V. 2–5.
25. Ibid., VI. iii. 7.
26. Ibid., III. ii. 3.
27. PI xii, 117.
28. Ibid., x, 106.
29. Ibid., xiv, 129.
30. Enn. V. v. 8.
31. PI xxiii, 198.

32. Enn. III. vi. 7.
33. Ibid., IV. viii. 1.
34. Ibid., III. vi. 13–14.
35. Ibid., III. vi. 16.
36. PI xxiii, 197–8.
37. Ibid., xiv, 139.
38. Ibid., xiv, 127, 140–1; xxiii, 197–8.
39. Ibid., xxxiii, 281.
40. Ibid., xv, 143–4; xxiv, 216; xxix, 251.
41. Enn. III. ix. 2.
42. Ibid., IV. iii. 31.
43. PI xxxvi, 298.
44x. Enn. VI iv. 3. The name Quested had already been used in chap. ix of *Howards End.*
45. Ibid., II. iii. 18.
46. PI xix, 167.
47. Enn. IV. viii. 8.
48. PI iii, 21; viii, 86; xiv, 127.
49. Enn. IV. iv. 44.
50. PI xiv, 127.
51. Ibid., viii, 75–7; xv, 143–4.
52. AH ii, 17.
53. PI xiv, 125.
54. Ibid., xxvi, 228.
55. Ibid., xiv, 127.
56. Ibid., xxiii, 281.
57. Ibid., xx, 181.
58. Ibid., vii, 56.
59. Enn. VI. ix. 5.
60. PI xi, 112.
61. Enn. VI. iii. 9.
62. PI xix, 251–3.
63. Ibid., xi, 112.
64. Ibid., xxxvii, 308–9, 312.
65. Ibid., xxxi, 265; xxxvii, 310.
66. Enn. VI. iv. 12.
67. Ibid., V. i. 12.
68. Ibid., IV. iv. 40.
69. PI xxxi, 260; xxxv, 292–3.
70. Ibid., vii, 60.
71. Ibid., xxxv, 293; xxxvi, 301–2, 303–4.
72. Ibid., xxxvii, 310.
73. Enn. VI. vii. 22.
74. PI xxxiii, 278.
75. Ibid., xxxiii, 275.
76. Enn. VI. vii. 22.
77. Ibid., III. viii. 6.
78. Ibid., VI. ii. 21.
79. PI xxvi, 235.

80. Ibid., xxxiii, 278.
81. Ibid., xxxiii, 275–9.
82. Enn. V. viii. 17.
83. Ibid., VI. vii. 22, 33, 35.
84. PI xxxiii, 276.
85. Enn. VI. ix. 7.
86. PI xxxiii, 276–7.
87. Ibid., xv, 142; Enn. IV. iv. 27; VI. vii. 11. Cf. also III. vi. 13.
88. Enn. VI. v. 11.
89. Ibid., VI. viii. 18.
90. PI vii, 68.
91. 'Passage to India', section 9, ll. 233–4, *Walt Whitman: the Complete Poems*, ed. Francis Murphy (Harmondsworth, 1975) p. 436.
92. PI xxxvi, 304.
93. Enn. VI. ix. 3.
94. Ibid., VI. ix. 3–4.
95. PI xxxiii, 278.
96. Enn. IV. iv. 6.
97. 'Toxaris', § 34.
98. *Stromata*, Clement of Alexandria, Book I, chap. XV; *Historia Ecclesiastica*, Socrates, Book I, chap. XXII; *The Indian Travels of Apollonius of Tyana*, Osmond de Beauvoir Priaulx (1873) pp. 171–4.
99. *Bardaisan of Edessa*, H. J. W. Drijvers (Assen, 1966) pp. 174–5.
100. PI xiv, 128.

CHAPTER 10

1. HD (1953) 19.
2. His Highness Tukoji Rao III, the Rajah of Dewas Senior.
3. HD (1953) 50.
4. Ibid., 10.
5. M 240.
6. HD (1953) 112.
7. M 240.
8x. Since this paragraph was written further light has been thrown on this and other matters relating to Dewas in the second volume of Furbank's biography (Furbank II, ch. iv).
9. PI xxxvi, 303.
10. HD (1953) 119.
11. Ibid., 133.
12. M 163.
13. HD (1953) 171.
14. Ibid., p. 116.

CHAPTER 11

1. TCD 285.
2. *E. M. Forster: A Tribute* (New York, 1964), p. xii.
3. *Encounter* (January 1962), XVIII, pp. 20–7.
4. PI xxiv, 207.
5. *Encounter* (January 1962), XVIII, p. 25.
6. Ibid.
7. Ibid., p. 27.
8. TCD 285.
9. 'Passage To and From India', *Encounter* (June 1954), II, p. 21.
10. TCD 286.
11. *Encounter* (January 1962), XVIII, p. 27.
12. HD (1953) 30–1.
13. Ibid., 30.
14. University of Bombay, 1933.
15. *The Achievement of E. M. Forster* (1962) p. 164.

CHAPTER 12

1. Quoted Furbank I, 15.
2. *International Social Science Journal*, 19, 4 (1967), pp. 493–516.
3x. Nirad C. Chaudhuri, 'Passage to and from India', *Encounter*, (June 1954) II, pp. 19–24. For a more sympathetic acccunt, see G. K. Das, *E. M. Forster's India*, with a Foreword by John Beer (London, 1977) and especially pp. 47–51 for parallels between the 'troubled situation at Chandrapore' and the 'actual situation surrounding the Amritsar massacre'.
4. Frederick C. Crews, *E. M. Forster: The Perils of Humanism* (Princeton, N. J., 1962) p. 142.
5. Quoted by John Colmer in *E. M. Forster: the Personal Voice* (1975) p. 11.
6. PI xxiv, 219.
7. PI xiii, 124.
8. PI xxv, 221.
9. PI xx, 181.
10. PI vii, 64.

CHAPTER 13

1x. 'Art for Art's Sake' (1949), TCD 87–93.
2. 'Our Diversions: 2, The Birth of an Empire' (1924), AH (1936) 44–7; 'The Challenge of our Time' (1946), TCD 54–8.
3x. A call echoed in Forster's need for a perfect Friend.
4x. 'Passage to India' (1871) in *Leaves of Grass*; 'India, The Wisdom-Land' (1890) in *Toward Democracy* (Swan Sonnenschein, London, 1911). In his essay, 'Edward Carpenter' (1944), Forster wrote: 'As he had looked outside his own class for companionship, so he was obliged to look outside his own race for wisdom' (TCD 207). It is open to conjecture that the predominantly

'feminine' nature of India's civilisations, their cultivation of the imagination and intuitions, the pursuit of the unseen, and an eroticism in the visual arts, myths and epics which is conceptually androgynous – the Absolute as the two-in-one, the male-female principles as coexistent – may have had an especial appeal to male members of what Carpenter called the intermediate sex.

5. Quoted Furbank I, 216.

6. Heinrich Zimmer, *Philosophies of India* (1967) p. 231 (first published 1952).

7. The significance of Jain cosmology to the ideas and images in 'Caves' is discussed in my *Delusions and Discoveries: Studies on India in the British Imagination 1880–1930* (1972).

8. 'Liberty in England' (1935), AH (1936) 62–8.

9x. In addition to the works referred to in these notes I wish to acknowledge a more general debt to the following books:

John Beer: *The Achievement of E. M. Forster*; Malcolm Bradbury, Editor: *E. M. Forster: A Passage to India: A Selection of Critical Essays* (Casebook Series) 1970; Frederick C. Crews: *E. M. Forster: The Perils of Humanism*, 1962; Furbank I; June Perry Levine: *Creation and Criticism: A Passage to India*, 1971; Wilfred Stone: *The Cave and the Mountain: A Study of E. M. Forster*, Stanford, California, 1966; Lionel Trilling: *E. M. Forster*, 1944; Peter Widdowson: *E. M. Forster's Howards End: Fiction as History* (Text and Context Series) 1977.

CHAPTER 14

1x. As far as non-fiction is concerned, *The Hill of Devi: being Letters from Dewas State Senior* (1953) demonstrates how intelligently Forster confronted the limitations of the role of an observer, and how consistently his imaginative sympathy enabled him to transcend them.

2. Cf. Benjamin Britten's essay 'Some Notes on Forster and Music', in *Aspects of E. M. Forster: Essays and Recollections written for his Ninetieth Birthday 1st January 1969*, ed. Oliver Stallybrass (1969) 81–6.

3. Epilogue, GLD 201.

4. Joseph Campbell, *The Masks of God: Occidental Mythology* (1965) p.3.

5. 'Gide and George', TCD 220.

6. *E. M. Forster: A Study* (1944) pp. 124–5.

7x. The descriptions of the Gokul Ashtami Festival in *The Hill of Devi* are more irreverent—Forster uses the word 'facetious'—than in *A Passage to India*: which is not to say that Forster doesn't permit a spirit of levity in the novel, but that it is subsumed into more serious explorations which the novel's contexts co-operate to render revelatory at points such as this.

8. G. Jean-Aubry, *Joseph Conrad: Life & Letters*, 2 vols (1927) I, 280.

CHAPTER 15

1. Virginia Woolf, *Flush: A Biography* (1933); Forster, 'Mr and Mrs Abbey's Difficulties', AH (1936) 225–33.

2. Quoted by S. P. Rosenbaum in *The Bloomsbury Group* (1975) p. 122.

3x. As it is of John Collier's (more knockabout) tale, *His Monkey Wife* (1930).

4x. See also the poem 'O Child of Uranus' in *Towards Democracy*, in which the Uranian is presented as a messiah.

5. TCD 305.

6. Max Beerbohm, 'Lytton Strachey' [The Rede Lecture] (Cambridge, 1943).

7. AH (1936) 85.

8. AH (1936) 77.

9. AH (1936) 57.

CHAPTER 16

1. The author thanks the Trustees of the Forster Estate – the Provost and Scholars of King's College, Cambridge – for their permission to quote from the letters, the Humanities Research Center of the University of Texas at Austin for the hospitality extended to her, and the Fulbright Committee for their financial support.

2. John Sayre Martin, *E. M. Forster. The Endless Journey* ('British Authors. Introductory Critical Studies', Cambridge, 1976).

3x. 'What I Believe' (TCD 71). It is worth noting that 'the wide-open world' belongs to Forster's 'aristocrats' whatever their nation or creed.

4. 'This £8,000 [Marianne's legacy to Forster] has been the financial salvation of my life. Thanks to it I was able to go to Cambridge. . . . After Cambridge I was able to travel for a couple of years, and travelling inclined me to write.' *Marianne Thornton, A Domestic Biography* (1956) p. 289.

5. See *The Lucy Novels. Early Sketches for A Room with a View*, ed. O. Stallybrass, The Abinger Edition, 3a (1977).

6. As quoted by Elizabeth Ellem in 'E. M. Forster: the Lucy and New Lucy Novels', *Times Literary Supplement*, 28 May 1971, and O. Stallybrass in *The Lucy Novels . . .*, p. 18.

7x. 'Philip, my tried and true acquaintance: who on this occasion, as on many others, feels and behaves as I do.' MS. of *Where Angels Fear to Tread*, in the British Museum. Note also that elsewhere Forster gave E. J. Dent as Philip's 'ancestor'.

8. See Furbank 1, 95 and Elizabeth Ellem, loc. cit.

9x. Such was the case for the little chestnut grove near Ravello where 'The Story of a Panic' came to his mind in a flash. See Forster's introduction to CSS (1947).

10x. Malcolm Darling had been Forster's contemporary at King's before entering the Indian Civil Service. He had served in Lahore, where Forster visited him during his 1912 tour of India, and had acted as tutor to the Maharajah of Dewas Senior, whose private secretary Forster became in 1921. Malcolm Darling was knighted in 1939. See also Forster's obituary article on him in *The Times*, 10 Jan 1969.

11. Letter to J. R. Ackerley dated 31 May 1947. This (as well as all the letters to Ackerley here mentioned) is in the Humanities Research Center of the University of Texas at Austin.

12x. 'It was architecturally necessary. I needed a lump, or a Hindu temple if you like–a mountain standing up. It is well placed, and it gathers up some strings' 'The Art of Fiction. E. M. Forster', *The Paris Review*, Spring 1953. The interviewers were P. N. Furbank and F. J. H. Haskell.

13. See HD 105 ff.

14x. Forster had met J. R. Ackerley in 1922 on the occasion of the publication of the younger man's poem 'Ghost' in the *London Mercury*. After Ackerley's stay in India, recollected in *Hindoo Holiday* (1932), they became close friends; an extensive and varied correspondence was exchanged for some forty-five years until Ackerley's death in 1967. See *The Letters of J. R. Ackerley*, ed. Neville Braybrooke (1975); and '"Dearest My Joe": Une lecture de lettres de E. M. Forster à J. R. Ackerley', E. Hanquart, in *E. M. Forster*, C.E.R.V.E. (Montpellier, France, 1977).

15. See HD 155.

16x. Once he apologised for the quality of his handwriting by telling a friend he was writing him the eighteenth letter on that day!

17x. In October 1923 Forster had already warned Ackerley, who was undertaking his own 'Passage to India', that 'the person in another berth in a cabin is always fairly pleasant and very dull.'

18x. Forster was indeed sailing in this Equatorial region which sailors associate with calms, light winds, and inactivity.

19. Letter to J. R. Ackerley dated 7 Aug 1929.

20x. William Plomer, the poet and short-story writer, was born in the Transvaal in 1903. He became a friend of Forster's and of Ackerley's in the thirties. *I Speak to Africa* came out in 1927.

21x. ' . . . a river several times the size of the Thames falls into a chasm deeper than St Paul's and what with the spray and the double circular rainbows and lying on one's stomach on shiny rocks over bottomless cauldrons . . .'

22. Letter to J. R. Ackerley from 'the Red Sea', dated 9 Sep 1929.

23. See LTC, p. xii.

24x. The British Protectorate over Egypt came to an end in 1922.

25x. C. P. Cavafy, the Greek poet of Alexandria, whom Forster had made friends with during the First World War, was famous for his capacity for self-withdrawal even in friendly company.

26x. For other anecdotes about this visit, see Alec Randall, 'E. M. Forster and Romania', in *Aspects of E. M. Forster*, ed. O. Stallybrass (1969) p. 51–60; Sir Alec Randall died in 1977.

27. See 'Recollections from Nassenheide', *Listener*, 1 Jan 1959.

28. 'The Eyes of Sibiu', *Spectator*, 25 June 1932.

29. The national *tvika*.

30. Letter to R. C. Trevelyan, 21 Feb 1947. I wish to thank the Master and Fellows of Trinity College, Cambridge, who gave me access to this correspondence.

31x. Letter to Provost J. T. Sheppard dated 21 May 1947, King's College Library. This young friendly couple were Noel and Marietta Vogues, who were also Ackerley's hosts when he visited the United States in 1962 (see *The Letters of J. R. Ackerley*).

32x. 'It is the most astounding natural object I have ever seen. It frightens. There are many colours in it besides crimson–strata of black and of white, and rocks of ochre and pale lilac. And the Colorado river itself is . . . still more sinister, for it is muddy white and very swift, and it rages like an infuriated maggot between precipices of granite, gnawing at them and cutting the Canyon deeper. It was strange after two days amongst these marvels, and terrors, to return to the surface of the earth, and go bowling away in a bus between little fir trees.' That Forster was riding a mule in the Canyon is recorded in a letter to Provost Sheppard.

33*x*. This word is coined from their friend, Prof. W. J. H. Sprott, who was to become Forster's literary executor.

34*x*. Paul Cadmus, the American artist, drew several portraits of Forster, in particular those reproduced in the first separate edition of *The New Disorder* and in the first American edition of *Two Cheers for Democracy*. E. M. Forster appears in Cadmus's painting called 'What I Believe' (1946).

35. Letter written to Ackerley in a train going through California on 31 May 1947.

36. See *Listener*, 4 Nov 1954.

37*x*. This was Forster's first trip to Germany since the war. I disagree with Philip L. Fry (*An Annotated Calendar of the Letters from E. M. Forster to J. R. Ackerley in the Humanities Research Center*, Ph.D. dissertation, The University of Texas at Austin, 1974), who dates this letter 'April 55' in spite of internal evidence to the contrary, and of its fragmentary date.

38. See 'Recollections from Nassenheide' and Forster's introduction to LJ (WC).

39. Letter to Ackerley dated 7 July 1957.

40. King's College Library, E. M. Forster Collection, vol. 21.

41. Three of these tours are recorded for the summer months of 1962, 1963, and 1964 respectively.

CHAPTER 18

1. From two letters to *The Nation and Athenaeum*, 29 March and 26 April 1930.

2. Published in *The Listener*, 30 April 1930. Reprinted in *D. H. Lawrence, The Critical Heritage*, ed. R. P. Draper (1970).

3*x*. *The White Peacock* (1911) from Part Two Chapter i, 'Strange Blossoms and Strange New Budding', pp. 197–200. I am grateful to John Beer for drawing my attention to the script of Forster's talk in the library of King's College, which confirms that this was the section of Lawrence's novel that Forster had in mind. An extract he read out began a little before and ended a little earlier than the quotation given here.

4. *The Plumed Serpent* (1926) from Chapter xvii, 'Fourth Hymn and the Bishop', pp. 265–6.

5. From Part One Chapter vi, 'The Education of George', p. 95.

6. See *Phoenix: The Posthumous Papers of D. H. Lawrence*, ed. E. D. McDonald, 1936, pp. 22–31.

7. From Chapter xx, 'Marriage by Quetzalcoatl', p. 332.

8. From Part Two Chapter ii, 'A Shadow in Spring', p. 224.

9. See *Phoenix* (cf. Note 6) p. 7.

10. See E. Delavenay, *D. H. Lawrence, L'Homme et la Genèse de son Œuvre* (Paris, 1969), p. 674.

11. See *The Collected Letters of D. H. Lawrence*, ed. H. T. Moore (1962) II, 799.
12. Ibid., 811.

CHAPTER 19

1. See my book, *Art and Order: A Study of E. M. Forster* (New York, 1964) pp. 73–6. Some of the points I make in this essay are more fully elaborated in that book and in two essays: 'Depths and Surfaces: Dimensions of Forsterian Irony', *English Literature in Transition*, (1973) XVI 257–74, and 'Desire and Consciousness: The "Anironic" Forster', *Novel*, (winter 1976) IX, 114–29.
2. *The Collected Tales of E. M. Forster* (New York: Alfred A. Knopf, 1952) p. 123.
3x. *Pan the Goat-God: His Myth in Modern Times* (Cambridge, Mass., 1969) p. 268, n. 2. For Merivale's objections to the use Forster's critics make of Pan, see p. 184. Her study, admirable though it is in its comprehensive examination of Pan, seems to me too restrictive in its approach to Forster.
4x. See Jeffrey Meyers's essay, '"Vacant Heart and Hand and Eye": The Homosexual Theme in *A Room With a View*', *English Literature in Transition*, (1970) XIII, 181–92. The remark referred to appears on p. 189. P. N. Furbank's illuminating account of Forster's reaction to a contemporary homosexual interpretation of the story (Furbank I 133–4) should also be consulted.
5x. 'Ansell' may possibly provide another example, and 'The Rock' presumably means to do justice to relationships in this world too.
6x. See Meyers' essay, and also Samuel Hynes, 'Forster's Cramp', *Edwardian Occasions* (New York, 1972) p. 116. Hynes describes the scene, correctly, as 'reminiscent of the pederastic bathing of Victorian homosexual writing and photography'. See too Paul Fussell, *The Great War and Modern Memory* (New York and London, 1975), chap. VIII, especially the sections called 'The British Homoerotic Tradition', pp. 279–86, and 'Soldiers Bathing', pp. 299–309. In *Sexual Heretics: Male Homosexuality in English Literature from 1850 to 1900* (New York, 1971) p. 8, Brian Reade writes: 'For John Addington Symonds the word Arcadian meant homosexual, and little more.' In a non-homosexual context, one may note the legitimating of male nudity by the seemly introduction of pan pipes into paintings and photographs. See, for example, *Thomas Eakins: His Photographic Works* (Philadelphia, 1969) pp. 55, 57, 58, 59, 63.
7. See 'Desire and Consciousness', pp. 117–22.
8. According to John Colmer, 'in 1928, Forster wrote in his Commonplace Book: "What a pity the poetry in me has got mixed up with Pan."' See *E. M. Forster: The Personal Voice* (1975) p. 40.
9x. My discussion is intended to focus on the five stories that, in Stallybrass' edition of *The Life to Come* (LTC), run from pp. 97 to 165, and I have used the title of the whole volume to refer to them. Of the remaining three late, homosexual tales, two were completed, one partly written, before the other five. It must be admitted that a shadow of the earlier Pan, the Pan of connecting, continues on in these three stories, with predictable results. The attempt to actualize love as well as desire leads, with a fatal inevitability, to disaster and death. Consciousness remains divisive: 'There was always a

barrier either way, always his own nature' (p. 95). For further distinctions between the two groups of stories, see 'Depths and Surfaces', pp. 266–7, and 'Desire and Consciousness', pp. 123–5.

10. Paul Valéry, 'Aurore', *Poésies* (Paris, 1942) p. 86.
11. *Speedboat* (New York, 1976) p. 73.

CHAPTER 20

1. PI xxxvii, 309.
2. Forster speaks of this significance which Krishna's birth had for him in the novel in a Paper entitled 'Three Countries', the manuscript of which I consulted in the archive of King's College, Cambridge. I am grateful to the Provost and Scholars of King's for permission to consult this material.
3x. It is an interesting coincidence that the prototype of Eliot's 'The Fire Sermon' was preached by Buddha near Gaya, where the Marabar (originally 'Barabar') episode too is based.
4x. The last words of Buddha to the priests were: 'All the constituents of being are transitory; work out your salvation with diligence.' (See H. C. Warren, *Buddhism in Translations*, Cambridge, Mass., 1953, p. 109.)

Eliot reproduces Buddha's words in *The Cocktail Party*, Act 2, where Reilly says to Celia:

> Go in peace, my daughter.
> Work out your salvation
> with diligence.

Again, Reilly to Julia:

> And when I say to one like her
> 'Work out your salvation with
> diligence', I do not understand
> What I myself am saying.

5x. Buddha's eight-fold path consists of: right belief, right will, right speech, right action, right means of livelihood, right effort towards self-control, right attention, and right contemplation.
6. See Thomas's speech to the Second Priest in *Murder in the Cathedral*, Part I.
7. 'East Coker', IV.
8. Furbank II, 328.
9. AH (1936) 332–4.
10. Ibid., 333–4.
11. Cf. Juan Mascaró, trans., *The Bhagavad Gita* (Harmondsworth, 1962) Canto xi, 3, p. 89.
12. AH (1936) 92.
13. See 'The Gods of India', *The New Weekly*, 30 May 1914, p. 338.
14. LJ (WC) vi, 69.

CHAPTER 21

1x. In addition to the works cited below there are discussions of the relationship by Robert Gish ('Mr Forster and Mrs Woolf: Aspects of the Novelist as Critic', *Virginia Woolf Quarterly* (1976) II, 255–69); by Wilfred Stone, in *The Cave and the Mountain* (Stanford, 1966); and in Furbank II.

2. E. M. Forster, *The Lucy Novels: early sketches for 'A Room with a View'*, ed. O. Stallybrass (Abinger ed. vol. 3a, 1977) p. xii.

3x. Virginia Woolf's childhood adventures at catching moths are recounted in some detail in her essay 'Reading' (Essays II, 22–5). See also her essay 'The Death of the Moth' (Essays I, 359–61).

4. I am grateful both to Mr Stallybrass for transcribing the note and to the Provost and Scholars of King's College, Cambridge for permission to reproduce it.

5. Leonard Woolf, *Sowing* (1960) p. 171; Furbank I, 66.

6. P. N. Furbank, letter to the present writer, 6 October 1973.

7. TLS, 22 Oct 1908, p. 362; reprinted in V. Woolf, *Contemporary Writers*, ed. Jean Guiguet (1965), pp. 49–50. (Also reprinted, along with some other reviews and articles cited in this essay, in *E. M. Forster: the Critical Heritage*, ed. Philip Gardner (1973).)

8x. See Walter Allen, *The English Novel* (Penguin, 1970) p. 77, and Robert Curtis Brown, 'Laurence Sterne and Virginia Woolf: A Study in Literary Continuity', *University of Kansas City Review*, (1959) XXVI 153–9. Incidentally, while Forster's comparison between Virginia Woolf and Sterne may have been the first to appear in print, another common friend, Lytton Strachey, had already suggested to Virginia Woolf a couple of years previously in 1925 that perhaps the ideal thing for her as a novelist was to 'take something wilder and more fantastic [than she had until then attempted], a framework that admits of anything, like *Tristram Shandy*' (AWD, 79). Sterne is, of course, one of the first few names in the long list of literary luminaries to whom Virginia Woolf facetiously acknowledges a debt in the Preface to *Orlando*, as Forster's name is one of the last. In any case, Virginia Woolf seems to have herself sanctioned the linking of her name with Sterne a year after the publication of *Aspects* when the World's Classics edition of *A Sentimental Journey* came out (1928) with an introduction by her. This was the only introduction she ever wrote to a work by another novelist, and many reviewers of this edition, not surprisingly, made a comparison between her and Sterne one of the main subjects of their comments. In fact, the review in the *TLS* (10 January 1929, p. 25) was even titled 'Mrs. Woolf and Sterne'.

9. Lionel Trilling, *E. M. Forster* (1970), 142n.

10x. Probably, Virginia Woolf would have found this description of her novels as 'little silver cups' particularly offensive, could she have read it. In *A Room of One's Own*, she had derided silver cups as puerile and characteristically male emblems of achievement, and mocked those who think it of 'the utmost importance to walk up to a platform and receive from the hands of the Headmaster himself a highly ornamental pot'. She had gone on to tell women novelists that 'to sacrifice a hair of the head of your vision, a shade of its colour, in deference to some Headmaster with a silver pot in his hand or to some professor with a measuring-rod up his sleeve, is the most abject treachery. . . .' *A Room of One's Own* (1929), pp. 159–60.

11. P. N. Furbank, letter to the present writer, 6 October 1973.
12. Virginia Woolf, *Roger Fry: A Biography* (1940) p. 294.
13. C. B. Cox, *The Free Spirit: A Study of Liberal Humanism in the Novels of George Eliot, Henry James, E. M. Forster, Virginia Woolf, Angus Wilson* (1963).
14. Ibid., p. 103.
15. Ibid., 74–116, *passim*.
16x. Very different in detail, they all share a common belief that there is only one view of the world, and one family; and invariably at the end the mirrors break, and the new generation bursts in.' Review of Walpole's *The Green Mirror*, TLS, 24 Jan 1918, reprinted in V. Woolf, *Contemporary Writers*, ed. J. Guiguet (1965), p. 71.

CHAPTER 22

1. Furbank 1.
2. AN vii, 98.
3. TCD 82–3.
4. Ibid., 84.
5. AN vii, 86.
6. TCD 84.
7. Virginia Woolf, 'The Russian Point of View', in *The Common Reader*, first series (New York, 1953) p. 181 (Essays I, 241).
8. AN iv 57.
9. Woolf, 'Modern Fiction', in *The Common Reader*, first series, p. 157 (Essays II, 108–9).
10. Chekhov, Anton, 'Gusev', in *The Portable Chekhov*, edited by Avrahm Yarmolinsky (New York, 1968) p. 268.
11. Woolf, 'The Novels of E. M. Forster', in *The Death of the Moth and Other Essays*, (New York, 1974) pp. 162–75 (Essays I, 342–51).
12. Forster, Letter in my possession, dated 21 Sep 1957.
13. Forster, 'Short Stories from Russia', *The New Statesman*, 24 July 1915.
14. The story is 'Agatha' (or 'Agafya'). Forster is quoting a translation by Marian Fell from the collection *Stories of Russian Life*.

CHAPTER 23

1. *Letters from D. H. Lawrence to Martin Secker 1911–1930* (privately published 1970) pp. 59–63. Quoted (with later dates) by F. R. Leavis, *Thought, Words and Creativity* (1976) p. 32. I am grateful to Carl Baron for drawing my attention to these references and for making available to me his wide knowledge of Lawrence's letters and other writings.
2. Letter to Linati, 8 August 1924 (*Letters*, ed. Harry T. Moore, 1962, II, 800).
3. Leavis, 'E. M. Forster', *Scrutiny*, 1938, VII. Reproduced in *The Common Pursuit*, (1952) pp. 262, 263.
4. Wilfred Stone, *The Cave and the Mountain* (Stanford, Calif., 1966) pp. 15,

121n, 227n, 379–87, etc., etc. Professor Stone makes a number of comparisons, some of which anticipate or supplement points in the present essay. See also Frank Kermode, *D. H. Lawrence* (1973) pp. 5, 25, 60–1, 137.

5. For the first, see E. M. Forster, *The Lucy Novels: Early Sketches for 'A Room with a View'* (ed. O. Stallybrass, 1977); for the second, 'E.T.' (Jessie Chambers), *D. H. Lawrence: A Personal Record* (1935) p. 116.

6. *The White Peacock* (1911), ch. iii, 43; RWV vi, 67–8 (and cf. WAFT ii, 18); *The White Peacock*, quoted by Baron above, pp. 188–90.

7. Cf. my *The Achievement of E. M. Forster* (1962) p. 90.

8. HE xliv, 337.

9. *The Rainbow* (1915) ch. xvi, 462–3.

10*x*. In a letter to Forster, 24 January 1915 (*Letters* (Moore) I, 315) Lawrence says that he has read only one or two stories of Forster's and would like very much to have *The Celestial Omnibus*. On 28 January he refers back to *Howards End*; a postscript by Frieda tells how she 'felt like turning somersaults' after reading *Where Angels Fear to Tread* (Furbank II, 7). (In a letter of March she says that The Longest Journey 'touched me on the quick' (*E. M. Forster: The Critical Heritage*, ed. P. Gardner (1973) p. 97).) In a letter of 3 February (quoted below, p. 254), Lawrence comments on *The Celestial Omnibus* in terms of the 'Only connect' motto from HE.

11*x*. On 23 June 1911, Lawrence wrote to Louie Burrows, 'Bring me Howard's End [*sic*] on Sunday, if you can' (*Lawrence in Love*, ed. J. T. Boulton, (Nottingham 1968) p. 114). He had evidently read it by that time, since he wrote to A. W. McLeod on the same day (in an unpublished letter), 'I'm bringing you Howard's End – it is exceedingly good and very discussable.' Paul Delany, in 'Lawrence and Two Rainbows' (*D. H. Lawrence Review* (1975) VIII, 54–62), points out that Lawrence's rainbow image in the closing pages may have been influenced by Forster's use in *Howards End* of 'the rainbow bridge in us that should connect the prose in us with the passion' and by the Wagnerian rainbow bridge in the title-story of *The Celestial Omnibus*, which was illustrated by Roger Fry for the endpapers of the book as a whole.

12. M. L. Raina, 'A Forster Parallel in Lawrence's "St Mawr"': *Notes and Queries* (March 1966) CCXI, 96–7.

13. Letter to David Garnett, 19 April 1915; *The Flowers of the Forest* (1955) pp. 53–4.

14. Leonard Woolf, *Sowing, an Autobiography of the years 1880–1904* (1960) pp. 171–2. For more light on the whole relationship see David Garnett's 'Forster and Bloomsbury' in *Aspects of E. M. Forster*, ed. O. Stallybrass (1969) pp. 29–35.

15*x*. GLD xiv, 179–80; C. Hassall, *Edward Marsh* (1959) p. 522. His short story 'The point of it', similarly, was, says Forster, ill-liked by his Bloomsbury friends. ' "What *is* the point of it?" they queried thinly, nor did I know how to reply' (CSS (1947) Introduction).

16. AN v, 66.

17. *Phoenix* (1936) pp. 398–516.

18*x*. Carl Baron points out to me that the name 'Pagans' derives solely from a memoir by D. L.'s friend G. H. Neville in the *London Mercury* shortly after his death, and that the assumption that the group actually called themselves by this name should not be accepted without question, therefore. The term 'neo-paganism' was in use by 1876 (*OED*); in Bloomsbury the group which included Rupert Brooke, Ka Cox, Gwen and Jacques Raverat, Frances Cornford and David Garnett was called the Neo-Pagans (See Virginia Woolf, *Letters* (1975) I, 460, note to letter of April 1911).

19. LJ (WC) xxiii, 225; xxxi, 287; xxxiv, 323–4.
20. 'The Machine Stops', CSS (1947) 163. For a fuller account of Orion, see my discussion in *The Achievement of E. M. Forster* (1962) pp. 91–4.
21. Kenneth Grahame, *Pagan Papers* (1894) p. 109.
22. Peter Green, *Kenneth Grahame, 1859–1932; a study of his life, work and times*, (1959) pp. 119–23.
23. 'The Olympians', *The Golden Age* (1895) pp. 1–7 (reprinted from *Pagan Papers*, pp. 113–18).
24. David Garnett, *The Flowers of the Forest* (1955) pp. 33–7. The stay, and its impact, are described in Furbank II, 4–13.
25*x*. Letter to Russell, 12 February 1915 *Letters* (Moore) I, 316. Frieda wrote in a letter to Forster (20–1 March 1915) that during the stay he and Lawrence had been 'on the brink of quarreling—watching each other like two tom-cats' (Furbank II, 11).
26. Unpublished letter to Forster, 23 July 1924. Quoted below, p. 264.
27. Angus Wilson, 'A Conversation with E. M. Forster', *Encounter* (November 1957) IX, 54. Cited Stone, op. cit., 381n.
28. HE xix, 172.
29. Letter to Forster, 20 September 1922 (*Letters* (Moore) II, 716).
30*x*. Unpublished letters to Forster of 2 June 1915, 30 May 1916; letter of 20 September 1922 (*Letters* (Moore) II, 716). Carl Baron points out to me that Lawrence read Edwin Arnold's *Light of Asia* in youth and sometimes quotes from it in letters: he still refers to it once or twice in *The Plumed Serpent*.
31*x*. In the letter referred to above (note 25) Frieda replied, to his complaints, that what Lawrence was preaching to him was 'just exactly what you say yourself in your books'; she told Forster 'You are *not* to mind L's "customs beastly, manners none"'; think, I have put up with them, and they have improved!' (Furbank II, 11 var.). For Forster's comments on the earlier 'dressing-down' see Furbank II, 13.
32. Letters of 11 February 1915 and 24 February 1915 (*Letters* (Moore) I, 315, 323).
33. Letter to Russell, 12 February 1915 (*Letters* (Moore) I, 319).
34. See above, pp. 77–8.
35. Unpublished letter to Forster, 3 February 1915 (quoted Furbank II, 8).
36. P. Merivale, *The Great God Pan* (Cambridge, Mass., 1969) pp. 194–219.
37. Unpublished letter to Forster, 23 July 1924, quoted in part in Furbank II, 124.
38. PI xxiii, 20.
39*x*. J. M. Murry, 'Bo-oum or Ou-Boum?', *Adelphi* (1924) II, 150–3; reprinted in *E. M. Forster: The Critical Heritage*, ed. P. Gardner (1973) 236–8. Writing to Forster after this, Lawrence said 'Saw Murry's Bou-oum crit.—but even that is better than his *miaow*—anyhow, damn the universe and its echo—*je m'en fiche—On peut toujours s'en fiche*, même de l'univers' (*Letters* (Moore) II, 793–4).

40x. See his letter to Secker, 13 August 1925, quoted above, p. 245. His previous letters to Secker had contained several requests to send copies of his books to Forster.

41. 'The Novel', in *Reflections on the Death of a Porcupine and other Essays*, 1925, pp. 105–6 (*Phoenix* ii, 417).

42. Letter to S. S. Koteliansky, 22 November 1927, *Letters* (Moore) ii, 1024.

43. AN vii, 99.

44. *Nation and Athenaeum* (29 March 1930) xlvi, 888.

45. Ibid, (5 April 1930) xlvii, 11.

46. Ibid. (12 April 1930) xlvii, 45.

47. AN vii, 100.

48x. *The Trial of Lady Chatterley, Regina v. Penguin Books Ltd.*, ed. C. H. Rolph (Harmondsworth, 1961) pp. 112–13. In the course of his evidence, Forster mentioned that *Sons and Lovers* was the novel of Lawrence's that he most admired. (In the 1930 broadcast discussed below it had been, interestingly, *The Plumed Serpent*.) He also invoked Bunyan and Blake as Lawrence's true antecedents: 'Lawrence too had this passionate opinion of the world and what it ought to be, but is not.'

49. 'The Cult of D. H. Lawrence', *Spectator* (18 April 1931) 627. This interesting piece is hard to summarize and should be read in full.

50. 'D. H. Lawrence', *Listener* (30 April 1930) pp. 753–4.

51. See, e.g., J. D. Rosenberg, *The Darkening Glass* (1963) pp. 30f., 35, 109ff. etc.

52x. 'E. T.' (Jessie Chambers), *D. H. Lawrence: A Personal Record* (1935), p. 107; *Letters* (Moore) i, 29–30. Carl Baron points out to me that in Lawrence's early story 'Goose Fair', published in the *English Review* in February 1910, the aspiring heroine is reading a copy of *Sesame and Lilies*, which is crushed by her mother when she suffers a heart attack.

53. *The Rainbow* (1915) iv, 101.

54x. Letter to Edward Garnett, 14 November 1912. *Letters* (Moore) i, 161. In *Fantasia of the Unconscious* (1923) x, 108, he wrote: 'When Mrs Ruskin said that John Ruskin should have married his mother she spoke the truth. He *was* married to his mother.'

55x. *The Lucy Novels: Early Sketches for 'A Room with a View'*, ed. O. Stallybrass (1977) p. 22: HE vi, 46–8. I owe the *Howards End* reference to P. N. Furbank's biography (Furbank i, 173–4). Furbank also mentions that Forster worked for a time at the Working Men's College, where Ruskin had earlier lectured.

56x. Since writing this I have come across the following in a letter to Ackerley: 'Although my mother has been intermittently tiresome for the last thirty years, cramped and warped my genius, hindered my career, blocked and buggered up my house, and boycotted my beloved, I have to admit that she has provided a sort of rich subsoil where I have been able to rest and grow. That, rather than sex or wifiness, seems to be women's special gift to men.' (Quoted Furbank ii, 217.)

57. LJ (WC) xxviii, 263–4.

58. LJ. (WC) xxxi, 296.

59. 'A View without a Room', *Observer* (27 July 1958) p. 15.

60. PI xiv, 138–41.

61. PI xxiv, 214 etc.; xxix, 249, 251; xxxiii, 276–7, 281.

62x. PI, xxxvi–xxxvii *passim*. The incident in the tank, when Stella Moore falls first against Fielding and then against Aziz, and the latter's reference to it in his letter to Adela Quested next day (p. 308) should be particularly noted.

63. Unpublished letter to Forster, 23 July 1924, quoted in part Furbank II, 124.

64. Letter to Forster, 19 February 1924, quoted in Furbank II, 163.

65. Virginia Woolf, 'The Novels of E. M. Forster', *Atlantic Monthly* (1927) cxv, 642–8. Reprinted *Essays* I, 348–9.

66. Ibid., 351.

67. Preface to CSS (1947) quoted above by Judith Herz, p. 19.

68. See his letter to Edward Garnett, 5 June 1914 (*Letters* (Moore) I, 281f.).

69. PI xxxii, 270.

70. *Aaron's Rod* (1922) xvi, 225.

71. Ibid., xvii, 246.

72. RWV iv, 40–1.

73. Letters to Lady Cynthia Asquith, 21 Oct 1915 and J. M. Murry, 25 Oct 1923. *Letters* (Moore) I, 371 and II, 759.

Index

307